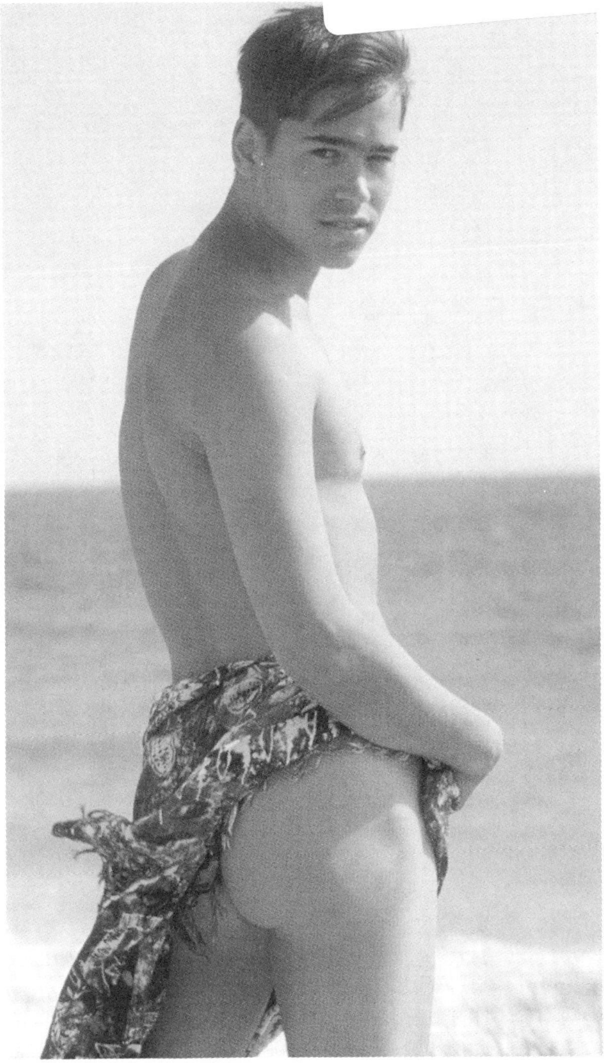

On preceding page, coverboy Johan Paulik, international porn video star of the year for the second year in a row, courtesy Bel-Ami, and seconday illustration courtesy Pride Video (see Acknowledgements and Sources). Johan's picture book, Euros No. 8, his videos and the Bel Ami Calendar available from STARbooks

Worldwide Praise for
The Best of the Superstars
Annual Reviews

"...Of course we love to hear about powerful people's sex life and penis size and sexual preferences and abnormal usage of tampons and ambiguous quotes about which gender they sleep with. 'The Best of the Superstars' is a game of spot the poof played against the backdrop of world media, and most people love it. ...The delightful things about the first part are numerous. ...Above all, you feel like editor John Patrick shows you his media clippings, gives you his pat summary of the news of the year, then tells you stories he's heard through his sources... The second part contains random information related to porn actors. Because of their more accessible sexuality, reading about porn actors is much easier on the intellect. Much easier. ...But the real subject of this book is titillation. The book assumes that media power is an aphrodisiac to the reader. It also implies that the ultimate in power comes through your certainty that the sex lives of American movie actors are just as sleazy and hypocritical as you want them to be. And that's comforting."
– Paul Veitch, *Screaming Hyena*

"'Superstars' is a fast read...if you'd like a nice round of fireworks before the Fourth, read this aloud at your next church picnic..."
- *Welcomat, Philadelphia*

"For those who share Mr. Patrick's appreciation for cute young men, a delightfully readable book...I am a fan of John Patrick's...His writing is clear and straight-forward and should be better known in the gay community."
- Ian Young, *Torso Magazine*

"John Patrick has one of the best jobs a gay male writer could have. In his fiction, he tells tales of rampant sexuality. His non-fiction involves first person explorations of adult male video stars. Talk about choice assignments!"
-*Southern Exposure*

THE BEST OF THE SUPERSTARS 1998: THE YEAR IN SEX

Edited By
JOHN PATRICK

*One in a Series from STARbooks Press
Sarasota, FL*

Books by John Patrick

Non-Fiction

A Charmed Life: Vince Cobretti
Lowe Down: Tim Lowe
The Best of the Superstars 1990
The Best of the Superstars 1991
The Best of the Superstars 1992
The Best of the Superstars 1993
The Best of the Superstars 1994
The Best of the Superstars 1995
The Best of the Superstars 1996
The Best of the Superstars 1997
The Best of the Superstars 1998
What Went Wrong?
(When Boys Are Bad
& Sex Goes Wrong)
Legends: The World's Sexiest
Men, Vols. 1 & 2
Legends: 3rd Ed.
Tarnished Angels (Ed.)

Fiction

Billy & David: A Deadly Minuet
The Bigger They Are...
The Younger They Are...
The Harder They Are...
Angel: The Complete Trilogy
Angel II: Stacy's Story
Angel: The Complete Quintet
(Expanded International Ed.)
A Natural Beauty (Editor)
The Kid (with Joe Leslie)
HUGE (Editor)
Strip: He Danced Alone
The Boys of Spring
Big Boys/Little Lies (Editor)
Boy Toy
Seduced (Editor)
Insatiable/Unforgettable (Editor)
Heartthrobs
Runaways/Kid Stuff (Editor)
Dangerous Boys/Rent Boys
(Editor)
Barely Legal (Editor)
Country Boys/City Boys (Editor)
My Three Boys (Editor)
Mad About the Boys (Editor)
Lover Boys (Editor)
In the BOY Zone (Editor)
Boys of the Night (Editor)
Secret Passions (Editor)
Beautiful Boys (Editor)
Juniors (Editor)
Come Again (Editor)
Smooth 'N' Sassy (Editor)

Entire Contents Copyrighted © 1997 by John Patrick, Sarasota, FL. All rights reserved. Every effort has been made to credit copyrighted material. The author and the publisher regret any omissions and will correct them in any future edition.

Annual edition published in the U.S. December 1997.

Library of Congress No. ISSN 1053-6671
ISBN No. 1-87798-98-1

Contents

Book I.
Sex, Scandal & Gossip
Gays on Film:
Jude Law / Rupert Everett / Jeremy Jordan
Lukas Haas / Tony Ward
The Great Beauties:
Tom Cruise / Keanu Reeves / Antonio Sabator, Jr. / Brad Pitt
& Awaiting Greatness: Jared Leto / Johnathan Schaech
Muscles Go Mainstream:
Steve Reeves / Kevin Sorbo / Dean Cain
Brendan Fraser / Marky Mark Wahlberg
The King and the Princes:
Michael Jackson / Prince William
Jonathan Taylor Thomas / Devon Sawa / Brad Renfro
The Gay for Pay Boys:
Brad Davis / Mario Lopez / Antonio Banderas
Leonardo DiCaprio / Ewan McGregor / Skeet Ulrich
Sex in Theater
Nude Boys On Stage,
And Other Spectacles, Including Porn Stars Ryan Idol
Johnny Hanson / Sonny Markham / Kevin Kramer / Hawk McAllistar
Sexiest TV Stars::
George Clooney and Noah Wyle / David Charvet / Chad Allen
Sex in Music:
Elton John & Liberace
Pansy Division / Pet Shop Boys / David Bowie
Hanson / Joshua Bell
Artists & Models:
The Brewer Twins / Tyson Beckford / Anthony Wayne
Book II.
The Sex Superstars
The Gay for Pay Boys:
Ty Fox / Adam Hart / Jeff Stryker / The Brothers Rockland
A Feast of Foreskin:
Lukas Ridgeston / Johan Paulik / Aiden Shaw / Marcello Reeves
Hot Couples:
Kurt Young and K C Hart / Matt Bradshaw and Todd Stevens
Derek Thomas and Logan Reed / Chad Knight and Cole Youngblood
The Hottest New-Cummers
Jim Buck / Jake Cannon
Book III.
Legendary Sex Pigs and The Big Hustle
The Best of the Best
And The Pictures of the Year
And The Superstar Index

Editor's Note

What follows is an overview of the personalities and entertainments that have helped mold our gay consciousness. My thoughts from a fan's perspective have been combined with the opinions of leading critics in their respective fields, including Michael Musto and others at the *Village Voice*, *The Advocate's* many columnists, *Adult Video News's* Mickey Skee and staff, Jerry Douglas and his staff at *Manshots* magazine.

And special thanks to the always entertaining *Filth* columnist Billy Masters, whose columns are weekly must-reads for thousands.

Many thanks too to our spies, Rod in New York and Dan in San Francisco, who keep me posted on what's happening in the real world.

In addition, I wish to thank the many readers of my books who have written expressing their opinions. Their enthusiasm for particular stars has spurred me to do further research which has added immeasurably to the scope of this book.

– John Patrick

Our Choice for Movie Star of the Year, for the second year in a row: Leonardo DiCaprio

*Outside William Burroughs' villa in Tangiers, Morocco,
July 1961: Peter Orlovsky, Burroughs,
Allen Ginsberg, Alan Ansen, Paul Bowles, and (seated)
Gregory Corso, Ian Sommerville.*

Dedication:
To Allen Ginsberg and William Burroughs

"... To the day he died, Allen Ginsberg remained a fierce advocate of free speech," Mikal Gilmore noted in *Rolling Stone*. "In recent years he even took up a defense of NAMBLA (and his) involvement with the outfit outraged many of his longstanding admirers. But Ginsberg would not be cowed. 'It's a free speech issue,' he said repeatedly, pointing out that to stifle the ability to discuss such a matter in a free society was perhaps its own kind of outrage. Also, apparently he stayed as sexually active as he could. In 'Death and Fame,' in *The New Yorker*, Ginsberg boasted about the many men he had seduced throughout his lifetime, and he detailed what it was he liked about his sexual intimacy with these partners. But for all that Ginsberg did or attempted to do, to this day 'Howl' still cannot be played over America's airwaves during the day, due to the efforts of Jesse Helms and the Federal Communications Commission.

"Since Ginsberg's death, I have seen and heard countless tributes to his grace, power, skills and generosity - but I also have seen and heard just as many disparaging remarks: what a shoddy writer he was; what a failure the legacy of his Beat Generation and the 1960s generation turned out to be; what an old lecher the guy was.

"Perhaps all this vitriol isn't such a bad thing. Maybe it's another tribute of sorts: Allen Ginsberg never lost his ability to rub certain nerves the wrong way when it came to matters of propriety, aesthetics, morality and politics.

"But I also know this: Allen Ginsberg won - against the formidable odds of his own madness-scarred childhood, against all his soul-crippling doubts of self, against all those stern, bristling, authoritarian forces that looked at this man and saw only a bearded radical faggot they could not abide. Ginsberg won in a very simple yet irrefutable way: He raised his voice."

"While Burroughs is known as a Beat writer," Otto Coca said in *HX*, "he is the odd man out within a group who prided themselves on being outsiders. Considerably older than the others, Burroughs' writings lacked the youthful enthusiasm that lightened the darkest works of his contemporaries. Considering that every adventurous college boy seems to find his way to a copy of *On the Road* – Kerouac's stream of consciousness novel about traveling America in search of love, freedom and beer – it's interesting to note that the implicit homosexuality of the Beat texts is often glossed over in deference to the concept of 'experimentation.' Kerouac may have been 'experimenting' (Gore Vidal's recent memoir relays details of a night that lack 'experimented,' playing catcher to Gore's pitches), but Burroughs made no such delineations. All of life was a chance to experiment, and he did so without apology. Unlike Ginsberg's Walt Whitman-esque rhapsodies to the boy beautiful, Burroughs presented homosexuality, not in a good light. but in an honest light. His work paved the way for future authors who would choose to write about sex unflinchingly. In 1997, William S. Burroughs might be best known as a personality, a human cultural signifier, something akin to a malevolent Quentin Crisp. But it can be assured that history will remember Burroughs as a raw, compelling writer who saw far, far past the boundaries that were placed before him, and who even helped remove some of them."

THE YEAR IN SEX: SEX, SCANDAL AND GOSSIP

With each of our books we aim to give our readers a strong sense of connection to the fact that there are many others who have the same feelings and fantasies that they do. So, within all the mixture and variety of new stars and new entertainments, there is a thread throughout our annual reviews for the nostalgic, the great performers and great films and videos of the past that will remain part of our shared experience forever.

The guys we feature may be "superstars" but they are, after all, human and that's what makes them believable, interesting, and full of connections to us. What makes them people we want to read about is that they connect to gay fans hungry for peeks into glittering lives, and it has become a steady diet of titillation. Perhaps *too much*.

"There are certain unspoken rules in the fun and frivolous world of gossip," Gary Socol of E! Television's *Gossip* says. "Never report the drug habits of a celebrity – unless he or she has officially entered the Betty Ford Center. Never divulge the details of a diva's plastic surgery – unless it's Joan Rivers, who boasts about it. And never, ever discuss the love life of a gay celebrity – unless he or she is out of the closet.

"Anyone who's in-the-know knows the names (and, in some cases, phone numbers) of the rich and famous who are gay. But out of respect, out of honoring their privacy, out of fear of being slapped with an ugly lawsuit, we don't gossip about their private lives on the air or in print. Still, I wish we could treat gay celebrities the way we do their straight counterparts. Reporting that Liv Tyler was kissing a gorgeous gent is fair game, but announcing that a male star was hot and heavy with some stunning stud is an invasion of privacy, so we leave it alone. Is this right? Of course not. But there's nothing we can do, short of discussing the incident in oblique terms or making it a 'blind' item: 'What macho-male leadin- man was locking lips with a guy half his age?' Let the guessing games begin!

"...I see a male TV star asking his lover to leave the house when a *People* magazine reporter is due, and a movie hunk who denies he's gay (or even bisexual), despite the fact that he has a propensity for picking up guys at the mall (and refusing to shower)."

And then *Movieline* ran this item: "On-screen, playing tough and sexy made this guy's fortune. Off-screen, he's notorious for mouthing off empty-headed machismo. When he's on location, though, those dusty boots have been known to take an occasional walk on the wild side. On a couple of recent movie shoots, the macho one appears to have hit on an MO for indulging his latent needs: he picks out and hits on a good-looking, hyper-masculine, possibly receptive dude from the crew. In a hotel-bound van after a long day of shooting on his most recent movie, the star shared the back seat with his designated stud and casually let his hand rest near the guy's crotch. Not sure how that worked out, but the sexy catering company guy who kept visiting the star's trailer for at least an hour daily was probably not discussing craft services. Meanwhile, the press is dutifully reporting how the star's longtime lady love visits his sets to keep a watchful eye on him and his *female* co-stars!"

"In the world of gay gossip, it's the best of times and the worst of times," suggests Michael Musto. "For every step we've gone forward – taking the taboo out of gay issues and making them reportable – we've also gone back, as the media retreats to a complacency that doesn't keep up with the way the real world is changing.

"To some degree, the celebrity press still thinks that homosexuality must be protected from public scrutiny. They equate gayness with such illnesses as alcoholism – a struggle the celebs must deal with privately. Actually, they think it's far *less* reportable than alcoholism. Stay tuned..."

All that said, gossip is undeniably a great deal of fun, and gossip about homosexuality can be particularly amusing. "Oh, it's hilarious," says columnist Michael Musto. "It's a great leveler of society: Even Oscar nominees are chasing transsexuals!"

"Hi, I'm Eddie Murphy. Here's $200. What type of sex do you like? Can I see you in lingerie?" That's what male hooker Atisone Seiuli told the *Enquirer* the "Nutty Professor" comic said to her after he picked her up early one morning in May. The duo was stopped by the cops, who had their eye on

Atisone. Since at that point Eddie hadn't done anything illegal as far as the cops were concerned, they let him go. Eddie turned on the charm to tell them, and, later, the press, that he'd just gone out to get something to read and offered the hooker a ride home. Trouble was, Eddie was headed in the wrong direction to take the 20-year-old Atisone home, and Eddie had dropped two hundred dollar bills in Atisone's lap, which he quickly slid into his purse. *The Enquirer* quoted Bill Mersey of New York's *Action* magazine – which runs ads from cross-dressing hookers – that he's known for a long time Eddie's taste for the unusual. "He likes to chat them up and watch them dance or strip, usually without engaging in any overt sexual activity. He's simply fascinated by transsexuals. He treats them with respect."

Eddie was livid at the coverage of his private life. He sued the *Globe* and the *National Enquirer* for $5 million each. He claimed slander and invasion of privacy, saying the reportage caused him "severe emotional and physical distress, requiring medical attention!" The *Enquirer* said a statement, "Mr. Murphy is attempting to rehabilitate himself at our expense." Murphy also sued auto mechanic Ioane Seiuli, 36, for $1 million for telling the *New York Post* that Murphy was a friend of his cousin's and had promised Atisone a role in a movie.

Eddie *didn't* sue Karen Dior, however. Johnny Depp Clone back-up singer and star of the film "He/She Cornholers," Dior was quick to ring-up the tabloids and jump on the "I've done it with Eddie" bandwagon. She managed to get her picture on the front page of *The Globe*. Dior, porn fans know, is really Rick Van. Dave Kinnick in *Adam Gay Video* recalls, "Rick is a very special case in the gay video industry. He is probably the only actor who gets as many women's roles as men's. For when he isn't fucking guys with his big dick as Rick Van he is donning a wig and any number of fetching diva-like gowns and is performing transvestite parts as Karen Dior." And this boy/girl also directs. This is a list of just some of his many male parts: "Brats," "Brown Paper Wrapper," "Delirium," "Delusion," "Fan Male," "Frat Pack," "Immoral Thoughts," "Personal Service," and "Summer School." Last year, Rick won Best Gay Specialty Release for "Orgy Boys" and Best Transsexual Video for "Red Riding She-Male" at the *Adult Video News* ceremonies in Vegas. As Karen, he has starred in a number of unforgettable videos including "Sharon and Karen" and "Steel Garters." Van also played a beauty queen in an episode of "Xena: Warrior Princess," a syndicated TV show popular with dykes.

Musto weighed in again: "As for 'The Drag Queen and I,' Eddie Murphy gave his most hilarious performance in years saying he was merely helping out that transsexual hooker by driving her home. What a selfless pal to the trannie community – you never would have guessed it from his homophobic humor! 'It's not the first hooker that I've helped out,' claims the smutty professor. No, it isn't – and it's certainly not the first transsexual. We've heard of his good deeds for years!"

In *HX*, Cathay Che commented, "Since the early days of Murphy's career, when he zoomed to celebrity on *Saturday Night Live*, the trannie underground has been rife with stories about Murphy's itch for she-males.

" I personally know several trannies who claim to have had sexual encounters with Murphy, each weaving a similar tale about expensive cars with tinted windows, hotel rooms, a fetish for lingerie, generous amounts of money and the downward curvature of the comedian's penis.

"In fact, it seems that every trannie from the West Side Highway to Santa Monica Boulevard is now claiming to have shagged the Nutty Professor, including accounts in the tabloids by porn stars Karen Dior and Summer St. Cerely and former Warhol superstar Holly Woodlawn. Murphy must have kept his dark sunglasses on during that last one). Murphy, of course, has denied all accounts, and in a classic case of celebrity spin control, has mounted a major P.R. counter-offensive, granting a number of 'exclusive' interviews loaded with powerful denials, including: On *Entertainment Tonight*: 'I love my wife, and I'm not gay.' In *Star*: 'Now everyone is coming out and saying, 'Hey, I slept with Eddie Murphy.' It makes me really mad. I have been totally faithful to my wife.'

"Wow, pretty strong stuff, huh? Not really. What does his wife have to do with anything? Everyone knows that half the male stars in Hollywood are married to trophy wives just to keep up a respectable facade. And whoever said Murphy was gay? Bisexual, perhaps, but not gay. And as for his denials of being a degenerate, well, the loathing in that statement speaks volumes. Don't throw stones if you live in a glass house, Eddie. Ironically, much of Murphy's early stand-up routines ridiculed homosexuals and their behavior, and many gay people are delighted by the comedian's public embarrassment. Just desserts, they smirk."

Billy Masters in *Filth* was one of those smirking the most: "My sources say the only thing unusual about this is that Eddie got caught - and no one had their pants down! And, while Eddie states he was only giving the trannie a ride home, he singled this person out of all the many prostitutes on Santa Monica Boulevard and they all knew him by name. Well, he *is* Eddie Murphy after all."

What the comic actor told *Playboy* in an interview some years ago now makes a lot of sense: "I think an orgasm is your thing, and you should fuck whoever the fuck you feel like fucking. Whoever makes you come the hardest, that's who you should be with. And all those people who say you shouldn't do that, fuck them, because it ain't their fucking business."

The same week Eddie was driving off scot-free in Hollywood, with his pants up, in New York, a nosy audience was paying $39 each to hear erstwhile porn star and Las Vegas preacher John Wayne Bobbitt give a "seminar" about having his manhood sliced off by his wife Lorena! An ad announcing the event promised that John would tell all about hls "spine-tingling ordeal." I don't think it was his spine that was tingling! Bobbitt himself once called the slicing "exhilarating!"

As good as the *Enquirer* reporters are, even these days, some gossip never makes it across the Atlantic. For instance, Philip Gambone, just back from Italy, mentioned in *Frontiers* that he had met a boy there named Marco, who came from the Italian aristocracy and lived in Milan with his boyfriend. "Marco regaled me with stories of obligatory tea parties and polo matches. I asked him if, as a gay man, he was out in that society, and he was. Being homosexual wasn't so much a problem among the nobility he said. Lots of men from European royal families were gay. He told me about the well-known affair between Prince Albert of Monaco (Princess Grace's balding son) and Aemone, the youngest son of Umberto, the pretender to the Italian throne, now in exile in

Switzerland. Apparently, neither their homosexuality nor the fact that, at the time of the affair, Aemone was 17 and Albert was in his 30s seemed to be a problem."

And we never saw Billy Masters's famous quote about John Travolta show up in the tabloids. As you'll recall, Masters quoted Maxene Andrews of the Andrews Sisters telling about John Travolta when he was a chorus boy in her Broadway show "Over Here": "I never expected him to hit it so big. I mean, he just seemed like a nice young man who was sleeping with all the other young men in the cast!"

Several years ago, Masters was way ahead of the tabloids, the first to break the news that Jeff Smith, TV's "Frugal Gourmet," was asked to leave his position at University of Puget Sound after complaints from male students of alleged molestation and/or harassment. Now the "Frugal" Smith, according to published reports, had been charged by six men of sexual assault after the Puget Sound incident. The suit stated that Smith had a pattern of pursuing teenage boys for sexual and other illicit activities as part of his hiring and firing process. As Masters said, "I don't know what he promised them, but I can't imagine any job is worth having to touch him. Slime!"

George Heitman, in an interview with *People*, said that his hands still tremble when he remembers that fall evening when he was 15 and Smith was his boss at the Chaplain's Pantry, the popular Tacoma, Wash., restaurant that Smith then owned. Heitman said, "As usual, leftover champagne brought back from that night's catered party flowed freely among the teenage boys who worked in the kitchen. Also, as usual, Smith dismissed the boys until he was finally alone with one of them. This time it was me. He said he wanted to eat me like a sugar cookie. And (then he) proceeded to pull my pants down and perform oral sex. I was shocked. I was too scared to resist."

When Smith was finished, Heitman says, Smith told him, "Get back to work.' I had distracted him.'"

People reported, "According to three civil lawsuits filed against him Smith was frequently distracted by the boys he hired. Claiming sexual abuse, eight men are suing the ebullient Methodist minister turned food evangelist. (Under Washington law, no specific amount of damages can be sought.) Another half dozen witnesses, including a former judge, have signed statements that they were subjected to sexual advances by Smith or saw someone else who was.

"Most of the accounts are strikingly similar. They claim that during the '70s, when the alleged victims were teenage employees of his, Smith hugged, kissed, fondled and even raped, using a combination of what one suit calls 'alcohol, coercion and force' to get what he wanted.

"Since suggestions of such unsavory behavior began surfacing publicly on Seattle talk radio two years ago, Smith has firmly maintained his innocence. 'All the allegations are denied,' says his attorney Ed Winskill. Meanwhile, Smith seems to be trying to give the appearance of going about business as usual, remaining a familiar presence at Seattle's historic Pike Place Market near his condo. (Wife Patty lives in the Tacoma home where sons Channing, 28, and Jason, 26, grew up.) But there are indications the heat may be getting a bit uncomfortable for him. The Odyssey cable network suspended his show. These days the bestselling cookbook author, whose popular programs were devoured for two decades on public TV by a weekly audience of some 15 million, can be seen only in reruns.

"Whatever fallout Smith may be experiencing, it pales next to the suffering some of his accusers claim they've endured, including drug problems and relationship difficulties. Two say they tried to kill themselves. Making the alleged assaults even worse, several plaintiffs say, was the fact that they came from such a respected authority figure. So well-regarded was Smith that a boy who did speak up at the time says he was told he must have misunderstood. Geoff McMahon, one of many teens placed in the Pantry through a work-study program at Tacoma's Stadium High, has not joined the suits but states in an affidavit that he once 'complained to the counselor (of the work program) that Jeff Smith was trying to molest me.' The result? 'He told me, 'It's probably just Mr. Smith's way to make you feel comfortable.'"

Another victim says a wine-sipping Smith cornered him in the back of the restaurant and demanded that he remove his shirt while doing the dishes. Additional tales of Smith chasing boys around his restaurant, grabbing their butts and crotches, forcing them to scrub the floors clad only in their Jockey shorts, and hurling containers of meat tenderizer when he didn't get his way are just the half of it. "...If these tales aren't enough to land Smith in jail they should at least result in a name change for his Odyssey network show," *Out There* said, "maybe to something more suitably decadent and rotting-sounding, like, say, The Frugivorous Gourmand."

Keith Thomas, who had worked for Smith in the 1970s as part of a high school workstudy program, said that at the time he had shrugged off Smith's hugs and kisses as "weird, but (I thought) maybe that's the way it is with people in the food business."

Speaking of being frugal, George Michael continues to tantalize us, especially after he told *The Big Issue* magazine: "My sexuality is no one's fucking business." Then he went on to talk about it at length. "Even though my sexuality hasn't always been dear to me, it was never a moral question. I've never thought of my sexuality as being right or wrong. I've wondered what my sexuality might be, but I've never wondered whether it was acceptable or not." Billy Masters said, "Could it be that I forgot to mention that during my last trip to LA, I bumped into my ex, George Michael? Could it have been at the gay dance club, Axis? And, could it be that the rags were correct saying that when he had to go pee pee, his security guards clear the men's room? Hey, Georgie - I was in the ladies room waiting! Know your friends."

Speaking of being tantalized, showbiz gossips love to tantalize us with the "blind item." *Movieline* magazine is the best at this practice. One that really got us going was this one: "That photographer is renowned for shooting astonishingly beautiful portraits of the astonishingly beautiful. But does he also occasionally act informally as matchmaker and pimp?" Well, look, in Tinseltown, who doesn't? But anyway, *Movieline* goes on to say that one of the world's better-looking actors posed for this photographer (quite possibly the famous Greg Gorman) and then was called by the lensman several days later, claiming car trouble. The shutterbug said he had pressing business and conned the star into driving him to the home of a famous producer who treated them to a lavish dinner after which the star received "a discreet offer from the photographer on the producer's behalf − a minimum $10,000 cash for sex, negotiable upwards." *Movieline* swears the actor declined and has since heard that the producer has a practice of phoning associates to find him "straight-studs-for-hire to feed his insatiable appetite." At least the offer was "discreet!"

"Like every other enclave of creative and would-be creative people in the country, the movie colony is thoroughly relaxed about homosexuality," Hendrik Hertzber said in *The New Yorker*. "The obvious justice of gay rights is no more controversial in Hollywood than the proposition that happy endings sell. Familiarity has bred tolerance and respect, and was doing so within the industry, if not on the screen, long before the Hays office packed it in. ...Ever since the closet door swung ajar, a generation ago, movie folk have been streaming through it. In the '90s, it's not just set designers and wardrobe mistresses and hair stylists who can afford to be openly homosexual. It's perfectly okay for directors and producers to be gay, too. Ditto screenwriters, moguls, agents, publicists, caterers, gaffers, best boys, script girls, and 'supporting' actors and actresses. But leading men and leading ladies? Hollywood doesn't think so. What's especially queer about this is that, while it's still not O.K. for stars to *be* gay, it has become O.K. for them to *play* gay. Doing so was once seen as a career-killer, but in recent years the list of well-known actors who have portrayed sympathetic gay characters on the screen and lived to tell the tale has included Antonio Banderas, Cher, Robert Downey, Jr., Whoopi Goldberg, Tom Hanks, Mariel Hemingway, Jonathan Pryce, Will Smith, Wesley Snipes, Terence Stamp, Patrick Stewart, Meryl Streep, Patrick Swayze, Uma Thurman, Jennifer Tilly, and Robin Williams. There are no important examples of this phenomenon in reverse. The industry evidently believes that audiences will readily suspend disbelief to watch a notorious Don Juan pretend to be a faithful husband, a nice Midwestern girl pretend to be a space alien, a bookish environmentalist pretend to be a psychotic serial killer, or, for that matter, a confirmed heterosexual pretend to be a raging queen. But under no circumstances can Romeo be played by someone who, off duty, might prefer Mercutio to Juliet.

"A Gallup poll that was commissioned by *Entertainment Weekly* found that the vast majority of moviegoers simply don't care about the offscreen, (or onscreen, for that matter) affection preferences of their favorite stars. Sir Ian McKellen, the gay-identified actor, predicted not long ago that 'the fit young actor of talent who comes out and stars in a movie and is a hit will be the most famous actor in the world and make a fortune for his agents and his managers and producers and the studio." We doubt it.

While reporters for the tabloids have a weekly deadline, biographers have the luxury of time, carefully researching before publishing their bombshells, usually long after the subject is dead. Still, some biographers don't add anything new to the stew. For instance, during the year, we had *two* new books about Cary Grant: *A Class Apart* by Graham McCann and *Dark Angel* by Geoffrey Wansell.

"As for McCann's insights," Brendan Gill, writing in *The New Yorker*, said, "the best of them are borrowed – with a scholar's conscientious attributions – from other writers. But perhaps the oddest thing about the book is his gingerliness in respect to Grant's sexual disposition. In a prim, old-maidish fashion, McCann cannot bear Grant to be anything but ruggedly heterosexual, and he goes to great lengths to derogate anyone who dares to suggest otherwise.

"This is to assume the same hypocritical posture that was once the universal rule in Hollywood in respect to the private lives of the people – actors, directors, screenwriters, and designers – who make up the so-called 'creative' side of the movie industry. It is a posture that remains formally *de rigueur* but is beginning to show signs of sagging. In the old days, the truculent tycoons who ran the studios tried to impose on their actors, under the threat of summary dismissal, domestic arrangements that with sanctimonious hypocrisy they pretended to believe were the norm for those wholesome American citizens who flocked to the movies at a rate of almost a hundred million a week and kept the industry booming. Egged on by an assortment of Mrs. Grundys of both sexes and by clergymen expressing the usual pieties, studio heads asserted that adultery, homosexuality, and other infamous sexual activities would cause the American heartland to boycott movies featuring actors base enough to practice them.

"In 1975, Pauline Kael wrote in these pages a celebrated Profile of Grant, nearly every word of which implied, in my judgment, that Grant's homosexuality – or, more accurately, his bisexuality – was an indispensable attribute of his professional success. Kael makes no direct reference to either homosexuality or bisexuality, though she hints at a personal relationship between Grant and Randolph Scott, as made fleetingly manifest in an exchange of glances in 'My Favorite Wife.' Kael writes, 'The presence in the cast of his close friend Randolph Scott (they shared a house for several years) may have interfered with his concentration.' A few weeks ago, I asked Kael why in her Profile of Grant she had kept so nearly silent regarding his sexual nature, and her answer was that at the time Grant was alive, and still obliged to uphold the Hollywood taboos that had made denial a necessity throughout his career.

"'Moreover,' Kael said, 'I have always had great confidence in allusiveness.' The difficulty, as Kael would agree, is that allusiveness will not serve when biographers falsify a man's life, to say nothing of his artistry, by insisting upon a state of affairs directly at odds with the facts and thus rendering both his life and his artistry inexplicable. Like the recognized ability of actors throughout history to move upward socially, homosexuality and bisexuality are historically a commonplace in the theater – and far more openly so, it is fair to say, in the British theater than in the American.

"...In real life, Grant was obliged by studio fiat to endure a quasi-comic role not unlike the roles he played onscreen. The New York photographer Jerome Zerbe, who, strikingly handsome and flirtatious, was a lover of both Grant and Scott, used to tell me of how Grant and he in the nineteen-thirties were obliged to honor the prevailing Hollywood taboos and at the same time generate favorable publicity in movie magazines and among Grant's doting fan clubs. To that end, Grant was reported in the press to be enjoying an impassioned affair with the starlet Betty Furness. Night after night, he took the good-natured Furness out to dinner and returned her to her apartment promptly at ten o'clock, after which Zerbe and he and assorted companions went out on the town. In *Dark Angel*, the second bio on Grant released during the year, we are given the usual facts, drawn from the usual sources, and again and again we are told of Grant's unquenchable desire for women. "Not very felicitously," Gill reminds us, "the author notes that Grant had 'an eye for a pretty girl,' that in age 'his attraction to beautiful women had never dimmed,' and that he hadn't 'lost his appetite for the company of pretty young women' – the pretty young woman in question being Maureen Donaldson, a girlfriend at the time, who was forty-five years his junior. Poor Cary Grant! What about all the men he was attracted to in his youth and with whom he sought to form permanent relationships, always in vain? The story of that struggle, often heartbreaking, remains to be told."

In the long but delightful biography *Secret Muses: The Life of Frederick Ashton* by Julie Kavanagh, released in mid-1997, we see the great ballet master made no secret of his attraction to dancers. For instance, Nicholas Magallanes, with his glamorous Hispanic appearance and masculine magnetism on stage, was exactly Ashton's type. "The choreographer needed little persuasion to use Magallanes," Kavanagh reveals, "but was also 'whipped up' by Lincoln Kirstein, who referred to him as Mr. Nick 'Basket' Magallanes and sent Ashton a full-frontal nude drawing of the dancer by Tchelitchew. ... 'You'd be blind not to have noticed but it didn't get in the way of anything,' said the ballerina Tanaquil LeClercq. 'Freddie just came in and flirted a little.' Which, in this case, was all Ashton was able to achieve. Magallanes 'liked his boys very young'. 'He was absolutely fixed about it,' said Dick Beard, who had himself been a lover. 'There was no give and take for the sake of career. He did exactly what he wanted to sexually and it didn't have anything to do with gain or loss.'"

The dance master's long-time lover, Alexander Grant, always accepted that Ashton had a world outside the dance and, unlike Brian Shaw, was not affronted by his exclusion from it. "At the time, though, Ashton was keen to educate him, and, when the company performed in Boston, he took Grant to an Isaiah Berlin lecture at Harvard... Despite their twenty-year age difference, Grant loved being in Ashton's company and was touchingly in awe of his social aplomb.

"To Ashton, Grant was 'Someone to Watch Over Me', his favorite song, who never minded being there when he was needed. 'Freddie expected it of me. He didn't like to be abandoned. He'd say, "Where are you going? Don't leave me alone." There had to be a certain amount of attention, but it wasn't an imposition for me - Freddie has always been part of my life.'

Later, though, colleagues noticed that "things were a little fraught between Fred and Alex." The problem, Kavanagh reveals, was that Grant, was as much in demand off-stage as on. "When you're young, attractive and everybody wants you," said Ashton, "you're not going to be restricted, you're going to enjoy it. Can you even *imagine* Alexander being faithful?"

"Sexual activity, for many dancers, is an extension of their occupation," Kavanagh states. "Their virility simply another form of athletic prowess. Not surprisingly, Grant, one of the most physically charismatic performers of his time, adored sex and was very good at it. People who knew him told me, 'He was extremely animal and prodigiously endowed which was a large part of his charm.' 'He was a loveable animal. So warm and gentle with marvelous hands.' 'He had a fabulous body - better than most dancers: chunky and savage and very physical. Like a wild animal in a way.' With Grant in the forefront of Ashton's mind, it was no coincidence that he used sexuality as a subject in his ballets and treated it more graphically than ever before. Yet however inspiring Grant's sexual dynamism was to his work, it was not easy to come to terms with in private."

Then one night in New York, to steady his nerves during one of the intermissions, Ashton went off to Bill's Bar for a martini. "There, talking to John Cranko, he spotted an alluring youth, with full lips and a quiff of hair flopping over one eye. Cranko introduced them, but Tony Lizzul, a keen ballet fan, knew who Ashton was. 'Hearing I was still in college, Fred asked what I was majoring in. When I told him it was chemistry, he seemed relieved I was not someone in the theater looking for his help.' They arranged to meet after the performance at a party, and after a 'wonderful night' together at the St Regis Hotel; they were almost inseparable for the rest of the New York season. If Ashton was committed to another engagement, Lizzul would go to his room. Ashton wrote him: 'Oh the delight of opening the door to you & to know that you would be with me for some hours, hours of bliss and happiness.' Ashton continued to take comfort from the fact that, although flattered by the attention, Lizzul had nothing to gain from him professionally.

"Lizzul was a thoughtful, earnest young man and had a

sweet sympathy' in his nature which Ashton appreciated: 'You seemed to understand me.' He was not only attractive, but an easy companion, 'a nice boy and cozy', and was considering a career in perfumer. He also had a romantic streak, which, naturally, appealed to Ashton, who was delighted to be given a personalized cologne, an infusion of lemon verbena in gin, and touched when, on his return journey to England, he found his cabin filled with his favorite flowers.

"They had been sitting in the King Cole Bar of the St Regis, Ashton drinking his usual dry martini, when Lizzul told him he had 'done it', meaning that the choreographer had made a profound impression on him. 'You did something to me and created something in me which I can never forget.' The phrase became a refrain in their letters and telegrams, with Ashton demanding constant reiteration - 'I feel I have done nothing *please* re-assure me' - and Lizzul obliging, 'Yes you did it, and it will probably die with me, please believe me.'

"Ashton was searching, perhaps even consciously, for someone 'to churn him up creatively,' in Billy Chappell's phrase, to make him experience once again the romantic's craving for the unattainable. His New York encounter with Lizzul provided him with a potent after-image, causing him hours of unfulfilled yearning: 'I think with a longing that hurts for those nights at the St. Regis when I could gaze on you as you slept & drank in those wonderful looks.' But, like an oyster conjuring grit into pearl, it would poetically transmute itself in his work.

"Yet, even though Ashton was elated to find his ardor reciprocated (in their first correspondence), subsequent letters were more cautious, and Lizzul's reticence - his 'Arctic breezes' - spread doubt and insecurity. Lizzul recalled,'I was more important to Fred than he was to me. At the time I was too young to appreciate the intensity of his love.'

"Lizzul led what they euphemistically referred to as a 'complicated' life, the focal point of which was Fire Island, then, as it is today, a sanctuary for homosexual men. Flamboyant, promiscuous and free, Lizzul's attempts to spare Ashton's feelings rarely took effect. Ashton wrote him, 'You say don't worry, how can I help it? With those big blonds forever making demands on you, of course I worry. Where do I stand?'"

Of course, Ashton's was a heart waiting to be broken and it was by Lizzul as well. Reflecting on his affairs, Ashton wrote, "I'd be in love with him and he'd go off and that was how the queer world worked. I wasn't promiscuous but they were. If I loved somebody I loved somebody. That was all I wanted, I didn't *want* anyone else. But anybody I loved wanted everyone else. They liked me but I wasn't enough for them and if someone said, 'Let's go to bed,' off they'd go. If I didn't put up with it they'd just go off, that's all. ...Nobody was prepared to be devoted to me. They wanted that and they also wanted to fuck around. Well I try to understand. I probably didn't satisfy them physically, so they were all onto something else. In the queer world, you can't expect fidelity, dear."

Occasionally, a new biography will be released which advances a bit of gossip that is quite startling. For instance, during the year, the suggestion came from Lawrence Quirk in his biography of Paul Newman that the hunky star, and close friend of Gore Vidal, had an affair with Robert Redford! Quirk says that Newman has been dogged by gay rumors all through his career and then offers the insight: "(but) he would be the first to admit that it makes no difference as to what kind of person you are."

Newman, star of one of our favorite movies, "Hud," was once asked if bobby-soxers would respond to the appeal of James Dean and he responded, "I don't usually go out with boys. But with his looks, sure...sure..."

"The more stars die, the quicker the dirt covering the world they glittered in is kicked up," Patrick Giles said in *HX*. "Boze Hadleigh has made a career of tracking down and asking probing questions of closeted gay celebrities. After the success of a first volume devoted to Tinseltown lesbians, *Hollywood Gays* consists of interviews with 10 closeted gay men from Hollywood's golden days contains a few revelations and some genuinely funny dish. But what comes across from the sessions with Cary Grant, Liberace, Tony Perkins, Paul Lynde, Cesar Romero, Brad Davis, Randolph Scott, James Coco, Billy Haines and David Lewis is the overwhelming awfulness of life in Hollywood for gay movie stars. Groomed and marketed as sex symbols for the world's women, these stars became seductive personae who threatened, wounded and finally engulfed their true sexualities. Straying too far from their straight scripts meant total professional and personal ruin. The fear, duplicity and exhaustion of a life hidden behind – and from – cameras seep through every page of these sometimes lighthearted but always wary interviews. ...Is any amount of fame worth such a life?"

The Advocate once asked ace biographer Donald Spoto what's behind the public's taste for sexual scandal. "In our puritan society, the hunch is that everyone else is having more and better," Spoto said. "Therefore, we've got to know what it is that they're doing – or did – and how they did it. At the root of this is a fierce, prurient curiosity that springs from jealousy and envy. We want to feel that we're more successful, more achieving, more attractive in sexual conquest than others. And if we read that people led very wild lives, then we feel that they're shallow or cheap or tawdry. Either way, the reader wants to feel superior.

"I can't imagine anyone wanting to write the life of a current Hollywood star," he says. "For one thing, so few of them are worthy of serious, complete biographies. For another, as long as they're alive, the story is not over."

As an author who takes pride in his insistence on the truth, Spoto knows that revealing a star's homosexuality, for instance, would be both required by the dictates of his conscience and impossible because of legal considerations. "We live in a very litigious society, and homosexuality is still thought of as a crime," he says. "People regard this as a smear on their character: So-and-so is 'accused' of being a homosexual – as if he were accused of being a Nazi or a serial killer. In Hollywood, with very few exceptions, everyone is completely terrified of being known as gay."

Gore Vidal seconds this, saying, "It is now the custom to establish that anyone worthy of an 'intimate' biography must be revealed not only as a homosexual but as an anti-Semite: plainly the two most dreadful 'preferences' of all."

Speaking of preferences, Anita Sarko in *Paper* noted that she was stunned by the number of people who approached her asking if Ellen DeGeneres was really gay? As if the whole thing had been a sweeps-week gimmick! One wag asked, "Do you know what they are now calling girls who are coming out of the closet? Ellens!" "Well," Sarko responded, "that's better than what they called them before!"

"Oh it's fun (to speculate about which celebrities are gay)," novelist Christopher Bram, author of *Gossip*, said in an interview with Christopher J. Hogan in *GCN*. "Actually, this ties to the general question of the importance of gossip among gay people. Gossip is important to everyone. It has a special importance to gay people because there were so few references – until recently – in the media, in print and television, to who was gay. You don't even get the 'so-and-so divorced their third wife this month' type of coverage. It's completely secret, so gay people have to share what they know with one another. It makes them feel connected to the world at large. Also, part of the appeal is that you're not sure if it's true or not. It's half imagined. It's not necessarily a hard, cold fact. That makes it like writing fiction. It's kind of like a communal fiction project.

"When gay people talk about celebrities who are gay, it's not out of a need for role models. There's a bit of dirt – a bit of a bite to it. It's fun. It's good to know something that the established media isn't telling you.

"Now with the Internet, gossip has been accelerated, and it has added new dimensions to it. You can now download nude pictures of Brad Pitt. Basically, it has escalated an activity that was already going on.

"In Hollywood, gossip is fairly harmless. It has a purely entertainment value, and it doesn't have any direct political results. It has some indirect and subtle political consequences, but no direct ones.

"It was during the fifties that *Confidential Magazine* started to run stories on who was gay and effectively destroyed several people's careers. Before then, the studios didn't care as long as you didn't get arrested, and even then sometimes it wasn't a problem. George Cukor once got arrested. The studio managed to cover it up, but it wasn't important to them. It became important in the fifties particularly with actors and movies stars. Then, only slowly in the sixties and seventies it went back to a more *laissez-faire* attitude the way it was in the twenties and thirties."

Yes, today's most popular exercise in prurience is speculation as to who among our notables has coupled with the same sex.

Suggests David Kamp in *GQ*: "Sooner or later, every name that attains the status of being 'household' acquires a trailing tail of homosexual innuendo, a swath of ribbon bearing the legend 'Frequented the bathhouses in 1981' or 'Shared more than a dorm room with school buddy' or, simply, 'What's his deal?' Often the speculation plays out as a kind of parlor game, wherein those purportedly in the know entertain the credulous by, say, painting all of Hollywood lavender: 'That actor – a queen! That actress – a dyke! That marriage – a sham!' In other instances, word circulates through a gossip item, or a politically charged 'outing,' or a McCarthyite smear... Homosexuality fascinates Americans as much as celebrity does, and the two combined inspire a sort of delirium."

On that note, we will leave the last word to Patrick ("Star Trek") Stewart: "In recent interviews...with the gay media, to my surprise, it's been put to me that I might be gay...I found myself curiously flattered by this."

"Everyone wishes to be Cary Grant. Even I wish to be Cary Grant," the late actor wrote. Two recent biographies don't even mention the star's bisexuality.

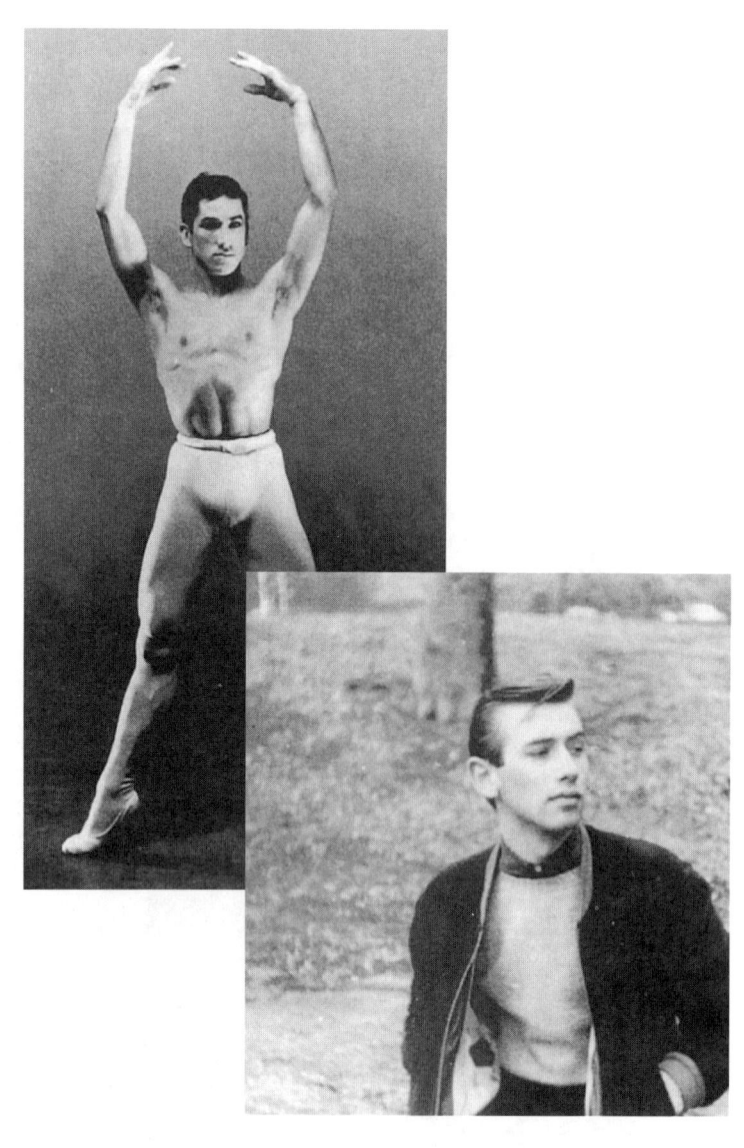

Great master Frederick Ashton developed stirring relationships with dancers such as Alexander Grant (top) but one of his most interesting was with the youthful American Tony Lizzul (bottom), as pictured in "Secret Muses: The Life of Frederick Ashton" by Julie Kavanagh

*Neophyte actor – and accomplished photographer –
Mike Ruiz is the hugely hung star of the low-budget film
festival favorite "Latin Boys Go to Hell,"
photographed for Next magazine*

GAYS ON FILM
(Or, Privates on Parade)

"When I told my friend George, who hates movies," Gary Morris says in the *Bay Area Reporter*, "that I was going to write a brief survey of frontal male nudity in this year's Lesbian and Gay Film Festival, he raved, 'Most movies are so horrible only *dick* could redeem them!' With this sentiment in mind, I've tried to catalog some cinematic sightings of our oft-discussed but rarely seen spongy-tissued little pal for male viewers who prefer a little anatomy with their artistry.

"...For fans of drag dick, 'Chocolate Babies' is *de rigueur*. Wiry Max spends much of his time getting drunk and screaming epithets from a rooftop, clad in a loosely woven net dress that hides none of his ample endowment. 'Latin Boys Go to Hell' moves into butch*er* territory – or as butch as one can expect from men who watch soap operas. The poster boy for the film is the gorgeous Carlos, whose hefty schlong is inexplicably rejected by Justin, a twink he covets. However, this entry also falls into the dreaded 'Where is the penis?' category when one of the characters is castrated. David DeCoteau's 'Leather Jacket Love Story' pays considerable attention to another handsome hunk in the buff. Mike is a thirtyish leatherman who falls for an 18-year-old blond *naif* who writes poetry. Don't let that angle put you off. Mike appears to be a true rarity in gay cinema: a convincing butch. He has numerous nude scenes in which he grinds away on top of Poetry Boy. Size queens will leave this one smiling." Carlos is played by Mike Ruiz, who said he "looked for something redeeming" in his character, but couldn't find it. He paused, then said, "He's *cute*." No, it's Mike that's *cute*.

Morris also liked "a film about a porn star that doesn't show the fleshy member... Hard to imagine, but William E. Jones' 'Finished,' about suicidal sex star Alan Lambert, somehow managed to make one. Perhaps the NEA credit at the end of the film explains why there are so many shots of ocean waves and industrial landscapes and so few of Lambert's drool-inducing body. Fortunately, the other two porn docs in the festival fill the void.

"Ronnie Larsen's 'Shooting Porn' reveals a variety of dicks on display, along with much reassuring cocksucking and buttfucking. England's archaic laws apparently allowed the makers of 'A Star is Porn' to show limp dicks, but no action (it's optically censored, like Japanese porn). On the other hand, even clearly visible hardons couldn't make these decidedly homely Brits appealing.

"Some of this year's films have minimal or discreet frontal nudity that only whets the appetite. Denis Langlois' 'L'escorte' has some extremely fetching French-Canadian flesh, but alas, we get only an eyestrain-inducing glimpse of the sacred tool during a naked stroll through a dark hallway. Nancy Meckler's 'Alive and Kicking' makes up in narrative power what it lacks in dick, so perhaps we shouldn't complain about this one. Yon Fan's 'Bugis Street' has a sexy, self-worshipping piece of trade whose endless hours in front of the mirrors prove only a tease when he fails to rip off his bikini briefs. John Greyson's 'Lilies' is one *of* many features in this festival that pivots on a beautiful man whose obtainability is in question. There are snatches of frontal nudity in this baroque production, but as always, never enough.

"Greyson is also the probable winner of this year's PPSI (penis per-square-inch) award for 'Uncut.' This challenging work is a virtual Shangri-La for the prick voyeur. Most intriguingly, the director uses Peter Greenaway-like window-box inserts to show circumcisions and dicks in various states of arousal. Call it cock consciousness."

Much interest was shown in the privates on parade in Terrence McNally's screen adaptation of his own play "Love! Valour! Compassion!" but, beyond that, it became yet another example of a dreary trend that movie critic Bill Kelley says has lately become a cottage industry: "'straight' actors mincing their way through embarrassing portrayals of flamboyant homosexuals. This time, it's Jason Alexander, *Seinfeld's* George Costanza, who has the heart-shaped sunglasses and love bears. Alexander demonstrates, as did Steven Weber ('Wings') and Patrick Stewart ('Star Trek: The Next Generation') in 1995's 'Jeffrey,' that some TV actors apparently will take any part in the off-season just to star in a movie. But even this isn't the most depressing thing about 'Love! Valour! etc.' What is? That this destitute man's 'The Boys in the Band' (Mart Crowley's exercise in '60s self-loathing that was dated the instant it opened) has been accepted, first on stage and now on film, as a work both legitimate and important. The truth is that to call 'Love! Valour! etc.' 'hackneyed' is to put it mildly. The narrative eavesdrops on a group of gay men who spend three weekends one summer at a country retreat in upstate New York. All the worst imaginable cliches are brought to wheezing life – at one point, several of the more free-spirited lads don ballerina costumes and prance about, performing an impromptu 'Swan Lake.' Like clockwork, the movie remembers at convenient intervals to briefly stifle the giddiness so that somber homilies about AIDS can be delivered by various characters. The contrivance trivializes a serious subject.

"It's a dreadful film, directed by Joe Mantello (who staged the Broadway production) with the grace of a jackhammer."

"Dicks! Butts! Handcuffs!" might have been a more commercial title, and a more accurate description of what you see on film, Steve Warren said in *The Front*. "Alexander pushes too hard with one hand while pulling his punches with the other. He plays gay as convincingly as Nathan Lane plays straight."

"The movie is more wordy than cinematic," Bruce Williamson said in *Playboy*, "but still works as a witty, tragicomic slice of the lives of a choreographer (Stephen Bogardus) and his friends. Among a slew of flawless performances, Alexander is a scene-stealer, and John Glover retains the glow of his Tony-awarded dual role as the diametrically opposite Jeckyll twins. While it all seemed funnier onstage, it is somehow more poignant and intimate in filmed close-ups. There's more male nudity here than moviegoers usually see, none of it exploited for shock value."

"This is the type of film that, I feel, makes a convincing case for the 'closeting' of plays: if they were written for the stage, leave 'em there!" said Kimberly Yutani in *Southern Voice*. "What do these eight guys do together? Most of the time, they talk about being gay. Or else they talk about their other defining characteristics: Latino, blind, they have AIDS, they're crusty and British. Fascinating. And though the dialogue can be bitchy and 'gay,' it's not smart. At one point a character says,

'I can catch a ball. I genuinely like both of my parents. I hate opera. I don't know why I bother being gay.' In order to liven things up they need some nudity (Randy Becker as Ramon caused quite a stir during the stage run with his massive 'talent'), hence, they often leap into the lake naked."

Talk about running naked! "Wild Reeds" and "Sebastian" finally became available on video and the traffic was heavy.

Set in Southwest, France, 1962, at the end of the Algerian War, "Wild Reeds" centers on the relationship formed among a group of teenagers (two local boys, Serge and Francois, and a girl, Maite) facing the pressures of their maturing sexuality, the formation of their political ideals during a turbulent period in French politics, and the stress of completing their Baccalaureate exam. Francois and Sergo develop an arrangement to help one another with their classwork. As their friendship progresses, their relationship briefly turns sexual. Francois realizes that, not only is he gay, but he is in love with Serge, who moves on from this fleeting intimacy to a relationship with a woman. It is the winner of four 1995 Cesar Awards; the Golden Globe entry for Best Foreign Language Film; and France's official selection for the 1995 Oscar. Upon the film's release in America, *The Advocate* raved, "Among the great international films about coming-of-age-and coming out."

And speaking of coming out, there's the quirky Norwegian film "Sebastian." This is the heartwarming tale of 16-year-old Sebastian, and his journey through the coming out process. Shown to 50% of 14-to-18-year-old Norweigians, it is not an educational film, but a charming, sexy coming out story.

Ian Bloomfield in *Vulcan* magazine says, "Our hero, Sebastian, is left alone with his friend Ulf for an evening, and they indulge in lots of sickly-sweet things like foam baths together, body painting and gobbling down home-made waffles. But at the end of the evening when Seb tries to get his leg over (well, a snog anyway), his mate doesn't want to know. Typical man. And it's from here that his journey begins. Once you've got used to the subtitles I know you'll enjoy it. I did. But then I'm a sucker for first love, happy ending, coming out tales."

Speaking of pioneers, "Tres gay Pierre and Gilles are French artists who have pioneered their unique photographic images into a minor *cause celebre*," comments Robert Julian in the *Bay Area Reporter* about the film "Pierre & Gilles, Love Stories." "Catherine Deneuve, Rupert Everett, and other luminaria waltz through this documentary, singing the praises of the artists referred to in the subtitles as 'P&G.' Their oeuvre is somewhat hard to describe, but it relies heavily on glitter, makeup, set design, leather accouterment, and cultural iconography that ranges from Biblical themes to Hindu actresses. Their photos possess a vaguely Robert Mapplethorpe-meets-the-Cockettes aesthetic, but to the uninitiated, they will simply be kitsch. It may help to recall that France is the country that adores Jerry Lewis. In 'Pierre & Gilles, Love Stories," the art and lives of P&G are documented by director Michael Aho in an outrageously queer fashion – this film simply screams.

"On the same program is Francois Ozon's 'Summer Dress,' a short subject that revolves around two scantily clad French gay boys, a beach, a strange girl, and a dress. The unforgettable opening has one of the boys vamping barefoot to a French version of Cher's 'Bang Bang (he shot me down).' To say more would spoil the fun, but this double bill is a Francophile's delight."

The Importance of Being Oscar (and Jude Law and Stephen Fry)

"One hundred years ago, Oscar Wilde was a prisoner at hard labor, serving a two-year sentence for 'gross indecencies with male persons,' his brilliant and meteoric career destroyed, his name vilified across the English-speaking world," Brian Caffall wrote in *PGN*. "Today, the great British poet, novelist, playwright and critic is the subject of wide-ranging re-appraisal and reconsideration. He even has a memorial window in Poet's Corner of Westminster Abbey, and a movement is afoot to ask the queen to grant him a posthumous pardon. This reconstruction of Oscar Wilde has been reflected in theater and film as well, although one of the most balanced of all depictions of Wilde's downfall remains Robert Morley's 1959 film, 'Oscar Wilde.'"

Over the past year, there has been an unprecedented

renewed appreciation for, and re-examination of, all things Oscar. Most notably, on stage there was "Wilde Spirit," "Oscar Wilde's Wife," and "Gross Indecency: The Three Trials of Oscar Wilde," and two biographical films.

"Gross Indecency" is constructed almost entirely of first-hand sources, including transcripts of the initial libel suit Wilde brought against the Marquis of Queensberry, the two subsequent criminal trials for "gross indecency," newspaper accounts, memoirs and biographies, and Wilde's own writings.

Notes Caffail: "The play posits that Wilde was brought down as much for his stance as an artist and an aesthete as for any dallying with members of his own sex. As constructed by writer and director Moses Kaufman, Wilde's real crime was challenging the comfortable Victorian status quo, of 'frightening the horses' to use Mrs. Patrick Campbell's famous phrase. As much as the gay movement may have adopted Wilde as one of its early martyrs, Wilde was not blameless in bringing about his own ruin, a point glossed over by Kaufman's adulatory script. While we may look back on British law of the time as having been repressive and puritanical, the fact remains that Wilde repeatedly left himself open for attack, and allowed his blind passion for Lord Alfred Douglas to color his judgment about the chances of winning a libel suit or being vindicated in answering criminal charges. He knew the rules, and he flaunted them. Wilde's tragedy was not so much that he was persecuted by the law as that he felt himself, by dint of his fame and position, to be outside it. Conversely, his heroism, if such it was, did not come from challenging the law as much as it came from his notion that he could redefine it. To use his own words, Wilde suffered the consequences of 'feasting with panthers.'

"'Gross Indecency' actually makes a stronger case for Wilde as a victim of outraged convention than it does in painting him as a protogay activist. Although the actual charges brought against him were for having sexual relations with men, the real hostility against Wilde was as a corruptor of young minds, not young bodies. ...'Gross Indecency' is never less than interesting, and is often riveting. ...Much as this play might have more impact if Wilde were drawn in a more balanced fashion – less plaster saint and more a man of human foibles – 'Gross

Indecency' is most definitely worthwhile. It's preaching to the choir, but the preaching is first-rate – and the choir can still use some saints."

In his review of the same play, Christopher Byrne in *L&G NY* says, "Oscar Wilde was not gay. Certainly he was homosexual, but he did not identify himself as a 'gay person.' Wilde was 'a lover of beauty in all its forms.' If those forms were sometimes young and male, and his appreciation went beyond dispassionate adoration and into the more carnal, that was simply part of experiencing the beauty. Wilde did not believe that anything was moral or immoral. Rather, he believed things were either beautiful or not beautiful.

"Sadly, 19th century British society did not quite share Wilde's sentiments or somewhat unorthodox definition of artistic appreciation. Wilde lived in a society that was rigidly divided between the moral and the immoral, clearly delineated and codified in law. Even the thought of two men together was so repellent that were two men known to be lovers and the knowledge became public, it would provoke enormous outrage and scandal. (One cannot help but hear harbingers of the polemic of today's far right in the castigation of homosexuality by Lord Queensberry, Wilde's accuser.) Wilde was first accused as a 'posing sodomite' by Queensberry, who Wilde took to court for libel. In the course of three trials, Wilde was subsequently convicted of 'gross indecency with male persons,' a crime whose punishment was two years' confinement at hard labor, torture for a man of Wilde's temperament. The conviction and incarceration destroyed the career of the man who was arguably the best writer of his generation, as well as his relationship with Lord Alfred Douglas, the love of his life for whom he risked all.

"...The tragedy, and the outcry it caused among the more enlightened people of the period such as George Bernard Shaw, set the stage for the evolution for what we know today as a gay sensibility. As gay people, we owe Wilde a debt of gratitude not merely for his achievement as a writer but especially for his courage and passion as a man. As Wilde himself said, some times giving into temptation, to follow the heart even when the outcome is surely destruction, is not weakness but strength.

"Wilde's wit, philosophy, passion, destruction by the 'secular arm, the instrument of God's vengeance,' and his ultimate humiliation are all spectacularly captured in this new play. ...It is an emotional and artistic experience of such intensity that you will be moved to your very core. ...So moved was I by 'Gross Indecency,' that I really couldn't speak for nearly half an hour afterward. I love it when that happens in the theater."

Even Michael Musto in the *Village Voice* enjoyed the play: "I was glad to like 'Gross Indeceny,' and that's coming from someone who's seen Oscar Wilde's life story done as a drama, and musical, a puppet show,and a Random House breakfast."

Meanwhile, in Hollywood, "Oscar Wilde's Wife" was playing to sell-out crowds. "In any era," Les Spindle said in *Frontiers*, "a straight woman marrying a gay man would certainly be setting herself up for heartbreak, but in the staid climate of Victorian England, such a plight was especially treacherous and humiliating. Such is the premise of Bonda Spinak's speculative drama on the trials and tribulations of Constance Wilde. Director Mark D. Kaufmann senses Spinak's literate script well, skillfully achieving poignant, lyrical drama, while sidestepping the pitfalls of weepy soap opera or campy melodrama. ...Scandal became a way of life for the repressed Constance, and that point is driven home by an amusing Greek chorus of spiteful young girls and dandy young gentlemen who periodically interrupt the play's action, strolling across the stage to chant out their judgmental and hypocritical barbs at the heartbroken Constance. ...A classy and thoroughly absorbing production."

Jeffrey Solomon in *LGNY* says, "This play is a long overdue education in queer and literary history. For those who are already fans of Wilde, they should find the play, constructed from actual trial transcripts, letters and other first-hand sources, fascinating. Wilde was an outspoken advocate for artistic freedom and an unabashed 'admirer of youth.'"

And speaking of being outspoken, "Believe it or not, the long arm of the law did *not* come after 24-year-old Brit babe Jude Law when he appeared nude in public," Marlien Rentmeester reported in *US*. "That's because Jude was on a Broadway stage, acting in a play called 'Indiscretions' opposite Kathleen Turner. Jude's bold and in-the-buff performance won him bravos in the form of a Tony Award nomination in 1995 and a smoking-hot Hollywood career. ('Gattaca,' the sci-fi thriller starring Uma Thurman and Ethan Hawke, 'Music From Another Room,' which costars Martha Plimpton, and as a Savannah hustler in Clint Eastwood's adaptation of the best-seller 'Midnight in the Garden of Good and Evil.'"

"Wilde" star Stephen ("Jeeves") Fry, writing in *The New Yorker*, says, "The irony – or the joke, perhaps – about making a film on Wilde is that it is a refinement on Wilde's own celebrity of a hundred years ago: a created thing that might be offered as a boilerplate for all the celebrity mania that was to follow. Wilde was nationally famous before he had written a single memorable work – famous as an undergraduate, famous for being famous, and pilloried in the cartoons and comic cuts for his exotic dress sense and his too utterly-utter aesthetic sensibilities. He was paid to tour the United States to publicize 'Patience,' a Gilbert and Sullivan operetta that guyed him and his circle. Certainly he earned his fame later, with the huge success and notoriety of his literary and dramatic works. But up until his trial, in 1893, the public view of Wilde was that the most famous thing about him was his fame – a logic loop all too familiar to contemporary celebrities.

"I can remember the first time I heard of Beatrix Potter. I can remember the first time I heard of Harriet Beecher Stowe. I can recall with piercing clarity the moment when the name Fyodor Dostoyevsky first came to my ears. (It was in a Norwich cafe bearing the improbable name Just John's Delicatique.) No matter how hard I try, however, I am unable to think of a time before I had heard of Oscar Wilde. It is as if he had been with me always, like Christ and the Queen. Not just with me, either.

"I was about seventeen when I emerged from my Firbank, Douglas, Acton, and Howard phases. I don't regret my teenage posturings and the fantasy years of collecting limp leather editions of decadent, consumptive poets and penning violet-inked diary entries, but these days I must confess that, if pushed, I would rather lose every Oriental silk dressing gown I own than a single pair of sensible corduroy trousers. *Autres temps, autres pantalons.* I still retain affection for that luxuriantly poisonous style, but it is, I suppose, not much more than literary drag, and, like so many drag acts, it can become tiresome. At any rate, it has nothing whatever to do with Oscar

Wilde or his works. Indeed, such images are only part of what the current jargon labels the 'self-oppression' to which we are all prey. Wilde's courage lay not in his 'alternative sexuality' but in the freedom of his mind. To picture him primarily as a gay martyr *avant la lettre* is, I think, to play into the very hands of those who brought him down a hundred years ago.

"Yet I know that it is the sexuality and, most especially, the sex that excites the interest of the press... I had advance notice. A few months ago, the Sunday edition of the *Daily Mail* published a piece on Jude Law, the astonishingly talented young actor in "Wilde" who plays Lord Alfred Douglas, Wilde's lover, the beautiful, petulant, and tempestuous youth known as Bosie. (It was Wilde's relationship with Bosie, the son of the Marquess of Queensberry, that brought him to trial and subsequent imprisonment.) The *Mail* decided that there was a story in the fact that I am gay and Jude is straight, and so it reported that during our 'love scenes' together I had to have my penis taped to my stomach to spare my own blushes, not to mention those of Jude Law and the crew. I stared at this story (apparently given to the *Mail* by an insider on the set) amused and amazed, quite undecided as to whether to be flattered or insulted. The fact is that I never actually had to take all my clothes off during the shooting of the film. Wilde, it is generally agreed, did not like to have Bosie Douglas see him naked, for Bosie was not much aroused by Oscar's generous helpings of flesh. So the story was entirely, wholly untrue. For the *Mail*, however, it was a story too good to check. The newspaper wanted it to be true: it had to be true, for it reduced Wilde and his nature (and me and mine, not that that matters much) to the level of sexual beast. Fry is a whoopsy. He had to lie next to an attractive young man, therefore he must have sustained an ungovernable erection. It stands, as it were, to reason. 'The penis mightier than the word' has long been the slogan of the British newspaper editor."

*Jude Law as Bosie,
photographed by Michael Roberts for Vanity Fair*

Rupert Everett, photographed by Paul Maxwell for US magazine

Rupert Everett

*"This is a man with enormous sex appeal.
He's handsome and clever and smart."*
 – Julia Roberts

"Rupert Everett insists he doesn't steal 'My Best Friend's Wedding' from Julia Roberts, and he's not someone you want to argue with," Marc Peyser said in *Newsweek*. "A few years ago, a woman found his performance in Noel Coward's 'The Vortex' hard to hear. She sent him a note to complain. He sent one back. 'I hope to avoid further disappointment,' he wrote, enclosing a lock of his pubic hair as compensation. 'She forwarded it to the newspapers,' says Everett. 'I was hoping she would.'

"There will be no complaints about his performance as George failing to register this time. Despite his protestations, Everett does something remarkable in 'Wedding': he turns the cliched role of the gay best friend into a charming, hilarious, gorgeous creature with just the right amount of bitchy common sense. Everett improvised many of the funniest moments, including a riotous taxicab scene where he mauls Roberts's breast in an inept attempt to make Dermot Mulroney jealous. That sequence was trickier than it sounds. 'Julia does not like people touching her tits,' says Everett, in a British mumble that might well be tough to make out onstage. 'She did get pissed off at me once – I did it again when we were playing around.'"

Roberts says, "He said I was his 'ultimate fag hag.' I adore him. And if there's any justice in the world, Rupert will soon be heralded as the comic genius that he is. People think of him in a very stuffy, British way, where he wears ties and (his) jaw only moves ever so slightly. But now there's just a whole new point of view."

Paul Rudnick, writing as Libby Gelman-Waxner, joked, "...Everett is a romantic hero for the women like me who have heard the rumor that Cary Grant's big amour in real life was probably with Randolph Scott."

Everett says, "We did a lot of improv. I make it up in the toilet before I do a scene. That's the secret to being a good actor."

So good, in fact, that David Denby in *New York* said, "The movie has nowhere to go; all it can do is spin around, though some of the spinning is highly entertaining. Everett, who has played highborn louts in his English movies, makes a triumphant appearance as Jules's gay editor. ...George makes wise and witty remarks, like someone's perceptive aunt. At a certain point, the filmmakers throw up their hands and let Everett take over the movie. We're not entirely ungrateful. Everett, at least, knows what he's doing."

Everett, the son of a British Army officer, grew up all over the empire. Then he was placed in boarding school. "When you get left at boarding school at the age of 7 by your mother, there's a kind of cauterization of emotion that numbs you forever. That's something all the English upper class have in common. I wasn't lonely at boarding school," he continues, "but I could never understand the rejection you have from the mother when you're just dumped away from home."

"When Everett was a boy he used to wander from his parents' house in the south of England to a secluded spot among the trees and rolling meadows, fall to his knees and pray for the Virgin Mary to appear," *US* revealed. "Aware of his burgeoning homosexuality, he wasn't, as might be conjectured, seeking divine intervention from the Blessed Mother to make what was bound to be a difficult life easier. In fact, he had an altogether different mission."

"I was determined to have my fucking apparition," the actor laughs now, "so that any minute there'd be, like, this huge, hideous basilica built there." Why? Well, he says, without the least bit of embarrassment or apology, to ruin his parents' favorite view, of course.

Rebellious Everett eventually he went to drama school but was thrown out at 19. "It was very character forming in a sense," he says. "Considering what my background is, if I hadn't been queer and gone into the club scene, I'd have lived the most incredibly protected, tiny little existence, and I think an actor needs to do things, have a life, be exposed."

Although he came to prominence as a homosexual boarding-school student in the 1984 film 'Another Country,' he's avoided the gay pigeonhole despite outing himself years ago.

Everett's played everything from Miranda Richardson's doomed lover in 1985's 'Dance With a Stranger' to a fashion designer who cheats on his wife with her sister in 1994's 'Ready to Wear.'

US found Everett surprisingly candid about his fall from grace in the '80s. "Of his reputation for being difficult, he acknowledges that it was well-earned but adds that it mustn't be overlooked that his best performances were given under circumstances in which he 'was incredibly strident about what I believed was right.' While his journey to Hollywood after his British successes was a bust ('I didn't fit into the Brat Pack vibe of the movies they were making at the time'), his pariah-like treatment back at home was disheartening. It didn't help matters that he made outrageous claims about his prodigious talents. ...In fact, the notoriously vengeful British press seemed to be in a competition to see who could most ceremoniously hang him out to dry. 'He's rude, difficult, intolerant, given to the sort of bad behavior that involves walking out of an interview, a restaurant or a relationship,' hissed the *Daily Mail*. 'If politeness were pounds he'd be penniless, and if petulance was pennies he'd be a wealthy man,' one-upped the *Times*. The more conservative *Observer* simply asked, 'Will Rupert Everett ever be as good an actor as he says he is?'"

"All those types of things, you get over them, don't you?" says Everett. "It's like being a prostitute. The first time out is fine, and then you get knocked about a bit on your third night of work, and you go back four days later with a bruise and you get knocked about again, but you've got a knife, so you're OK. It becomes second nature."

Interesting analogy, considering the actor has admitted to, but never elaborated on, being a member of the world's oldest profession. At the time he was a struggling actor in London who simply got propositioned outside a subway station one day and 'sort of fell into it.'

"I didn't set out to hustle," he explains, "but this guy offered me such a massive amount of money, well, it was like a year-and-a-half's pocket money, and it just came in really handy." And while to some it might appear to be just an extreme form of rebellion against an upper-crust upbringing, Everett says it was hardly anything of the sort; it was a lot more practical than that. "Like a lot of upper-class people, I was given no money," says Everett, admitting once he got the hang of it he had "all sorts" of clients and basically relied on the work as his main source of income for a year or two.

Perhaps, then, this explains his rather strong reaction to fellow thespian Hugh Grant, when his name comes up. "Hugh Grant I was kind of with, until he said that getting sucked off by Divine Brown was – what was the word he used on his big apology tour? 'Abominable'? " asks Everett, referring to Grant's infamous appearance on *The Tonight Show* shortly after he was arrested for lewd conduct. "I thought how fantastic for him to have been given head by Divine Brown and how brilliant a career move it was, but the moment he said it was an abomination, he really lost me. Because that poor prostitute, having to suck his meaty little dick anyway, why should she be roped into his apology? I think that's one of those moments when you just say, 'If you don't want me, you don't have to have me. That's what I did. I got a blow job – what of it?' When it's suggested that maybe this was the only way Grant could get back his girlfriend, Elizabeth Hurley, Everett rolls his eyes and says, "Oh, please! She's like a boomerang, darling, she's always going to come back."

Using his life experiences as a base, he's also created a thriving second career as the author of two campy, semi-autobiographical novels that were best sellers in England in spite of some critical evisceration. "Everett made the most of those complaints, too," *Newsweek* reported. "When The Times Literary Supplement described his *Hello Darling, Are You Working* as 'deplorable,' Everett blurbed it on his dust jacket. 'If someone was brave enough to put something like that up on a theater, I'd go straight in,' he says.

"Thanks to 'Wedding,' people are going straight into theaters in droves, and the critics are calling Everett the gay Cary Grant (if that's not redundant). He appreciates being a new homosexual role model. He's less thrilled by the Grant comparison. 'It's what they say about all British actors when they're discovered,' he says. 'A few years ago, Hugh Grant was Cary Grant. Now it's me. Doubtless there's a Cary Grant in embryo waiting to burst out of swinging London and take the crown next year.' We'd like to contradict him, but we're afraid of what he'd send us in the mail!"

"Everett brings a tart, distinctly pink twist to this comedy cocktail in the role of George, the gay confidant of Julia Roberts," raved Cathay Che for *Time Out*. Knight-Ridder's Chris Hewitt also raved, "Everett is a hoot and a holler in scenes when Roberts forces him to pretend he's her straight fiance and he makes her pay for it by going way overboard." Indeed, Everett seemed to get more dialogue by the day as the filming progressed. George Meyer, esteemed movie critic, went so far as to predict an Oscar nomination for Everett: "Given the movie's best lines and sharpening them with aplomb and quick delivery, he steals the show."

Everett explained the point of the movie to Che in an interview in New York: "I suppose beautiful women get tired of men punting on them all the time. It's a macho myth that women only think about getting laid. It's *men* who think about getting fucked all the time, because our brains are actually lodged in the heads of our dicks. Women are much more complicated and profound than that. In 'My Best Friend's Wedding,' the message is that love comes in many shapes and forms. In the relationship between Julianne and George, there's a bit of ambiguity. We're not going to get married and we're not going to have sex, but it's an old-fashioned love. In the film I'm (a) bookish, (b) English and (c) homosexual, so I'm not going to have a sugared outlook on Julianne's trysts. She's like a beautiful, exotic bird flapping around in a room and bashing her head against windows, and I'm the one picking up the pieces."

"What happens to most people who get a huge success like this," Everett says of "Wedding," "is that the bubble bursts in about 10 minutes and they're back to summer stock in Connecticut, swatting mosquitoes as they play Sir Toby Belch." Not that he minds adulation. "An actor," he declares, "never gets tired of people telling him how fabulous he is."

Everett says that his current success is due to the fact that American cinema has changed. "When 'Another Country' and 'Dance With a Stranger' came out in the mid-'80s, I wanted to come over here right away, because we didn't have much of an industry then. But it was the time of John Hughes and 'Pretty Poison' and 'St. Elmo's Fire,' and there wasn't a place for someone like me, with a European sensibility and an exotic kind of look. And that has changed. If those films had come out, say, two years ago, they'd have been major mainstream films, and I would have had a totally different career."

Everett admits his first novel was semi-autobiographical. "There are many things that are similar. I had a really nice childhood, but it's part of the past. My generation was, in a way, the last of the Victorians. My grandmother was a real Edwardian lady. My grandfather was an admiral in the navy. I suppose all the male members of my family were very, very cold. We used to have to go hunting, and the first time you kill a fox, you are 'blooded' – they take the paw of the fox and cut it off and rub it all over your face. The funny thing about the English upper class is that they're pretty unsophisticated people, even though they are surrounded by incredible wealth and beauty. My great-uncle is one of five people in the world who has a private Michelangelo picture in his collection."

Everett was educated by Benedictine monks. "The upper-class English boy is sent away to boarding school, and probably the most lasting effect of my childhood – if I ever get bored enough to go into analysis – is the rejection I felt from my mother when, at seven years old, I was taken to the monastery and left there. It sort of calcifies your heart. But everyone was treated as I was. The monks were quite nice, actually.

"When I left school at 15, I wanted to live in a completely different way (from the upper class). Show business was disappointing in the end, because it was as insular and provincial as being in the upper classes. I had this image that show business was a kind of gas-lit netherworld of passion, sex, hysterical laughter, hysterical tears, traveling, enormous heartbreak and exultation. That the acting world is so bourgeois is a disappointment I've never quite gotten over. No one is trained anymore to be mad or crazed – actors now have to be the most normal people and represent family values.

"The exciting actor for me was the 16th- or 17th-century actor, who was a kind of criminal. When they came to town, daughters were locked up, stores closed – but there was a sense of excitement. And when everybody came to see *Macbeth* by the glare of the torches, the guy playing him was probably a murderer. You saw in his eyes something that really scared you. Now you have these actors who are dead-eyed corporate sharks swimming at you in the cold waters on-screen, and you're not getting anything from it. I think the thing most lacking is truth. You're always being forced to hide behind a more acceptable version of yourself."

Everett came out in 1989, because, he says, his bisexuality had come to an end in 1986 and he couldn't be bothered to lie. "I didn't admire the society that despised homosexuals enough to lie, I suppose. As soon as you lie, you're agreeing with them. I'm pleased to be homosexual, because if I'd been heterosexual, I would never have gotten out of the home counties of England. So from my point of view, if I hadn't been gay, I wouldn't have done anything.

"I'm an actor, after all, so I like to be appreciated and I don't mind if (people) like me for things that are really about me. I'm happy to be appreciated for what I am. I get people saying to me, 'Now that you're 'openly gay,' – which is a kind of hideous phrase – 'do you think you'll ever be able to be successful in the movies?' I think maybe if you were a gay man and you were 21, it might be difficult, because young girls might not be able to get their heads around the idea that there wouldn't be a sexual rapport. But I'm a 38 year-old actor, and the audience I probably appeal to is between 18 and 30, so it doesn't matter. I must say, I've been very lucky. Maybe if I'd been straight, I'd have been luckier, but I've never felt restricted at all. When I look at my work I think that, for the most part, my films will stand the test of time.

"I hate the word *gay*. *I* don't particularly want to be accepted by society. When we talk about gay culture, we're still talking primarily about men – and that's the problem. Men are facing a very difficult time, and I think gay culture is facing a difficult time as well. In gay culture, there is this obsession with being a man, but it's superficial. I think that being a man – in the best, classical sense – is obviously about things other than having a good body; it's about courage, truth, honor. But no one values anything except what you can touch and take to bed. Personality has become a belt and a haircut.

"But I think men's positions in general will be changing dramatically over the next 100 years. If you think of the existence of the world in terms of a 24-hour clock, then man has existed for four minutes – and what women have done in the last millisecond is totally mind-boggling Women have radically changed their position; moving from being servants to taking over health care and charity, establishing suffrage and, in the '60s, finally burning the bra. Women are on the move. Women have changed and men have to change as well."

Everett's newest book, *Guilt Without Sex: A Jewish Bestseller*, is about Hollywood in the future. "It's about the same thing happening to the actor that happened in the '80s to the drurnmer. All bands used to have a live drummer, and then computers came in and the drummer who couldn't program was a drummer who simply didn't work anymore. The ones who were successful were the genius programmers. So it's about a really bad actor who is a genius programmer. He's got samples of every actor throughout history, and he can morph them."

In the past, Everett, who maintains homes in Miami's South Beach, England, Paris and New York's Greenwich Village, has told inquiring minds that he doesn't believe in relationships, or at least doesn't have time for them (currently, he's not in one, he admits). "I have a crashingly huge ego," he's been quoted as saying, "and when you boil it down to bones, in the bed and relationships it all has to be about me."

But now, as he approaches middle age, he seems to be softening his anti-relationship stance, well, at least a little. "Maybe homosexuality is better casually," he muses. "Maybe it's just an extension of buddydom."

*Tony Ward makes a date in "Hustler White,"
photographed by Rick Castro, the co-director.
Photographer Reed Massengill wants to shoot Tony: "He's a
great eternal beauty...the construction of his face. He has a
great body, but it's his face that I love."*

Tony Ward

"If dicks earned frequent-flyer points, Tony Ward could've been to the moon and back five times." – Blue magazine

"I related to 'Hustler White' because I had lived that life," the film's star Tony Ward told *The Advocate*. "I wasn't on the streets, but I was naive, and I thought I had to trade sexual favors for photos.

"The man who first scouted me introduced me to a whole ring of guys who sort of swapped young boys around," he continues. "They were sweet men, cool people, and respectful, but they wanted sex in return for what they did, which was make a pretense of photographing you in order to get a modeling book together. Then they'd throw you $70 or $80 to boot, so it really was like hustling. I never told anybody about it. For a while I was like, *What the fuck's wrong with me?* I had a girlfriend too, so I had this double life. But I didn't stop it, I was working a shit-ass job making $200 a week, and I liked making a little extra cash on the side."

"Ward, a mix of Portuguese, Scottish, Irish, English, and Swedish descent, grew up in a poor San Jose neighborhood," the magazine reported. "His was the first generation in his family that did not have to work picking fruit. Naive though he was, as his photographs began appearing in such gay skin magazines as *In Touch* and *Blueboy*, he realized that his looks might be his passport to an escape from a life spent, as he puts it, 'delivering paint or working for Kmart. I really wanted to be a model but didn't know how to do it. I went to one agency in San Jose that told me to come back in a year, after I'd gotten a nose job. I even got a doctor's number.' But a gay mentor Ward had met put the kibosh on that idea. 'He stopped me by showing me all these pictures of Roman statues with my nose. I didn't know.'

"A move to Los Angeles brought about the meeting that would jumpstart his career in the far more rarefied world of high fashion. When Herb Ritts spied a Polaroid of Ward on his first agent's desk, they began a collaboration that would produce some of the most spectacular male nudes of the '80s. 'We weren't lovers, but we were very close and spent a lot of time together,' says Ward of his relationship with Ritts. 'Then he got jealous because I brought a girlfriend over to his studio, and I never went back.'"

The film "Hustler White" came along, says Ward, when he had just about given up the idea of acting. Given its explicit nature, the film might have been a hard sell to a more image-conscious performer. But when Bruce LaBruce's co-director Rick Castro got in touch with Ward, he got an affirmative answer only hours after giving Ward the script. Though he acknowledges that Ward initially struck him as "the sexiest man I'd ever seen," Castro points to another quality as the most valuable aspect of his performance. "He has a magnetism, of course," Castro explains, "but it's the naive charm he has, an innocence he still has at 33, that's so unique."

"They wanted me to really have sex. They wanted me to blow my co-star, they wanted me to really fluff him, they didn't want me to just jerk him off. And I said to them 'I can't tell you (whether I will). I have to get in this situation, feel it out and see how it goes'. It ends up being all simulated ... it's not a porno because there's no penetration. But that's Bruce's thing, he wants to put it all in (the audiences') faces. What ended up happening made it more commercially accepted than it ever possibly could have been if there was actual penetration shown. The shocking stuff, I mean, it's completely boring. People go 'Oh, they just wanted to shock people with the stumping' (where an amputee fucks another man with his stumpy leg). But you know what? This is reality. This is a man with no fucking foot. They tried to soften it up a little bit and humanize it by trying to make everyone laugh at it. It's a heavy image - but it's reality. This is a family movie. It's about sitting there and watching your fantasy up there on a screen, or, if you like, a nightmare. But if you compare it to some of the grotesque crap that Hollywood makes - the gratuitous, senseless, abusive sex, violence, death - what we saw up there was a fucking picnic. And it was done with humor."

Ward has no discomfort with the adulation he's found among gay men. "I've been asked how I feel being a gay icon or pinup boy, and I'm proud of it," he says. "I'm happy to be that. It's just about appreciation. I appreciate pictures of men on many different levels too – on sexual levels. It doesn't matter to me how people look at my pictures – or who does."

In fact, his interest in male sexuality has not been exclusively photographic. Though he is living happily with his girlfriend in the Silver Lake district of Los Angeles, Ward says he's never "labeled" himself in terms of sex. "I have had affairs with men from time to time but not really a relationship," he says. "It's about liking the person. I've had a lot of, you know, fun. There's a lot of experiences I would just put in the mindless-sex category. I've had good things with both male and female, (but) I've always been in relationships with women." That freedom may go a long way toward explaining the hypnotic sexuality that Ward's best photographs exude. "I do what I want to do," he says. "With whoever I want to do it with."

Now, all that directors want him to do is to fuck boys again. "You can't avoid it. Every role that I've been offered is a gay role. I don't mind. That's fine with me, for now, and eventually I'll go into an arena where it's a little bit less closed-minded. I'm going to the south of France (for a film) called 'The Cuckold's Desire.' I play a character called Chevalier. He's a courtesan in the early 17th century and he goes in and basically screws this whole family. He goes in for a pre-arranged marriage to the daughter of the Duke. So I go in and I fuck the mother in the first scene and then I'm banging her for a while. I meet the Duke and I ask for his daughter's hand in marriage and I end up fucking the Duke and then I'm fucking the daughter and it ends up crazy. It's great and it's actually kind of a dramatic thing, like 'Dangerous Liaisons.'"

There's talk of a part in "Flowers For Algernon" as well as a blossoming sideline in international television commercials. Ward revals, "Then there's this script written by Tennessee Williams back in the '60s. It's called 'One Arm' and it's about a prize-fighter who loses his arm in a car accident and becomes a hustler who ends up on death row. It's been buried (for so long) because the lead character isn't gay but becomes a male hustler. So it was a little too controversial to be made.

"I'm not going to be an actor," Ward concludes. "I'm not going to be like Johnny Depp or Brad Pitt. I've never wanted to be anybody but me. I never was that big a fan of anybody that I wanted to be like them. I just want peace."

*Lukas Haas, the star of "Johns,"
earlier in his career*

Lukas Haas

"Limpid, liquid, tactile – they beckon as guilelessly as a cool lake on an August afternoon. They distract and disarm, make it difficult to concentrate. Haas seems to know this."
– Detour magazine, about the eyes of Lukas

"'This is a story that begins and ends with shoes,'" Michael Bunch commented in his review of "Johns" in *4Front*. "We hear this as one of the lead characters is having his sneakers, along with all his money, stolen while sleeping on a neighborhood lawn. 'Johns' is the latest entry into the suddenly popular genre of male hustler films. Although unlike its recent predecessor, 'Hustler White,' which not only took risks but jumped head-first into oncoming traffic, this falls a bit flat.

"The story follows a day in the life, Christmas Eve, of two hustlers on Santa Monica Boulevard. The streetwise John (David Arquette) wants to spend his birthday in the best hotel in town and with the help of his young protege, Donner (Lukas Haas), sets out to make the three hundred dollars needed to accomplish this. We are then introduced to a series of dates, or rather johns, they encounter on this quest. From the Hollywood producer going for the noontime blowjob to the seemingly harmless old man who wants to spank Donner then ends up beating the crap out of him. Actor Elliot Gould even makes a memorable cameo appearance as a flamboyant musician who chases John around the bed, hoping for a quickie while his wife is out shopping.

"Soon we learn that John is straight, has a girlfriend and by the number of watches he is gifted with through the film, constantly late. But we also discover that Donner is hopelessly in love with him. So while John is busy dodging drug dealers, turning tricks and making excuses to his girlfriend, Donner is making plans of his own. His family can get them both a job as lifeguards at a hotel in Branson, Missouri, room and board included. Now all he has to do is convince John to go away with him.

"...The best thing about the film is John, played by David Arquette. From the first moment he is on screen you can't take your eyes off him. He is like a spring wound too tight and provides a perfect balance to the painfully sedate but effective performance of Lukas Haas."

Effective certainly does describe all of the performances of Lukas Haas. You may remember him as the adorable little Amish boy Samuel in "Witness," made in 1985 when he was 8. Since then he's remained busy, acting with the likes of Robert Duvall, Jessica Lange and Winona Ryder.

Not only does Lukas Haas act, he has written a script, has directorial aspirations, writes songs, and plays, he says, "keyboards and drums and guitar and bass and stuff." He also has, Joy Ray of *Detour* magazine says, "the biggest eyes in Hollywood:" "Limpid, liquid, tactile – they beckon as guilelessly as a cool lake on an August afternoon. They distract and disarm, make it difficult to concentrate. Haas seems to know this; whether by instinct or by Machiavellian intent, he rarely blinks. It is said of Brigitte Bardot that her first brilliant moment on screen came when the director told her to 'stare at the camera and think of nothing.' That lesson is one that the 20-year-old Haas seems to have been born knowing."

"I'd love to be able to keep on working as an actor," Haas says. "That'd be wonderful, you know, maybe if I can write or direct, or go from one to the other, use different forms for one piece or whatever."

"The drive to diversify," *Detour* noted, "was perhaps what led him to portray a gay teen hustler..."

"I don't have some kind of idea about worldly changes that will happen because of the film, because films haven't affected me that way, necessarily," Haas explains. "My reason for doing it was the character."

"Male hustler movies are a rare breed" Tom Dolby said in *X Y* magazine, "prone to a bizarre combination of gritty reality and psychedelic fantasy. From Warhol onward, filmmakers have tried to capture the sexual ambivalence, the violence, and the sadness with which male hustlers turn tricks and pass the time. A welcome addition to the fray is 'Johns,' an auspicious debut from director Scott Silver.

"...While David Arquette plays John with a goofy surety, the lithe Haas is the true star of the film, portraying Donner with a grace unseen in most actors his age. It is Donner's sadness and longing that remains after the film has ended, a feeling which captures the hustling experience as well as the alienation of gay youth. While all John (who is straight) wants is to spend the night at a posh hotel for his birthday, Donner seeks a more permanent refuge from the life of hustling..."

When Silver started doing research on the local youths, he became fascinated with his subjects. "At first, they thought I was a cop," he recalls, "but slowly I gained their trust. I would pay them $20 each to hear their stories. Practically every story in the film is true." Although the tales he heard sometimes surprised him, Silver soon found a common thread. "What these kids want," he says, "isn't that different from what everyone wants: friendship, a sense of belonging. As a filmmaker, I wanted to let people know that the human experience is universal. We are all more alike than not alike."

"This town likes to stereotype people," Silver says. "Wilson Cruz only gets cast as gay, which is ridiculous. But it's a closed-minded business. It's all about the money. There's a perception in Hollywood that gay stars just aren't fuckable to the public." Although Silver laments the lack of positive gay images in the media, he is quick to note, "The gay character in my movie is the strongest character. That wasn't all accident..."

If Haas had been selling his body when the film debuted at the Sundance Film Festival, he'd have made the most money, according to Paper. "Arquette's cute, but Haas was the night's most drooled-over male."

Haas looked good enough to drool over in "Boys," opposite Winona Ryder, who was playing an older woman to Haas' youth. Trouble is, the fuss the story asked us to believe, *Rolling Stone* pointed out, didn't work because "Ryder still looks like jailbait no matter how much she smears on lipstick and badass attitude."

"Now is a low point, really," Haas insists. "I think I'm on an in-between kind of level. There's other actors that get offered bigger-money type of roles, and I'm not at that level. But something could pop up in a second and change all that. I feel established, that's the one thing, just 'cause of all the work. So I feel like I can just hold my ground."

The oldest child of an artist and a screenwriter, Haas got his start in acting fortuitously at the age of five. "Months before I got the chance to do it, I was telling my parents every day that

I wanted to be an actor," he remembers. "In kindergarten, I was always into dressing up and being the clown. When the casting director (of 'Testament,' his first film) was casting, they called up my kindergarten and said, 'Who is the best actor in all the school plays?'" His teacher recommended him, and he "went and auditioned and got the role."

"Parts have been trickling in steadily since then," *Detour* said, "and he even seems to have navigated the treacherous teen years with flair."

"I haven't actually changed, really," Haas reflects. "They say there's this period where most actors don't get through it. But I find that exists all through the ranks, it just depends on individual careers. I feel like I've made it through so far, although I still feel like people think of me as younger. Which I am. So that doesn't bother me."

He goes back to his home in Texas when he's not working. "When I'm (in L.A.) for too long, I start to feel the competition more strongly," he says. "I'm much more anxious to get a film. A lot of people think I'm snobby because I'm not outgoing. I don't talk to people I don't know, and so they think since I'm just back there not saying anything, that I'm avoiding everyone. But I just don't know how to approach people very well." *Detour* insists that doesn't mean he's not watching: "Every situation, every movie, every director is under the careful scrutiny of his trademark gaze."

*Jeremy Jordan posed for the
famed Bruce Weber in Interview magazine*

Jeremy Jordan

"...an incredibly cute, blond, buff singer crooning his way through 'Right Kind of Love' video shirtless."
— Billy Masters in Filth

The other night on cable there appeared a film called "Live Nude Girls." I winced, but before I switched the channel, I noticed that one of the cast members was Jeremy Jordan. I have to admit I have been obsessed with the cutie ever since he was a teen idol with one hit record. Now he takes small parts in small projects. My patience with the movie was rewarded when Jeremy finally appeared, as a volunteer for Greenpeace who calls on a neighbor, a frustrated housewife, for a contribution. Nature takes its inevitable course and Jeremy hastily fucks her on the dining room table. This provided us with a sensational shot of the actor's luscious backside. He was certainly perfectly cast! We saw him a few months earlier in an episode of "The Gun," playing a rather smooth criminal, and that too was another case of perfect casting. (Wil Wheaton, looking sexier than ever, also had a role in the episode.)

But it was "Nowhere" that provided Jeremy his showiest role yet. Lydia Marcus in *Frontiers* said that Gregg Araki's "Nowhere" has "plenty of style but basically no substance. The film is made up of close to 20 empty-headed, predominately pleasure-seeking teen characters who've got nothing to do but eat, blab and screw. The film begins with a naked and showering Dark (James Duval) experiencing a sexual stream of consciousness masturbation fantasy that involves hetero, homo, and bondage and domination sex. But Araki is just teasing us with a sensuality that the film never ends up delivering. Instead we get inane teen conversation, sex scenes that are generally comic but never erotic, and tons of loony acting that relies on people contorting their faces in a style reminiscent of silent movie theatrics. A few actors stand out despite their lack of storylines: Guillermo Diaz, who has amazing screen presence but never enough screen time; a dreamy and androgynous Nathan Bexton as the boy of Dark's dreams; a practically unrecognizable, geeked out and braces-wearing Christina Applegate; and Thyme Lewis' Tom of Finland-like character, complete with perfectly groomed chest hair, leather chaps and a hot motorcycle.

"When Araki lets Duval talk and be a little fleshed out, Dark becomes an empathetic lead, but when Duval is forced to emote, the character loses intensity. Like Araki's previous feature, 'The Doom Generation,' the production design is inventive, and whereas that film was practically black and white, "Nowhere" is Bubbliciously bursting with Starburst fruity colors. There are fun cameos from John Ritter as a fiery TV preacher and from Traci Lords, Rose McGowan and Sharon Doherty in a hilarious parody of val-speak. For all of Araki's considerable talent at finding intriguing actors and his knack for making creative imagery, it's really too bad he's telling the story of a bunch of mostly boring and wasted youth."

"I admit that after suffering through the first half of 'The Living End,' (I chose dinner over the second half), I vowed I would never see another film by Gregg Araki," Nora Burns said in *HX*. "Having heard mixed reviews of 'Totally Fucked Up' and 'The Doom Generation,' I again chose dinner. So, needless to say, my expectations going into 'Nowhere,' the finale of writer/director Araki's 'Teen Apocalypse' trilogy, were less than stellar. Well, you can guess the rest. I liked it.

"For 'Nowhere,' Araki has finally hired some decent actors, and there are enough great cameos and colorful sets to hold the audience's expected short attention span for 85 minutes, or until the movie breaks down with an unfortunately silly ending."

"'Nowhere' unfurls on-screen like a trashy kaleidoscope of youth gone haywire," *Genre* magazine said. "Yet this supertasty eye candy still packs a punch – conveying underneath its glossy exterior the awkwardness and aimlessness of our teen years. And any movie that opens with boy-babe Duval yanking it in the shower can't be too bad."

"All the guys in 'Nowhere' are all very young and very cute," John Price noted in *4Front*. "Araki has a knack for steamy erotic scenes like opening the film with a naked James Duval masturbating in the shower while intermittently fantasizing about his African American girlfriend and a hot 17-year old boy with one bright blue and one bright green eye. It's one of the most beautifully titillating film experiences I've ever seen. Of course the porn aficionado will ultimately be upset because there's no penetration. It's erotic, but beautiful – not guttural and graphic. James Duval, however, is a delight. He is plagued with the dilemma that he looks exactly like Keanu Reeves. He does. And what's wrong with that? The good part is, he's a better actor than Keanu. He gave an admirable performance in 'Independence Day' as the kooky-trailer-trash that saved the world. He certainly has a great future. However, for a really good actor, he sure was naked a lot in this movie...

"Also, are there *Tiger Beat* fans out there who remember the lovely Jeremy Jordan? He is delightfully cast out of type in this movie. Now, he's tattooed, ODing on intravenous drugs and cheating on his BOYFRIEND. Those are some startling images you may not want to miss."

"'Nowhere's' ensemble cast is filled with some sicko surprises," Peter Davis said in *Paper*, "including *Teen Beat* staple Jeremy Jordan playing a pierced, tattooed gay junkie with a death wish..."

All the publicity accorded "Nowhere" got gays interested in Jeremy again. "A popular question in my E-Mail recently revolves around singer/actor Jeremy Jordan," Billy Masters noted in *Filth*. "You may recall Jeremy as an incredibly cute, blond, buff singer crooning his way through "Right Kind of Love" video shirtless. He later abandoned singing to act in such films as 'Leaving Las Vegas.' Connoisseurs of such heavenly bodies swear that Jeremy (who's real name is Donnie, incidentally) is featured in Greenwood/Cooper's 'Boy 2.' Not so says one of the producers who assures me the guy in question is actually a model from Bratislava! But, if you wanna see more of Jeremy, take a look at 'Live Nude Girls' where he has sex with Dana Delaney. She seems to have all the luck!"

"Young Gun" Tom Cruise at a press conference in 1983 to promote his first big hit, "Risky Business."

THE GREAT BEAUTIES

"It used to be that when women cooed, 'He's *beautiful*,' about fine male specimens, nearby guys would ask them to please, *please* refrain from using the B-word," Louisa Kamps said in *Elle*. "The exotic, gender-bending connotations of masculine beauty made straight men nervous. But in the '80s, with more women making business decisions and growing mainstream acceptance of gay aesthetics, overly beautiful men started to appear in increasingly provocative ads. For the first time, men were being used to market goods to financially independent women (the way women had always been used to sell to men), and men, dragged in to consume products (or self-images) they weren't necessarily asking for, found themselves touched on a nerve that had never before been so blatantly exposed.

"In 1992, when the pumped rap singer Marky Mark modeled tight briefs in ubiquitous Calvin Klein ads, male objectification was certainly complete. In a scene undoubtedly played out elsewhere, one ordinary Joe had his moment of clarity when confronted by the ab-and-groin specter of Mark looming in Times Square, and his girlfriend saw him furtively poking his own belly – as much, she supposed, to test its strength as to confirm that he himself did in fact still exist. American men are overwhelmingly expressing new concern – even anxiety – about their appearance.

"Marketers, are turning men into eager, sophisticated consumers of vanity products. Today, men spend roughly $9.5 billion a year on grooming aids and plastic surgery, and men's designer collections, long-scaled-back sidelines to womenswear, are being met with greater enthusiasm each season."

"As far as beauty goes," declares Paul West of Boss Models, an agency that made the prescient decision to nurture male talent when it started in 1988, "men are the women of the next century."

Katharine Rosman in *Elle* recalled "a surreal moment of cinematic slow motion" when she attended a party in Manhattan and a model she recognized from the pages of *GQ* sauntered in. Said she, "Without moving, I was transported to a sexually charged cosmopolitan event.

"Jack is about six-foot-three, with chiseled cheekbones, a strong jaw, and thick eyelashes surrounding sleepy brown eyes. A semicircle of women sipping Bud Lights flocked around him giggling and nervously fixing their hair. I kept my distance, irritated that someone 'deserved' attention solely because of his looks." Yet an hour later, Rosman found herself with Jack, on the street, in search of a club: "As we walked down the street, heads turned, and all at once I understood the arrogance of the fat, short, balding man who strolls into a bar with a leggy blond on his arm. Suddenly, I was sultry and alluring because of my fabulous babe; I was a sexy woman who accessorized like a champ. I was drunk on myself, intoxicated with how his beauty reflected upon me. At the club, we flirted, we danced, we kissed, but being *seen* with him was the biggest turn-on."

"Essentially, the beautiful male is a version of the beautiful female," Lisa Shea said in *Elle*, "who has been vaunted, vamped, and vampirized by men and women alike. These men's looks aren't dependent on any particular of manliness; their appeal derives not from the obvious masculine arenas of money, power or athletics, but from the more feminine province of pure looks. Their beauty is singular and passive, existing on its own without need of or attachment to skill or status or achievement.

"In my experience, beautiful men often are indifferent to their appearance and to the effect that it has on those around them. One ex-boyfriend swore he never noticed people staring at him. And he never really seemed to look at himself except in a workmanlike fashion – brushing his teeth or combing his hair in front of the bathroom mirror. He received the avid attentions of men and women in equal measure, with women tending to be teasing and aggressive in his presence and men tending to flatter and fawn. It all made him yawn.

"On the other hand, a close friend of mine is muscled but lithe, and has exquisite features, which he knows makes him look androgynous – he isn't – and which he offsets by wearing scruffy work boots, smoking cigarettes, drinking beer out of the bottle, and walking like a cowboy. For all his subterfuges, he still comes across as beautiful to behold. But he is a man whose beauty, I think, makes him feel hopeless. He reminds me of

Marilyn Monroe, in that he seems harried and hounded by his looks rather than loved and protected.

"...I love the looks of beautiful men, their heads, their gaits, the color and texture of their hair, their lips and eyes, the backs of their necks, their hips and buttocks and feet; the parts creating a powerful stimulus, the sensuous play of which I never tire. The intense watching I do becomes a vital activity, unfrivolous, charged with mystery and meaning, an erotics of the visual that produces in me a larger sensation of well-being. Fantasizing, projecting, daydreaming – this free exercise of the imagination is the real seduction behind all the looking."

We agree with Ms. Shea when she writes, "...My love of beauty is a willed enchantment, something I need knowledge and experience of all the time, the way other people need money, religion, art, sex."

In pursuing our own love of beauty we are constantly intrigued by polls. One of the most interesting during the year was the poll conducted by *Elle*. "Who's beautiful?" *Elle* asked their readers. And based solely on physical appearance, the winners were: #1 Tom Cruise; #2 Brad Pitt; #3 Denzel Washington; #4 Antonio Sabato, Jr.; #5 Keanu Reeves and Johnny Depp (tied). Tom Cruise and Denzel Washington were by far the favorites of readers thirty-five and up; eighteen- to thirty-four-year-olds preferred Antonio Sabato, Jr., and Keanu Reeves.

Brad Pitt, who sued to keep nude photos of him in *Playgirl* hidden, was the most fantasized-about male star on the internet in a survey conducted by the on-line service Prodigy. They say the second most fantasized-about stars on the internet are the Baldwin brothers, lumped together, which is a bit unfair, and third in the poll was George Clooney, with a major movie and a TV series going for him.

The London-based gay magazine *Vulcan* asked its readers to name their IDEAL MAN. The 1997 survey showed the top film idols for Brits to be: 1. Keanu Reeves, 2. Brad Pitt, 3. Tom Cruise. The magazine asked its readers to describe their "IDEAL MAN" and found, not surprisingly, a strange similarity in the answers.

"In fact," the editor commented, "so many of them seem to describe the same guy, we thought we'd entered Stepford

Country. Freaky! So what we've done is pull the most popular 'features' the things which were constantly mentioned when describing your 'ideal man'.

"So here you have it: 'He would be about 6 ft tall, aged 18 - 21 years old. He would have a cute, baby-ish face, tanned, with firm cheek bones, sprinkled with a very light, innocent boyish stubble. He would have short dark blond cropped hair, bright blue sparkling eyes and moist soft lips. He would have a firm, muscular, smooth chest with chiselled pecs and a well-defined washboard stomach. He would have an inviting line of hair running from his naval to his groin and a nine-inch dick with shaved (low-hanging) balls. His legs would be fairly hairy, his thighs strong, powerful, full of muscle. He would have a tight firm arse. He would be straight-acting, a lad-next-door type. He would wear Calvin Klein underwear and faded 501's. He would be sporty and would look fabulous in football kit. He would be versatile, quite happy being active or passive, and he'd love kissing and cuddling. And finally, he would have a charming personality, a fab sense of humour and loads of money. You don't want much do you?"

One *Vulcan* magazine reader spoke for a lot of us when he wrote that he wanted "to have Robbie from Take That all to myself, strip him, handcuff his hands behind his back, suck him off, then force my ten-inch cock up his hungry hole while he begs me for mercy..."

Another reader fantasized about being "tied to the floor while at least a dozen Bel Ami boys wank above me, covering my face in their hot boy juice and then forcing me to lick their cocks clean..."

Meanwhile, over at London's *Gay Times*, "corpses littered the male icon of all time category in the Readers Awards, with the face that made Athena millions, James Dean, topping the poll. River Phoenix, the Nineties take on Dean - i.e. not alive, not bad looking and not very talented - snuggled up to him in second place. The list of female icons rounded up all the usual suspects, with Madonna being followed by corpse after corpse after corpse: Marilyn, Bette, and Judy. Your next most favored fags were Oscar Wilde and, inexplicably, Alexander the Great.

"But above them in third place and the first still breathing male icon - was Brad Pitt, making him 'the most fuckable man on the planet.' Which isn't quite the same as Icon in my book, but never mind. Brad - sorry to have to break it to you girls, but he's just got engaged - was also voted the sexiest film actor. He beat off Keanu Reeves and everyone's favourite dreamy dwarf Tom Cruise. The cute boy vote went to Leonardo DiCaprio, but East European porn star Johan Paulik came in a close second, and the big hairy man vote here went to Antonio Banderas."

London's own sexiest film actor was Ewan McGregor. "As if you couldn't guess," the magazine declared. "Greatly helped I reckon by the 'Trainspotting' poster where he looked like he'd just been pissed on (and loved it!) and by the fad that when you saw his cock in *The Pillow Book* it was gi-bloody-normous.

"Glen Berry came in a little behind, thanks to his role as Jamie in 'Beautiful Thing' - one of several actors here who played gay roles. A lot of you also expressed a desire to see Scott Neal (who played Ste)'s beautiful thing. And blow me, if Hugh Grant didn't come third, one of a number of clean cut (well, he looks clean cut) posh boys...including the two Ruperts - Graves and Everett."

We know all about Everett's success recently and Graves, who blessed us with full frontal views in 1987's masterpiece "Maurice" and, earlier, in "A Room with a View," appeared in one of the more interesting films of the year, "Different for Girls," playing Paul, a scruffy, motorbike-riding delivery boy living in London who literally runs into an old school chum (Steven Mackintosh) who has changed a bit in the 16 years since they last saw each other: He is now the transsexual Kim. They attempt to renew their friendship, but Paul's unruly, punked out ways threaten the prim and proper lifestyle Kim has carefully constructed for herself since her operation. But after an ugly arrest, during which they are brutalized by the cops, Kim has to decide whether to come to Paul's aid, as he gallantly did for her in their youth. "Graves," Dennis Dermody notes in *Paper*, "gives a full-throttled performance as Paul - he's the ruffian on the stairs with a great heart. He's exasperating, but irresistible. And Mackintosh is utterly believable as Kim. Her apartment, clothes and job (writing greeting-card rhymes) reflect her self-imposed exile from life."

Tom Cruise

"You guys think everybody's gay. You think Tom Cruise is gay. If Tom Cruise was gay, don't you think somebody would have told the tabloids they'd slept with him by now? You think he shoots everyone he sleeps with?"
- Roseanne

What more can you say about Tom Cruise? If you were standing in a check-out line at the supermarket at the end of May, you were tempted by an issue of *National Enquirer* screaming, "Who's Gay, Who's Not," and featuring photos of the likes of Cruise, plus Rosie O'Donnell, Matt LeBlanc, Cindy Crawford, and John Travolta. But inside... nothing any self-respecting gay or lesbian person didn't know already. And, of course, the denials about Cruise and Travolta continued.

Maybe the question should be, "Did you ever let your dick be sucked or did you ever – ?" Remember, Tom said, in *Vanity Fair*, in late 1996, "I'm going to work my ass off and do whatever it takes – "

Whatever Tom had to do to get where he is, a lot of us love him. We love him no matter what he's doing. We loved him in "Jerry Maguire," even though he wasn't particularly sexy in the part. "The screenplay gives all of the characters some great lines, but the film is really all Cruise's, and he does some of his best work as a man suddenly having to re-build his whole life from the ground up," David Almeida said in *Filme Fatale*.

Another gay critic said, "Tom, Tom, Tom... how can you not swoon? The film gives us a few shirtless shots and even a quickie butt shot just to tease us. He is dreamier than ever in his doggedly romantic role. I don't know who this Zellwegerchick is, but I hate her."

Amy Taubin in the *Village Voice* wasn't buying. "Suspension of disbelief has its limits; I can sooner buy Denzel Washington as an angel than Tom Cruise as a lover of anyone except himself. ...The story falls apart. Part of the problem is that Cruise is always Cruise. He's very good at portraying a vampiric hustler who has a little epiphany about warm and fully human relations, but he's incapable of convincing us that Jerry ever does more than give lip service to that epiphany.

...Unlike, say, Clint Eastwood, he seems unaware of his inexpressiveness. He's not self-conscious about being empty. He just is. And it's his emptiness that makes him irresistible. Because we imagine, watching him, that by pouring our feelings into him, we can make him whole."

"Tom Cruise makes love to Tom Cruise for over two endless hours in this dreadfully inert and superficial comedy," *Frontiers* joked. "Since he has little chemistry with the stereotyped characters, and even less with the cardboard-cut-out women, nothing he does carries the slightest sex appeal or honesty."

"The new Cameron Crowe film is charming and good for a few laughs, but does not really pay off," Reed Jordan said in *4-Front*. "It's a perfect role for Tom Cruise. He is in his element as a phony guy clamoring at adolescent ideas of maturity. Fortunately, he looks as good as he did when his career began. He's even in the same sunglasses as 'Risky Business,' and the old line need not be spoken to ring in our heads. Sometimes you just got to say . . ."

The lesson is, "Instead of learning to be oneself, one should find a mate who completes them. While sputtering about playing for the love of the game, the personal rewards are postponed until the money is made. What's really unnerving is that Jerry finally wins back his wife with the same shallow rhetoric I heard Tom utter about Nicole Kidman on *Oprah* - 'Someone to share it all with.' Apparently the point is, unless you love everybody, you can't sell anybody. We really want that to be true and for Jerry to say the right thing, but this film ends up not supporting its own thesis. Despite the misogynist vision of divorced women as chocolate-eating harpies, the sexual humor is engaging. One can't help but long for the kind of denial that would make this all true."

In a cover story for *Vanity Fair*, Jennet Conant says that people have "trouble taking Cruise seriously as a genuine thespian. Perhaps, like Robert Redford before him (Cruise may fairly be considered the Redford of his generation), he hasn't seemed to suffer enough to be perceived as really actorly. At his worst, there's a chill beneath his charm. But you don't see that very often. He is cursed with the talent for making everything look so easy, as though he were always simply playing himself. Many people don't understand how hard it is to appear so casual and spontaneous in the middle of a multi-million-dollar production where the police keep stopping you and the budget keeps accelerating.

"...He doesn't apologize for his luck, perhaps because no actor of his generation has worked harder at being lucky than he has. Originally cast in a small part in 'Taps,' he got the part of the trigger-happy cadet when another actor failed to make the grade during the mock-boot-camp rehearsals for the movie. He succeeded because of his gung-ho dedication. 'He attacked it that day with such incredible confidence all our heads turned around,' recalls Timothy Hutton, who co-starred as a fellow cadet and has been a friend ever since. 'He worked incredibly hard, and that continues to be the case. He approaches every movie like it's the first one.'"

His first wife, Mimi Rogers, divorced him, saying he was always working. He had no children by Rogers, who reportedly complained that Cruise had no sex drive, at least directed towards *her*. "It's a lot of stuff to deal with," says Cruise of his early stardom. "In the beginning, I was always afraid. 'This is my one shot. I'm going to lose it, so I've just gotta *work, work, work.*' The first ten years . . . that was it – work, work, work."

Cruise says his past experience has made him "more committed." He and Kidman have never been separated for more than two weeks. "I go where she's going. Or she goes where I go," he says resolutely. "We're always working and on the road, so my best friend is Nic." He acknowledges that traveling together is more complicated now that he and his wife have adopted two children – Isabella, three, and Connor, one. But he maintains that it's not impossible. "I went to 15 different schools growing up," he says, a passing reference to the difficult adolescence that followed his parents' divorce when he was 12. Cruise, his mother, and his three sisters were on their own. "We stuck together and, to this day, are very close," he says. "I think what's important is that kids see parents who love each other." Cruise admits he can't imagine what it would be like to have two movie stars as parents, and knows "normal" home life for his children is a challenge. Both he and Kidman find the celebrity culture of Los Angeles a less than ideal place to raise a family, and Cruise says that when he hears "nightmare stories" about kids carrying beepers and quoting their fathers' box office, he's ready to pack his bags. These days, Cruise is always surrounded by family. His big sister Lee Anne works in marketing and publicity for his company, and one of his cousins sometimes functions as his assistant on location. (Another sister has a teaching degree and lives in Florida, and the youngest owns a restaurant in New Jersey.) Kidman is very close to her parents and sister in Australia, and she and Tom recently purchased a town house in Sydney where they can stay during extended visits. Given everything, Cruise and Kidman keep a very low profile. They live in a big, comfortable house near the Palisades, in a residential neighborhood that doesn't attract many movie stars. Their one real movie-star indulgence is a very private mountaintop retreat in Vail, Colorado, the home away from home of an increasing number of industry heavyweights.

Then there's the matter of the religion of Tom and his wife. "In Hollywood these days, Cruise is God. And John Travolta, who played an angel in a hit movie, ranks among the Apostles," Russell Watson said in *Newsweek*. "Beyond an ability to fill theater seats, what they have in common is membership in the Church of Scientology, an aggressive, high-tech religion that occasionally gets into fights with governments and law-enforcement agencies. ...Scientology claims 8 million members worldwide."

A story in *McCall's* quoted an anonymous source as saying that Kidman married Cruise, who has denied rumors that he is secretly homosexual, only to 'squelch the gay stuff," and alleged that in return he "would make her a movie star." The magazine published a complete retraction, but Cruise says it was very hurtful. "I feel very angry about it," he says. "I just try to remind Nicole, it's like a mantra – 'You have me, you have the kids, it doesn't matter what anyone else thinks.' I know it's all part of it. But sometimes, when it's beyond what anyone . . . " he says, his voice trailing off. "It's hard."

In July, Cruise figured in a bizarre twist to the story of Andrew Cunanan, alleged killer of designer Gianni Versace and four others. Cunanan's gay roommate Erik Greenman gave an exclusive interview to the *National Enquirer*, and divulged that Cunanan's fixation with Cruise was part of the warped behavior that helped spark his cross-country killing spree. Greenman lived with Cunanan for 12 months, between the time Cunanan left his sugar daddy and when he began his killing spree.

"Andrew's mind was warped beyond repair," said Greenman, who is 25. Although some news accounts have depicted Cunanan as a charming figure, in fact he's a sadistic deviant crack addict who loves inflicting pain, Greenman confided. "Andrew was passionately in love with Tom Cruise and wanted him sexually. He was totally obsessed," Greenman told *The Enquirer*. "He had pictures of Tom plastered all over his bedroom. He'd rent five Cruise videos in a single night and spend the whole evening stopping the films frame by frame, studying Tom's every nuance and gesture.

"One night Andrew watched the early Cruise film 'Risky Business,' then the mid-period movie 'Top Gun,' and finally the film 'Mission: Impossible.' He told me, 'Tom ages like fine wine. He's the perfect boy toy.' Andrew especially loved the 'Risky Business' scene where Tom dances wearing only his briefs. Tom was everything Andrew wanted in a lover – hairless, boyish frame and incredible smile. Andrew said, 'I want to tie him up, use him and make him beg for more!'

"He described bizarre sexual fantasies about dressing Tom in full leather bondage outfits and dominating and humiliating him. Andrew loved male S&M videos, especially one that showed a boyish-looking porn star being tied up and tortured with an electric wand. More than once I came home to find Andrew privately watching that shock-torture scene. He said several times, 'I'd love to use that wand on Tom Cruise!'

"Andrew even kept a 'shrine' to Tom – a plastic carrying case loaded with pictures, movie reviews, articles about him and ticket stubs to Cruise movies. He was so nutso over Tom that every time he headed to the bathroom, he'd grab an article from his 'shrine' and reread it in the john.

"Cunanan constantly played the theme from 'Mission: Impossible' and was always quoting famous lines from Tom's movies. But Andrew hated Tom's actress wife Nicole Kidman. He told me, 'I'd like to knock her off so I could have Tom all to myself.'"

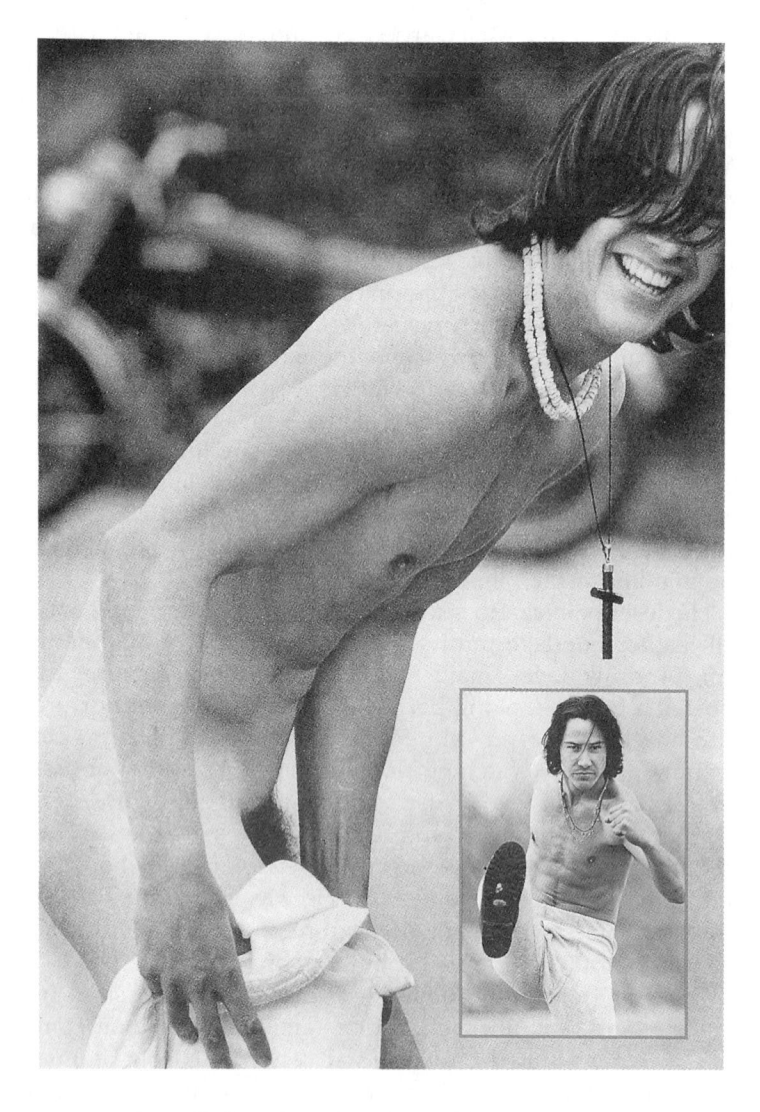

*Our all-time favorite view of Keanu Reeves,
originally appearing in Detour magazine,
photographed by Greg Gorman.*

Keanu Reeves

*"There's nothing wrong with being gay,
so to deny it is to make a judgment.
And why make a big deal of it?"*
– Keanu Reeves

After a couple of years of disappointing films, Keanu Reeves appears to be back on top – just where we want him. "Last year was not a good year for the commercial success of Mr. Reeves," Reeves admits, laughing. "It was hard, because not only commercially, but also, I felt, in the end, artistically, (those movies) were either compromised by editing or some choices that producers wanted to make."

Reeves's longtime manager, Erwin Stoff, who met the star when Reeves was 13, said, "Staying concentrated on the struggles at hand isn't always easy in the odd life Reeves has made for himself, a life lived from a suitcase, in hotels and on motorcycles and on the tour bus of his band, Dogstar." His agent insists that Keanu's fiercely devoted to his career and to the concept of having a career, and I think it is one of the things that is misunderstood about him. Yet, put on the spot, Reeves seems a little less fierce: "I'm not considered like, you know, actors like Brad Pitt, or, let's say, Tom Cruise. I don't have that kind of draw."

During 1997, he toured with his band, Dogstar, earned $8 million appearing opposite Al Pacino in "Devil's Advocate," and guest-starred in the low-budget indie film "The Last Time I Committed Suicide," in which he was shockingly overweight. But he didn't keep those pounds on for long, as noted by Peter Davis in *Paper*: "Reeves is no longer chubby. In fact, he looked almost rock-star skinny as he hopped off his Hog and made his way to the Chateau Marmont lobby." Yes, by June, on the TV entertainment shows doing promotion for both films, he was back to looking sensational, apparently just off a diet. (Or maybe he'd been having more sex?)

"Suicide" imagined the final days of Neal Cassady's life as a private citizen – before he left Denver and was reinvented by Jack Kerouac as Dean Moriarty. Hovering on the verge of beatitude, Cassady is torn between the need to prove himself a man by settling down with a fuckable wife and the desire to find his authentic self by cutting loose of ties and responsibilities.

"In the universe of strange career moves, no one is likely to top Keanu Reeves' latest choice," Robert Julian said in the *Bay Area Reporter*. "...There is lots of homoerotic subtext here, but most of it is subliminal (with the exception of Adrien Brody as Ben, Cassady's queer friend and part-time roommate)... Stephan Kay's screenplay is something of an anti-romance in which men behave badly and women are left in the lurch.

"...Although turning down 'Speed 2' now seems prescient, Reeves' appearance here is somewhat puzzling. The film is an interesting trifle at best, one that never quite catches fire; and Reeves' Harry does not provide the kind of material that will leave much of an impression on anyone. One can only surmise that Reeves must have a significant other lurking somewhere in the cast or the creative team behind this film. At least Thomas Jane gets lots of mileage from his Neal Cassady turn. Jane is sexy in the irresistible fashion of bad boys like James Dean or Brad Pitt. After the credits roll at the end of 'Suicide,' the image you're likely to recall is that of dishwater blond Jane in his sleeveless T-shirt, covered with grime, working the midnight shift at the Goodyear plant. Think Michelangelo's David, blown through a trailer park."

Ronnie Burk of San Francisco disagreed: "I went to see 'Suicide' expecting a bad film. I was delighted to have been thoroughly engrossed by the camerawork, the music, the narrative, and the studied characters. This portrait of the political and sexual overtones of conformity and repression during the Eisenhower era, with its use of language and jazz, creates a quintessentially 'Beat' film. The contextualization of the proletarian Neal Cassady seeking love, freedom, a way out of the stale banality of his time comes off heroic as ever. The silhouette scene between Jane and Reeves smoldered with repressed desire. The photography of Bobby Bukowski is superb. ...Julian wastes his time, and ours, looking for dirt where there is only light. Disbelieving that Reeves may have chosen this role over a Hollywood Schlockbuster for reasons of artistic merit and political engagement, he bores us with the usual innuendo and gossip-mongering... "

Village Voice's Amy Taubin says, "As Cassady, Thomas Jane looks vaguely like James Dean and has about as much complexity as a Calvin Klein model. Jane's blandness might have worked for the film if Kay had been interested in deflating the Cassady myth, but his intention seems to be quite the opposite. 'The Last Time I Committed Suicide' is a done-to-death romanticization of the beats, albeit from a Gen X perspective. Excepting Jane, the actors are quite good, particularly Adrien Brody as an Allen Ginsberg type and Claire Forlani and Gretchen Mol as two of the women Cassady beds and abandons. Keanu Reeves is his enigmatic self as Cassady's pool-shark buddy. I've never been sure whether Reeves is such a riveting screen presence because of, or in spite of, the woodenness of his acting."

Reeves defended himself on *E! Online*: "You know, some people like what I do, some don't. There's not really much I can do about it. I'm trying, you know? I'm not the best actor in the world; I know that. But I'm trying. That doesn't mean anything, I guess – just to try." Try *harder*, we'd suggest.

"It's odd: For a movie star, Reeves has a surprisingly neutral presence," James Kaplan noted in *Premiere*. "He doesn't suck all the air out of a room; he hangs back and ponders the options. In his scuffed hiking boots, wrinkled black jeans, black V-neck sweater, and dark gray T-shirt, he might be your brother, home from college for the weekend, or the painter from down the hall, over for a friendly game.

"Acting, at least acting a la Keanu, can be tense stuff. This seems to have been especially true of 'Devil's Advocate,' an updated Faust tale in which Reeves plays an ambitious young southern lawyer, Kevin Lomax, who comes to New York City to work for a huge firm headed by the Mephisthophelean John Milton, played by Al Pacino. 'It was an exhausting shoot,' Reeves says, 'both mentally, and physically, and 85 working days long.' Cast and crew also had to deal with the logistical difficulties of filmmaking in New York, and budgetary pressures from Warner Bros., which could use a big hit and may not consider a $57 million nonactioner starring Pacino and Reeves a sure thing. In addition, there were reports of strain between the co-stars."

"He's the last one to give himself a break, to know when the work is good," says Steven Baigelman, who wrote and directed *Feeling Minnesota*, the disappointing 1996 noir comedy in which Reeves starred. "There were days when that kind of thing would piss me off. He wears his pain on his sleeve, no question. Nobody stands in Keanu's way more than Keanu."

Reeves's Dogstar gigs continued to draw big crowds and get lousy reviews. At a gig in L.A., Kaplan said Reeves, in black T-shirt and jeans, seemed "both distant and present. He chops his hand on his bass, windmilling his arm and looking off to the side as though wanting to fade to some unattainable background where fame and responsibility don't exist. He puts on a little stocking cap, grinning goofily at nobody. Then the song is over and the band troops offstage, Reeves staring straight ahead, at no one, moving on to whatever the next thing might be." Our local music critic, Eydie Cubarrubia, had good words for the music, despite some problems with the publicist: "Sorry, Dogstar – or rather, Keanu Reeves – fans. Between Dogstar's road manager hardly ever getting back to their publicist, and their publicist giving them an incorrect phone number after the manager finally did get back to her, and two-thirds of the band having left for Graceland by the time a reporter did get in touch with one member (who was reluctant to speak without the others present, as many bands are) – dude there just must've been some bad Karma down the line.

"Oh well, such is the adventure of interviewing any band on the road. And Dogstar is a real band, despite the snickers of those who love music and hate actors. The trio – guitarist/vocalist Bret Domrose, drummer Rob Mailhouse (once of *Days Of Our Lives*) and, of course, bassist/requisite 'cute member' Reeves – last year put out a four-song EP, *Quattro Frommage*, which a press release said has sold more than 50,000 copies worldwide. Then, the fate that has befallen many a band – even critically acclaimed ones – befell Dogstar: Their label (Zoo Entertainment) was purchased by another (Volcano Records) and 'differences' ensued, resulting in the yearling band leaving the stable. By then, they had already recorded *Our Little Visionary*, which was supposed to be released around the time of the band's March departure. No matter – they've taken the same D.I.Y. approach that has sustained many a label-less band.

"Dogstar embarked on a two-month tour to promote and sell the CD, which can only be purchased at shows and from the band's Web site. Paying to get into the show to buy the CD may require more money than it's worth. But there have been worse debut albums than *Our Little Visionary*. When the band isn't trying too hard to be deep (*The History Light*), sweet (*Bleeding Soul*) or pop-grunge (*Honesty Anyway*), they manage to prove their musical adequacy. There's an unassuming attitude that today's music snobs could probably identify with, perhaps unintentionally a jump-start on what will likely be the next pop culture nostalgia kick – the retro feel is best expressed on *And I Pray* and *Goodbye*. Even when the band quotes Soul Asylum (*Enchanted*) and the Gin Blossoms (*Forgive*), the effort sounds radio-worthy – perhaps because of the production, which here and there retains just enough fuzziness to give the disc that warm, analog sound lacking in some of today's records.

"Even on the weakest cuts, Dogstar's material sounds heartfelt."

Heartfelt? That's certainly describes every word we write or utter about this exotic beauty. And we are not alone! Do you recall last year we reported that Billy Masters in *Filth* was claiming that more and more people were coming forward every week with their own Keanu stories? Billy said, "I have almost as many of these as Tom Cruise stories! Anyway, the most popular one alleges that Keanu goes over to cute guys and says something along the lines of 'I'm not homosexual, I'm not heterosexual, I just like sex. Come home with me.' Boy, was Keanu disappointed when two of my sources turned to him and said 'Well, I'm gay and only sleep with gay men,' and walked away!'"

"More than most of us," Kaplan finds, "Keanu Reeves is a mass of ambiguities: He's masculine and feminine; decisive and waffling; focused and goofy; crisp and turgid. Some men become movie stars by dint of looks, a scrap of talent, and sheer, dogged persistence. But every once in a while, a star comes along – a Montgomery Clift, a James Dean – who has such an elusive, help-me quality that audiences are drawn into the vortex of an enigmatic soul. Keanu Reeves has all this, but what he has in addition, as the world first discovered with 'Point Break' in 1991, is the ability to play action heroes, men of little hesitation, anti-Hamlets. His easy physicality is a side of him that – in an age of action pictures, and layered over the subtext of his sensitivity and exotic good looks – is pure gold."

For his part, Reeves simply "thanks the gods." That's what he said in September, 1987, in Karen Hardy Bystedt's book *Before They Were Famous*: "One thing that's cool about being in Hollywood and doing movies is that somehow if you happen to be in a film that makes a lot of money, you get power. I don't want too much power, man, (so that it) is no longer feasible to be an actor. But I would like to have enough things so that people would be curious. I'd like to have my say and not be screaming at the walls. I guess I'm successful in that I'm getting a chance to do what I want to do. What sacrifices have I made to do that? I don't know if they're sacrifices because I've gotten to do what I wanted. Privacy. Yeah, man, obviously, because it's a public domain. You're in a movie and people see it. That's not a major thing for me. I haven't experienced fame yet. My sacrifices are still pretty much in my small world. I'm not really out there yet. Life hasn't really been affected by that. How does my image differ from who I am? I'd like to say that I'm not all that naive, but I am. And I'd like to say that I'm not all that innocent, but I am. In terms of misconceptions about me, probably that I'm clean or that I'm short. What do I like best about acting? I almost said, 'CHICKS AND SEX AND FUCKING AND MONEY,' but that hasn't happened yet. The best thing about being an actor is acting. I mean, what else is there?

"...I don't involve myself in any organized religion. I checked it out when I was 11. Since then I haven't needed it. I totally don't want to bum anybody out. Here we go, God! My own God? Do I believe in my own God? Well, I seem to pay petty respect, whenever I talk about my success, I talk about retribution for my success, that you must pay for it. I guess in some sort of deep-rooted way I feel I haven't. I don't agree with that. Maybe I'm paying tribute to irony. It's the sort of thing that can make you bitter. But, yeah, I guess I believe in God. No, I don't believe in God. I don't know. Those are things that are still in turmoil.

"I'd rather laugh than be in a corner crying. But you know everything is a flash, man. All I can say is that there's a poem by Walt Whitman that goes, 'In my youth I thought long long thoughts.' I am sort of a sensory hound. I've been a sensory hound ever since I can remember.

"I live very simply and that is something I want to do. I'm basically a pretty rudimentary fellow.

"Who would I like to fuck the most? Meryl Streep, because even if I wasn't good, she would fake it the best. No, I haven't slept with most of my leading women. I'm practically a celibate monk.

"How do I fit in? I guess I'm just doing what I'm doing, trying at least. I'm trying to pursue what I'm curious about, trying to survive and hopefully not be fucked up the ass by irony and the gods."

Speaking of being fucked up the ass, in June of '97, Oily in *The Bay Area Reporter* had yet another story: "Keanu has been spotted around Santa Monica in the company of a scruffy, skateboard-carrying wag. Of course, Oily knows it means nothing, and he's trying desperately not to make anything of it. But it's not been easy in light of the intriguing rumor that Keanu pulled out of 'Speed 2' because he didn't want to work again with Sandra Bullock, who apparently put lots of pressure on the actor to, ahem, perform."

Antonio Sabato, Jr., for Calvin Klein underwear

Antonio Sabato, Jr.

*"If someone likes the way I look,
or they call me sexy,
that's flattering."*
– *Antonio Sabato, Jr.*

Three years ago we reported that Antonio Sabato, Jr. was interviewed by *Detour* magazine's Michael Castner and revealed he wanted to be the Calvin Klein model. At the end of the interview, Antonio invited the interviewer to go surfing. As they got ready to go, Sabato stripped and revealed that he indeed wears white Klein briefs. "You know," he said, "these Calvin Kleins are comfortable. When I'm big enough, I want to be the Calvin man."

At that, Castner gazed at the bulge in the hunk's briefs and said, "You don't think you're big enough now?"

"I mean bigger *fame*," he laughed.

Well, as we all know, fame came to Sabato and he became *the* Calvin Klein model. During his first year, he had that infamous billboard on Times Square, was signing skivvies at Bloomingdale's and genuinely revelling in his dreamed-of role of a lifetime. The second year brought new poses and, by golly, he looked better than ever.

"It was exciting to the max," Sabato says now about the billboard. "I don't perceive it as me. The guy on the billboard is a lot tougher than I think I am. I would have picked a smiling picture."

"More to the point," David Colman in *OUT* said, "was the colossus-size poster of a soulful Sabato in a black jockstrap hung in Times Square: His goods are even more startlingly outlined than in most of the designer's previous ad flings. It's all right there."

Bruce Bibby in *OUT* said he didn't think Sabato was particularly attractive until he interviewed him: "...While I was having a cheeky poolside chat with the taut-cheeked Calvin Klein poster boy, who glistened with sweat from a fresh workout, I reconsidered. Bear in mind that the Rome-born beauty (his family moved to Beverly Hills when he was 12) is not perfect, but this is precisely why he is so captivating. His nails are rough and bitten. Unsightly hair sprouts from his shoulders, marring the Asian designs tattooed there. But, baby, that 6-foot-1-inch bod – not to mention his anywhere, anytime bedroom eyes – turns those imperfections into icing on the cake."

When asked how it felt to have men and women salivating over him, Antonio replied that he finds it amusing, considering he tried to date girls in high school, "but I couldn't get a date if I paid someone. I was a very dorky guy, and I couldn't speak to anybody." Sabato regards it as "just a job, and it's over. I am who I am. Whatever they think, they think. 'Entertainment Tonight' asked me, How do you feel about being on the cover of a gay magazine? Well, I don't care about those stupid things. If you're gay or straight – it doesn't matter. Americans are very intolerant. I see a lot of negativity in this country. I have close friends who are gay and I never see them as being gay. I see them as human beings. Also, I don't feel that I have to explain myself all the time, if I'm gay or straight. You kind of know. It's all a bunch of bullshit. Know what I'm saying?"

Hollywood is not only anti-gay, it's anti-black, anti-Chinese, anti-women, and in some places, anti-Italian, feels Sabato. "They've got labels for everything, and that's wrong. You've got to be who you are and not give a fuck about anybody else."

Sabato says his sex drive is "quite above" average, and he said he didn't mind being called a himbo. "In a way, I take it as a compliment. But I also take it as an insult because it automatically implies you're stupid. It's a hazard of modeling underwear."

He's made a career of taking off his shirt. When he played the kindhearted Jagger on "General Hospital" for two years, any excuse would do. "The producers would say things like, 'OK, you're in a boat, and there's a leak. Take off your top and put it in the hole so you don't sink,'" he says, laughing. "I didn't mind if it was justified. But I wouldn't just walk into the hospital, wave and take off my shirt.

"I want to do good stuff and work with really good people, but it takes time. I mean, I'm so naive about a lot of things. You've got to really keep your eyes open and be on your toes in this business."

Speaking of doing good stuff, it is interesting to note that

Sabato may well have played his finest role, that of hustler John Hawkins in "If Looks Could Kill," a movie-length episode of TV's "America's Most Wanted." He was perfect casting for the part of the gorgeous hunk who had a tremendous power over men and women.

Sabato was flattered Klein ask him to pose, but admits that "I do wear Donna Karan and Giorgio Armani. I'll model for them when I go out on a date."

And what gender would that date be? One wonders when one reads an item such as this from Billy Masters in *Filth*, coming to him from a recent political science meeting in Los Angeles: "Since when do I care about such a meeting? When it is attended by Richard Sabato, better known as Ricardo and brother to so-called actor Antonio Sabato, Jr. Ricardo, who is gay, happened to mention that his brother is bisexual. He also said, 'But you know, he's also Italian,' whatever that means!"

Masters also revealed that Sabato let the execs at Klein know that he would no longer do public appearances in his underwear unless the local gay press was notified. "Seems he feels the gay fans are more fun," Masters concluded.

Nowadays you can download nude photos of "the most fuckable man on the planet," Brad Pitt, on the Internet but this is our favorite, from his early days in Hollywood

Brad Pitt

"Brad Pitt is a pretty downhome basic boy."
- Janice Johnson, high school drama coach

It became *Playgirl's* biggest selling issue of all time: "Brad Pitt Nude!" It didn't hurt that Brad decided to sue the magazine on the very day the magazine shipped to bookstores and magazine stands, getting incredible coverage on TV. Magazine sellers reported they had more orders than they had magazines, and they weren't about to return any! The photos were the ones taken back in 1995 by the snoop who, using a telephoto lens, was able to spy on Brad and galpal Gwyneth Paltrow on vacation. A couple of months before, *Celebrity Sleuth* magazine had featured most of the same photos, plus dozens of other celebrities in the buff, and nobody noticed!

Even more shocking to some than the sight of Brad in the buff (which was quite lovely actually - succulent, cut dick, etc.) was the word Pitt and his once-beloved Paltrow had split: "The couple seemed blissful whether in high society (they went to the White House for a screening of *Emma*) or low (she danced for him on the bar at Hogs & Heifers)," People said. "They finally became engaged - after months of speculation - when she visited him in Argentina, where he was shooting a historical story "Seven Years in Tibet." Then at Christmas he took her home to meet his father, Bill Pitt, who used to own a trucking company, and his mother, Jane, a school counselor. (In celebration of their anticipated union, the family dined at the local Red Lobster.)"

Pitt rhapsodized to *Rolling Stone* as he envisioned their wedding day: "I can't wait, man," he said, ". . . walk down the aisle, wear the ring, kiss the bride. Oh, it's going to be great."

Gossip Walter Scott laid the heaviest blame for the breakup on the shoulders of Paltrow: "Our source says that, despite her public reputation for sweet reasonableness, the actress has a hidden mean streak. It was Paltrow's petty and selfish ways, we're told that finally killed the relationship."

Curiously, at the end of summer, the *New York Post's* Page

Six was reporting that Paltrow had moved in with pal Winona Ryder. They said the two roomies were seen hand in hand at the premiere of "Cop Land." The column, however, made no Sapphic love connection.

Whatever derailed the momentum toward that all-important walk down the aisle, everyone who knows the couple interviewed by *People* magazine agreed on one point: There is virtually no possibility that Pitt was putting his charms to work on another. "Brad is not a womanizer," says one friend, "and he doesn't cheat. He always has one girlfriend." At worst he has a tendency to fall in love – one at a time – with his leading ladies.

Paltrow seemed to be happy with Pitt, even if hers is a more genteel sensibility than Pitt's, with his love for country music and beer. But for all the well-documented nights out in Manhattan with Pitt, Paltrow has usually emphasized the snugly domestic in their relationship. During a typical day, she told E! Online, "we hang out alone, read papers, have coffee, watch *Unsolved Mysteries* or have friends over for dinner and laugh and play Pictionary." And she has been quite vocal about having children, even if that might mean putting her career on hold. "I love acting," she told *New York* magazine. "But it's not the most important thing to me." To understand what is important to Pitt, it is interesting to go back a few years.

"I'd always dream about being an actor but I never thought of it realistically 'cause it's just not something you think of back home in Missouri," Pit said in 1989, as reported in the book *Before They Were Famous*. "You're going to be an accountant or an engineer or you're gonna open up a lawn service. That's what there is. And I used to be bummed because I figured I wasn't getting an opportunity, growing up in Missouri. But now that I live here and I see how messed up things are out here, I'm thankful I'm from there. Everything works perfectly, you know. Like the big guy takes care of things, right? So I'm out here at my right time.

"...I dreamed of opportunity because I knew things could happen. There's more, I'll be honest. When I was sitting there in my little backyard, playing with my puppy or whatever, eating Twinkies and drinking Kool-aid, I'd dream of fame. It sounds so frickin' cheesy, but there were flicks that moved me, that kind of shaped me as a kid. ...I'd dream of fame and fortune. The lifestyle of the rich and famous is very attractive to someone out there. I'm being perfectly honest, that was part of the attraction at home, to be the number one guy.

"Then you get out here and you just want *to be* good. You start to get into it. I didn't know anything. I didn't study acting at home. I got out here and I had so much frickin' stuff to learn.

"...My philosophy was, all I need to see is forward. I'm heading west and that's all I need to see. I was such a dork. I just remember driving out and each time I passed a state line, I'd be like, Yeah! I was so excited.

"And then I pulled into town (L.A.) and I had my first meal at McDonald's and it was like, Now what do I do? I met these eight guys who had this crummy apartment and I crashed there for about half a year. I did all sorts of odd jobs, like dressing up as chickens, being a delivery boy and driving strippers around. I did anything that was flexible...

"You grow up with heroes and you come out here and meet them. I've been kind of disappointed. So now my philosophy is, Keep your heroes, they're important to have, just don't get to know them. It's very sad. Yeah, they're just people. They're just frickin' people.

"My first job was a recurring role on 'Dallas.' Then they started to throw me in these *Teen Beat* magazines. Man, it was a nightmare. That's such a huge trap, you know. You burn out so hard. I was in there like a month. I just didn't know these things. Then I yanked myself. I said, Yank me, keep me away from them. Yeah, I think it can hurt you.

"...You've got to stay low, do quality work and cruise and do your own thing. ...The key is to rely on that and not to worry about things. You do not worry. Everyone worries out here. Worrying is the biggest waste of time because things will work if you have faith. That's the word, that's the only word. If you start thinking you're too cool, you're gonna lose it. That's why it's good just to hang out with your buddies and your family and stay low. STAY LOW."

Of course, it is rather hard to STAY LOW when you are Brad Pitt. As The Lady Chablis put it in his/her memoir *Hiding My Candy,* "That boy gets me all fluttery inside."

Teen idol pin-up of Jared Leto

Jared Leto

"Jared walked in, and you went 'whoa,' this is somebody who really has something. It's easy to believe someone that beautiful doesn't have much going on upstairs, but he is a very funny, smart guy."
– TV producer Marshall Herskovitz.

In naming Jared Leto one of the World's Most Beautiful People, *People* magazine said, "Sure, he can run – as evidenced in the biopic 'Prefontaine,' about Olympic track star Steve Prefontaine, but the actor can't hide from millions of teen girls who still see him as the dishy-but-distant Jordan leaning against his locker in 'My So-Called Life.' With MTV periodically re-running the series, they won't stop swooning any time soon."

And, according to the unofficial Jared Leto Web site, maintained by legions of smitten Leto-heads, the adorable high school dropout "doesn't eat Spam, his first kiss was bad and sloppy, and he hates shaving."

Chris Mundy of *US* waited and waited for Leto to show for an interview. "Finally strolls through the door," Mundy wrote. "You assume he's a flake.

"It has been two years since Leto's television series, 'My So-Called Life,' died its premature death, and during that period he has bided his time, hoping to find the right projects to help melt the Jordan Catalano mystique. The problem is that, like his fictional alter ego, the more Leto hides out or keeps quiet, the more that aura grows, and there remains the possibility of real depth behind his stare. Or not. Which means Jordan Catalano's great mystery has become Jared Leto's."

"You have to remember – and I have to remember to tell myself sometimes – that my part on that show was really small," Leto says. "A lot of people talked about it, but sometimes I had just a couple of lines an episode. So I haven't really done anything. I don't expect that a director is going to be saying that he *has* to work with me.

"I said to myself a long time ago, even before I knew better, that I wanted to do good work," says Leto. "What I didn't realize is that when you set up those boundaries, you don't work much."

Wandering, it turns out, is what Leto does best, what he grew up doing. A self-described "weird kid," he and his older brother, Shannon, were raised by their young, single mother in, among other places, Louisiana, Colorado, Virginia, Wyoming and Haiti. "It was just that whole nomadic, hippie kind of thing," Leto said. Leto dropped out of high school briefly in 10th grade, only to return to get his diploma, then moved on to study painting at the University of the Arts in Philadelphia, but quit to learn filmmaking at New York's School of Visual Arts. Finally, at 20, he drifted to Los Angeles to take up acting. Perhaps this peripatetic upbringing accounts for the fact that his favorite activities are solitary – playing guitar, hiking with his dog, Judas – and that he doesn't mind checking out of his life and his relationships for long periods of time.

"That doesn't faze me," says Leto. "I spend most of my time by myself anyway. I concentrate on the work."

Karen Hardy Bystedt confirmed this in her book *Before They Were Famous*. She says she met Leto in 1993, before he was famous, of course, and said, "Not only is he blessed with beautiful looks, he is also incredibly focused, smart, talented and creative."

When Leto arrived for his interview with Mundy in downtown New York his hat was pulled too far down over his eyes, a patchwork beard spread across pale cheeks and his long hair was dyed blond – it was clear the actor had done all he could to look less like his former TV character. Mundy observed, "It becomes clear that Leto is comfortable and focused only when talking about his fictional characters. When the conversation turns personal, his attention strays and he uses his spaciness as a shield, content to let you believe he is yet another actor housed within a flaky outer shell. Which means, of course, that he's probably not such a flake after all. We make our way indoors to talk about what he wants, his fascination with character study and how he assigns himself a different task during each film to help him learn – an Irish accent in 'Last of the High Kings,' no unnecessary mannerisms in 'Going West.' When he talks about acting, Leto comes alive, his voice turning animated while his hand touches your arm every time he makes a point. Which is often. It was with

'Prefontaine' that Leto met the greatest challenge of his short career. Shot documentary style, the film is one of two Steve Prefontaine bios – the other is produced by Tom Cruise and stars Billy Crudup – but the only one endorsed by the runner's family."

Stiff competition, that Billy Crudup, who, you'll remember, co-starred in "Inventing the Abbots." "He can invent my Abbott anytime," Michael Musto said in the *Village Voice*, "Even in the otherwise humdrum potboiler 'Grind,' he manages to radiate matinee idol magnetism, infusing real meaning into absurd 'Can you roll your tongue?' boudoir games with Adrienne Shelley and much cavorting with a rabbit. The camera loves him, and so do I."

Like Leto, Crudup is one of Hollywood's hottest rising stars. He also appeared in "Noose," "Everyone Says I Love You" and was Tommy in "Sleepers." Crudup won the Outer Critics Circle award for outstanding newcomer for his work on the New York stage, in "Arcadia" and "Bus Stop."

Meanwhile, Leto was charming reviewers himself: "Marvelously tanned Jared Leto plays the cocky hero of 'Prefontaione,'" Reed Jordan said in *4Front*, "charting his thoughtful performance with emotional energy. With barely a wisp of ice blue in his dreamy eyes, Leto takes the individual sportsman and makes him a team player, joyfully embracing his sweaty teammates. He's a memorable lover with the women in the film as well. Legs, legs, legs, in the shower scenes keep up the pace."

"I'm rarely proud of what I've done," he says. "I hated everything I did on 'My So-Called Life.' It was a great show, no thanks to me. But I think there's some pretty decent moments in 'Prefontaine.' I worked really, really hard at the running. I trained really hard. And I worked really hard to look like him."

Mundy said it was impossible not to notice the actor's head swiveling to look at every woman who passed by, so he asked if he has a girlfriend. "I'm sorry, what was the question?" he said. The question was repeated, loud and clear. "I'm sorry, what was the question?" Leto grinned slightly, once again keeping quiet, and the writer realized that maybe he was on to something: "After all, Jordan Catalano never said a damn thing but remains one of the most alluring men in recent pop-culture history. And he wasn't even real."

Leto has a fabulous future. He is not only beautiful, he is "absolutely fearless," says *MSCL* creator Winnie Holzman. "He's somebody who totally does not rely on his looks, but wants to be a good actor. What's great about Jared is that he knows he's much more than his face."

Indeed, it's Billy Masters in *Filth* who asked, "Could it be that Jared Leto is telling the truth and is not gay? If you read the interview in *Details* magazine, Jared (one of Billy's personal favorites) makes it pretty clear that he isn't gay. That may indeed be true, but I can personally attest to his presence at several WeHo gay dance clubs. Of course, that doesn't mean anything - if I were at a straight club, it wouldn't make me straight. Now, if I could just remember the last time I did that!"

Johnathon Schaech posed for Bruce Weber early in his career, and Interview magazine published the results.

Johnathon Schaech

"It's too early yet to tell whether or not Johnathon Schaech is going to be a great actor," *Interview* said. "What is obvious, though, is that he's capable of unleashing an intensity that can burn holes in floors – or in flesh. That ability is compounded by his ironic awareness of this quality, which comes across most palpably in his Luciferian performance (as a bisexual) in Gregg Araki's 'The Doom Generation.' If Schaech uses his knowledge sparingly and chooses the right roles for himself, he could turn out to be a mighty dangerous movie presence."

"I pretty much played a psycho in everything. Everyone seemed to think I was completely insane," he laughs now.

"He was dramatic even as a kid," recalls best buddy Adam Elliott, who can't remember not knowing Schaech. "We used to play whiffleball as kids, and even that was a show. We couldn't just go out and play. Before the games, he had a neighbor raise the American flag, and we had a stereo that played the national anthem. We were big Baltimore Orioles fans, so we pretended we were all the Orioles players. John would go to the plate and imitate their swings, and he'd stick his tongue in his cheek like he had a bunch of chaw. We had music between innings and built an outfield fence out of plywood and sleds. It was the 10-year-old's equivalent of major-league baseball."

Schaech says, "Acting was always in my mind, something that I knew ever since I was a little boy. I would tell my mom, and she would just kind of look at me. It was kind of like this awareness. I kept seeing where I was supposed to go. When I was a kid, I kept saying I was going to go out to California.

"I kept thinking, There's got to be something else. I actually left (school) in my junior year. It was the week before finals, and I went to every one of my professors and said, 'Look, I don't want to be here anymore. I'm going to go away, and I'll come back, possibly, but I just need to go.' Then I went out (to Hollywood) for a week and I met some of the right people."

He came to Hollywood and met Terry Hinckley, who was a models' agent at Wilhelmina West. "He signed me up and gave me a bicycle. I still ride one. Great photographers like Bruce

Weber and Herb Ritts took some pictures of me. But I was already studying with (the late acting coach) Roy London and I'd got the acting bug. He taught me a great deal about acting, but he also made me believe in myself. I remember one time he just threw down the material we were studying and looked at me and said, 'Can you do anything else with your life except acting?' And I stood up and said, 'No, I can't.' From that point on, I knew I couldn't walk away from acting."

Schaech appeared in Franco Zeffrelli's film "Sparrow" in 1993 and says, "Zeffirelli really pushed me hard. I was so green, and I was scared to death. Zeffirelli's a very passionate man, and as well as trying to build you up and give you support, he can lose his temper and then not get along. But I think we made a good film. And boy, did we have some great meals out there. You know, when I stayed at Zeffirelli's home, he told me I slept in the same bed that Laurence Olivier had, and he would tell me stories about Elizabeth Taylor and Richard Burton making love in such-and-such a bed. This was in his villa in Rome."

A European Diet Pepsi ad paid the bills for a while, as did a stint as a stalker on the Aaron Spelling schlockfest flop *Models, Inc*. "You learn a lot what *not* to do," Schaech says of the latter, clearly an unpleasant experience. "I learned how to get it on the first take, because they weren't gonna give you a second."

Following his role in "Doom Generation," he smouldered as Winona Ryder's love interest in "How To Make An American Quilt."

Jock Johnathon trained strenuously to get the bod we fell in love with in "American Quilt." "He took a lot of teasing from the male crew when he did the pool scenes with his shirt off," says director Jocelyn Moorhouse. "He was quite embarrassed, actually."

Schaech said, "I've noticed people looking at me, but I don't know if it's a physical thing."

"Some gay boys may snap while viewing the sexy poses into which Mr. A. works his male leads, young James Duval and luscious Johnathon Schaech," *Bay Area Reporter* said. The gay relationship is never consummated, but, reminds Araki, "neither is the menage," which comes to a halt when Rose Mc-

Gowan gets up to pee at the crucial moment. Schaech played a swaggeringly violent and sexy drifter who insinuates himself between two teen lovers.

"He has a real ambisexual vibe," says Gregg Araki of Schaech. "He appeals to men as well as women. There's something about him – a feline quality – that guys and girls both find appealing. He's not just some macho blockhead."

About the NC-17 movie, Schaech says, "I didn't have a problem with any of it," though, when pressed, he admits his parents are banned from seeing it and says he wouldn't take a similar role today. "That's not what's making my heart beat, that's not the songs I hear, that's not part of my life right now."

Steve Reeves was delighted to find this early photo of himself, "Perfection in the Clouds," on Cecil B. DeMille's wall when he went for an interview for the role of Samson

Muscles Go Mainstream

While Disney's version of "Hercules" flopped at the box-office, it ignited interest in the it's-so-bad-it's-good TV show and the old movies starring Steve Reeves. Locally, we found Vince, Central Florida's favorite go-go boy, quite an attraction, dressing up as the muscleman at Disney World (worth the price of admission alone).

You could say that muscles have gone mainstream, but the well-muscled physique has been a fixture of gay-male culture for many years. Indeed, "it is difficult to imagine a time when we celebrated any other body type as the ideal," Brendan Lemon noted in *The Advocate*. "But it was only a generation ago that gay men had to hide their fascination with muscles for fear that it would too blatantly reveal their sexuality. In the '70s, however, muscle stereotypes began to change. It became compulsory for the urban homosexual to go – proudly – to the gym to acquire a V-shaped torso, taut abs, and bulging biceps. Gay-identified photographers like Bruce Weber began publishing photographs of underclad athletic male models in small-circulation magazines like *SoHo News*. Mainstream advertisers soon picked up on the trend – to the point that today the man with muscles is viewed as a gay archetype and the media's ideal favored body type is seen as an appropriation of gay taste. That straight hunks like Antonio Sabato Jr. are willing to appear in underwear ads or married rock stars like Jon Bon Jovi now pose in Versace fashion layouts has a lot to do with the fact that gay men tilled this territory beforehand, making it more acceptable.

"Half a century ago it was enough for a Hollywood icon like Gary Cooper to possess only a colossally handsome face; today a young actor striving for such stardom must also have a worked-out body: He never knows when a director might ask him to strip for the camera.

"Assessing this crossover of the gay muscle aesthetic into mainstream imagery, the sexfantasy guru Nancy Friday, author of 1992's *My Mother/My Self: The Daughter's Search for Identity*, last year wrote, 'We are a different culture where...beauty is linked to male homosexuality; as the power of beauty has shifted increasingly into men's lives, the star of homosexuality rises.' If, in Friday's sentence, you exchange the word *muscle* for *beauty*, it would still make a lot of sense...

"A historian might wonder whether all this activity is not so much a victory for the gay aesthetic as it is a return to much earlier ideas about male vanity. In Renaissance Florence, Italy, for example, it was the duty not only of women but also of many men to appear ostentatiously attractive in order to pique the interest of possible conquests. In that era interest in strong, well-proportioned bodies did not necessarily denote that the admirer was attracted to men; the muscle connoisseur had no automatic sexual orientation. ...It is only in the past two decades – since influential artists and designers and photographers came out of the closet and gay men began going to the gym en masse – that an avid interest in portraying or attaining muscularity has helped make the muscular body itself seem gay."

Classic: Steve Reeves

One of our favorite musclemen of all time is Steve Reeves, who starred in the 1959 "Hercules," frequently broadcast on American Movie Classics and available on video.

"Reeves seemed to lead as Spartan an existence as one would assume a man devoted to physical fitness might," *The Perfect Vision* magazine said. "There were never any tabloid scandals, so instead there were rumors: He was five-seven, and the producers of his films had to hire actors two inches shorter than him to make him look larger (untrue); sets had to be scaled down to further pump up his stature (wrong again); his voice was dubbed, therefore he had a high voice, or a Brooklyn accent, or no voice at all due to steroid use (all false)."

And then, as suddenly as his film career began, it ended in the late Sixties, and Reeves retired into the relative obscurity of private life. He had served for 15 years as a role model to millions of physical perfection and of living proof that self-made stardom was possible and then it was all over.

Reeves tells how it all began: "In 1947, when I won the Mr. America title in Chicago, I got back to my hotel and there was a letter from an agent in New York City. It said 'If you're interested in show business, I think you have potential. Give me a call or write me a letter and I'll see that you go to acting school on the GI Bill of Rights. We'll find you a little apartment, and on weekends we'll get you into vaudeville acts so you can make some extra money.' I had got ten out of the army six months before and was attending California Chiropractic College in San Francisco. Chiropractic was my major, and my minor was physical therapy and massage.

"When I got that offer, I said, why not? I went back to New York and went to Marlon Brando's coach, Stella Adler. I was in her class and one day she gave me the project of acting pigeon-toed. I was walking around like she wanted me to, and she said, 'You're not doing it right.' I stopped and said, 'From the age of six to the age of ten I had to *force* myself not to be pigeon-toed. So don't tell me I'm not doing it right. Most of the people in this class want to be character actors. They *like* to walk pigeon-toed, stutter, and lisp. But I want to be a leading man. I want to learn how to walk well and speak well.'

"She said, 'Would you see me after class, please?' So I went after class and she said, 'You know, you're disrupting the class. I think I'll have to give you your money back.' I said, 'Yes, I think you'll have to!'

"Then I enrolled in the Theodora Irvin School of the Theater, which wasn't all theory and gave us little plays to perform. And during the time I was there, I was doing a vaudeville act with a comedian named Dick Bumey. We would go to all the different circuits on weekends. One of Cecil B. De Mille's talent scouts saw me and brought me into Paramount, New York City, for a screen test for "Samson and Delilah." I did the test in my street clothes but I passed it, and he sent me a seven-year contract. So, on my 22nd birthday, I left New York City on a plane to Hollywood and got myself a little apartment within walking distance of Paramount Studios, because I didn't have a car.

"I arrived at Paramount and walked into Mr. De Mille's office. He had five two-foot by three-foot blow-ups of pictures on his wall. The pictures were of Bob Hope, Bing Crosby, Dorothy Lamour, Alan Ladd, and me, in a pose called 'Perfection in the Clouds,' where I'm standing with my hands over my head stretching toward the sky. And he said, 'This is my Samson.' "Then he added, 'But you must realize that the motion picture camera puts on 15 pounds, so you're going to have to lose 15 pounds. You understand?' I said, 'Yes, sir.'

"He gave me a coach who would spend a couple of hours a day with me and he'd invite me to have lunch with him every day. All the starlets on the lot came up to me and said, 'Why don't you take me to lunch today?' I couldn't figure out why they were so interested in me. I thought, I'm a pretty good-looking guy and all, but not this much. I found out later the main reason was that they wanted to have lunch with Mr. De Mille, because they'd been there for years and never even met the man.

"So I'd lose five pounds, then I'd go out to the beach on Sunday and all my friends would say, 'Steve, you're looking terrible. You're ruining yourself. You're the world's greatest; what do you want to be just another actor for? Why don't you stay in this field.' Then I'd go back to the studio and De Mille would say, 'Look, you've only lost five pounds, and I've got to start the picture about three or four months from now.'

"Once a week I would have to do a skit for him. I would study it, and they'd give me other actors to work with. I was on a stage where they had a glass window between the seats and me, and I couldn't see him. I did this on and off, I guess, for about three months. Then he called me into his office and said 'You've lost seven pounds in three months. Some days your skits are really good; and some days they're terrible. It looks like you're preoccupied with something. I'm going to start the picture a month from now, and I'm going to have to use Victor Mature. He's not ideal for it, but he's an experienced actor, and I can depend on him.'

"I have nothing against Victor Mature, but I learned that a person has to have the sympathy of the public. In 'Samson and Delilah,' in the scene where they blinded him, there were little 'oohs' and 'ahs,' but within six months I saw 'Captain From Castille' with Tyrone Power, where he gets wounded on the side of his head, and all the women in the audience went 'Ohhhh!' Tyrone Power had the sympathy of the audience and Victor Mature didn't – at least in that picture."

One of the rumors circulating about Steve was that he toured with the fabulous Mae West, but he says he never did. "I never toured with Mae West. That's a fallacy that's always reported about me. During the time the 'Mae West Show' was on, I was playing in *Kismet* on Broadway."

He did, however, appear in Ed Wood's infamous film "Jail Bait." "The picture was originally called 'The Hidden Face.' It's about a criminal who goes to a plastic surgeon who changes the criminal's face to resemble his own. Somewhere in the film there was something about 'jail bait,' so they decided the title *Jail Bait* was more commercial. It was my first film, and I got my Screen Actors Guild card for it. The shoot lasted two or three weeks for me, off and on. I played a young detective, and I had a suit on at all times. I even had a tie. Only took my shirt off once. Those were the days, huh?"

Pietro Francisci, the director of "Hercules," had been looking for Hercules for about five years, Reeves says. "Around Italy, he'd find somebody who was good-looking and tall, but had no body. Or someone who was good-looking but short, and had a great body. He just couldn't find the right combination. One day his daughter, who was 13, went to the theater and saw 'Athena' (MGM, 1954, starring Jane Powell, in which Reeves appeared), which had gotten to Italy by then. And she ran home and said, 'Daddy, I think I have your Hercules.' He went to the theater the next day, pictured me with a goatee and moustache, and felt I would be his man.

"At the time I was working for American Health Studios in public relations. I'd go to Riverside and open up a fitness studio with the mayor and Miss Riverside, then wait another two weeks or so and open another one some place else. I had a good job with them, it didn't use too much of my time, and the owner made me promise I'd forget about show business if I worked with him. So when the Hercules offer came, I just ignored it. Then Francisci wrote me another letter and said 'Look, this is serious. Here's an airplane ticket.' There was also an advance of $5000, which in those days was quite an advance. I realized the guy was serious.

"I started growing a moustache and goatee on my job. This way I didn't have to have something glued on, which is terrible. My boss asked me what I was doing it for, and I said I wanted to look more distinguished.

"I was only paid $10,000 for 'Hercules' and I had no

percentage. The film cost a half million to make, and it earned $40 million in the United States alone. It was the box office champion of 1959. It was made in the summer and fall of '57. It didn't get to the States until the summer of '59, and by the time it opened here I'd already made four other films, and had committed myself to others. At the end I was making $250,000 a film, which was good in those days. Sophia Loren and I were the highest paid actors in Europe."

Amazingly, during the 15 years Reeves worked in Europe, he would work out possibly one month a year, usually the month of May. He lived in Switzerland most of the time and would go skiing and take walks with his dog. "But the food there was so great that I would gain maybe 10 pounds during the winter. So during May I'd work like a son-of-a-gun. Run through the mountains there, use the weights, and get in top form that month, and that would last me through the season. During filming you're too exhausted to get a decent workout, and I really didn't need it because the stress that there is in acting kept the fat off me and the muscle didn't want to go away.

"When I was going to high school the football coach would tell the players, 'You can't swim because it softens up your muscles. You can't lift weights because it makes you musclebound. You can't ride a bicycle because it makes you run slow. All the things that professional football players do today, hit the weights, ride the bicycle, do some swimming to loosen up, I had to fight for every inch of the way. Similarly, people weren't accepting bodies like mine on the screen, and if I'd had a face that wasn't, shall we say, noble, it probably wouldn't have happened for me either, because people weren't ready for just the body.

"I retired for three reasons. One was the stress. Two actors who were friends of mine, Errol Flynn and Tyrone Power, died young. Flynn died at 50, but he drank a lot. But Tyrone Power hardly drank at all, and he died at 45. I thought, if those guys go at 50 and 45, I want to have a good life. I want to do exactly what I want in life, so I'm going to retire at 45.

"When 45 came, mythological films and action films were going out of style, and the Westerns were starting to come in. It wasn't difficult for me, because it wasn't like I was at the top of my career and they wanted me for everything and I really had to resist.

"Also, I had hurt my shoulder on 'The Last Days of Pompeii.' The film was two days from being over and there was a scene where a chariot was running away with the hero and heroine in it, and I was supposed to ride up, grab her off the chariot, and throw her on the back of my horse. An Italian stunt man was driving it, but the hood of the chariot blocked his view. They hit a bump and he was thrown off, and it really *became* a runaway. I had a fast horse, and I actually swung onto the chariot like in the movies, and was able to pull the horses to a stop. But the chariot skidded and my shoulder hit a tree. Boom! My index finger was bent the opposite way, up towards my wrist. So I pulled it down, straightening it out. And my shoulder was jammed, so I put my fist between my knees and pulled up, and it sounded like a cannon going off when my shoulder went back in.

"The next day I woke up sore, but it wasn't really bad. It was the last day of filming, and there was a scene where Pompeii is burning. People are fleeing for cover. I'm in the harbor after getting all the people out of the town, and the sea is on fire. They had put diesel fuel across the water, and the scene called for me to jump off the wharf, dive under the flaming sea, and swim underwater and out to the waiting boat. I dove in, and when I did my first breast stroke, my shoulder ripped. And every stroke was rip, rip, rip. I would have been burned if I'd come to the surface, so I just kept swimming until I got there. "After the shoot, I went into physical therapy, and it never did get right. On each picture it would get a little worse. On my last picture, 'A Long Ride From Hell,' we used to warm it up with hot towels before each scene, then ice it down afterwards. Fifteen years ago I saw in a magazine that Tommy John, a famous pitcher, had the same thing I had, but he was going to have it operated on. So I went to the same doctor as he did and my operation was successful.

"For all those reasons, I decided to retire. Also, I was getting lonesome for the States. I had a ranch in Oregon before this one, where I spent vacations, but I wanted to spend my full time there. I was very good at picking stocks, and I made quite a bit of money that way in the Sixties. I had the right amount in the bank when I retired. And I'm in good shape. I weigh a solid 200. I get up in the morning about six o'clock and go power walking for about a half hour, then go back in and do the weights for about a half hour, and then, in the summertime – at least nine months a year – I do pool exercises. Then I go and ride my horses for about an hour, so from about six till ten it's all exercise, but pleasurable exercise. Years ago I used to use comparably heavy weights and maybe 10 repetitions for each muscle. Now I lift lighter weights and do about 15 repetitions. It keeps me where I want to be and it's no great stress on the body. I feel good, I look good, I'm in great shape, and I don't have any injuries."

Kevin Sorbo

Kevin Sorbo, a former Budweiser pitchman, nearly passed up the opportunity to play Hercules on the syndicated series *Hercules: The Legendary Journeys*. The actor figured, with his comparatively teensy-weensy 6-foot-3, 215-pound frame, couldn't fill the sandals of recent no-neck Herculeses like Reeves, Arnold Schwarzenegger and Lou Ferrigno. "When I got the script, I thought, 'I'm not going to waste my time or the producers'," says Sorbo. Luckily for him, his agent urged him to go to the audition, where he was snapped up. "We were looking for a Joe Montana type," says executive producer Robert Tapert. "Kevin has that immediate Midwestern accessibility."

A native of Minnesota, Sorbo looked like a geek as a kid. He played basketball and baseball, but didn't dare act. "I grew up in a jock neighborhood where you were considered a sissy if you were into that." He didn't discover his artistic side until he had dropped out of college and, encouraged by a girlfriend, took up modeling. Says he, "The people who knew me back in school are probably pretty surprised!" Before getting his big break as Hercules, Serbo finished second to Dean Cain for the part of Superman in *Lois & Clark*, and starred in several never-picked-up television pilots. He even made an appearance on *Cybill* as Zsa Zsa Gabor's boytoy.

"As played by Kevin Sorbo," Ken Tucker says in *Entertainment Weekly*, "Hercules is the sort of muscular adventurer who, walking down a leafy lane, meets a little girl who suddenly turns into a two-headed monster. After slaying this creature, Hercules tells his friends about it this way: 'I met a kid on the road. She turned into a thing – totally unprovoked.' *Hercules is* meant to be a period piece. The opening-credit voice-over helpfully informs us that the show is set in 'a time.. .when the ancient gods were petty and cruel.'" (You know, as opposed to the present-day Republicans.)

"The plentiful, exaggerated action scenes, combined with Sorbo's low-key, I-know-I'm-a-big-dumb-guy attitude, make this show a magnet for kids and a soothing brain-cooler for adults slack-jawed in front of their TV's."

"If Hercules ever sat down at Kevin Sorbo's breakfast table," *US* magazine reported, "there might be rumblings on Olympus. An egg-white omelet, bowl of granola or dish of yogurt would hardly fuel a leisurely morning on the Mount, let alone an afternoon out slaying Hydra or the Nemean lion.

"But Sorbo, who plays the mythical superhero, has concerns of a more mortal nature. Like a stomach he wishes 'could be more washboard,' he says, and keeping his chest – his prized body part – in divine condition."

"'I've always had girlfriends tell me they like my chest," says Sorbo. The six-three, 215-lb. Sorbo confesses to Zeus-given genes. "I don't have that fat-kid story," he says. "The metabolism in my family is pretty high. Even my dad, Lynn, who's a teacher, is in great shape at 66."

Sorbo started lifting weights in high school, and now spends an hour and a half a day in the Les Mills World of Fitness gym in Auckland, New Zealand, where he shoots *Hercules*. "He also puts superhuman effort into watching his diet," *US* reports. "That means six small meals a day, easy on the meat and heavy on the pasta, and laying off the alcohol and caffeine. But every now and then he splurges, he says, 'on a double-chocolate syrupy thing. Just add a banana for potassium.'"

Sorbo, next to be seen as "Kull the Conqueror," says he doesn't think it strange a man his age (38) is playing a strongman. "As long as you keep yourself in shape. I don't want to be 50 and playing these guys. I hope to graduate to more sophisticated dramatic roles. I feel like I did the groundwork. I played by the rules – and they're tough rules to play by. There certainly are shortcuts in this business, but that's not the way I played it. I took my chances."

One chance Serbo didn't take, just so you know, was on the casting couch. He said it was "alive and well in Hollywood, but he just didn't do anything about it."

. . .

Even the latest Batman nemesis Arnold Schwarzenegger has appeared as Hercules. In fact, he made his film debut as the superhero, billed as "Arnold Strong." The 91-minute, 1970 film was called "Hercules in New York," and was re-released a few years later in a 75-minute version as "Hercules Goes Bananas."

Another famous Hercules, Mickey Hargitay, who played the role several times, including one hysterical feature with his then-wife, the late sex-bomb Jayne Mansfield, appeared last July at Outfest in L.A. peddling a new documentary of considerable interest, "Hercules in the American Underground."

And, proving you can't keep a good man down, now Steve Reeves himself is featured in Tapeworm's "Hercules Recycled," a "What's Up, Tiger Lily?"-style spoof that re-edits footage from "Hercules" and its sequel, dubbing in a loopy story about power struggles in the chariot industry.

Dean Cain

"Gossip, gossip, gossip! Hunky Dean 'Superman' Cain is working out with *Friends* star Matt LeBlanc!" Jim Provenzano revealed in the *Bay Area Reporter*. "Seems LeBlanc, who plays the dopey dago stereotype on the hit show, has become a chub. Cain, who shows off his bod in tights on *Lois and Clark*, has offered his services.

"How nice for them. How nice for everyone. Now, I'm not one to perpetuate unfounded rumors (much), but only recently, Dean Cain was supposed to be 'workout buddies' with star quarterback and rumored-to-be-homosexual Troy Aikman. What gives? Did those nasty rumors force a break-up? Matt, we all know, nearly put the Spartacus Gay Guide out of business a few years back when he sued for being put on the cover of the international gay guide, since he never signed a model release for that shoot. A warning for all, but not me. 'Matt's grateful for all Dean's help,' says a 'set insider,' according to Jennifer Pearson in *The Star*, a tabloid that actually does not lie. From my old *OutWeek* days, I'll let you folks in on a secret. This article about Matt 'n' Dean is what's known as 'a near outing.' Lucky little Matt. I hope his gluts are getting a good workout by Dean's spinus erectors. I get inspired enough to go to the gym just thinking about the pair. I like to lay back on my bench press and imagine the baggy shorts of Dean Cain offering me inspiration as he spots me, his muscular thighs leading up to the magical wonder of his Super gonads. Ah, exercise is so healthy. What I wonder is, do Dean and Matt shower together after their sweaty workouts? Do they sit together in the sauna? Do they towel off together? Do they comb their hair in the mirror while comparing their six packs?

"This all springs to mind as I contemplate the advances in Gym-ology I have made with the help of numerous workout partners over the years. Some were boyfriends who wanted to sculpt me into a larger version of myself, thus to satisfy their own ends. Others had my best interests at heart. This has included a few heterosexuals. Trainers at gyms can be very helpful. There's nothing more tedious than a workout you hate, but there's nothing more ridiculous than pumping iron in a way that doesn't work. You've finally renewed that gym membership, or else got the bike you wanted, or made a decision to work out, run, jog, or even do a few pushups with a friend or roommate. Now what? We don't all have Dean Cain's pecs to inspire us."

Provenzano, in *XY* magazine, also reveals that while *Men's Workout* is quite possibly the lamest workout magazine of the ever-widening field, it nonetheless "gets credit for visually admitting that most, if not all, readers of exercise mags are fags."

Provenzano finds that all of the other magazines avoid homo angle at every possible point, stooping so low as to include sex articles that basically amount to "How To Pick Up Babes."

"*Men's Workout*, the latest and most obvious pseudo-sports jockaholic mag, uses as their workout models the exact same guys who show off their cocks and butts doing what cums naturally in your favorite porn videos," Provenzano contends.

"This I find to be a truly subversive act. Although staff listings may be fictitious when it comes to workout magazines, we bet *Men's Workout* is financially related to porno as well, or in the words of my friend who works for both workout and porno magazines, 'duh!'

"*Men's Workout's* subtext is as subtle as a Marky Mark billboard. Get the buns of a Colt Model! Pump yourself along with Lex Baldwin! If you really want to do your boyfriend with all the skill of these human oil wells, then you'd better work on your abs *their* way! Of course the porn performers think they are 'breaking out' into what they say is merely another kind of 'modeling' – the kind with clothes. You'll excuse my dumping the term porn 'stars,' since one of the members of our wrestling team, a terrific professional actor, got upset with calling them 'stars.' I have since corrected my vocabulary. My post-porn and present-porn pals agree – 'porn performer' is more accurate, since like trained seals, the tasks are limited and specific. But as to the athletic skills of porn performers, *Men's Workout* fills a uh... hole in the market.

"Having always wondered how Marco 'when will he ever bottom' Rossi got that big butt, readers are treated to the exact steps the porn performer (using yet another fake name) uses to keep his huge body in camera-ready proportions. And while some may snicker at the blatant hypocrisy of Marco bragging how he loves stripping at Ladies Nights, when most of us have videotaped proof of him being rimmed by Zak Spears, as well as enjoying the genitals of many boys, *Men's Workout* is an excellent source of supermarket neo-porn.

"This crossing of borders, from real porn to porn pretending it is sports to real sports, is the point of it all. Athletics allow easy escapism ('I don't wanna grow up') in our 'be a man yet act like a boy' culture. Grown men are allowed to play with each other for a living. Like prison, being on a team also includes straight guys considering (or being asked to consider), homosexual activity as part of their lives. Not that different. An October 1986 *Chicago Sun Times* article, which has been cluttering up my pile of junk for years, waiting for some fabulous use like this article, is about then-new Chicago Bears player Doug Flutie, whose cute looks and tight butt interested me even back in my school days. Although very short by football standards Flutie was highly accomplished as both a player and sex object.

"The article certainly considers his balling skills in both departments. It asks, 'How will Flutie get along with his new teammates?' A veteran Chicago Bear, Otis Wilson, answers. 'We got a lot of characters in this locker room. If he's a straight, tight guy, he's gonna be in for a long year. We're gonna loosen his ass up.' What could this possibly mean? Maybe *Mens' Workout* could share some information about Flutie's current status, and let us know the looseness of his ass."

Kevin Sorbo

A newly-buffed Brendan Fraser, photographed by Bob Frame for Premiere magazine

Brendan Fraser

"Fraser's girlfriend (who I'm told, is rather 'ample') is open-minded about his ambi-sexual dalliances..."
- Billy Masters in Filth

"Thus far, Brendan Fraser has been most remarkable for turning in excellent performances in films that are, well, unremarkable," Chris Mundy said in *US*.

For instance, Fraser played the gay son in "Twilight for the Golds," and his performance sparkled "with wit and intelligence," raved the *Advocate*, but Robert Julian in the *Bay Area Reporter* found the whole project distasteful. "Brother David (Brendan Fraser) is an unsuccessful artist who lives with his lover Steven (Sean O'Bryan). David's relationship with his sister is strained, and he resents the fact that his parents don't invite his lover to their home. David and Steven are attempting to mount a post-mod production of the entire Wagner Ring Cycle when Suzanne's little secret leaks out. ...Brendan Fraser's David has a perpetually wild-eyed expression that suggests he did his character research at Bellevue. This allows Sean O'Bryan's Steven to emerge as one of the few relatively normal humans in the cast... Director Ross Marks throws this mess together in an undistinguished fashion, but there isn't much anyone could do with this material. ...The film version, like the play, provides a cast of characters who make much ado about precious little. The motion picture, however, rewrites the ending of the original play. The new, superficially optimistic conclusion allows for the birth of the child and implies an uneasy reconciliation among the Golds. Suzanne will raise her queer baby as a single mother society be damned and full speed ahead through a mist of tears and soft-focus photography. This places the audience in the awkward position of being grateful to the Golds for allowing the child to be born - as if their grudging willingness not to terminate a queer life somehow makes them huggable. Gay and lesbian viewers will probably find this conclusion as warm and fuzzy as a Hallmark card featuring Hitler."

And then there was "Mrs. Winterbourne," which had Fraser

with Shirley MacLaine and Ricki Lake. This was heralded as "a real turkey," according to *Bay Area Reporter's* Oily, "but it's very entertaining, and Brendan Fraser is drop-dead gorgeous throughout." Leah Rozen in *People* liked Fraser but said the slimmed-down Lake suffered "from a severe case of the cutes. The onetime John Waters camp icon morphed into TV talk show host scampers through every scene as if she was campaigning for votes in her high school's Miss Popularity contest. In contrast, Fraser, usually just a big hunk in lackluster youth comedies ('Encino Man' and 'Airheads'), glides along debonairly, bringing to mind a younger Tom Hanks."

Fraser also appeared in the seldom-seen "The Passion of Darkly Noon," set in the American sticks but filmed in Germany. Empire's Patrick Humphries called it a "weird fable" that has the titular bible-clutching Darkly Noon ("an intensely irritating Fraser") stumbling through a forest with a head full of ideas which are slowly driving him insane. "He is rescued by the sultry Callie (Ashley Judd) and her glowering, mute coffin-maker lover Clay (Viggo Mortensen). Sleeping in their barn and earning his keep by helping out Clay, the shy, stuttering religiously fanatical Noon slowly becomes obsessed by Callie.

"...Sadly, its reach exceeds its grasp. Too top heavy with symbolism for its own good, this has coffin-makers and stigmata, revenge and redemption, all jostling for attention within a plot that's a bizarrely incoherent cross between Tennessee Williams-style sexual tension and A Nightmare On Elm Street-esque horror."

Mundy said he asked Fraser about his choices and Fraser indulged, as he often will, in a long pause. When he answered, it was with an earnestness that was both commendable and more than a little unnerving. "Each new sortie, each new undertaking, I strive to make it a personal declaration about who I am," he said finally. "You can only grasp at moments. To dominate an entire project is desirable but not always obtainable. Rather, you can't always execute it."

Mundy said that the majority of Fraser's time is dominated by the arts – theater, classical music, jazz, film. And when he needs a break from these activities, he usually indulges in making creations from the old Polaroid cameras he hoards. "I love them," he says. "There's a quality that comes with Polaroid film that's unique. It's like an antique from the future." Oh, yes, he also draws. "The first thing I ever noticed about him is that he's a really fantastic cartoonist," says Lisa Gonzales, one of Fraser's best friends from his days at Cornish College of the Arts, in Seattle. "He's very visually artistic. "

That's probably why Fraser was so delighted to be photographed by Bob Frame to promote his biggest film ever, "George of the Jungle."

Leah Rozen in *People* magazine said, "'George' just may make Fraser a star. He's darn cute and manages to convey George's fundamental dimness without cutting down on his likability. And it doesn't hurt that he has the best pair of male legs to grace a screen since a kilted Mel Gibson pranced across the heath a couple of years ago in 'Braveheart.'"

"WOW!" Liz Smith gushed. "Wait till you get a load of Brendan Fraser in *Premiere*. The 'George of the Jungle' star obviously wanted to keep a record of his buff bod before the results of his 'George' exercise regimen – four months of weight training – slipped away. Fraser posed for photographer Bob Frame in costume as Adonis, Poseidon and Mercury. Perhaps 'in costume' isn't quite correct. Fraser is nude as Mercury (except for his cute winged cap), draped in an aquamarine loincloth as Poseidon and has a gold glitter cup attached to his nether regions as Adonis. Fraser looks like he's enjoying himself, and why not? You're only this young and good-looking for a short while. Make hay while the sun shines..."

"This film is represented by a real powerhouse of a company (Disney) hooked up with sponsorship, and it will heighten perception about Brendan Fraser," says Fraser. "That's an agent talking, but I do concur. And, forgetting all that, it's a lot of fun. There's no harm in that."

"I'm a big guy, so I looked like a jock even though I never really was one," says Fraser. "But I threw the javelin as a kid, and I was good at it. What I loved was that you didn't need to be really strong. It's all physics, it's a dance. All you're trying to do is throw it farther the next time. It came down to competing with yourself and whether you were satisfied with how you performed. That's the same thing I strive for in my adult life."

As an interesting footnote to this, Billy Masters in *Filth* noted, " On my way back to the east coast from Los Angeles I found my peaceful sleep disturbed by the flashing images of what appeared to be a NAMBLA propaganda film playing in first class. Further investigation proved this was actually 'Jungle 2 Jungle' which I happily missed in the theatres. I am shocked that Jesse Helms somehow missed this film which depicts a virtually naked mid-pubescent boy being chased by grown men. ...Give me 'George of the Jungle' any day! I know Brendan Fraser only had that body for about three days of his life, I know the hair was a wig and the tan was body make-up but, quite frankly, I just don't care!"

More satisfcation is on the way, for Fraser and audiences alike. His latest role, as a lovestruck artist in "Still Breathing," scored him the best actor award at the Seattle International Film Festival.

And we have another great Fraser potrayal to look forward to: Christpher Bram's *Father of Frankenstein* will be made into a film. Bram says, "The screenplay was already written by the director, Bill Condon. I've read it and I really liked it. It's supposed to be really rare for writers to like the adaptation of their work. I like the director, and I think he's got a great cast. Ian McKellen will play James Whale. Vanessa Redgrave will play the housekeeper, and Clay Boone will be played by Brendan Fraser."

Marky Mark Wahlberg posed oh so provocatively for David LaChapelle's camera in photos that appeared in Detour magazine to promote "Boogie Nights"

Marky Mark Wahlberg

"Those who know him – directors, actors – say he is, at the age of 24, as sweet a boy as now lives."
– Details magazine

Marky Mark, the street urchin from ghetto Boston who had a hit rap record and became a sensation in concerts by dropping his pants, attained his greatest fame as the Calvin Klein underwear poster boy. Nobody looked better in a pair of white cotton briefs than Marky! And then he endeared himself by dedicating a photo book about himself to his penis. Now, we all said, that was a boy we'd want to get to know better.

But then he got in a brawl with one of Madonna's pals and called the guy a fag (imagine!) and that was that. He lost his Calvin contract and more records, although promised, never came. He even grew tired of dropping his pants for teenage girls.

He missed his gay fans, though, and did an interview with *The Advocate* to prove it. He adamantly denied being a homophobe. Nobody seemed to believe him, but it didn't matter. Marky's a fighter. He got a small part in "The Substitute," a made-for-TV movie in which he basically played himself, and he was so good it led to parts in "Renaissance Man" and "Basketball Diaries." He was on his way to becoming a movie star!

In the scary film "Fear," he played with utmost conviction the murderous Lothario nightmare of *every* dad with a *sweet* teenage daughter. Apparently, as long as he's threatening, he's perfect. But the part did present problems. For the love scene, for instance, the stud said, "I had to tape this thing around myself, and the little pubic hair I had was gone. Then I couldn't get the thing off. It was torture."

Promoting the movie, the actor refuted any notion that's he's a homophobe. *Details* interviewer Erik Hedegaard says, "Those who know him – directors, actors – say he is, at the age of twenty-four, as sweet a boy as now lives, one who deserves all that is customarily bestowed on those who attain movie stardom. I wouldn't know about that. What I do know is that for days on end he tried to let me see for myself.

"For instance, he graciously allowed me to watch him sleep. From this I can honestly report that his slumbers are blissfully free of teeth-gnashing and drooling – two of your more common signs of moral turpitude. For many other hours, I watched him watch TV. From this, I pass along the news that he does not stay on any one channel long, unless it has the good sense to air 'The Waltons,' 'Barney,' 'The Munsters,' or basketball. We talked cunnilingus; he didn't know the word, but once I explained it, he stated with grim vehemence, 'Man, I ain't into that!'" Asked why he shuns cunnilingus, Marky pointed to his trousers. "I keep thinking about him (his penis) being down there, you know what I mean (inside a woman), and then maybe somebody else's dick having been down there, too."

Even when the star's fully dressed, there's lots to feast upon. Hedegaard says, "Because it's a face that begs to be studied, I study Marky's face. It's pretty amazing. With his hair all messy, he can look like a sleepy little boy just up from a nap, toddling around the corner with soggy stuffed monkey in hand. At other times, his eyes narrow into slits, cold and dismissive, with the flesh around them thickening; they could be boxer's eyes. Then he smiles and all that drops away. Not to gush, but his smile is dazzling in the way it breaks across his face, opening up the hardness there, making him seem penetrable and warm, friendly even. Such considerations, however, cause Mark to tug on his ear and utter unhearables. When I ask him about his face, about all he says is, 'I see what I see and what I've seen for a long time.'"

Whatever the looks of Marky's thing, the star thinks his feet are his best physical feature: "They're soft, but they're ticklish as a motherfucker!"

While making "Traveler" with Bill Paxton, Marky appeared one day dressed in a nice white shirt half-buttoned, his Timberland bootlaces untied, his new khakis bagging down, his belt unbuckled, and a big fat grin. Paxton was delighted. "We love your style, kid!" he yelled. "You're coming out large, baby. You're nationwide!" To top off his look, Mark slapped on a furry Cossack-style hat and said, "Motherfuckers in one place was ragging on my hat. It's the shit right here. My pop gives the best gifts."

"I'm cashing the Kid like a check," Paxton said, laughing. "I'm going to the bank with your ass!"

Marky's ass wasn't the subject, though, of the actor's next project, "Boogie Nights," based on the career of one John Holmes, otherwise known as Johnny Wadd in the golden days of porn.

Ingrid Sischy, editorializing in *Interview* says, "It was remarkable, Marky's success, because a kid from so-called nowhere, who doesn't speak the language of success, isn't supposed to make the big time, let alone become an object of desire. There was such a ruckus around Wahlberg that the question of what his own desires were has only begun to be sorted out now.

"...It didn't help that the hoopla around Wahlberg for a while only seemed to make him confirm others' preconceptions about him. Prejudice and pride got so twisted up that the next thing that started up was stories of Wahlberg's own prejudices – against people of color and homosexuals. It was a mess, and I don't think he would argue with the characterization of himself back then as also a mess. He was *playing* music, but it didn't feel as though he was hearing the music. The first note to break all that, eventually leading to 'Boogie Nights,' was when someone had the inspiration, as the saying goes, to 'put him in pictures.'

"As an actor, by getting into other people's skins, Wahlberg was able to get into his own in a way that didn't deny his past yet also allowed the rest to come out. The process of acting, and all the examination of character that goes with it, has been a vehicle for Wahlberg's own processes of self-discovery and self-awareness, as well as for his own sense of others.

"...The movie will get the Moral Majority all worked up, but in fact the movie's about humanity, the very thing these folks claim to care so much about. What makes Wahlberg so authentic in it is his obvious, from-the-gut understanding of all that this film and his part – as a kid who becomes Dirk Diggler, porn star – entails.

"The film itself is an achievement because it doesn't treat its material exploitatively, coyly, or naively. It isn't selling anything, it doesn't sensationalize, or fall into some agenda of condemning or promoting pornography. It simply tells a story of a group of people, who for one reason or another, can't find comfort or survival in the mainstream world, and end up in this 'under-the-counter world' – where, by the way, people treat each other both terribly and beautifully, as they do in the rest of the world.

"Wahlberg plays his part with the kind of depth that's rare. He can do this because he looks the subject – and himself – straight in the face, and that's also what allows him to show us so much that we need to know."

The Bottom Line noted, "In promotional interviews, Marky made it clear he was cast for his acting talent (well, okay, his buffed body too) but not because he has monster meat. Apparently he's no Woody Harrelson. He describes in tantalizing detail how the producers had a special effects company build a giant prosthetic penis for him to wear. It was so elastic, in fact, he could insert his own inside it with gratifying comfort. This may launch a whole new line of tie-in products, and why not? If they can sell hamburgers with dinosaurs, penises and porno should be a natural. Just ask Jeff Stryker."

"I feel blessed," Wahlberg told Dale Brasel in *Detour* magazine, "and I know that there are a lot of other hard-working people out there, but I really feel like I'm dedicated to doing the right thing, and that's why it's all possible. People that don't know me and have just read the bullshit must think I'm a really angry, arrogant, unapproachable person. In actuality. I use it to my advantage because I do have a sense of humor. If people are that simple-minded, you know, I kind of throw it at them every once in a while. Most people say, 'Oh, God, you were nothing like what I expected.' What did they expect? That I was going to attack them or something?"

For "Boogie Nights," Wahlberg says he went to the set of an adult film, "basically just to get the feel of how the whole thing works. The looseness, the kind of normality, the nudity, stuff like that. We watched certain films just to find out how bad the acting really was. ...I did meet Ron Jeremy. Like, 'Hey, what's up,' you know? He just kept telling me about his rap record. I'm not a huge fan of adult films. I was kind of uncomfortable

– I think sex is something that's private and should be done behind closed doors."

Wahlberg insists the movie is not all about his penis: "I think about his realization at the end of the film. That he's not everything that he thought he was, or everything that people made him believe, but that he still does have something special. He carries on with a certain amount of those beliefs, but not so much the egotistical side. But at the same time, he thinks he's Al Pacino. In his own right, he was a star.

"I was actually getting at the technical side of this strange attachment. It's a little too weird to explain, but that was the character. Philip Seymour Hoffman is so good in the movie, he turned his character into the most pathetic thing on two legs. He's amazing. When I read the script, I loved his character, Scotty J. And look who gets kissed by another man! Shit, I'd kiss Phil Hoffman any day of the week. I would, I really would."

"It is a movie that is not just jerking you off when it asks, as Burt Reynolds's character, porn director Jack Horner, does, 'How do you keep them in their seats after they come?'" said Paul Thomas Anderson, the director. "But…the strongest tug through the movie is Mark Wahlberg's character, who's just sort of a beautiful kid who's seventeen years old and has a really big penis. As Burt Reynolds's character observes, there s something wonderful in his jeans just waiting to get out. Or words to that effect. Tell me a prosthetic anecdote. I feel that what we need here is a naked-actor story. I mean the thirteen-inch prosthetic penis. It's odd that people think it's a prosthetic. That's Mark Wahlberg's penis! I'm not sure where all this prosthetic talk comes from. That s kind of amazing, since Leonardo DiCaprio was supposed to do the part before. Who knew that all these young actors were walking around Hollywood with their big…. Well, that's kind of how it happened. You know, Mark came to me and said, 'I've got an inch on Leo.' I said, 'Really?' And he showed it to me. And then I hired him!"

"One reason Wahlberg's gotten so far in movies is that the camera rarely fakes him out," Brasel says. "He radiates urban authenticity. 'I'm definitely as honest as possible,' he asserts. 'I just try to be natural. If you begin rehearsing, you're not even starting out really listening to other people's lines and stuff.'"

Wahlberg recalls working with DiCaprio in "The Basketball Diaries:" "We both went into it with a chip on our shoulder. Being, to a certain extent, from the world (author) Jim Carroll describes in his book (from which the film was adapted) gave me the position to say, 'Hold on. Why is this guy doing this? He's from Hollywood.' And, him being a great actor, with lots of experience, and the star of the movie, he was like, 'Hold on. We don't want this rapper/underwear model fucking up our beautiful art movie from this classic book.' We both got over it and got along well. I've been on movies where there's this fake, 'I love you,' then you see somebody later and they don't even want to look at you. It just wasn't like that here − it was genuine, and it's still like that today."

Brasel concludes, "Wahlberg strikes me as one of the straighter-talking guys I've met in some time, which is a neat trick for someone who's pretty much grown up in public. Where would he say his head is these days? 'I think I'm pretty fortunate to be who I am inside,' he asserts. 'I'm at a stage where I'm letting it an out. It's the first time I've ever been able to talk about personal feelings, to be honest in personal relationships, to say how I feel without hiding it, without acting cool or like I don't care. I'm just growing up.' Staring off for a few moments into the middle distance, he continues. 'I used to feel like the cops were watching me all the time.'"

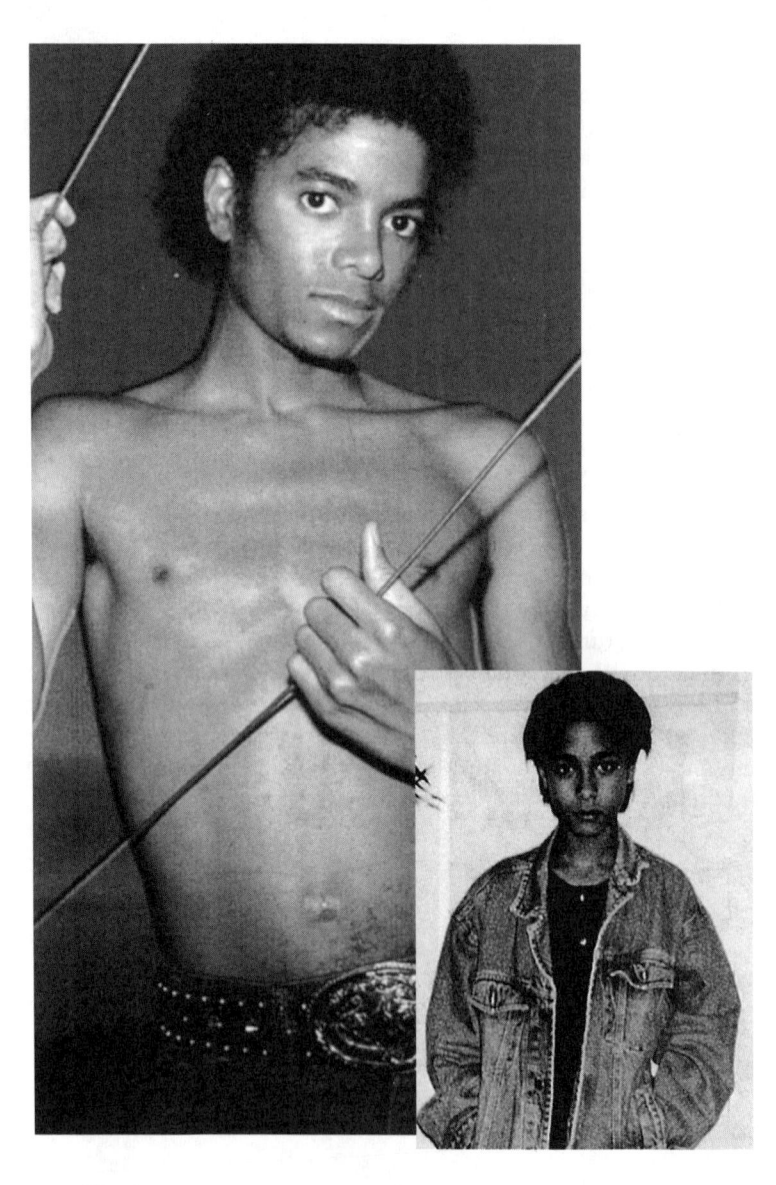

*"'Before I put it in, close your eyes and count to ten."
– Lyrics from a song on Michael Jackson's latest album;
above, Jackson when he was indeed "The King of Pop;"
(inset) Jordie Chandler's exotic looks captivated Jackson*

THE KING AND THE PRINCES
(The Saga Continues)

Michael Jackson

"I'd hate to be Michael Jackson."
"Imagine waking up as Michael Jackson."
"Kafkaesque..."
"He's circumsized. I know because I know someone who stood near him in the toilet and noticed."
- The Pet Shop Boys

"There was a time when Michael Jackson could legitimately call himself the King of Pop," *Entertainment Weekly* declared. "Alas, those days have gone... Between his diminished productivity and the ongoing psychodrama of his life, the guy seems like a sad relic from another era, as removed from mainstream pop as Rosemary Clooney. One almost wishes he'd retired after 1982's *Thriller*, a watershed he can only dream of topping.

"...Forget the music; armchair psychologists will have a field day with the words. 'Who gave you the right to share my family tree?' Jackson asks on 'Ghosts,' a line that should give pause to the mother of his new son. And add Susie - who stabs the protagonist of the title track - to the list of women who've drawn Jackson's lyrical bile. Yet even more criminal than his apparent misogyny is the way Jackson's essence is buried beneath the studio manipulations of *Blood on the Dance Floor's* hired guns. For several years the pallid one has looked like a ghost of his former self. Now he sounds like one."

"Given Jackson's recent 'image problems' and disappointing record sales, the strategy behind his latest album appears to be sound: Lower expectations and get people dancing," commented Nathan Brackett in *Rolling Stone*: "...Unfortunately, it is largely a joyless affair. Jackson's siege mentality hasn't lifted; when the King of Pop really *tries* to be 'dark' here, he ends up being truly disturbing. Every reference to sex on *Blood* contains some creepy twist, from the double-entendre: 'Before I put it in, close your eyes and count to ten.' ...There's no escaping Jackson's pained public persona.

'It was blood on the dance floor,' he sings on the title track, 'and I just can't take it.' At this point, for the most part, neither can we."

However, there was some good news for Jackson during 1997. "Michael Jackson's career in the United States seems becalmed," *Newsday* reported. "His 'Blood on the Dance Floor' album is flopping spectacularly. But overseas Jackson remains mega. According to Billboard, his 'Blood' is Europe's top-selling disc, occupying No. 1 or 2 spots from France to the Netherlands and beyond. No wonder Michael lives abroad now. He needs adoration – and over there he's still adored." And, on the legal front, a Santa Maria, Calif., judge ordered five former employees of Jackson to pay nearly $1.5 million in legal fees Jackson incurred while defending himself against their wrongful dismissal lawsuit. The five, who claimed that they were forced out of their jobs and had been harassed by Jackson's security detail, lost their case. And then there was the birth of his baby, Prince, who is staying with his father in Europe and not with the mother in California.

"Is there anything Michael Jackson won't do to make us think he's normal?" asked *The Express* in London when the marriage to Debbie Rowe was announced. "Is the man this desperate or are we being unfair?" asked Jane Warren. Then, reported *The Sun*: "Michael Jackson's pregnant bride issued an amazing statement last night, declaring: 'I'm not a lesbian!'"

Unfortunately, the one book that might actually have helped his cause was largely ignored. "About a year ago," *Paper/Planet Pop* reporter Fenton Bailey says, "a friend handed me a copy of *Michael Jackson Was My Lover: The Secret Diary of Jordie Chandler*. The book was falling apart – not because it was well-thumbed, but because, just like Madonna's *Sex*, it came that way. But unlike Madonna's volume, this was no high-end publishing venture. On the contrary, the production values were so entirely absent that the thing was simply coming unglued at the seams. In fact, there was no publisher associated with the book at all. (The book was self-published.)

"I flicked through it looking for the dirt. There were the to-be-expected snapshots of the pop star with the boy, and then, over the page, a cavemanesque doodle. This was the infamous telltale description that the boy had given of Jackson's penis. It looked like some kind of mushroom, and scrawled alongside it was a description of how it was spotted pink and brown like a cow's udder. I think I laughed – partly because it was so absurd and partly because I felt silly gaping at the King of Pop's cock, albeit a crudely figurative version.

"As I leafed through the book, I remember thinking it would trigger another outbreak of the media virus that has plagued Michael Jackson. I could see the headlines, not just in the tabloids, but on CNN as well. The book was sure to become an instant bestseller and launch a thousand more media-generating lawsuits. In short, it would be a never-ending story for the beleaguered inhabitant of Neverland. But instead of a media tsunami, there was silence. There were no reviews, no headlines, nothing. From time to time I looked for the book while browsing in book stores, but it was nowhere to be found. Eventually I gave up. And then last month I came across it in A Different Light in New York. It was the second edition – presumably the first had either sold out or completely fallen apart. This time around the binding was stronger. I grabbed it.

"Much of the content is familiar, and if it's dirt you're looking for, you won't be disappointed, with one chapter baldly titled 'Jackson's Use of Enemas and Tampons.' Almost 10 pages are dedicated to Chandler's description of Jackson's genitalia, police verification of which gets its own chapter.

"However, the book is not really the tawdry expose you might expect. In fact, it is almost sympathetic to Jackson. After a preface from author Victor Gutierrez, which ends with the request that you read with an open mind because you will need one, the book begins with this disarming sentence: 'Jordie Chandler, a slender, dark-haired boy of 13 with beautiful Polynesian features, knew that he was in love with Michael Jackson.' At the time, Chandler is in the DA's office being interrogated for the details of how he was abused by the King of Pop. 'Abused?' Jordie thought. 'I have not been abused!' He hung his head, put his hands on his knees and wondered how it had come to this. Reading on, it all becomes swiftly and tragically clear. Chandler appears less abused by Jackson than he was by his parents, who could not be characterized as loving. Some could take the line that the mother countenanced the relationship once her misgivings were allayed with luxury gifts and other attentions.

"Then there's the estranged father, who plays the role of the mad Hollywood dentist. While filling the cavities of the rich and famous, Evan Chandler tries everything to advance his burning ambition to get into pictures. He would be funny if he wasn't so venal. Determined to get to the bottom of the relationship between Jackson and Jordie (so he could profit from it), he confronted his woozy son as he came 'round after having a tooth removed: 'Lie to me and Michael will be destroyed,' he reportedly said. 'Tell me the truth and you save him.' Only when Evan promised his son that he would not tell anyone did Jordie spill the beans.

"Dad promptly repayed his son's trust by betraying it. His efforts to cash in brought lawyers into the fray, then the authorities and the press, as events quickly spiraled out of control. Even when Jordie became suicidal, Evan thought it was because of 'the abuse.' But according to the book, Jordie was not upset 'because he felt shame for his sexual acts with Jackson. He was depressed because his father had promised him that nobody would know.' He was also depressed because he was separated from Jackson.

"As Jordie Chandler blew out the candles on his 14th birthday cake, he wished for his nightmare to end. But a few days later, when his father agreed to a multi-million-dollar payoff from Jackson, the real nightmare had just begun. To wrest control his $20-million windfall out of the hands of his free-spending parents, Jordie had to sue them. Today he spends his days sitting alone in his room in a house that has become a fortress even more bereft of love than it was before. He barely speaks to his sister and mother, with whom he lives. Jackson's gifts are all gone, and the bedside poster of him has been replaced by one of Antonio Banderas in 'Desperado.'

"Jordie Chandler's not-so-secret diary reads like the lovelorn cry of a gay teen who has been betrayed and exploited by the very people who were supposed to protect and love him.

"...It is truly heartbreaking to see Chandler sitting alone in his room reading secret messages from Jackson into the titles and lyrics of songs like 'They Don't Care About Us.' But it's true: They don't. And this explains the mystery of the book's lack of profile. Irrespective of the legal minutiae that have deterred Jackson's lawyers from suing the book's publishers from here to kingdom come, the overriding fact is that the public would never entertain the version of events put forward in this book. The only acceptable version of the story is of Michael Jackson the evil pedophile who abuses young boys. So when Chandler protests, 'It wasn't the games or the expensive presents...it was the attention and love we received from Jackson,' the truth is that no one believes him and no one wants to face this reality. And that's the real tragedy."

And the drumbeat never seems to end. Billy Masters in *Filth* reported that Jackson celebrated his 39th birthday with a special televised concert in Copenhagen. "At Michael's request," Masters said, "the world famous Tivoli Guards performed. In case you don't know, this is a marching band made up exclusively of pre-pubescent boys. Now you know what to get the (alleged) pedophile who has everything!"

Prince William

"William, neither movie star, rocker, nor sports star, has become one of the most sought-after teen idols in the world."
– Smash magazine's Leesa Daniels

In the book *Prince William*, Randi Reisfeld says the future King of England was "to the spotlight born, and will to the spotlight always be drawn – even if sometimes, it seems, he's kicking and screaming all the way. (But) for now, Wills, as he is called, has his hands full just trying to be a normal teenager, making friends, studying for exams, listening to rock music, going to dances, going on dates, and dealing with his divorced parents. Imagine having it all – every word, every step, every accomplishment, goof, embarrassment, and failure – reported on and gossiped about the world over. Wills doesn't have to imagine what that's like: that is his life. What's more, he knows it will always be his life.

"Prince Charles's distance from both his sons was becoming an issue, but it didn't mean William spent no time with his dad. Indeed, one of Charles's friends said that it was a case of quality over quantity time: 'When (Charles) does see the boys, he's all over them. But then, he might not choose to see them again for a month or so.' Another added, 'Charles is treating William pretty much the same way his own father, Philip, treated Charles' – in other words, they just didn't see very much of each other. No matter how rare, William's visits with his dad were well chronicled. They usually involved the kinds of outdoorsy activities for which the royal family is known to be passionate: hunting, fishing, shooting, and riding. All of which Wills seemed to enjoy and even excel at. With his father, he dressed in the conservative style expected of a future monarch and took his meals, which were prepared by the palace staff, at home.

"...Aside from riding lessons, William took private instruction in tennis, swimming, rugby, and piano. A favorite sport continued to be 'let's elude the bodyguards.' William took great pleasure in confounding his security detail by hiding behind bushes or mounting his pony at Balmoral and riding off by himself. After trying to ditch his bodyguards once too often, he was given an electronic homing device to wear – so his location could be pinpointed at any time.

"The royals agreed to allow William to spend a few summer weeks with a friend at a Montana ranch in the USA, far away from the prying eyes of the British media. There, William learned to ride cowboy style, to lasso, and even to square-dance. He made a good impression on his U.S. hosts, who declared Prince William's horsemanship impressive, his manners and friendliness even more so. Naturally, however, William had become even more wary of people's motives in getting friendly with him.

"William (has) continued to take on more royal duties, including such state functions as the fiftieth anniversary of V-J day. William won accolades for his professional handling of the situation. 'He's very self-possessed' was the verdict of his performance. ...William took his father's place by Diana's side on many of occasions. At her Christmas party for the staff at Kensington Palace, it was Wills who got up and made the traditional thank-you speech. He'd also become quite savvy when it came to the press. On a skiing holiday with his mom and brother, William refused to pose for photographers who'd upset Diana the day before.

"It has been suggested that tabloids were offering William's schoolmates substantial sums of money to 'act as correspondents' at Eton: In other words, tell on Wills, risk expulsion, but make money. So far, only a handful of the boys at Eton have ratted out their most famous peer. Reports have leaked that William is teased and taunted mercilessly, almost always on account of some parental indiscretion or other. But if he's accomplished nothing else in his fifteen years, William has learned to become thick-skinned and to stand up for himself. 'He's tough minded,' claims an insider, 'and gives as good as he gets.'

"...These days he's a fascinating combination of wary and watchful, yet relaxed and cheerful; steely, and self-confident, yet sensitive and shy; a typical teenager, yet poised beyond his years. In fact, what many observe about William is that after all the public family strife he's endured, he seems to have inherited the *best* qualities of each of his parents."

"All my hopes are on William now," Princess Diania told *The New Yorker's* Tina Brown in June. "I don't want to push him. Charles suggested he might go to Hong Kong for the handover, but he said, 'Mummy, must I? I just don't feel ready.' I try to din into him all the time about the media – the dangers, and how he must understand and handle it I think it's too late for the rest of the family. But WIlliam – I think he has it. I think he understands. I'm hoping he he'll grow up to be as smart about it as John Kennedy, Jr. I want William to be able to handle things as well as John does."

In his book, *The Decline and Fall of the House of Windsor*, Donald Spoto describes Prince William as "reserved and serious, a cautious and introverted boy who has grown wary of all the publicity. Conscious of his position and his future, he is becoming a dignified, somewhat stern teenager, his eyes often have a premature, prescient sadness."

"They say that every picture tells a story – and every picture of Prince William says that the boy knows how to dress," Reisfeld maintains. "While he might require constant Scotland Yard protection, it's a sure bet the fashion police aren't after him. Of course, looking good is part of the 'job,' such as it is: If you know you're going to be photographed constantly, you might as well dress up. And Wills does. So well, in fact, that he was named one of *People* magazine's Best Dressed People of 1996. 'He looks and dresses like a model,' they trumpeted. 'He makes no mistakes.'

"While William's budget allows purchases from the most expensive stores, a sense of style is something that can't be bought, and William seems to have inherited his from his flawlessly dressed, fashion plate mom.

"What he doesn't enjoy, and he's made it perfectly clear, are his constant chaperones. Being tailed by detectives and security guards was bad enough when he was little; it's ten times worse now that he's a privacy-intense teenager."

"He loathes being chaperoned at every waking minute," according to *Hello!* magazine. "He's been heard to ask, 'Why do I have to be surrounded by policemen?" And even though he has, for the most part, outgrown the "game" of trying to hide from his handlers, Prince William is still pretty good at giving them the slip when he's determined to.

"Money is something he not only has," Reisfeld says, "it's also something he doesn't have to think about very much. He'll always have it. ...He recently opened up his first bank account and made a deposit of five hundred dollars. Of course, Wills doesn't need to hit the cash machine very often: Nearly everything he needs, in a material sense, is provided for him, from clothing to cars, to concert tickets, CDs, books, movies, videos, restaurant tabs, and any other item he might covet. Money is only one aspect of William's life of privilege.

"Prince William doesn't have a girlfriend, but he does lead an active social life. In spite of his natural shyness and necessary wariness, he goes out frequently, to parties, dances, mixers, and tony teenage balls.

"Of course, wherever he goes, the media spotlight follows. William attended his first teen dance on October 23, 1995. It was the La Fiesta ball, held at the Hammersmith Palais nightclub and was not open to the public. Invited guests, who paid thirty-five dollars a ticket to get in, were limited to one thousand private-school students. Wills attended with his friends from school – and two detectives from Scotland Yard."

Wills isn't technically a star, but it's a good bet he understands the concept well. Being able to afford anything your heart desires is beyond most people's imaginations, but William was born into just that kind of privilege. Stickers bearing his image are affixed to the notebooks of schoolgirls all over Europe. The first time *Smash Hits* magazine printed a princely pinup – not that William posed for one, of course; the shot had been taken on the Queen Mum's birthday and sold to the magazine – sales went through the roof. Any tidbit, factoid, gossip item, or rumor regarding the teenage prince is hungrily scooped up by his adoring fans.

"What is it about Britain's royal heir that turns girls to mush?" Reisfeld asked. "Though looks aren't everything, few would disagree that great looks do a teen idol make – and snogable (kissable) Wills has been declared 'mad cute' by his legion of fans. Nearly six feet tall, blue-eyed, blond, and broad-shouldered, he'd be popular with the opposite sex whether he was a prince or the Baldwin next door.

"Of course, the fact that he is royalty doesn't hurt. William is wealthy, he's famous, and any way you look at it, he's looking at a pretty awesome future. One British teen magazine printed a list of the top ten reasons Wills is so cool, or 'fanciable.' Among them: He's loaded (rich); he likes (the rock group) Pulp; he knows how to partee!; he wears trainers (sneakers) instead of sensible shoes; he's not scared of going on scary theme park rides; and he's an all-around, dead normal, diamond geezer (he's down to earth – and really, really cute)."

A columnist opines, "Girls go after him because he's handsome, kind, funny, and because he's pretty on his pedestal, a glittery target."

Target is right. As we reported last year, "Even in England people are taking note of NAMBLA and its *Bulletin* and the problem of child kidnapping and sexual abuse," Mike Echols said in *Brother Tony's Boys*. "The miniseries 'I Know My First Name Is Steven,' based on my first book of the same title, was telecast in over one hundred countries, but nowhere was it received with more interest and acclaim than in the United Kingdom, where BBC-1 premiered it in 1990. The person responsible for that broadcast – and for the 1993 rebroadcast – is Mark Dietch, BBC-I Editor. In February 1993, Mark visited me for two days in Carmel, California. During that time I showed him some issues of the *NAMBLA Bulletin*, including the September 1992 issue whose back cover featured a photo of ten-year-old Prince William and his parents. And at Mark's request I made a copy for him to show associates back in London."

Wills has been voted Britain's Number One teen idol and "Most Handsome Royal," and pinups and posters of the prince proliferate in teen magazines.

While he hasn't spoken up publicly, he has made it known that he isn't very comfortable with his new teen idol status. Not that he isn't flattered by his popularity, he's just embarrassed by it. "He cringes at things like the *Smash Hits* poster," reveals *Daily Mail* correspondent Richard Kay. "He doesn't revel in the attention." That modesty, of course, only adds to his shyguy appeal. "This is the first time a member of the royal family has been popular with teenagers," asserted the editor of *Live & Kicking* magazine.

So what is next for this appealing young man? "As a child,

William reveled in military pomp, pageantry, and uniforms," Reisfeld comments, "but in recent years, he seems less gung-ho about all that regimentation. *Majesty* magazine once reported that William confided to his mother that he most definitely did *not* want to enter the navy. However, he has several years to reconsider and very well might change his mind. What happens after a possible military stint is hazier still. After all, it's not as if Prince William will have to go out and find a job. One awaits, of course."

With the tragic death last summer of his beloved "Mummy," Royal-watchers fear Prince William will become the focus of the tabloids. Photograph by Tim Graham of Sygma.

Jonathan Taylor Thomas looked great in several sexy poses for Andrew Macpherson in Detour magazine

Jonathan Taylor Thomas

"Not every kid wants to go out and be crazy."
– The too-good-to-be-true Jonathan Taylor Thomas

Teen idol Jonathan Taylor Thomas "is very uncorrupted by his success," his "Home Improvement" co-star Patricia Richardson told *US* magazine. "He has an innate cool. He's alarmingly adult, but then, he was alarmingly adult when he was 9. He would bring a newspaper to the set with him every day and read it cover to cover, and then he'd want to discuss it. And he could."

Amiable and unpretentious, Thomas will tell you he likes school (he gets straight *A's*), loves fly-fishing and, though he has his driver's permit, still uses his mom's car. Nonetheless," *US* magazine says, "he is one of Hollywood's most bankable child actors, with a consistently top-rated show and a deal at Disney. Hollywood execs have realized what tens of thousands of crazed *Teen Beat* readers have known for years: This kid is a *star.* "

"Showbiz Today," on CNN, followed him around on his promotional duties for "Wild America," the film he made during his summer "vacation" from "Home Improvement." Even in the short segment you marvelled at the youth's masterful handling of the thousands of fans who showed up at his every stop and who called in to talk shows. "How old are you?" Thomas asked one caller. "Eight," came the answer. "Eight?" Thomas said, grinning, appearing to be having more fun than is legally allowed.

In "Wild America" he stars with Devon Sawa and Scott Bairstow. Thomas said that while making the movie he had to put up with more than his fair share of grief from his two older co-stars, both on and off the set. "They would try to justify it by saying that it would build my character!" In addition to some serious character building, the guys got to do some major brother-style bonding during the two and a half months they spent filming the movie, according to *y/m* magazine. "They went to movies, out to eat – and got a kick out of the funny looks they occasionally got from fans who got a triple dose of the three drop-dead gorgeous-dudes out on the town while on location."

"The trio of young men is handsome, and all but Thomas give shirtless time to the camera," John Stephen Dwyer said in *In Newsweekly*. "This flesh has made it to the brief television commercials for this picture, along with a teaser for a skinny-dipping scene. The poster for this movie depicts the boys as idealized, airbrushed, wet-lipped vamps. Despite this, the movie context has a very duplicitous 'we hadn't noticed' attitude about the boys' sexuality. Warner Brothers publicists would be loathe to admit that ticket sales for this movie will be fueled by teenage lust and not by pictures of mountains and deserts."

So what does the young actor think is the reason for his success with fans world-wide? "Gosh, I have no idea," he deadpans. "I'd like to say that it's raw talent." He laughs. "I guess it's because my character on the show has always been very humorous. I've had great material. And part of it has been that I've never played a character that kids don't like or don't relate to." Since Thomas gets most of the scripts for actors in his age range, it can be tough to choose. "It's been a struggle, because scripts are either very, very broad, stuff I've done before, or they're too dark," he says "And no, I don't want to play a 15-year-old ax murderer. But I would like to do edgier material, because that's what seems to be respected."

"Wild America," the true-life story of three brothers who leave their hick town in the late '60s and hit the road to pursue their dream of becoming wildlife filmmakers, was just the type of project that appealed to Thomas. "For one thing," *US* said, "the story line deals with moviemaking, one of his favorite subjects. (A budding director, Thomas spends his free time on set deluging the director and cinematographer with questions.) It also has action and adventure." The filming was difficult at times, but Thomas didn't complain. Of course, Jonathan is no tantrum-thrower. He jokes, "I'm not one to toss my weight around – I'm only 110 pounds."

"In playing the unlikely heroic 12-year-old in 'Wild America,' Thomas does nothing new," critic George Meyer noted in his review of the film. "He remains an impish, cute, moptop. But he gets all the best lines and acts as narrator." *Entertainment*

Weekly's Owen Gleiberman said, "Thomas has become a bona fide teen idol, but he'd better enjoy it while it lasts. Teen idols tend to fade as quickly as they sprout (Leif Garrett, we hardly knew ye!), and it's easy to imagine Thomas, with his honey gold moptop and thick lips that curl into an angel's smile, going in one of two directions – he looks like he's about the turn into either Val Kilmer or John Denver."

"In one of the movie's most powerful moments," *US* commented, "Thomas' character, Marshall, confronts his indifferent father. It's a scene one suspects is near to the actor's heart. When asked if he sees his own father (who was divorced from his mother when Thomas was living in Sacramento, Calif., before he was discovered), the actor looks at his feet and answers, 'Um...no. Not much.' But his love and support for his mother, Claudine Thomas, who acts as his manager, is palpable. 'My mom could parent a hundred people,' he says. 'She's so strong. I definitely would not be here if it wasn't for her.' After college, Thomas hopes to start his own production company."

"Around the set we joke that he's going to be another Ron Howard someday," says Richardson, referring to how the child actor went from appearing on TV to making big-budget films. Howard, however, was not a teen idol.

In the book *Totally JTT*, Michael-Anne Johns says, "Ironically, Thomas found himself under fire for just being himself." Indeed, in some press accounts his articulateness has been termed "jarringly erudite," as if he were a phony because he's such an intelligent conversationalist. Instead of being impressed with his maturity and understanding, Jonathan was accused of being "programmed" and having "well-rehearsed" answers to questions.

Perhaps the biggest sacrifice to stardom is the trade-in of a normal lifestyle. The star's proud mom told the *National Enquirer*: "I work hard to keep Jonathan a normal kid." But the truth is Jonathan's life thing but normal compared to others his age. "I've had to give up a lot of things," Thomas himself admitted shyly to a journalist. Not the least of which is his beloved soccer. He simply has no time to be at practice or even go to all and Thomas deeply misses being part of a team – being just "one of the guys." Now Thomas always has to be on guard when he meets new people. It's always in the back of his mind that new pals may just want to hang out with him and be his friend because he's on TV, not because of his personality. He told *People* magazine, "You have school, friends, learning your lines, and making sure your performance is up to speed. I can't tell you how many shows I've done with full-blown migraine headaches."

One reporter who was on the scene during the filming of "Tom and Huck," Deborah Storey of the *Huntsville Times*, was very impressed with his professionalism and wrote in one of her articles, "With extras, camera, and everything in place, Jonathan steps into position after pausing a moment to pat a horse that keeps sticking its nose into my back.... Jonathan is a real pro. He'll joke around until just the moment before he is to act, and then he is right on his mark."

Thomas is mature enough to know he can't be a teen idol forever. In the meantime, girls follow him wherever he goes. "I don't know how they know," he says, "but they always know." His fans have an uncanny ability to track him down. "It's sometimes distracting to look over and see a whole group of girls staring and giggling. I understand I am part of their life, and there is a lot that is owed them. It's difficult because you want to make everyone happy, but if you try to do that, you're setting yourself up for failure."

"No form of celebrity seems to have quite so much to deal with as child-star celebrity," Stephen Rebello said on the occasion of interviewing Thomas for *Movieline*. (Nice work if you can get it!) "Face it: most 15-year-olds neither know nor care about contracts, labor laws, line readings, photo shoots or shopping-mall diplomacy. For years, journalists have tripped all over themselves declaring Jonathan Taylor Thomas the perfect young Hollywood citizen, normal as from-scratch apple pie despite all of the hoopla, exceedingly likable, a pro. And right here in front of me, he's animated, articulate and clearheaded. ...He is not remotely like any 15-year-old I've ever encountered in the real world. His eyes already know things, and the set of his newly forming jawline suggests a shrewd customer, however friendly."

"You know what?" Thomas said. "I'm comfortable with who I am. I mean, I am cut loose. People have this conception that there must be this inner person that just wants to go and cause trouble. (But) I love to fly-fish, to travel, to sit back relaxing in my room with the fan on, reading. Not every kid wants to go out and be crazy."

"Thomas certainly appears uncannily comfortable in his own skin," Rebello said. "His TV screen persona, a spunky, good-underneath-it-all wise-ass not unlike that of the young Michael J. Fox on 'Family Ties,' is a natural extension of this easygoing manner. Can he broaden and deepen the colors of his palette? Can and will, Thomas seems to say."

"I'm a balance," the young actor observes. "I can do dramatic material and at the same time I can make you laugh. I don't think that's a quality you see in many young actors. Usually, it's one or the other. I'm also experienced for a person my age. The director doesn't necessarily have to tell me technical stuff like where to turn or move." He is so grounded because he started in the business when he was eight. He's also grounded because of his doting mother. "She's a mom and a very bright business partner and, number one, a great friend. She's a lot of why I'm sane. Whatever my future is, my mom will be in it."

He says, shrugging, "I've spent a lot of time with adults. Basically, if you want to do well in this business, you have to be able to function intelligently in an adult world. You have to learn to relate to the adults on the set or you're isolated. When I'm with my friends, I can have conversations about meaningless things. (But) I've always been a bit older than my friends. I think a lot. I don't do things without thinking first. I'm a very rational human being. A lot of young actors put acting before education. We've not done that. We've tried to balance both, which is tough because acting in the series and doing movies is a full-time job for me. Throw in a social life with family and friends, and it's a full plate."

"I'm not into the Hollywood scene. I don't go out and party. I'm not trying to seize and suck the life out of every moment. I'm not trying to take all this entertainment business stuff and completely absorb it. This business has a lot of great things to offer, but it can be completely immoral. All the qualities that apply in regular life don't necessarily *apply* in the entertainment business. I think it's just that I have a plan. I have goals. I have too many things I want to do in life to burn out."

When it comes to his love life, he says, "I've gone out on a couple of dates. I look forward to dating, having a relationship, but I'm not necessarily going to go out there and look for it. And the girls I have dated are never in the business."

"Since we're batting around the subject of romance and sex," Rebello noted, "I mention how impressed I was with his aplomb at last spring's ShoWest convention when Ellen DeGeneres rocked the packed house by jibing that Thomas had hit on her and obviously 'didn't know.' Did he actually get the joke?

"Thomas cracks up, widens his eyes, and regards me as if now I were the alien life-form. 'Actually, I must have been doing a really good job, because when she said that, all of a sudden the blood in my body drained. Oh, I got it completely. Completely. I'm not *that* young. I thought what she said was hilarious."

Yes, Thomas is "built to laugh," April P. Bernard said in *Seventeen*. "Even at his most earnest, he seems just nanoseconds away from flashing that blinding grin and those tremendous dimples."

Thomas says that, besides his having to deal with fans, he thinks the worst problem in our country today is AIDS. "I just pray this whole thing will end soon," says the star thoughtfully. "It's already plagued too many of our people."

The main complication in Jonathan's love life is his work. His acting career is such that his schedule, keeps him busy much of the year. So when it comes to getting out and having the opportunities to meet girls, he says, "I really don't. It's not really a priority of mine right now. But I do have girls who are friends, I just don't happen to have a girlfriend."

*Rare glimpse of
Devon Sawa
with his shirt off*

Devon Sawa

Devon Sawa is still fresh enough to count the enormous fan attention as the "surprise bonus" of stardom. He says he doesn't mind the occasional problem he gets from an over-enthusiastic admirer. "The fans are definitely the best thing about my career," Devon says. "I am getting a tremendous amount of mail and that's so cool. Except sometimes I don't know what to do with it all!" (5,000 letters per week and counting.)

Occasionally a fan will even find her way to the house that he shares with his parents and his sister, Stephanie, and brother, Brandon, in Vancouver, British Columbia. "A few people just showed up the other day. They drove from a very far distance, but, as usual, I wasn't home. Then there was a girl who would hang around the hotel in Savannah a lot for me while we were filming 'Wild America,' and she would send gifts and show at the set. It was cool at first, and I talked to her a few times, but she didn't get it that we had to work. It got to the point where she wouldn't give up – stalking isn't going to do anything for me! That was scary."

Despite the occasional unexpected guest, Devon says Vancouver has been a great place to live, especially now, since no one really recognizes him.

Sawa has enjoyed (or endured) years of adulation for his turns in movies like "Little Giants," "Casper" and "Now and Then" (with a great shot of his backside). Sawa said baring it all was "horrible. That was the first thing they told us when we were signed for the movie, that we'd be doing a nude scene. It was just embarrassing – there was nothing we could do about it. It wasn't like they sprung it on me, but it was probably the most embarrassing moment of my life. You got the camera guy there, the key grip... I don't know if I'll ever do another nude scene. But if I do, I want to beef up a little first!"

So along with getting mauled in malls and put-upon by paparazzi, Sawa now has to deal with how casting directors perceive him. "In a way, it's painful," Sawa sighs. "One casting director told me, 'You're the next Leonardo DiCaprio,' and when I heard that, I said, 'Let's talk about how I don't want anything to do with being like Leonardo.' He's an amazing actor, but the films we're pushing to do are different. I'm going my own way. In a big way. In all fairness to the casting directors, Sawa used to share the same management as DiCaprio and he does look somewhat like the recent Romeo."

Yes, more and more lately, the actor has been hinting that the stress he sometimes feels has caused him to think about whether he really wants to stay in Hollywood forever: "I feel a lot of pressure now. I'm constantly thinking of where I'll be in my career in a couple years, and if I want to continue in this business, because it is a hard, nerve-wracking business."

Still, he loves Los Angeles. "Really. It's great there. It's so big and there's so much to do and so many people to meet!"

Brad Renfro

Brad Renfro

When casting director Mali Finn (who also discovered Edward Furlong for "Terminator 2" at a California youth center) was working on "The Client," she contacted alternative schools, boys clubs, YMCAs, churches, and even police departments and asked if they knew any tough kids who showed acting ability. "Not that we were looking for a delinquent," explained Finn, "but a tough boy."

A policeman in Knoxville, Tennessee, contacted Finn and told her about a ten-year-old boy who had just played a drug dealer in a school production sponsored by DARE. It was Brad Renfro.

Finn, who had met about 5,000 boys and interviewed nearly 1,500 of those, recalls when she met Brad, "He was mesmerizing. From the second he walked in, I had the feeling this was it. I usually taped each applicant for ten or fifteen minutes. I let the tape run an hour with him." Not only was the casting director impressed with Brad, so was the director, Joel Schumacher. Brad fit all the requirements, all the way around. Brad was an only child, who's lived with his grandmother since the age of three. His father works in a factory in Knoxville, and his mom had remarried and moved away to Michigan. Brad, young though he was, had definitely known some of life's hard knocks. All that – and more – translated onto the screen.

After earning outstanding reviews for "The Client," Renfro was cast in "The Cure." Again Brad won rave reviews. But director Peter Horton also remembers something else about working with Brad – the emergence of a young heartthrob. Brad had turned twelve during the filming of "The Cure," and Horton told the *New York Post*, "He was becoming a movie star with this incredible gaggle of girls, mostly thirteen-to-twenty-four-year-olds, who would follow him from location to location."

"Tom and Huck" co-stars Jonathan Taylor Thomas and Renfro had very little in common. They came from vastly different backgrounds, family situations, and showbiz experience. Jonathan was his naturally talkative and friendly self, while Brad would go off by himself and play his guitar.

Slowly, though, the boys began to talk – Thomas was very interested in Renfro's guitar playing and song writing. He was impressed by the poetry Renfro wrote. Soon Jonathan's natural friendliness and good nature engulfed Brad. They warmed up to each other and a few weeks into filming could often be found joking around together. Their relationship was soon evident on-screen. Renfro took his role to heart and grabbed an ax and chased a casting assistant around the office – because, he said, "if I couldn't have her, then nobody could."

And during filming of "Tom and Huck", he and his electric guitar stayed out well into the wee, wee hours playing "Anarchy in the U.K." at a club in Huntsville. The producers were paying an "acting coach" $10,000 a month to keep him in line, but neither she nor anyone else could stop the packs of cigarettes, or the girls in his trailer. When the bouncers at Hooters wanted him to leave, Renfro told the bouncers, "Hey, I'm the kid with the kid from 'Home Improvement'."

Brad and J.T.T. make a stunning study in contrasts, but the teen idol magazines love the bad boy as much as they adore the sweetheart. They have become America's two princes. *BOP* magazine gushed, "If your letters are any indication, you are obsessed with the babe-ly, talented, and ever-mysterious Brad Renfro." *Teen Beat* says, "Aside from melting hearts with his adorable face, this boy can act!"

In 1996, Brad's career slipped into overdrive. He got great reviews for his part playing Brad Pitt as a youth in "Sleepers," then headed to Louisiana to shoot "Apt Pupil," about a young man "at a crucial point in his life where he had to make very adult decisions." In other words, one of our favorite film genres, a coming-of-age tale. It's a psychological drama based on a Stephen King novella about an escaped Nazi (played by gay actor Ian McKellen) who reveals his identity to a young boy, played by Renfro. Renfro becomes obsessed with the man, and many in Tinseltown have become obsessed with the trouble-plagued production. The film garnered much publicity early on when local jocks were hired for a nightmare shower scene. Originally, the boys were to wear flesh-colored G-strings, but when the time came to shoot the scene, they were asked to remove them! Several of the boys complained and it became known as "the minor problem" around Hollywood. Lawsuits were filed.

Filming *any* movie is a bit of chore for Renfro. He says, "I'm a coward and a half. I'm afraid to go into Planet Hollywood alone. *[Laughs.]* When I first saw a bat, I almost fainted! But I think they leave you alone if you leave them alone."

Brad defends himself: "At times, I just want to hang out and do nothing – and I might have a bunch of homework and a ton of things on my mind, like my agent telling me I should take this or that part. And I just go out, call up some friends, go hit a few tennis balls against the garage wall and disappear for a few hours. But I know that at one point, I have to put the fun behind me and get to work. When you're on the set, you're in this little bubble of people who live and work together. It's not too much like reality at all! But in general, my grandma Joanne keeps me in line – and I have to go to school and do boring stuff that all kids have to do. In some ways, being an actor is harder because you have to go to school, or get a tutor on the set, do your homework, take your hour of phys. ed. per day, and learn your lines. And you have the time you spend on the set, a lot of which is 'down time,' but you have to spend it signing pictures or doing phone interviews. I try to sneak in calls to my friends, but I usually don't have the time. I love what I do – don't get me wrong – but it is hard work."

Does he date? "I have only done what you call 'group dating.' I don't think my grandma wants me dating yet. I still live with her in Knoxville, Tennessee.

"I would like to do every type of movie there is," Renfro says. "Personally, I would like to become the world's greatest guitar player and have lots of friends, which I already do, actually."

Leonardo DiCaprio dressed as a "gay-for-pay" Hollywood hustler for David LaChapelle in a series of photos for Face

GAY FOR PAY

*"I like them all. Men, I mean.
And a few chicks now and then."*
— Sal Mineo

Why should straight actors get to glory in playing gay while homosexual performers are limited by their orientation or forced to hide it, gays say.

"I have no explanation for it, but it's one thing to see me kiss a man and say, 'Well, he's playing a part,'" said Jason Alexander, who took the part Nathan Lane made famous in the film version "Love! Valour! Compassion!" "It's another thing to see a gay actor in a heterosexual romantic scene and buy into it, for most people."

"It's a very strange double standard," said Jeffrey Friedman, co-director and co-producer of "The Celluloid Closet," a documentary on Hollywood's treatment of homosexuality.

"There has been an unquestionable allure in gay roles in recent years," industry-watcher Lynn Elber said. "Some 40 actors, for example, competed for the drag queen part that Patrick Swayze won in 'To Wong Foo, Thanks for Everything! Love, Julie Newmar.'"

"The actors were beating down our doors," recalled producer Bruce Cohen.

But expecting a similar reaction to films featuring gay actors in straight roles may be wishful thinking, according to Doug Chapin, a manager and producer of "Love! Valour! Compassion!"

Joey Lauren Adams, a straight actress playing a bisexual in "Chasing Amy," notes that actors fret about how many issues, not just sexual orientation, might affect their careers. "I knew an actress whose agent told her she couldn't tell anyone she had a daughter, because then she would only be cast in mommy roles," said Adams. Anne Heche's own honesty might have less impact because of her gender, some suggest.

"The culture is much more used to selling the romantic fantasy of sex between two women, and men don't find it as threatening; they find it somewhat titillating," said Chapin.

"And I don't think women are as threatened by gay women as men are by gay men."

Cohen agrees that homosexual women are better positioned for acceptance, but he believes that is because of the gumption they've already shown. "When you look at k.d. lang, Melissa Etheridge and Ellen DeGeneres and Anne now, there's sort of this whole line of brave women pioneers, and the boys are still in the closet quivering," he said. When an actor finally does make the leap, "if they're accepted, everybody might say, 'Guess what? The public doesn't have any harder time with men than with women,'" he said.

There is a kind of retro example available: Rock Hudson, whose homosexuality became known shortly before his 1985 AIDS-related death, seems to be accepted as a straight romantic star in TV reruns of his many movies.

"I've never heard commentary from viewers suggesting otherwise," said Ken Schwab, vice president of programming for Turner Classic Movies.

GLAAD's Levine notes that several top male stars repeatedly have been the subject of gay gossip and yet haven't seen their careers disrupted. He predicted the same results for an actor who reveals his homosexuality. "If they're cast correctly and they're talented, you will get drawn into the story and it will resonate for you. Are you really going to sit in the movie theater and say, 'I'm not going to believe this story, he's really gay'?"

For those who take gay roles, there may be, in Tom Hanks's case, for instance, Oscar gold. For others, being gay-for-pay has other advantages. Indeed, some actors seem to become beauties when they take on gay roles. Consider Ian Hart. "Most actors know a little something about psychology. It's a rare actor who understands how people are defined by the contingencies of history. The young British actor Ian Hart brings that understanding to every role he plays," Amy Taubin said in the *Village Voice*. "Add in his concentrated energy, inventiveness, chameleon-like powers, and his uncanny abiliy to let you know what's going on inside his cbaracter's head without a word or a discernible gesture, and you have one stunning actor, someone who pulls your eyes whenever he's onscreen."

Hart appeared as the young John Lennon in both Christopher

Munch's "The Hours and Times" and Iain Softley's "Backbeat," and lately in Angela Pope's "Hollow Reed," as the ardent gay lover of a divorced doctor who's fighting for custody of his young son. Based on a true story, "Hollow Reed" is a slightly didactic suspense film about child abuse played against a landscape of homophobia. Martin Donovan plays a doctor who divorces his wife when he falls in love with Hart's character, a gay bookstore owner. When the doctor discovers that his son is being physically abused by his wife's new lover, he sues for custody. Desperate to protect his child, the doctor is torn between going back in the closet or trying to convince the court that his son is better off living with his openly gay father than with a mother who refuses to recognize that her properly heterosexual but psychopathic boyfriend has been beating the kid to a pulp every time he's left alone with him.

In his role, Hart seems to have metamorphosed into a Greek god, Taubin says. "The characters he played in previous films, however extraordinary, would never get checked out on the street. But here, his features look finely chiseled, the lines of neck, shoulders, and torso perfectly proportioned and aligned. He's a babe, and an unmistakably gay babe to boot. (Hart and Donovan have a love scene that's all the hotter for being brief.) But what's interesting is that, for all his beauty, there's no narcissism in the performance. Hart's transformed himself specifically to show how little investment this character has in his own beauty. No one-night stand, Tom's the guy who's around for the long haul; he's good-humored, loyal, emotionally generous, and far too honest to lie about his sexuality even for his lover's sake. For him, being openly gay is a moral choice, one that at the end of the 20th century is still subversive."

Meanwhile, in America, especially on TV, actors aren't so concerned about their image. When he began playing "All My Children's" gay hero Michael Delaney, actor Chris Bruno said, "I was worried about what people would say. Now I don't care." Nor should he: "All My Children" won the 1996 GLAAD award for outstanding daytime TV. But did success open him up to, say, a same-sex TV kiss? "No way," said *The Advocate*. "The actual physicality of having a relationship with a man is a step I'm not sure I want to go through in my life,"

Bruno told them.

In the movies, A. J. Jacobs reported in *Entertainment Weekly* that Kevin Kline had been signed to appear in "In & Out," about a star who, in his Oscar acceptance speech, outs a small-town teacher. (Tom Hanks, that *is* your beeper). Incredible as it may seem, Tom Selleck was reported to have signed to play an E-News reporter who is attracted to Kline! There'll be no frilly dresses and no sad ending. But promises screenwriter Paul Rudnick *(Jeffrey)*, there *will* be kissing.

"In fact," Jacobs said, "attitudes that were commonplace just a few years ago – including the old saw that playing a gay character could hurt an actor's career – seem to be eroding as well." TV's Superman Dean Cain, who chose to spend his series hiatus playing a gay bank robber in a low-budget drama called "Independence," said: "I probably wouldn't have taken a gay character at the beginning of my career. But now it's a much easier choice. This character is an action guy – that's a really comfortable place for me. The fact that he's gay is secondary."

"There are still taboos," says Richard Jennings, executive director of Hollywood Supports, a gay advocacy group. "Especially intimacy between two men. It's like the old taboo against interracial romance. But I think that will disappear over the next couple years."

New gay-for-pay boys keep popping up everywhere. Adorable newcomer Douglas Spain appeared in "Star Maps" as Carlos, an immigrant who works for his father's business. "The front is," *4Front's* Jeffrey Epstein revealed, "they sell maps to the stars' homes. The truth is that they sell sex to high priced clients booked out of the sleazy smoky bar in the Hollywood Roosevelt Hotel. It's a very bizarre premise that leads young Carlos down a treacherous path toward his unreachable goal of stardom.

"Spain, in his feature film debut, does a tremendous acting job as our leading man. He plays the ambition and the delight that this star-struck young man feels in coming to America to pursue his dreams. It also doesn't hurt that Spain is absolutely gorgeous and does plenty of sex scenes with both men and women. He's playing a hooker after all! But the darkness of the script and the role doesn't keep young Spain from shining through. His ambition and his imagination make this story work and make it fun to watch, all the way through. He is bright eyed and enthusiastic from beginning to end and is a pleasure to watch."

The last word on this goes to Rupert Everett. When asked if his being open about his sexual preference cost him roles, he said: "Probably, but do you think it's worth thinking about?"

*Brad Davis and director Rainer Fassbinder
confer on the set of "Querelle."*

Brad Davis

*"I don't know why everyone wants
to believe Brad was gay."
- Brad's widow*

Brad Davis, in his heyday, was the epitome of gay-for-pay. Some of us insisted he was, and most of us just wished he was. But now we are told the truth - or is it? "Brad Davis was not gay. Just ask anyone," comments Robert L. Pela in *The Advocate*. "His best friend, a gay man, insists that 'just because Brad had sex with men doesn't mean he was a homosexual.' His former colleagues refuse to go on record saying that Davis wasn't straight. And his widow - who in her memoir of the late actor, *After Midnight: The Life and Death of Brad Davis*, admits that he worked in a gay hustler bar and lived with a drag queen before making it big - says, 'I don't know why everyone wants to believe Brad was gay.'"

For an answer, we turn to a respected menswear designer, John Bartlett, who said in *OUT*, " 'If my libido had its own theme restaurant the plunging tank top that Brad Davis wore in Rainer Werner Fassbinder's gay-sailor classic 'Querelle' would hang there prominently. And the bathroom scene from 'Midnight Express,' with Davis and a fellow convict doing nude yoga in a steamy Turkish prison sauna, would play continuously.

"A stoic and elusive figure, Davis always remained on the outskirts of mainstream society, one of the few actors courageous enough to tackle roles of ambivalent sexual and moral persuasion. In contrast to most leading men of the '70s and '80, he chose to embody the dope smuggler, the criminal, and the outcast, before AIDS claimed his life in 1991. Brad Davis is a modern tragic figure - a man who was forced to hide his HIV status in order to climb the ranks of homophobic Hollywood. The actor revealed his illness in an angry open letter to the movie industry, released posthumously and widely publicized. Though married to a woman, Davis played characters who embodied the painful solitude and angry defiance so often associated with gay experience. Masculine, virile, and introspective, Davis' persona is the antidote to airbrushed sexuality, an icon in an era of homogeneous homosexuality."

Perhaps we want to believe Davis was one of us because of the many gay roles he played during his nearly 20-year career. Or maybe it was the sexed-up vulnerability he expressed in so many of his performances. Or maybe it's the stories that have surfaced since his death about his six-year battle with AIDS, an ordeal he kept secret and with which many gay men can identify. Whatever the reason, Davis was haunted by rumors about his sexuality during his life, and since his death he has become a gay icon whose assisted suicide in 1991 only adds to his tragic memory.

"Whatever Davis's declared sexual orientation, his hard-partying, promiscuous image has been well-documented since his death, and this profile, so much like that of a stereotypical gay man, has further fueled our connection with Davis."

"Brad was a bad boy for a very long time," admits his widow, Susan Bluestein Davis, speaking to *The Advocate* in an exclusive interview. "He was always partying, always very promiscuous. For a lot of *people*, that meant he was gay."

In the magazine's opinion, while most of us reject such negative stereotypes of gay men as promiscuous party animals, it's hard to overlook the growing popularity of gay circuit parties, which seem to promote drug use and multi-partner sex. "If these parties had been around when Brad Davis was a young man, he'd have been dancing his ass off at every one of them," says a former colleague of Davis's who prefers not to be identified. "Barring that, he'd be playing these party boys on the screen."

In the words of writer and friend Rodger McFarlane, Davis was 'the perfect '70s clone: "He was scrumptious. Anyone who ever had a budding gay libido – including me – saw him on the screen and projected all their post-adolescent fantasies onto him. Long before we became best friends, I had a huge crush on him."

So did most of the rest of us. In gay role after gay role, Davis teased us with possibilities: There was his homoerotic shower scene in a Turkish prison in 'Midnight Express' (1978) And his gay sailor in 'Querelle' (1982), in a scoop-neck tank top and white jeans so tight that the film's legendary gay director, Rainer Werner Fassbinder, declared that the trousers "revealed what religion Davis wasn't." Even Davis's stage roles were queer: He appeared in Larry Kramer's *Sissies' Scrapbook* early on and later starred in Kramer's AIDS-themed *The Normal Heart* in New York. "On the stage and screen, Brad said everything gay there was to say at the time," says McFarlane. "Plus, he was the last example of that decadent free-love era." That connection with a long-gone age of innocence is part of the reason Davis, for many, symbolizes our gay past. According to activist and writer Michelangelo Signorile, who documents the gay circuit party scene in *Life Outside: The Signorile Report on Gay Men: Sex, Drugs, Muscles, and the Passages of Life*, that's a dangerous model we can do without. "When Davis was portraying gays on the screen, drugs and promiscuity were less a threat than they are today," he says. "Now the drugs are more potent and more destructive, and with AIDS the dangers of multi-partner, casual sex are greater than ever." If Davis represents anything for gay men today, Signorile says, it should be a warning about the perils of excess.

Davis can also be held up as an example of the consequences of leading a closeted life. If he was gay, it's possible that Davis's carousing was a means of "acting out" against the pressures of the Hollywood closet. "The pressure for a Hollywood actor to remain closeted is 10,000 times greater than for the rest of us," Signorile says. "It's very possible that, if he were gay, Brad Davis resented that condition of his career."

"Those closest to the late star want us to believe that Davis literally partied himself to death," Pela states. "Bluestein Davis writes at length of her husband's drug abuse, and McFarlane suggests that Davis may have contracted HIV from 'passing around needles at A-list parties.' Neither makes much of the fact that Davis worked as a prostitute when he first moved to New York in the early '70s. His widow doesn't mention that in her memoir; McFarlane dismisses it by saying, 'He hustled, but so did a lot of struggling young actors back then.'

"Although Bluestein Davis contends that 'Brad was amused that so many people questioned his sexuality' and McFarlane insists that 'Brad didn't give a flaming shit that people thought he was gay,' the effort to present Davis as a naughty heterosexual continues. 'It's just that when you talk about Brad's being gay, it makes Susan look like a beard, and she deserves better than that,' McFarlane says. 'Their marriage was forged from great love and hard times, and their daughter doesn't need to be hearing that her dad was gay when he was not.' On the other hand, McFarlane gives Davis credit 'for never saying he wasn't gay when someone asked.'"

Greg Louganis looks great during a 1987 photo shoot and instructing Mario Lopez during the filming of his autobiography for TV

Mario Lopez (as Greg Louganis)

"Is history repeating itself?" Billy Masters asked in *Filth*. "Last summer the gossips were a-buzz with news of a new gay couple - Greg Louganis and E!'s very own Steve Kmetco - when their relationship went public with hand-in-hand photos surfacing from Cannes. Well, despite a messy separation and Steve's returning to his long-suffering spousal equivalent, I hear Greg and Steve are once again in Cannes together. Don't look for any photos this time, though. They seem to conveniently separate when the paparazzi are around."

As we reported here last year, Masters was the first to reveal the lovebirds met the year before when Greg was promoting his autobiography which was eventually made into a movie for television, starring Mario Lopez.

Masters quipped, "At the time, Greg was quite interested in Steve and I ask, who wouldn't be interested in a cute guy who does the television news in a spandex T-shirt, and looks good in it? But, of course, Steve was taken. Greg, however, kept trying to bump into Steve casually, but Steve was not really receptive until a few months ago when Greg got the nerve to ask Steve out (an act which makes Greg an 'honorary top.') They showed up together at the Daytime Emmy Technical Awards in L.A. back in June and, later, Cannes (where Steve did the better part of an E! broadcast shirtless - hello?). They also went to an L.A. screening of 'The Cable Guy,' and a couple weeks ago, zipped to N.Y.C. for a performance of the off-Broadway hit, 'The Boys in the Band.' At each stop, reports say they were holding hands and acting quite lovey-dovey. The big question now is, will Steve's lover of 17 years move out of the house they bought together? Not without a fight, say insiders, who know Greg is not the first to be Hooked on Phonics."

Masters was also among the first to break the news that Lopez, the hunk late of "Saved By The Bell" would play Louganis on TV. "Greg and Mario met when Greg was a guest on Mario's Saturday morning TV show 'Adventure.' The down side (so to speak) is that the much buff Mario has had to train down to get the lithe and limber look of peak-form Louganis.

If he were really a Method Actor, he would also have to turn up face down in the pillow of a certain Mr. Kmetco."

After the movie played on TV, Masters reported that Lopez wasn't the only actor capturing hearts of viewers: "I know you all saw 'Breaking the Surface: The Greg Louganis Story,' and many of my readers have inquired as to the sexuality of both Patrick David (who played Greg at 15 - yeah, sure), and Mario Lopez, who played Greg's later years. Well, I'm not gonna ever get into the whole Lopez situation, but I do have a story about Patrick David. First off, if Patrick is 15, so am I! That said, he was spotted at a San Diego gay bar! (Is he old enough to drink?) He was a little drunk (Midori Sours) and in the company of a significantly older man (agent, daddy, who knows) who he dirty danced with. He was very cute and flirty with the other patrons and seemed to enjoy the attention..."

Meanwhile, Lopez's career didn't seem to suffer a bit from playing the role of a lifetime.

And, last August, Louganis joined such high-profile gays as Mitchell Anderson, Michael Jeter, Chad Allen, and Bruce Vilanch in a special 30th Anniversary reading of the play "The Boys in the Band" at the Hudson Theater in Hollywood. Greg played the character "Larry."

Antonio Banderas

Antonio Banderas

"Everything about the man, from the sultry way he moves to his low, caressing voice, is permeated with a heady voluptuousness that makes other men seem like mere copies," *Cosmopolitan* magazine gushed. "Watch him eat a dozen oysters, and it will feel like the best oral sex you ever had. (You may even *faint*.) To the sensualist, life is there for the tasting. His appetites are prodigal, and he has no qualms about indulging them to the fullest. If, after three transporting amorous encounters in an hour, you politely plead exhaustion, he will raise himself on his elbows and gaze uncomprehendingly down at you – eyes soulful, hot bod ready for more. The man simply doesn't *understand* that not everyone has his capacity for lust. You will surely *try*, however, to live up to his expectations...for the paybacks, in terms of heightened awareness, enjoyment, *ecstasy*, are unmatched. True, his excesses may cause problems (with other women, for one), but where else would you find a lover who kisses you *slowly*, from the soles of your feet on up to your lips and after a lovemaking session that leaves you feeling deliciously ravished, feeds you lush strawberries in bed?"

"When he was born in the south of Spain," *US* revealed, "Antonio Banderas dreamed of being a soccer star. He spent hours kicking a beat-up leather ball through the back streets of his hometown of Malaga, fantasizing about the crowds that would one day chant his name. He was 14 years old when the fantasy died, when he broke his left foot and could no longer play the game he loved.

"'Do you believe in destiny?' Banderas whispers, leaning in close. 'I believe very much in these sorts of things, in how one little thing can change your whole life. The reason I am probably here now, talking to you, is because I broke my left foot.' Destiny, for Banderas, meant becoming the best-known actor in the history of Spanish cinema, coming to America, flirting with Madonna, falling in love with Melanie Griffith and finding himself turned into a tabloid-fueled household name, blowing through Hollywood like a sudden sirocco wind. There were times in 1995 when it seemed as if the 35-year-old

Banderas was in every movie being released. In fact, there were five: 'Miami Rhapsody,' 'Desperado,' 'Assassins,' 'Never Talk to Strangers' and a wacky cameo in 'Four Rooms.' It was an incredible range of performances, everything from sweet romantic comedy to operatic violence. He played villains and heroes, cold-blooded killers and lovable innocents. But in America, we want our stars to have more than talent. We like a little taste of scandal, and Banderas gave us that, too. It wasn't just his Valentino-like screen presence that turned him into an A-list occupant of Planet Hollywood.

"He can live with this. For now, he says. 'This is like a knife of two blades,' he says of the invasive media attention that has focused more on his personal life than on his acting accomplishments but has made him famous – and more marketable – in the process. 'If it would have just been an affair, a crazy romance that took three months, destroyed a family and, after that, nothing, that would have been one thing. But I believe in this relationship. It is something I have to do. I'm really excited about being a father. Everything is just gorgeous.'" You can say that again!

Michael Musto in the *Village Voice* noted that "Two Much," the first English-Language film by Fernando Trueba ("Belle Epoche") was the movie responsible for Melanie Griffith and Banderas being so personally entangled and Mutso's waking up screaming that they were making out next to him in bed.

"In an early morning press conference for the film," Musto reported, "Trueba was asked how he felt about the two having fallen in love on the set. 'I've never done a movie where there are *not* people falling in love,' he claimed. Then Melanie and her man were asked about the time they first knew they were falling. 'He asked me how old I was,' said Melanie, in that cute, perpetually girlish manner. She told him – and they fell. They both wantonly needed someone at the moment they met, and were ready to mutually avoid a pre-midlife crisis ('Don't lie about your age. Defy it,' as Melanie says in those Revlon ads). She's charming but has a slightly clingy edge and is all over him like a poncho, as if wanting witnesses.

"And he's hot in person too, wouldn't you know. In town to shoot the awfully titled 'Two Much,' Banderas met the press the next day, and even after two hours' sleep, proved to be devastatingly charming and self-mocking, though perhaps I'm a little biased. 'Please don't see me in the morning when I wake up,' he said. 'It's really a disgusting image. ...I know I'm gonna get fat,' he added in a similar vein. 'I'm gonna lose my hair, and if I'm a (real) actor, I'll continue working. I have to have a sense of humor about it.' Well, *then*, of course, we'll have to throw you out, big fella, but let's not cross that bridge till we come to it, OK? One promptly set to wondering if Antonio's personality has changed to match his imminent physical demise (and current stardom). 'Oh, I live all the time in limos and expensive suits and drink champagne in the morning,' he deadpanned. 'No, I'm still the same guy I was.' And he's still willing to play tons and tons of gay characters, thank heavens. 'I don't have any problem with homosexuals,' he said, 'and I'm not going to have problems to play them in the future. I'm not playing homosexuals being a queen (meaning with stereotypical mannerisms). I play a guy like me. It's not so far from what I am.' Hmm. *Now* we were getting warmer. When he played gay men in Almodovar flicks, Banderas noted, people really *believed* he was gay. 'I said, 'What does this prove?' He mused, 'That I'm a good actor!'"

"In 'Evita,'" Robert Julian said in *Bay Area Reporter*, "as in the play, Eva's story is told by Che (Antonio Banderas), a sardonic, Brechtian narrator inspired by the Latino revolutionary Che Guevara. Che's observations illuminate Eva's struggle while simultaneously questioning her motivations and success. This technique serves the story well, both dramatically and musically, providing an opportunity for point/counterpoint commentary as well as some interesting duets. As written, Che's role is limited to basic recitative with no big numbers or singular musical moments. The unexpected miracle of 'Evita' is the fact that Antonio Banderas is pitch-perfect as Che.

"In his previous appearances in English-language films, Banderas has been highly decorative but frequently unintelligible. In 'Evita,' he steals the film. Banderas has good diction, good looks, a good voice, and he demonstrates the thoroughly convincing political passion essential to making the fiction come alive. Banderas brings the kind of incendiary quality to this role that makes everyone else seem disconnected."

"'Evita,' like all Webber and Rice collaborations, is a mixture of the pretentious (Webber) and the schmaltzy (Rice)," movie critic Bill Kelly said. "... The film's strongest acting is in the performance of Antonio Banderas, as a skeptical narrator Che Guevera, who variously taunts Eva and comments on the action. The only authentic Latino actor in 'Evita,' Banderas commands attention in every scene he's in without trying to upstage Madonna. (The best actors are the generous ones. They share the movie, even when it would be easy to walk away with it.)"

"Madonna tried to get John Travolta to play the film's narrator, Che, " Colin Richardson said in London's *Gay Times*, "but, fortunately for us, had to settle for Antonio Banderas, the man who made her look foolish by rejecting her advances in her quasi-documentary, 'In Bed With Madonna.' ('Truth or Dare' in America). The opening half-an-hour in particular, encompassing Eva's escape from rural obscurity and her exuberant arrival in Buenos Aires, is a triumph. And Antonio Banderas is worth the price of admission alone."

"If anyone rises out of this film as a bigger star, it would be Banderas," John Price said in *4Front*. "We all knew he was sexy, but who knew he could sing like that? Even though his character Che is one dimensional, locked into narrative posture and always angry, Banderas manages to breath a sense of humor and a true passion into every scene...

"This movie will certainly be adored by lots of people: musical theater fans, Alan Parker fans, Lloyd Webber fans, Banderas fans and of course, Madonna's 87 billion fans. If you're not a Madonna fan, however, if it's any consolation, you do get to spend the better part of two hours watching her die."

"Antonio Banderas's magnetism is breathtaking, his singing is terrific, and his interpretation – by turns ironic, angry, and empathetic – is ideal," raved *Theater Week's* Ken Mandelbaum. *Buzzin's* Lee Hartgrave agreed: "Banderas smolders on the screen as 'Everyman,' the Che character who is in every scene as the man who is unseen by the other players. This role will do wonders for his career, and get him legions of new fans. As Eva said to Peron, 'I would be good for you.'"

It was Spain's filmmaker Pedro Almodovar who was good for

or sexually-ambivalent stud. "Antonio had arrived from Malaga," Almodovar explained. "He was an extra in a play. I saw him, arranged a screen test and knew at once he'd be a movie star. It was his first time in front of a camera and it was clear he was born to do it. We were lucky enough to have met at the right time.

"He has a fantastic emotional power in 'Law of Desire.' He's overwhelming. His animal quality is fully developed in 'Law of Desire.' I last saw the film on television. Every time I see it, I'm staggered. My reaction has nothing to do with the fact I directed the film. I've never seen performances of such intensity. It's as if Antonio and Carmen Maura were flayed alive. I'm not sure they know themselves how they attained such a level of performance. I remember that during the shoot they seemed as if in a trance. For a director like me, who enjoys working with actors, it was an extraordinary experience to watch them work like this. I was their first audience, and a privileged one too, because I knew best what they were trying to do. It was very impressive and I have shivers every time I see the film."

Critic Leonard Maltin calls "Law of Desire" a "surreal, hedonistic, and hilarious comedy focusing on a gay love triangle. Maura is a stand-out as a free-thinking transsexual."

For Banderas, his stand-out role was in "Evita." *Movieline* quoted the star: "It was a big role and a dream of mine. (My career) started at the bottom. And I went little by little. I never had, Boom! I never had the kind of movie where someone said, 'This is it! You are going to be remembered because of that movie.' But I felt people would remember this role, because it was so important to me." Yes, Antonio, we'll remember.

Leonardo DiCaprio

"He's a great-looking kid, with deep-set eyes, great lips and great bones. But there's a lot going on behind the eyes - very tortured on one hand, with a lot of warmth and humor and sexuality on the other."
– Casting director Risa Bramon on DiCaprio

"Leonardo DiCaprio isn't one to take any easy-money part that comes along, and that's why we think he's such a superstar," Carole Braden said in *US* magazine. "And for those deep-as-the-ocean blue eyes, we're in the front row every time."

Seventeen magazine's survey named Leonardo DiCaprio "Movie Actor of the Year: (Sorry Tom and Brad - not even close. His emoting as Romeo got you all fired up." In addition, the magazine readers selected the talented young actor as "Celeb You Could Totally Deal With Dating: Runners-up Gavin Rossdale and Jared Leto will have to sit this one out."

Some girls won't sit it out when it comes to Leonardo, however. The star says, "Suddenly all these teenage girls have bceome hysterical. What they do is shocking, climbing over walls and stuff."

Seventeen's readers, whether they actually seek the star out or not, mirrored the attitudes of many a gay male, despite the fact that there are just so many "cute boys all over the movies these days," to quote Michael Bronski in *The Guide*. "They pop up in the most surprising places. Like cheesecake poster girls from the 1940s, they are becoming ubiquitous. But unlike those smiling, leggy, lovingly coifed Hollywood nymphs of a half century ago, these young men - for the most part - are also dramatic stars.

"There was a point a decade ago where pretty boys seemed to be the up-and-coming Hollywood commodity. Think about the Brat Pack. Here we had the comely Andrew McCarthy, the lovable Anthony Michael Hall, the butch Judd Nelson, and the sensitive-but-tough Emilio Estevez. These types spawned a whole range of imitators. But none of them managed to find roles that gave them any real acting." Today, young stars seem to find more roles that challenge them, and no one has been as successful as what Bronski called "Hollywood's boy-of-the-moment," Leonardo DiCaprio, named by a teen fan magazine as one of the 25 Cutest Guys *Ever*. Bronski said, "Besides a terrific screen presence, DiCaprio has ambitions far greater than most young actors. As the young Arthur Rimbaud in Christopher Hampton's 'Total Eclipse' he managed to deliver a powerful and effective performance." For us Leonardo Lovers, this film is now available at a collector's price of $19.98.

People magazine said Leonardo "brought new heat to Romeo," and called him "a rising star, a reckless charmer." One of the highlights of this new version of "Romeo & Juliet" is the ball, wherein Mercutio is a black drag queen with a white afro. Leonardo explains: "Romeo meets Juliet at this ball. Romeo's on drugs, and that's him tripping out on Mercutio. Mercutio's wearing the afro as part of his costume, but I trip out on him, and it grows about three feet. That's a wild scene." *Premiere* magazine said the film was "all very self-consciously hip and MTV-ready. (But) the raw emotional power of the play comes through, thanks mainly to the impassioned performance of DiCaprio."

Bronski also liked Leonardo in "Romeo and Juliet" and "Marvin's Room." Said Bronski, "(Leonardo's) Romeo was severely hampered by the fact that he could barely speak Shakespeare's language it stuck on his tongue like ill-cooked taffy. But that impediment aside, he conveyed a rare vitality and passion. DiCaprio seems to work best when his emotions are on his sleeve. The flamboyant and crass Rimbaud was shocking, his love-struck Romeo is both impatient and innocent. In 'Marvin's Room,' DiCaprio plays a disturbed youth who does things like set his house on fire. His performance is effective and calculated. It works, but feels nowhere close to what he might do with better material; the film's emotional range feels like television."

"The most talented work comes from DiCaprio," Anthony Lane said in the *New Yorker*. "(He is) becoming a sort of elongated James Dean; he uses his lankiness beautifully, sending out that true adolscent rage at being the wrong shape for the world. ...I wish he had more to chew on."

Carrie Rickey, film reviewer for Knight-Ridder Newspapers, disagreed, saying, "Tears cannot tarnish the sterling performances in 'Marvin's Room,' a sandwich-generation stress-fest relieved by truly magical acting." In the movie, based on the play by the late Scott McPherson, whose observations were rooted in his own experience of having AIDS while taking care of sicker HIV-positive friends, Leonardo plays the most dysfunctional one of two sons and Rickey calls him "the most magnetic brooding juvenile since James Dean."

Indeed, Leonardo has long been rumored to be everyone's first choice to play Dean in a major biopic. Thus far, however, the project has not moved beyond the talking stage. Meanwhile, Leonardo filmed a new $100 million version of the Titanic adventure under James Cameron's direction in Mexico. Leonardo plays a third-class passenger romancing a first-class passenger played by Kate Winslet, as if ANYTHING about Leonardo could be less than first-rate! Leonardo said, "It's an epic love story. Huge special effects. I don't know. I'm just going to do it, and we'll see."

What we see is that Leonardo is really a superb actor. Consider his love scenes in "Titanic." Says Winslet: "I love Leo to bits. We had a great time swimming around in the water tank, trying to look drowned. But the first time our lips touched we were both like, Ohhh...yuck! I told him, 'I feel like I'm kissing my brother!'" Hmmmm!

Part of the problem for DiCaprio might be that there are really few good scripts for an intelligent, talented actor of his age. Bronski said, "Teen movies – comedies and shockers – are the main venue for youthful performers, but he is far beyond them. He also looks young – in his early 20's, he can appear as young as 16 – and this limits what he'll be asked to play. And though ethereally beautiful, you can't imagine him in Skeet Ulich's shoes in 'Albino Alligator' or the Edward Norton role in 'The People vs. Larry Flynt,' both serious films that ask for real acting and emotional content. Talk about getting cursed by good looks. Like beautiful female actors who find it difficult to get solid parts, DiCaprio – and to a lesser degree Ulrich and Norton – may find themselves trapped in an industry less interested in their talent than their looks." The Marilyn Monroe syndrome lives on!

Southern Voice said, "*Vanity Fair* coverboy Leonardo DiCaprio (who protests a bit too much that he is not gay) stars in Agnieska Holland's 'Total Eclipse', a very (homo)sexually demanding role. As 19th century French poet Arthur Rimbaud, who at age 16 embarked on a volatile, sexual and intellectual love affair with the much older poet Paul Verlaine, DiCaprio certainly took a risk with this role, especially for someone so concerned about his image. (It involves kissing and a scene of Rimbaud grinding it to Verlaine).

"The only career-damaging thing about 'Total Eclipse' is that DiCaprio is so horribly miscast in this Euro-production. You can never quite make the mental leap to believe DiCaprio is anything but a 20th century American kid in a ruffley period costume. Far more compelling is actor David Thewlis... His Verlaine is effectively snarling, capricious, drunken and libido-driven as he leaps from his wife, Mathilde to Rimbaud and back and forth again. Thewlis' memorable performance is the result of experience and range. DiCaprio is simply pretty and energetic."

That was plenty for Vivian Holland at *Playgirl*, however. "Leonardo is one of Hollywood's hottest new stars," she said. "He's also one of its hottest nude stars, which is why I call him Leo-nude-o. Though his body is thin, pale, hairless and hasn't much muscle tone, I still find him unbearably sexy. Those bee-stung lips, those large, languid eyes; those high cheekbones – and that butt!"

Holland thought that he showed his "ass-ets off to great effect" in "The Basketball Diaries." "In one unforgettable scene, Leo and his pals are sunning themelves in their boxers when they decide to moon the Circle Line cruise ship that's passing below them. To view these four callow hunks with their shorts around their ankles and their beautiful buns raised to the sky is like seeing a stud-muffin Mount Rushmore. Marky Mark's ass is the largest and most muscular, but Leo's butt, while smaller, is just as impressive.

"Later on, these four himbos-in-training play strip basketball in the rain. They run around soaking wet, screaming and tearing at each other's clothes...

"But to really get a good look at Leo's loins, see the otherwise dreaful 'Total Eclipse.' The theatrical release contained one great shot of Leo's rump.

"...In the video version, his circumcised wee-wee hangs out

for all the world to see-see. It looks small compared to the rest of him, but the scene was shot from below, and it looked plenty cold. Leo's package is sort of like a Toyota: compact, economical and cute.

"In another scene, he falls naked out of a bed and onto the floor, lying there on his stomach, with his purplish cock and balls clearly visible between his spread legs. The penis and hairy buttocks of co-star David Thewlis are also quite visible in the video version."

Holland said the European version contains even more nudity. The two men went about the business with a sense of humor. "There was a sequence of me being sodomized by Leonardo," Thewlis recalls. "When we filmed that, it was hysterical. I'm lying facedown on the bed naked, Leo's behind me with a cushion between us, and I'm screaming my head off. I don't know, it was just fun!"

"I told him I wasn't thrilled to do it," admits DiCaprio. "I wasn't exactly *nervous* about it, but I was a little *queasy*. But it was cool because... just the fact that David... he was right there for me...." A pause. "I don't know, this is sounding weird." Another try. "He was just very honest... I don't know what I'm saying. I have to think about it, I guess."

What isn't fun, obviously, are the rumors that are being spread about him. Ones he's heard: "That I'm gay. I heard a rumor that some guy said I was passed out in front of his home after a party for the whole night after doing too much coke. I wish I could have found that guy, face to face. I heard that I was going out with Ellen Barkin. That I'm an alien. Nothing that odd, I guess."

One of the delights of having DiCaprio make a new movie is the prospect of his getting some much-needed attention by doing yet another interview with one of the major film magazines. Sure enough, *Premiere's* Christine Spines did the job last fall before "Romeo and Juliet" opened. As we always say, having these veteran journals "cover" Leo is the next best thing to being there ourselves.

For the interview, Spines joined DiCaprio and his co-star Claire Danes on a jaunt around Griffith Park and a visit to the zoo, and a couple of museums – one devoted to trains, the other to cowboys and Indians. Spines says: "He's dressed in a baggy T-shirt, baggier shorts, and some ugly Shaquille-style Reeboks that he got for free, just for being himself. DiCaprio loves getting stuff for free. Danes hates the hassle of star-hustling to save a few bucks." Danes and DiCaprio are *not* a couple, Spines declares; Leo claims to be currently involved in a yearlong relationship with someone who's not in the industry. Says Danes, "He's paranoid now because everyone thinks he's gay. He's not gay. He's *not* gay!"

"The first stop on the tour is the train museum," Spines continued, "which can't come soon enough, as it is starting to bake inside DiCaprio's silver BMW coupe. He nervously points out the notable sights as he speeds through the park's narrow roads. 'Uh, there's the observatory, where lovers sit in their cars and smooch,' he says with a wave. He seems jittery. 'Oh, let's go there, since that's where they shot *Rebel Without a Cause*,' says Danes, and then, with mock enthusiasm, 'Leo is the next James Dean.'

"DiCaprio keeps driving, silently accepting the needling. He reaches for one of the many pairs of $5 sunglasses strewn around, opting for the mirrored ones. His backseat is covered with a layer of arrested-adolescent detritus: bubblegum chewing tobacco, empty Fruitopia bottles, a map of Six Flags Magic Mountain, a weight-lifting belt. The conversation is flowing like gallstones. Ahead, some big fellow at a bus stop has the misfortune to be sitting next to one of those cardboard signs movie-production location managers put up to show the crew where to go. It reads simply, BEAVER.

"The car screeches to a halt, down slides the driver-side window, and out pops DiCaprio's head. 'Hey, dude, where's beaver at?' In a roar of laughter, he peels out. An unfortunate, desperate moment for DiCaprio, who was grabbing for an icebreaker and panicked. All passengers in the car roll their eyes. Danes slumps in the passenger seat with her nose to the window. In her black T-shirt and mirrored wraparound sunglasses, she looks vaguely dangerous. Terminatoresque. Finally she lets out a small sigh. 'I feel all this pressure,' blurts DiCaprio. 'I don't know if you're having fun. I feel this responsibility to be a good little tour guide.'"

The movie set, Spines reveals, was "filled with a planeload of Hollywood's young, gifted, and rakish, who would spend their off-hours boogieing in local raves, turning themselves into prunes in the hotel pool with epic matches of Sharks and Minnows, playing Taboo in DiCaprio's room, and, of course, videotaping hotel-room parties. 'I think it *was maybe a* little *more* wild than it needed to be,' says Paul Rudd, who plays Paris, Juliet's other suitor. 'DiCaprio's best friend, walking around the hotel naked, was asking the security guys for a key to his room, and we're all sitting there filming it. It was insane.'"

Sounds pretty great to us!

But after spending some time with DiCaprio, Spines had to admit that the actor is a punk: "Despite what must be hours of coaching from his publicists, he can't contain the wisenheimer within. On another day, DiCaprio shows up an hour late for a cover-story interview with a buddy in tow. DiCaprio, in blue shorts and a blue T-shirt, one of those retro '70s jobs with an iron-on '3' on the front, looks as long and sleek as a deer rifle. His friend Jerry, who barely looks old enough to buy cigarettes, sits at the next table reading a book about dungeons or dragons.

"During the 'Romeo and Juliet' shoot, DiCaprio passed time between takes doing Michael Jackson impersonations and imitating the rest of the cast as they tried to say their Elizabethan lines with some realism."

Entertainment Weekly's made note of this when they named DiCaprio one of the 100 Most Creative People List. They called him "the Serious Movie's boy of choice," but he's hardly the Boy Serious. Consider: "He gets relaxed on the set by being funny – Jim Carrey funny," says "Romeo & Juliet" director Baz Luhrmann.

"...DiCaprio squeezes every last drop of juice out of his celebrity," Spines went on. "After all, even Elvis reveled in the Elvis treatment. All the Mexican girls were going mad over him on location for 'Romeo' and, back home, DiCaprio is a well-known party hound around Los Angeles, and gets considerable play in the gossip columns for being a constant attendee of fashion shows and any and all functions involving models."

"I'm written up in tabloids because I go out a lot to places," says DiCaprio. "I won't stay cooped up in my hotel room. Most famous people aren't out except in, like, their bullshit little dive bars or whatever. I don't want to become a strange person. I don't want to give up the life I already have. My career should adapt to me, and if it doesn't, then . . . Fame is like a VIP pass wherever you want to go.

"I mean, I haven't gone crazy yet, and I really do think I'm pretty well balanced being in the position I'm in. I think it has to do with me not investing everything in my job. All these actors think that the blood through their veins is fueled by acting. I'm happier when I'm not working, hanging out with my friends, doing something I love.

"You just get the feeling all the time that, like, you've gotta have more. And no matter how good it is, it's never enough. It's weird – I think the public expects that from you. They want you to keep going, otherwise you could fade away."

No chance, Leonardo. No chance. But in his efforts not to fade away, last summer the actor was in New York filming the new Woody Allen movie. Some of the scenes were filmed at the Stanhope hotel, and one guest was upset when the elevators stopped: "There was no air conditioning, and we were holed up for ten minutes while Woody went to work." Owner and manager Richard Born responded: "The most guests were delayed was ten seconds while a scene was actually being filmed. And I don't think standing around for ten seconds looking at Leonardo DiCaprio is a tragedy." Only ten seconds? Give us ten minutes...ten hours...ten days...

Ewan McGregor, photographed by Nigel Parry for Entertainment Weekly

Ewan McGregor

Ewan McGregor, the 26-year-old actor seemed destined to rival Sean Connery as Scotland's most famous export, said he entertained the notion of heroin for a while, "but as soon as we started working with the addicts, I realized it was unnecessary. But I think I see why people think it's cool." About having his body painted for English writer-director Peter Greenaway's "Pillow Book," the actor says, "It was nice being painted, it was a very nice feeling. I'd get to sleep while they did my front, and then they woke me up and I had to stand up while they did the back of me. It's very sensual, but it took a long time and I had to get up early for it."

In "Pillow Book" McGregor plays Jerome, a bisexual, frequently naked writer with a body-painting fetish, whose pale flesh appears ornamented with exquisitely-rendered Japanese calligraphy. "The painting took 4 1/2 hours," McGregor revealed. "I'd sleep on my back for the first two, then I'd have to stand up for the rest. All these beautiful Japanese extras would just come up and read me." He says he was cowed not by the film's nudity or the graphic sex scenes but by the basic beginner's jitters. "You know, I shot the movie long before 'Trainspotting.' I didn't know what I was doing, and Greenaway won't tell you. But after awhile you're just doing your own thing, and it's brilliant."

"Dazzling visual effects push 'The Plllow Book' to the limits of Greenaway's feverish imagination," Bruce Williamson said in *Playboy*, "...Greenaway goes overboard with this tale of Nagiko (Vivian Wu), a modern woman obsessed by an erotic tenth century literary classic. Nagiko's fetishism and kinky proclivities begin in childhood when her father (an eccentric calligrapher who annually inscribes birthday greetings on her face) consents to a homosexual relationship with his publisher. By the time she is an adult, Nagiko prefers lovers who will write things on her body – until a decadent English translator named Jerome (Ewan McGregor) urges her to turn the tables and adorn male flesh, to become the painter instead of the painted. Subsequently, Jerome becomes a sort of manuscript of erotic poetry, submitting his naked torso to the same publisher's scrutiny. It all culminates in lots of bare flesh, a suicide and several grisly sequences about a male corpse being flayed, filleted and reassembled in book form."

"With its black and white, color and monochromatic picture-within-a-picture-within-a-picture imagery that utilizes differing framing sizes, and through its use of traditional Japanese music and contemporary rock, 'The Pillow Book' is always a marvel to look at and listen to," said Lydia Marcus in *Frontiers*. "There's constant movement or change on the screen, but luscious cinematography and sensual images of painted bodies only carry the film so far. Greenaway directs his actors to be emotionally aloof, so that even when they're passionate or upset, it's hard for the viewer to feel the heat or the tears. The story centers on one woman's quest to find her own literary and personal voice. Nagiko searches to recapture the serenity and love of her childhood experiences with her father through a series of liaisons with calligraphers. First, she needs them to literally write on her own flesh, then later she becomes the body painter, seeking out human canvases. Along the way her most significant relationship occurs with a bisexual man, Jerome (McGregor), who she initially uses as a liason to a publisher (Yoshi Oida) who is Jerome's much older male lover. Nagiko always comes off as petulant, the publisher is a bizarre tyrant who is constantly seeking a carnal experience, and Jerome is a lightweight boy who doesn't seem capable of great lust, let alone love. In 'The Pillow Book,' Greenaway has defimtely challenged the medium of film. He changes and juggles frame, perspective and color so much throughout the film ... leaving the viewer with the feeling that they've practically experienced a living, breathing, three-dimensional film instead of the flat, two dimensional one we're accustomed to. The film itself is full-bodied, but its characters, unfortunately, never rise above their one-dimensionality."

"McGregor, a painfully withdrawn student who quit school at 16 to pursue acting, never lacked for work," Maureen Callahan said in *New York* magazine, "but 'Trainspotting' dramatically changed his lot both at home and in America. He suddenly found the mercenary Brit press camped outside his London house, inquiring after his wife and baby girl, who was sick at the time."

"They wanted me to talk about her illness," recalls McGregor, "and I was like, 'Fuck you.'"

"Handsome British actors may not have the naked animal magnetism of Marlon Brando in a torn T-shirt," Stephen Farber in *Movieline*, "but they have a more subtle kind of sex appeal, often combined with virtuoso acting skills. Some of the U.K. imports who have stormed Hollywood – from Cary Grant and Laurence Olivier to Daniel Day-Lewis and Hugh Grant – have become superstars, while others have remained arthouse darlings... But overall the migration has been fairly steady, and among the new wave of smoldering Brits, Ewan McGregor is the hippest candidate for superstardom, primarily for his turn as the barely decipherable drug enthusiast in 'Trainspotting.' McGregor more recently demonstrated his romantic allure in 'Brassed Off,' and he showed off considerably more of his, well, gifts in Peter Greenaway's erotic manual, 'The Pillow Book.' 'Nightwatch' is McGregor's first direct entry into the American market. Judging from this film, he needs to be more careful in choosing his vehicles. Other British actors have stumbled when trying to play the Hollywood game so the misstep is hardly surprising. And, as a matter of fact, McGregor himself actually comes off very well in 'Nightwatch;' the camera dotes on him, and he gives a natural, engaging performance as a hospital night watchman who gets embroiled in a series of gruesome murders. It's the film that's the problem. It takes an awfully long time to get to the grisly thrills, the script has gaping holes, and Ole Bomedal's direction is stronger on atmosphere than sense. All in all, 'Nightwatch' is too cheesy to push the gifted McGregor from promising to proven commodity."

In mid-1997, Ewan was named to *Entertainment Weekly's* 100 Most Creative People List. Said the editors, "Diving into a toilet to retrieve an opium suppository in *Trainspotting* made him the flushest young actor in England... (He does it with) a steady diet of beer and cigarettes and by staying far away from Hollywood. 'I hate it there,' he says. 'All the restaurants are the same. And why is everyone so fat there? It's the land of the fat-free diet, but everyone is huge!'"

He was mortified when the tabloids named him "Britain's Hunkiest Dad," then ferreted out old girlfriends, who recounted their glory days with a sensitive yet driven

McGregor. "All of that, in my eyes, is not on," the star says, who is quick to add that he's grateful for his sudden fame because it got him the part of Obi-Wan in the new "Star Wars" prequels.

"I want to do it, they want me to do it, so I'm doing it," said Ewan McGregor. "Actually, I really want to play Princess Leia. Stick some big pastries on my head. Now that would be interesting."

Skeet Ulrich, one of Empire magazine's "20 Hottest Faces of the Year," courtesy Outline

Skeet Ulrich

*"My biggest nightmare is
being labelled the next Keanu Reeves."*
– Skeet Ulrich

Skeet Ulrich is *not* Johnny Depp, Melanie Mannarino claimed in *US* magazine: "Sure they both have that stringy-haired, brown-eyed charm. But that's where the comparisons end. The 27-year-old from North Carolina is his own man with his own career."

To clear up the confusion, *US* cited these differences between the two actors: While Depp is multi-tattooed, the only mark on Ulrich's slender body is a scar left over from his open-heart surgery. And while Depp collects dead bugs in glass boxes, Ulrich keeps busy reading golf magazines and doing crossword puzzles. No dummy this Ulrich, who studied marine biology at the University of North Carolina for two years before transferring to the drama program at New York University. And while Depp just bought a house in Hollywood, Ulrich says he prefers living in New York because he enjoys the city's energy.

So far the films Ulrich has appeared in have ranged from "stinker to middling, making little impact on the moviegoing public," David Handelman wrote in *Details*.

Then Bryan Ray Ulrich (nicknamed "Skeet" by his Little League coach in North Carolina) scored good notices as a psycho terrorizing Drew Barrymore in "Scream."

Many teens who saw "Scream" during its first release, came back when it was re-released the following March, making the movie an instant cult classic. "Teenage girls especially return again and again to catch the bits they've missed and relive chase scenes and skewerings," movie critic Thomas Becnel said. Ulrich also scored as a former monk in "Touch" with Bridget Fonda, romancing Winona Ryder in "Boys" and with Sharon Stone in "Last Dance," and as a hostage in "Albino Alligator," directed by actor Kevin Spacey.

But perhaps Ulrich's greatest notices will be as a gay street hustler obsessed with actor Brad Pitt (who's not in the film) in

"Old Friends," which also stars Jack Nicholson and Helen Hunt. "I see my character as the gay version of Brad Pitt's part in 'Thelma & Louise,"' Ulrich says. "The outsider who comes in and rolls the lead (Greg Kinnear), uses his sex, and takes the money." He says he took the part "because it's not something you can roll out of bed and start playing," he says. "It takes work, research, a leap of consciousness."

He's hoping to play another gay character, in Todd Haynes's "Velvet Goldmine," about the glam-rock scene. Skeet says he hopes to avoid what he calls "cinematic reality" – the fake, limited repertoire of expressions usually depicted onscreen. "There's been a boiling down of real emotion into a set pattern instead of individualism."

He has proven himself a bona fide actor. He's strong yet vulnerable ("A girl could fall in love with him," says director Wes Craven, "or he could be purely psychotic") and oozes the enigmatic charisma that confers movie stardom. "Skeet's got a light touch," says co-star Bridget Fonda, "and he's mysterious – he's not offering everything – which makes him incredibly watchable."

"In this business," Ulrich says, "you're either Brad Pitt right away, or you're already going down the ladder, so there's no process, no learning." If there's one message he wants to impart, it's that "I'm disappointed in acting as a craft. I want everything to go back to Orson Welles and fake noses and changing your voice. It's become so much about *personality*. A lot of Hollywood, they don't work on acting, necessarily. They don't see you're gonna fall, make mistakes." Ulrich is ambivalent about revealing himself; he's still figuring everything out. "I'm not the most talkative guy in the world. And there are things I just don't want to talk about. I've never been one that was jumping out of my socks at every woman I saw – and I'm not opening the door to why."

Rumor has it that Calvin Klein is interested in having Ulrich replace Antonio Sabato Jr. as his underpants poster boy. We can hardly wait!

SEX IN THEATER: CUTE BOYS IN & OUT OF THEIR UNDERPANTS

Gay theater's obsession with cute boys in and out of their underpants continued unabated in 1997, but as *L&GNY's* critic Christopher Byrne put it, "defined pecs and defined character are not the same thing."

Pecs or no pecs, one actor who caught our eye was young Tony Meindl, who gained quite a following during the runs of the hits "Party" and "Love! Valour! Compassion!" (in which he bared all) and "Message to Michael".

In 1997, he scored wearing only a towel in "Queens Blvd." Raved David Bahr in *HX*, "Watching Meindl act is indeed a treat. Besides possessing a body sculptured from years of competitive swimming (he is the winner of 10 gold medals at the most recent Gay Games), the actor has a comedic goofiness that's rare for a guy with his looks."

Says Meindl, "If I'm going to be the trailblazer for gay actors doing gay stuff, then so be it. How can you be an actor if you're completely closed off to the public. What can you bring to your work if you don't live honestly in your life?

""Queens Blvd.' also explores middle age, through the story of Frank and Jules (Steve Hayes and Russell Leib), ex-lovers who live together in a tchotchke-filled apartment in Queens. When a young stud of indeterminate sexual orientation, David (Meindl), answers their ad for a third roommate, Frank and Jules approve, and 'Queens Blvd.' becomes an 'Is he or isn't he?' farce. David is asked to quote from 'The Wizard of Oz' and choose the right fabric for a slipcover from a pile of swatches.

Gregory Young in *HX* said, "Our duo has a room to rent in their queer little apartment, which Jules only rents to lesbians. Frank, however, wants another gay man to inhabit their abode, so they advertise and soon attract David, a jobless freeloader, to their place. Because David is played by Tony Meindl, Frank and Jules drool over themselves and give David their room with reduced rent, on the condition he will walk around the apartment naked from time to time. Paul Corrigan's sitcom-inspired script lacks any sparkling humor or intriguing character insight into these potentially fascinating creations. It's hard to tell if these men are truly vapid or just being presented as such. The character of David is even more appalling. It's one thing to create a lighthearted dumb bunny whose butt we get to occasionally see; it's another thing for him to waffle from straight to gay – and from masculine straight-edge to Fire Island queen – just for some slight comedy. ...Unfortunately, Meindl is wasted in a vacuous role, but I've never seen him look better."

Meindl stars in a children's video series, "Hard Hat Harry." He plays Harry, a hunky genie who takes kids on outdoor adventures and owns more butch outfits than the Village People," said *HX*. And, for adults, Meindl is on view in the indie film "Minor Details," playing a polymorphously perverse porn star. Just our kinda guy!

A straight actor who caused a stir in Manhattan was Maxwell Caulfield, remembered as the sexy star of the film "Grease 2" and a one-time "The Colbys" ("Dynasty" spin-off) regular. In "My Night With Reg," Caulfield plays John, a campy, aging Lothario head-over-heels in love with the eponymous Reg. Trouble was, as played by Caulfield, this just didn't ring true because, obviously Caulfield could have whomever he wanted. However, Caulfield was the star who made it all worthwhile. Harry Forbes in *Manhattan Spirit* said, "No stranger to nude scenes on the New York stage, Caulfield does it again, in a sensuous interlude with a young house painter, well choreographed (that's the only word for it), which masterfully conveys John's self-recognition of aging."

Ron Lasko in *Next* said Caulfield was "top notch, perfectly cast" but that the real star is "sexy young Sam Trammell as a much-coveted boytoy who longs for something more than he sees around him."

L&GNY's critic Christopher Byrne thought Caulfield a disappointment. "As a limited actor, playing a limited character, the performance swiftly approaches laconic, and might well have a sleep-inducing effect. However, you do get to see him naked, and he's just as handsome as he was in 'Entertaining Mr. Sloane' more than a decade ago, but as we keep having to learn this season, defined pecs and defined character are not the same thing."

Gregory Young, the Drama Queen, says, "If we *HX* staffers were as coitally interconnected as the industrious sexpot friends in Kevin Elyot's 'My Night With Reg,' why, we'd never have *time to* produce the quality literature that you're reading now! Playwright Kevin Elyot has engineered the fear and apparent randomness of AIDS in the mid-'80s by creating a theatrical petri dish. The layered and often terse dialogue prevents any moralizing, however, and though the play's soap opera shenanigans seem trite at times, it never reaches long into melodrama (the exception being an incredibly attractive but gratuitous nude scene near the end).

"Still, I can't really imagine it working without a sturdy cast, and this production has fortunately been blessed. ...Splendid is Caulfield, who's slowly turning into '70s *Tarzan* stud Ron Ely. The decision to cast him was a wise one; there's something in his features that's dangerously sensual and – maybe it's *The Colbys* connection coming through – very '80s. By the time the host finally reveals his love of Caulfield's character, it's no surprise to learn everyone else has already had sex with him (or is just about to)."

The dean of American critics, John Simon in *New York* magazine, thought Trammell "as the naif who is quite a manipulator in his own right," "outstanding, histrionically and accentually," but thought that Caulfield had "forgotten his English accent."

"The new arrivals on New York's gay theater scene – 'My Night With Reg' by Kevin Elyot and 'Queens Blvd.' by Paul Corrigan – have two things in common: naked (as in full, frontal) hunks and middle-aged blues," Dick Scanlan said in *The Advocate*. "Caulfield is well-cast as the pretty boy whose thinning hair reminds him and us that time is running out."

No matter what city you're in, playgoers love nudity. Some even say that there should be more of it! Take the case of Felix A. Pire's "Man on the Verge of a His Panic Breakdown," the Los Angeles-transplanted, one-man spectacle written by Guillermo Reyes that has hoisted the virtually unknown Pire into New York stage notoriety.

"Felix is a cat," says Gregory Young in *HX*. "He slinks,

purrs, pounces and shifts moods with an open eye or raised hair. He's as savvy as an alley cat with the taut, detailed form of a Siamese. He doesn't clean himself with his own tongue, however, and he prefers banana pancakes to Fancy Feast. But Felix A. Pire can afford to take a few liberties...

"Felix is also a chameleon. As a physical performer, he could pass for any number of well-toned ethnic types, while his voice is watermarked with a hint of Cuban ancestry even as it casually transforms into dozens of spontaneous creations during conversation. In 'Men,' Pire portrays a diverse selection of Hispanic gay characters with rubbery dexterity, leaping from differing ages and personalities with the ease of a performer such as Robin Williams.

"The part allows him to show off that lithe, little body in a series of fluid, sensual and scantily clad dance sequences that link the characterizations. 'I've actually had people complain that I didn't take off more clothes during those scenes,' he says. 'But I'm a classically trained actor and a well-trained dancer. I am not a go-go boy! It's not about me just shaking my ass up there.'

"'I'll definitely do more solo performances because I love working with myself. I don't want to ever be the boring leading-man type.'

"Observing Pire's zany, flamboyant style of humor, it's difficult to imagine him as merely a bit player on television and in films, yet that's been the extent of his Hollywood experience thus far. His movie debut was in 'Twelve Monkeys' as a member of Brad Pitt's maniacal animal protection gang.

"'The only direction that the director ever gave me was in my one big scene with Brad Pitt," Pire says. "You can't miss me. It ends with this really big close-up of my face. Anyway, the director says, 'Make it all about you, make it about the fact that you're having a nervous breakdown.' How was I to know that was to become a theme in my life!'"

Meanwhile, in Orlando, The Acting Studio presented "Party" and one attendee, Chris Murphy, said, "I enjoyed looking at the naked cast, almost as much as the cast (particularly 'Weenie boy' Dalton) enjoyed displaying their bodies. The Acting Studio has done the full frontal thing more than once, more than twice I think, and perhaps more than that. Male nudity has appeared to be the focus of their productions, and judging from the number of audience members at last night's performance, it has served you well. ...(But) I would prefer to spend $15 watching a gay 'Romeo and Juliet' or some other adapted classic – a rich and thoughtful costume drama. I can rent erotica at the video store for three bucks and fast forward through the dreadful dialogue." Yes, but seeing Weenie Boy "in person" – now that's worth $15 isn't it?

Meanwhile, in Boston, "*Dirt*," a comedy by Theater Offensive artistic director Abe Rybeck, is "so dirty it delights," according to critic John Stephen Dwyer. "A cheeky look at police, politicians and their prostitute bedfellows, *Dirt* delves into the muddy garden of gay politics with daring irreverence, just what we should expect from Theater Offensive. Juicy, tantalizing and scandalous, *Dirt* is centered around a fictional mayoral liaison to the gay and lesbian community (played by Michael Lopez-Saenz) and his latest hustler-turned-houseboy (Michael McNeal). The city politics and situations depicted in *Dirt* might seem especially familiar to Bostonians, but 'Thank goodness,' playwright Rybeck assures, 'it couldn't happen here.'

"While the suit-and-tie gay elite try to maintain the status quo, a brassy madam (played with style by Adam D. Morris (aka Ms. Eve Adams) stands at the top of another power structure. Soon we see the two worlds are one. Through dryish parody, the sacred cows of the gay and lesbian community are put on the block. AIDS-funding tycoons and the Log Cabin Club intertwine destinies with a 15-year-old hooker boy (Yogen Kushi) and a lesbian charwoman (Catherine Clark). Unless the liaison and his icy partner (Paul Outlaw) can sweep all their dirty secrets back under the carpet, the gay community gets no parade. Some might be embarrassed to see the gay community's dirty laundry strung across the theater. However, for a good-natured look at some mean topics, *Dirt* is paydirt."

"It's been a constant struggle," playwright Rybeck told Adrian Saks in *GCN*. "It wasn't just at that moment when we went from United Fruit Company to The Theater Offensive. We are bad boys and bad girls doing this funky work. Every step of the way we get better at what we do. Part of that is a growing professionalism, which is important, but also strange. There's much responsibility that comes with establishing yourself. Providing people with diverse, radical queer culture – it's not as if there are many places to do that. With the formation of The Theater Offensive, it upped the ante on our responsibility to the community. 'Dirt' is about insider gay politics and housecleaning. I first conceived of it as a long sketch United Fruit Company could perform; that must have been in 1989. So here I am eight years later racing to finish the final draft of the script.

"It's been fun hearing people's reactions. So many things have happened that I never knew about, yet they parallel what I wrote. Many scandals don't get out. Everybody I talked to about it said, 'Oh your inspiration for that must have been so and so.' It's been fun that it hits home for so many people's experiences, but more than that, it has been terrifying. It's horrifying that there is such a high level of bullshit in our community that doesn't get named. Naming it is not an unhealthy thing at all. Our movement is at a time in its development where it is really important to critique our work. In some ways I feel that we've already missed the boat on that. We've made some enormous strategic errors. 'Dirt' is about who has a place at the queer table."

Someone who has a place at the queer table even though he's straight is Randy Becker, who at 26, has no hangups about appearing in gay-themed works. As Glenn Sumi noted in *Icon*. "Luckily, that lack of inhibition translates on screen. Regardless of his future acting decisions, there's no denying his electric pouty presence, as palpable in person as it is onscreen.

"...In 1995, he played the dangerous Latino stud who humps the hero while cheeseburgers sizzle in Wally White's low-budget flick 'Lie Down With Dogs.' Now, he's reprising his Obie and Dramatic League Award-winning role as a dangerous Puerto Rican hunk in the film version of Terrence McNally's 'Love! Valour! Compassion!' in which he spends a great deal of time lounging around naked."

"My acting school teacher told me not to take the role in 'Lie Down With Dogs.' She said I wouldn't work in Hollywood. But it was a good role and I needed film experience. If I can't work in mainstream Hollywood for the next ten years, I can work elsewhere. Even within my agency, some people have a problem. One friend didn't audition for this because he wasn't comfortable kissing another man. Another friend wasn't comfortable being naked. Frankly, I'm glad I'm able to explore different roles.

"It was a challenge to make these objectified characters human. When people call me a himbo, I feel like I haven't quite done my job. With both roles, I tried to find moments of vulnerability, to suggest there was more beneath the bravado and sensuality."

About the on-stage (and on film) nudity in "LVC," he says, "It was all a little absurd. Here was this play with important issues, and some people just wanted to see the nudity. Every night, I'd look at the audience and there were all these men with binoculars. One night there was a guy in the front, taking pictures! I guess people go to the theatre for different reasons. There's nothing bad about it, it's just silly. It's like getting off on a piece of sculpture. But hey, some people do that."

We certainly do, and two stage shows have recently kept many porn performers busy flexing their muscles proving it: "STRIP!" and "Making Porn." The latter has travelled the country with stars ranging from the original, Rex Chandler, to Kurt Young. Young is included elsewhere in this book, but the others are detailed in this section. Now, when they say one of these guys is a "star of stage and screen," they aren't kidding.

Kevin Kramer, during a performance of "Bare-ly Legal!"

Hawk McAllistar,
another popular porn performer featured in "Bare-ly Legal"

Kevin Kramer

After several sold-out months in Hollywood, our favorite toyboy Kevin Kramer went to San Francisco with the show *Strip! Bare-ly Legal*. For those who read my book about Kramer (included in the *Beautiful Boys* anthology), I was delighted with the play, presented at the quaint surroundings of the little Globe theater. Apparently the play lost something in the transfer to the City by the Bay.

The *Bay Area Reporter's* Chad Jones commented, "With a ticket price of $40, *Strip! Bare-ly Legal* is a theater experience that's about $38.50 too much. Like *Tony 'n' Tina's Wedding* before it, *Strip!* is one of those interactive (oooh, a buzz word!) gigs that demands its audience play along with the actors until everyone is convinced they're having an 'authentic' good time.

"The premise here is that when you enter the Rococo Showplace on 10th Street, you're really entering the Cat Club, a strip joint run by drag queen Ms. Kitty (played by the show's creator and director Steven J. McCarthy in his drag persona, Madame Dish) and populated by the Tomcats, a retinue of five men who perform various stripteases throughout the 90-minute show. Mixed in with the real folk are cast members playing a gay couple celebrating their 18th anniversary, a straight boy waiting for his girlfriend who never shows up (and guess what, he ends up stripping by the end of the show, *quelle surprise*); and several game men who participate in the amateur strip that closes the show. When a show relies so heavily on audience participation, it had better make darn sure it has a fall back position. Miss Kitty had a devil of a time getting the largely dull audience whipped into an appropriate frenzy. Even the stripping – which goes beyond the usual g-string phase – was less than stellar. Porn star Kevin Kramer (last seen under Jeff Stryker) was the most polished stripper of the generally undistinguished lot. Like a real strip club, the audience is encouraged to stuff the g-strings with dollar bills, which results in a lot of embarrassing butt wriggling until the patrons pony up. This sort of thing may work at the Nob Hill Cinema, but as theater, it's cringe-inducing.

"*Strip! Bare-ly Legal*, which ran for eight months in West

Hollywood, is bland, unexciting, and about as erotic as a stroll through Utah."

Our own spy in San Francisco wrote, "Well, I finally made it to see *Strip!* after planning to go many times to the theater but was just too busy with other stuff.

"Actually, I can't call it a theater. They turned some warehouse into a so-called theater. The stage was very tacky – the seats were those white plastic things from Target spray painted gold.

"I must say that I was very disappointed. First of all, Kevin Kramer was not in it and they did not say it in the ad that was still running in the newspapers nor when I called to get a ticket. I honestly think that if I had at least seen *him* that it would have made the whole thing less difficult to handle.

"I thought that it was basically amateurish and embarrassing. Now I must say that I've never been a big fan of drag. Over the years I have seen various performers – some better than others – and for the most part I find it entertaining for a very brief time. There is a famous place in North Beach that really exists for the amusement of heterosexual tourists.

"The major portion of the show was Dish going around through the audience (I would say 40 of us total and that includes the planted couple) making up the lines as he went. I was certain that the long-haired guy (Matt Newman) was a part of the whole thing early on and did not know about the other plants until after. I guess for this I should give them some credit for their acting. I did think that the couple was celebrating an anniversary. You see, they said Hello on the sidewalk out front and asked that we join them for cake before we were let inside.

"I think there are really only two songs ("Fornication" and "Hurt You So Bad.") Neither one anything special. The boys stripped to their thongs, ran around collecting cash, then pulled the thong off, and dashed off stage. The only person who was truly good at dancing was Tho Vong. He was Beau in this occasion (There was no Precious and there was no Mr Mephistopheles). He is very pretty and has a beautiful body – including a perfect ass to rival Kramer's. Golden Boy was played by Johnnie Phoenix. Now he is a cute guy but was doing this God-awful phony French accent throughout – even before the show on the street – and it got real old real fast. Euri did nothing for me; he would stomp around, none too gracefully, and holler out some Portuguese word over and over. It bordered on Neanderthal.

"Hawk McAllistar is very handsome but again he should stick to porno. He was jumping around like he was supposed to be a cowboy and it wasn't working.

"Then came the worst part! From the start, Dish kept telling people whom he insisted would be in the strip finale. He went from person to person asking questions of them, at times trying to embarrass them as best he could and then announcing whether or not he had decided that they were to be part of his show. I think one of the reasons I don't care for drag is that it always seems to go hand in hand with insults, cheap jokes, degradation. The two guys to my right were both artists and Dish was prying more and more into their lives and artwork and insisting that one was going to strip later; they sneaked out when the lights were low. So did another pair behind me.

"In the end, Dish had, in addition to the guy playing Matt and the guy playing Todd, five other guys who stripped. They had to be dragged up on-stage. They acted completely uncomfortable. All tried to hide their dicks after removing their underwear but Dish and the dancers tried to expose them. And, oddly enough, this must have been a collection of some of the smallest dicks in town. Johnnie Phoenix and Tho Vong were both tiny. And I swear I've seen Hawk in sexvids and he seemed to be hung average or better, but he must have been suffering from stage fright. Of course, I'm used to the obviously excited, hugely-hung guys dancing at the Nob Hill!"

Sister Dana Van Iquity apparently loved the show. In her (his) review in *Bay Times*, he said, "Now you know that Sister Dana would never ever ever reveal any secrets, but trust me – this thing has more twists than Chubby Checker at the Peppermint Lounge. Twists and bumps and grinds and dancing penises! When they say 'Strip' they mean bare, and when they say 'bare-ly legal' they mean strip! ...It's rude, crude, lewd, and not for the prude. It's also a helluva good time. Bring the whole family, as long as they're total perverts! Ms. Kitty's stable of sexy strippers includes two headliners: Golden Boy (aka porn star Kevin Kramer), so named because of his gold-moussed hair, gold-glittered torso, and gold spray-painted boots; in fact, the *only* part of Golden Boy that isn't gold is his dick; and Julio, Ms. K's exotic and passionate lover (a brazen Brazilian who in real life is Euri Oliveira, the show's superb producer/choreographer/assistant director and totally nekkid performer).

"This nasty, sexy show is surely destined to become a cult classk. Once you've seen it, you'll want to bring your friends..."

Hawk McAllistar

Hawk McAllistar's best known for sexvids such as Jerry Douglas' award-winning "Flesh & Blood," partnered with star Kurt Young, and "Cram Course," "Law of Desire," and "Clothes Make the Man," but he's also done some specialty videos for his pal Karen Dior. He admits to enjoying dressing up as Anita, his drag alter ego. "Every breath of mine is gay," Hawk says. "I love being gay – that's me. All my co-workers know I'm gay, they know I do drag. Some know I do porn.

"My last lover's friend is a producer, Karen Dior. I did four or five movies for her. 'Dildo Pigs' was the first one. With Tanner Reeves. I did a shaving video: no sex, just shaving. It was fun. But it was a long day – thirteen hours! Working with Tanner, working with these gorgeous men... I'd never been near another naked man – the first movies I did with my ex-lover, because he didn't want me to do movies with anyone else. I ended up taking a muscle relaxer, I was so nervous. I looked like I was stoned, but man, that dildo just goes in and out! It was funny, because Tanner and I were next to each other, like laughing and talking about the weather, while those dildos were being shoved up our asses. But it's hard work."

You just never know what to expect next from the boy from Boise, Idaho. We certainly never expected to see him in "STRIP! Barely Legal," but there he was, playing a high-stepping cowhand, which was not far from the truth.

In an interview for *Manshots* with Lucas Kazan, McAllistar said, as a kid, he often got up to milk the cows.

Hawk said, "I see lots of people who can't cope with what they are. Like Rex Chandler. I mean, okay, so he's straight, he does it for the money. That's fine with me. He can do me anytime! I know who I am. And I am completely comfortable with myself. Because lots of gay men fantasize about straight men. It's taboo. You always want what you can't have.

"Me, I like Chase Hunter. He's absolutely perfect, except for the moustache. He's got a beautiful body, beautiful face, incredible, perfect dick. His body is a little thin, I usually like very muscular men, but his dick is the most beautiful dick I've ever seen. Perfect size, perfect proportion, incredible length. He really excites me. I used to have his picture framed in my bedroom."

One of our favorite scenes featuring Hawk can be found in "Men Only," from Jocks. *Adam Gay Video* describes it: "A day in the life of one of those inns where the staff is gay and the guests are gayer. Hawk has an attitude problem that gets rectum – no, rectified by Kurt Young and Steve O'Donnell's cocks. Hawk even sucks both at once..." Hawk looks as if he's really enjoying it, at least in that scene, but he admits to having had sex with people he wasn't attracted to. "It's all about performing," says he. "Sex is about pleasing, whether it be pleasing the director, or yourself, or your partner. I focus on myself, instead of focusing on what that person looks like. Focus on myself as a very sexual, stimulating person."

The best part of being a porn star is the recognition: "I like being recognized, that's a big part. I need that. And the money."

Ryan Idol

Speaking of nasty, "What is it about Ryan Idol that makes you want to hate him, even though you secretly love him?" asked Sticky Remote in *HX*. "Could it be his claim to be straight, even though his dick is rock-hard whenever he's in the presence of another guy's face, dick, ass or boots? ...Or could it be that we're just jealous of his huge success and beautiful face and body? Whatever the reason, 'Idol in the Sky' proves once again why it is that, despite everything, Ryan Idol remains one of the great gay video superstars of all time. He's more than just hype. He delivers all the hot sweaty sex of our fantasies, and more.

"In this new feature, Idol plays Commander Ace Idol, the bad-ass pilot of an L-39 fighter and chief of a corps of some of the hottest cadets around. Idol works them over well (when they're not too busy working over one another, that is), and we get to share in their training, both in the 'cock' pit and out.

"...Well, if Idol claims to be straight, he gets 18 out of 18 for acting. Although his asshole is still virgin cinema territory, he sucks, rims and fucks with abandon. His dick is so hard every second of this film, veritably twitching whenever his face is near another guy's dick or ass, that you've got to believe he's a homo. If you're lucky enough to be one of his partners, especially Joshua Sterling, you couldn't care less who or what else he's screwing. He knows how to please a man. Acting kudos also to Kyle McKenna, whose year-long perfection of the role of 'submissive military bottom' really shines in this flick.

"(This is) a mixed bag, with some real scorchers and a few duds. The scorchers: A torrid threeway with McKenna, Aaron Austin (as hot and beefy as ever) and Adam Wilde getting it on in the military classroom; Jordan Young's eager devouring of super hot J.T. Sloan. Idol's final assault on dark, hairy, beefy dream boat Joshua Sterling will leave a permanent impression on your remote control's rewind button. A chunky Dino DiMarco is a disappointment as is Idol's endless solo jerk.

"...Idol approaches each of his scenes with abandon, and the combination of his energy, looks and power dick proves him the superstar that he is."

Icon's reviewer said "Idol in the Sky" was a fun, almost campy satire on the masculine conventions of the army. "Obsessively cigar-toting Idol is a narcissistic flight captain shouting at trainees, screwing new recruits, and jerking off for all to see. A few other scenes are inserted here and there to break up the Idol worship... Idol's cocky attitude is total fetish fare here; the most hypermasculine of manners to complement the most hypermasculine professions. The *uberstar* is simultaneously hateable and lovable, which makes for a unique and mind-stretching porn experience. Most notable, however, is the opening credits, complete with a ten-minute rock video of clips from the film, sampled lines from the script, thrusts, push-ups and fighter jet lift offs all in synch to the beat of the song."

When Ryan wasn't making porn he was "Making Porn," the play, on stage in New York, San Francisco, and Chicago.

After attending a presentation of "Making Porn" in New York, Homo Dish in *HX* said, "Ryan plays the role of a porn stud quite convincingly. Shocking, huh? Later, we were invited to a reception in honor of Ryan's big night at the home of director Jerry Douglas, who was proudly displaying all those *Gay Video Guide* awards he won for his new movie, 'Flesh & Blood.' Playwright Ronnie Larsen made a lovely champagne toast to Ryan, and Ryan thanked everyone for being so nice. Blue Blake (Ryan's co-star) chimed in about how great Ryan has been. So much love in one room!" The good times were not to last, however. At one point in the run, Ryan came to blows with Blake.

While appearing in "Making Porn" in San Francisco, Ryan was interviewed by Will Shank for *Bay Area Reporter*: "I found him a complete pussycat. Charming and articulate, he was a pleasure to be with, the only difficulty being the distraction of his perfect looks. Born Marc Anthony Donais 30 years ago in Worcester, Massachusetts, Idol today is maturing into an Alec Baldwin look-alike, with the same great hair, chiseled features, smoky voice, and mesmerizing eyes. He is also an actor on the rise!"

The play is a perfect vehicle for Idol, being the story of a frustrated straight actor who resorts to making gay porn, and it takes full advantage of Idol's marvelous stage presence. We can personally attest that Ryan is a beauty. His exotic appeal is due to his mixed heritage. Says he, "I'm French, Irish, and American-Indian. Mostly French and Irish I grew up in Massachusetts until I was 13. Then I moved in with my mother's sister in New Hampshire for a while. She showed me a different side of life in an *Eight is Enough* kind of family. New Hampshire was conservative, an ideal kind of place, with no crime, no homelessness, no poverty, and it showed me that there is something to live for. In Worcester I grew up on the streets, and it was tough. I've struggled over the years, but now, at 30, I'm in a place I really like."

His sexual ambiguity has made his career what it is, he thinks. "There's a mystery there. Everybody who wants me to be gay thinks I'm gay, and everybody who wants me to be straight thinks I'm straight. I'm not evading the question, but I would prefer to maintain the aura of mystery. I will say sincerely that I'm into the pleasures of the flesh, but I've never liked labels.

"I always wanted to be a movie star. I don't mean to knock the movies, but I think it's so *hard to get* into. It's hard to get into the theater, but I'm hooked on performing live, in front of an audience. You can grab your audience and you can lose your audience – but you can also get them back. That's the challenge."

Speaking of challenges, during his *BAR* interview, Idol revealed that his "last video" was going to be "Idol Gods," which should be released in the spring of 1998. "We've talked about it for many years, and it's finally gonna be a real thing. I'll be writing and co-directing with Jerry Douglas, and I'm handling the budget and casting. It'll be one of the best videos I've ever made, and one of the best in the business.

"The movie takes place in an art museum. The gods are porn guys who were turned to stone because the government wanted to show that they could get control of the Sexual Revolution. So 20 years later it comes back to where it started at the Los Angeles Museum of Modern Art (*sic*). These guys are released from bondage and they come alive, and it's a big sexual expression. When the gods are released from bondage the message is even greater. This is going to be my last piece, and it's going to be a piece of art. I want to go out with a statement, a nice piece of work, an art piece. I'm not going to put an end to the Ryan Idol career, but I have other things I want to pursue." That, we take it, would be a life on the wicked stage, which would be perfect for Ryan. "I definitely want to pursue my theater career. I'd love to play Danny Zuko in *Grease* and Tony in *West Side Story*. *I* foresee doing *Grease* in about a year and *West Side Story* in two years. But it's kind of a dream."

Gene Price in *Bay Times* says, "After extended runs in New York, Chicago and Los Angeles, Caryn Horwitz, producer, and Ronnie Larsen, writer and director, have brought *Making Porn* back to the Cable Car with video superstar Ryan Idol as the would-be actor Jack turned porn Jock. The scene is San Francisco. The time is the early 1980s.

"Jack (Idol) is straight and married to Linda (Joanna

Keylock). Unable to land a legit acting job, Jack auditions for a porno. It is clever and great fun. There's nudity, dildo jokes, cum rehearsal shots with the guys spewing mouthfuls of milk over each other... Characterizations are well-drawn and there's enough substance in Larsen's script to rescue it from the typical drop-the-pants gay comedy. ...Idol was fine as the no-talent actor with the well-equipped body."

By mid-June, Mark Adams in *Video View* said he was anxiously awaiting the final flick for Idol: "Late fall seems to be the latest release date for the upcoming Ryan Idol feature. This will be the Idol's anal debut, so it should be a hot item for whichever studio decides to release the video, which has yet to be made. Reports from La La Land indicate it may be a bisexual feature. I don't know what this means, and I shudder to think who might be strapping on some apparatus just to give it to good ol' Ryan!"

Prospects of seeing that flick began to dim because, during the same period, *HX*'s Homo Dish was reporting that Idol, appearing in "Making Porn" in Chicago, was arrested after allegedly attacking the director: "We hear that Idol came offstage in a rage following the first act and proceeded to pin down Ronnie Larson on a table, hit him in the mouth and throw a garbage pail at him. Concerned cast members (including Dan Renzi from MTV's *The Real World*) called the police, who came and took Idol away in handcuffs. The confused audience watched as the leading man was led through the lobby and driven off in a police car. They seemed to think this was all part of the action since the fictitious porn epic being filmed in the play is titled *Cops!* But reality soon set in when they were told that the rest of the performance was canceled and their money would be refunded. Idol spent the night in jail and is being charged with battery. Ronnie Larsen tells us that he will *not* be dropping the charges and is through with using porn stars in his plays. From now on, he'll only use actors. What a novel idea!"

The show's producer, Caryn Horwitz, told the *Chicago Sun-Times* that Idol "came into town in a bad mood." New York actor David Gordon was flown in to replace Idol, but there is little word on what really caused the fight in the first place. Horwitz suggests jealousy on the part of Idol: "He didn't like it that his co-star (Elizabeth Storey) was getting the laughs."

Billy Masters had this to say: "What is this world coming to? My E-mail box has been flooded with stories from my Chicago friends regarding that great thespian, Ryan Idol, currently appearing in the bus and truck tour of 'Making Porn.' Seems that although he did the first two shows of the run, he suddenly was 'indisposed.' When looking into the situation more carefully, it seems that Ryan just went nuts during the intermission and starting beating up the other actors, including author Ronnie Larsen (who is no skinny-minny, by the way). Audience members who thought this was part of the show (one person quipped 'This is the best acting I've seen all evening!'), were jarred into reality when police arrived to escort the somewhat tarnished Idol off to the pokey (make your own joke). He later posted his own bail and abandoned the rest of the run."

(Another great video idea: "Ryan on the Run!")

And speaking of Larsen, in The *Bay Area Reporter's* resident theater critic Robert Julian's review of the playwright's "Shooting Porn," a documentary film, he said it was "destined to be a festival favorite for gay boys – even those who don't rent porn. Larsen seems to have developed something of an obsession for this topic (and) allows the actors, directors, reviewers and merchandisers of pornography to speak for themselves as his camera follows them from the initial filming in Los Angeles, through the promotion and marketing process, and into hallowed Las Vegas convention halls for an adult video awards ceremony. The featured porn stars are Blue Blake, Bryan Kidd, Adam Rom, Hunter Scott, Rip Stone and Adam Wilde. And yes, there are some hard-core action sequences, but the relentless eye of Bruce McCarthy's camera captures so much of the related production activity that the sexual liaisons are about as erotic as walking the dog.

"There are many wonderful moments in the film but my favorite is the detailed demonstration of an actor's fleet enema before his close-up. None of the insights here penetrates much father than nine inches, but this isn't rocket science. And one of the brilliant qualities of the film is that it never delves too deep because, essentially there is no *there* there.

"But it is porn director Gino Colbert who takes the prize for gratuitous one-liners when he remarks, with pride, 'I'm known for my toilet movies.'"

Elloitt Stein in the *Village Voice* said the movie "offers such a rosy view of the business, however, that it almost seems as much a fiction as the director's feel-good stage piece."

"Playwright/filmmaker Larsen is on a personal mission to turn hard core pornography into mainstream entertainment," David Cohen says in *Reel Thing*. "While his off-Broadway hit 'Making Porn' still inspires hard-ons downtown, his new project, 'Shooting Porn' – a hilarious and fascinating documentary about the gay porn film industry – should create many new converts to his cause. Larsen's noble intention is nothing less than the legitimization of this niche industry into a respectable profession. In 'Shooting Porn,' the director uses his considerable contacts to create a film that enlightens as it entertains. Larsen and his crew are given intimate access to the sets of two well-known porn directors, Chi Chi LaRue and Gino Colbert. The intelligence of these men and the musings of their cohorts, as *well* as the marked differences in their directorial styles, give 'Shooting Porn' much of its remarkable depth. LaRue, a sometime drag queen who resembles Divine's much younger, sexier sister, is a star on the contemporary flesh-for-film and emotional involvement in her work are contrasted with that of the more staid Colbert. Also a porn legend, he is detailed, direct, professional and devoid of the hysteria often surrounding a bunch of naked male actors. LaRue and Colbert, who are observed directing models in intimate coital clutches, are bewitching in remarkably candid interviews.

"Let's get one thing straight – 'Shooting Porn' is as graphic as its subject and as nasty as it needs to be. The film answers questions you didn't know you had: Actor Hunter Scott illustrates the do's and don'ts of douching. Adam Rom shares tips about getting and staying hard under hot lights; and Bryan Kidd breathlessly describes his first on-screen appearance. You'll laugh, you'll cry, you might even cum.

"You also might never watch porn the same way again after seeing Blue Blake get repeatedly slammed by a bullish boner. Screaming from pain, but biting the bullet, he is seen getting ready for his close up like the pro he is. Along the way we learn what a Hitler mustache is and the sordid truth behind stunt dicks. You will be enthralled."

Sonny Markham

One of the porn stars taking over the Rex Chandler/Ryan Idol role in "Making Porn" was Sonny Markham. Jeffrey Solomon in *LGNY* says, "This play is a very funny farce about the gay, male porn industry. Sonny Markham plays the straight actor who can't land a 'legit' gig. English porn star Blue Blake does a very funny and bitchy turn as an old porn pro. The play is full of yucks in the first act, but does an about face for act two and tries to become an AIDS drama. Come on, guys. You brought us into the theater with the promise of beefcake and laughs, so don't try to get deep."

"When Sonny Markham decided to come out, he did so in a big way," Mickey Skee reported. "The 24-year-old buffed, rippling muscled go-go dancer on the Chicago nightclub circuit was engaged to be married to a girl. He knew that men liked to watch his bubble butt wiggle, but he never understood that. He also had plenty of gay friends, but never really was attracted to them – well, not back then anyway. Suddenly, while dancing nude at one of the country's longest-running gay bathhouses, Man's Country in Chicago, Markham took the dive and gave gay sex a try. He came up wanting more. Club owner Chuck Renslow immediately contacted his friend, John Travis of Studio 2000, and told him about Markham's sudden turnaround, and how he might now do porn movies. Travis knew about Markham and had wanted him nude in front of a camera lens for years, but Markham always resisted, claiming he was heterosexual."

Travis not only put Markham in his first porn video, his cohort in porn, Scott Masters, wrote a script of Markham's true-life coming out story – sexual encounters and all – and decided to film it at the actual bathhouse where Markham's 'conversion' occurred. The video, "In Man's Country," became one of the hottest renting videos of the year, and Markham went on to do several for Travis.

Markham says he's proud of doing porn: "I just enjoy sex. I love sex," he says. "And the adult business taught me how to have the safest sex because they always use condoms." He smiles. "I like when people appreciate my body. And that's kind of the ultimate thing, for someone to see you having sex."

Skee noted that Markham always took care of his body, which is why he danced for the Meatpacker's dance troupe. He danced for women, but he also danced at clubs where the tips and money were better. He often rebuffed the advances of the men at the clubs. "I never tried to be rude because, in a way, I was always curious," says Markham, who has a particular penchant for drag queens of all shapes and sizes. "A year ago I started looking at pictures in men's magazines, *URGE* and *Manshots*, and wanted to be in the magazines with those handsome guys. Now I am and it's kind of strange for me."

Markham adds, "It may be a strange way to come out, but there's all kinds of coming out stories."

Johnny Hanson

Before appearing in "Making Porn," Hanson had appeared totally nude on stage only twice. "I was very, very nervous and scared – swore I would never do it again. But in the play ('Making Porn') it's different, though....I mean, I try to stay in character."

Hanson told *Manshots*, "I think everyone's an exhibitionist in one way or another. Anyone who puts himself onstage is an exhibitionist, whether they're going nude or not. Anybody who has to open up to an audience is an exhibitionist."

He signed with Falcon and on the set of his first video he said, "Listen, I know I'm a good fuck." (Laughs) "And they didn't believe me. I really don't think they believed me. John Rutherford didn't believe me. I remember doing my first fuck scene with Chad Knight (in 'Aspen 3'), and I remember them just dying. They were like, 'Oh, my God. When you said you were a good fuck, you weren't lying!'"

Hanson did not suck Chad's cock, nor did he get fucked. He says that he has experienced these things and didn't like it. Chad was very patient and very sweet: "He was a nice guy, yeah."

In "Download," Hanson worked with another legendary bottom, Danny Sommers. "He's adorable. He's sweet, very sweet, very nice. He's great! Very cooperative, very flexible. You can do anything to him – roll him on his head, fuck him on his head, fuck him on his back, slam him against the wall. Adam Wilde is a good bottom. But J.T. Sloan is my favorite to this point. He was the best. Actually, I asked for him. Yeah. he's hot! Has a great little hole. J.T. was definitely my favorite."

Hanson commented about his record: "I wanted to do something really sexual. I wanted to do a rap. I was on the road dancing, and I got tired of just perforrning to everyone else's music. I wanted to do something more creative. I wanted to bring it to a different level. I have a girl doing back-up chorus singing, and I went on the road with my demo, and I wind up getting a record company to pick it up. Actually, it started off just in a deejay shop, 'cause they wanted to see how it goes just in a deejay shop, so they only put it on vinyl – twelve-inch vinyl. I don't consider myself a singer. No, I don't. I can hold a note, and I have a great vibrato, but... I studied it for a little while with a coach. I'm a baritone voice, but I don't really consider myself a singer." Those listening to the record might well agree with him. A fan says that he was playing the record when a friend showed up. The fan left the room briefly and when he returned, the guest had turned it off.

Hanson says, "I'm proudest of the record. Probably the record, because I wrote it, it was all my idea, did it all on my own – something that I created and achieved to a degree. I mean, I would have liked for it to have gone further, but it's a very sleazy, sexual kind of record, and it could never get air play because of the words. (Laughter) But I put the whole thing together. And I shopped it around, I got a label to pick it up, and then when it got written up in *Billboard* - that was the best reward to me. It was like winning an Olympic medal or something."

Sonny Markham,
courtesy Studio 2000

Ryan Idol, tormented star of "Making Porn"

Johnny Hanson says he's most proud of his dance record

*David Duchovny,
voted the "Sexiest TV Actor" by Gay Times' readers*

SEX IN TELEVISION

The London-based *Gay Times* Readers' Poll for 1996 found "X-Files" star David Duchovny the favorite sexiest TV actor (non-UK). One London fan wrote that David is equally potent on film, as in "Kalifornia," with Brad Pitt. The magazine's readers wanted to be more than just friends with the entire male cast of "Friends," with Matt Le Blanc (Joey) first, followed by cute, monkey man David Schwimmer (Ross), and then wise-cracking, wise guy Matthew Perry (Chandler). In third place here was Batman/"ER"-star George Clooney, and fifth was Dean (they don't call me Superman for nothing) Cain.

Sexy or not, what fascinates us about TV stars is that there seem to be more of them who are out, about to come out, or only partially closeted than even in the music industry. The leading authority on this subject is Billy Masters of *Filth*, once he got over his moral dilemma on outing people. For instance, Billy reported: "...A.J. on 'General Hospital' will now be played by one of the most beautiful men alive, Blly Warlock, late of 'Baywatch', 'Capitol', 'Days of our Lives' and Marcy Walker. That is, of course, before he turned his interest to men. Once again, another story."

Another story was John Wesley Shipp, whom Masters called "the incredibly humpy actor" who "most definitely deserves a permanent section in *Filth*. You may remember him from when 'Guiding Light' had a 'The' in its title and John played the very hunky Kelly Nelson (did he always have on that black Speedo?), or, more recently, his own series 'The Flash' which was a flop, and his very attractive body on display in an episode of 'NYPD Blue' (including bare buttocks in the men's locker room). For years I waited for someone to tell me he was gay and, then some Atlanta fans told me of a Shipp-spotting at Atlanta's very own Armory on New Year's Eve where he was accompanied by four other equally humpy guys. I would just write this off as wishful thinking, until a New York waiter in L.A. (don't ask) told me he used to work with one of John's exes. Like me, he was skeptical - until John came by to say hi and proceeded to hit on my informant. My source gave John his phone number, but is still waiting for Johnny to come marching home.

"Well, now word comes that this is the man known as 'the guy half of West Hollywood has slept with' (the other half, I'm sorry to say, had to settle for Chad Allen). You may have heard that John was dating the heir to the Fiat fortune (they made a fortune with those lousy cars?, the 31-year-old Giovanni Alberto Agnelli. Old news. He's now dating actor Sam Jones. Someone out there may say 'Who is Sam Jones? That name sounds SO familiar.' Think back to your youth and you'll remember the very buff Mr. Jones as 'Flash Gordon' (ironic that he's now dating someone who played 'The Flash,' eh? He was also in '10', and posed nude for *Playgirl*, but you knew that. You may ask what the 43-year-old Mr. Jones has been doing lately. Well, aside from some acting in films not even I have heard of and still looking good, he's also done other work on film sets, like 'still photography' and 'set decoration.' How cute!

"Anyway, John and Sam have been showing up everywhere together: at a screening of 'Love! Valour! Compassion!', cuddling at a private party in the Hollywood Hills, even shopping for underwear on Rodeo Drive. That smells like commitment to me. However, Sam better be ready to move east since, rumor has it, John is going to replace Sam Harris in Broadway's 'The Life.'"

And speaking of "Love! Valour! Compassion!", *Entertainment Weekly* must get the award for most unexpected outing of the season by running a quote from Jason Alexander, who was promoting the film version of 'Love! Valor! Compassion!" Jason says, "I'm the only straight actor that I know of who has played this role!" As Masters put it, "Well, I guess Nathan Lane's closet is wide open now, regardless of how hard he has tried to keep it shut!"

John Price in *4Front* said, "Broadway legend and Robin William's' co-star in 'The Birdcage' Nathan Lane was at the Motherlode. At first he was enjoying his anonymity as most of the pool hall-minded bar patrons aren't really up on their Broadway credits. He was just another pudgy guy with a mustache having a drink until he was spotted by entertainment lawyer John Tobin and then the cat was out of the bag. Local actors and theater buffs Johnny Nicoloro and Jon Philip Alman cornered him against the bar seeking autographs and star-dust. After having just done the interview with his Broadway co-star

Randy Becker, I thought it would be fun to tease Lane and tell him that I thought his performance in the film 'Love! Valour! Compassion!' may be his best work to date. (The joke, of course, being that Lane created the role on Broadway, but the part was played by Jason Alexander in the film.) Nathan didn't laugh. He wasn't amused, and I thought it was appropriate that I didn't talk to him anymore after that. As soon as I walked away, 'Passion of Carmen' super dancer Marco de la Cruz – sporting a beautiful diamond and sapphire ring given to him by one of his fans – moved in on Lane and bent his ear for awhile about mutual friends and dancers. By the time Lane left the 'Lode 14 musical theater queens were belting out hits from 'Forum' and he was literally running across Santa Monica Boulevard in terror. Just remember, stardom can have its drawbacks!"

"My California sources have been working overtime on one of our favorite 'friends' - Matt LeBlanc," Billy Masters noted in *Filth*."I'm sure you know that Matty brought his 'best friend' (who is a very cute male, incidentally) to the Emmy's as his 'date.' This past year he bought a house which he is renovating with said friend. Doesn't mean a thing, right? Then how do we explain the recent sighting in Hillcrest, California where Matt and his special 'friend' were recently shopping at Ace Hardware and the managers were nice enough to close the store for their exclusive use. My question – what did they have to hide? It's not like someone was going to whip out that *Spartacus Gay Guide* from a few years ago which features a familiar cover-model – Matt!"

Masters was first to break the news of Simon Rex's "starring" role as a masturbator in gay porn. *OUT* followed up, saying: "Gay porn's leading graduate to date may be Simon Rex, 21, until recently one of MTV's best known VJs and host of MTV's *Most Wanted*. His story illustrates how the right choices can make all the difference, and points up the thin lines between porn as scandal, as news, or merely as colorful biographical detail. At age 19, Rex, under the *nom de porn* Sebastian, masturbated in three solo videos aimed at the gay market. When the tapes came to light in April 1996, *Newsweek*, *New York* magazine, *The Village Voice*, and television's *Hard Copy* all did pieces on MTV's handsome court jester and his porn past. The Internet carried his semi-nude photos. Not since Brad Pitt's bare balcony promenade had there been such a flurry of downloading.

"Rex has never attempted to deny or repudiate his past – he simply declines to talk about it. And while gay-baiting visitors to the chat room in MTV's Website occasionally flame over Rex's Xrated videos, they are usually told to get lost by others in the room. In the words of one online female fan, 'Who cares? He's gorgeous!'"

"Young people's attitudes are different," explains Jon Murray, the gay cocreator and producer of two of MTV's most successful programs, *The Real World* and *Road Rules*. "Besides, my guess as a producer is that it's the people putting up the money who have more misgivings than those watching." In fact, there are those who believe that MTV, with its carefully cultivated image as the rebel network, didn't mind the notoriety. Although the channel took Rex off the air at the end of March, it was for reasons of programming, not punishment; caught in MTV's overhaul of its entire schedule, Rex left with a sweet development deal.

"It's important to note the fact that Rex's videos were solo affairs with no man-to-man contact, allowing him to escape with his hetero credentials and bad-boy persona intact. Contrast Rex's experience with that of Jeff Griggs, once an actor on NBC's *Days of Our Lives*. In March 1996, six months after Griggs came on as Jude St. Clair, the tabloid press made the connection between Griggs and Tony Sinatra, the name under which Griggs appeared in hardcore gay videos such as 'Hole in One' and 'Secret Boys Club.' Griggs' contract expired when his character was killed off (as NBC notes had always been planned), and he left the soap – without significant success thereafter. The message was clear: Real man-to-man pornography is still a little too much for middle America to swallow."

George Clooney & Noah Wyle

"That's why Superman works alone!"
– George Clooney as Batman

In "Batman and Robin," as a mad scientist intent on breeding plants capable of taking over the world, Uma Thurman has all the best lines. "There's something about an anatomically correct rubber suit," she coos huskily upon spotting Batman (George Clooney) in his hunky duds, "that puts fire in a girl's lips."

The other villain, Mr. Freeze (Arnold Schwarzenegger, bald and resembling a giant tube of glitter in his silver-blue body paint), *People* magazine joked, "has come to the wrong movie. But then, you already knew that. What you possibly didn't know is how easily Clooney slips into Batman's glossy rubber boots. There's nothing showy about his performance, but he exudes a comfort level with the role markedly higher than that of predecessors Michael Keaton and Val Kilmer."

"When did straight people become such drag queens?" The Reel Thing asked in *HX*. "'Batman & Robin' is the most expensively produced dragfest I've ever seen. That makeup. Those eyes. And not to mention all the gender enhanced costumes. Is this supposed to be Gotham City or a Susanne Bartsch party?

"From the beginning, it's evident that this is a different kind of bat flick. The opening credits have plenty of self-mocking shots of bat butts and bat bulges. And for the most part, tongues remain firmly planted in cheeks throughout. ...As for the caped crusaders, George Clooney has a waggish charm that jibes with the film's tone. Unfortunately, that playfulness is often compromised by a noble but superficial subplot about how families are more about love than biology. Neither the stylish Clooney nor threadbare script satisfy on that front. Chris O'Donnell, on the other hand, doesn't even have style to coast on. The only thing not flat about this clueless frat boy is his butt."

Billy Masters in *Filth* said, "In 'Batman and Robin,' Chris does appear shirtless once, and George looks much better in his suit than out of it, and that's all you'll get out of me."

"George Clooney *is* a movie star, the real goods," agreed Lisa Schwarzbaum in *Entertainment Weekly*. "In 'Batman and Robin' he slips on the old rubber ears as comfortably as he suits up in surgical scrubs on TV each week on *ER*. In Clooney's first scene with Chris O'Donnell – himself fully installed, at this point, as the perkiest of frat-brother sidekicks – Robin, enviously eyeing his mentor's Batmobile, whines that he wants wheels too. 'That's why Superman works alone,' mutters Batman as he zooms away, solo. Clooney delivers this bit of commentary with such gracious oomph that we relax immediately, instinctively recognizing that unlike Michael Keaton's Batman (a brooder) or Val Kilmer's Batman (a scowler), this superhero is accessible, urbane, TV-friendly. He's Batman, the Guy!

"...The double trouble of the icy and the hot, the frigid and the sexual, has an elegant symmetry to it. But each character is such a one-dimensional idea – and each actor is such a dramatic clunker – that they slow down the works every time they appear. Schwarzenegger, in particular (billed above Clooney, stepping into a fancy Bubble Boy suit and intoning 'quote me' punchlines like 'The Iceman cometh!') is a monolithically heavy presence. Thurman ain't heavy, but neither is she the chlorophyll-filled femme fatale she aspires to be. Separately or together, the two are distractions rather than attractions. And that spells trouble in Gotham City.

"It's in our interest in the mature suaveness of Batman, the blooming hunkiness of Robin, and the nymphy possibilities of Batgirl that the franchise has a heartbeat. It's an odd day in Tinseltown when Schwarzenegger in sci-fi makeup is less exciting than a TV actor who does battle in his tights. But, as they say in the comics, that's charisma, baby."

"...For those of you who haven't followed this burgeoning romance, George Clooney and Noah Wyle have been virtually inseparable since 'ER' began," Billy Masters reported in *Filth*. "When it was Emmy time, rather than bring dates, they went together. This led Joan Rivers to quip that for their first official date, they were the most attractive couple at the Emmys. Noah and George made light of the rumors, all the while fueling them with sharp denials of any female dating partners in their present or future. Still they could just be best friends – right? Well, I have a best friend, and he never bought me a car. Yes, George bought Noah a car."

Later, Masters reported, "You know how much I like to talk about the George Clooney/Noah Wyle romance gossip. Noah certainly doesn't do much to stifle the rumors..."

Well, he did, finally , react. In the tacky tabloid *The Globe*, it was reported that "ER Heartthrob's Fury Over Gay Smear - Noah Wyle Blasts Rumormonger." Masters says, "Need I tell you who the 'rumormonger' is? If you didn't know, one paragraph into the article they name the 'catty columnist' as Billy Masters. There are now three things I know for sure - 1) *The Globe* never asked my permission, 2) *The Globe* never paid me, 3) Noah's NEVER gonna put out for me now!

"(But) here's a story you WON'T read in *The Globe*. I'm told that when Noah was performing the play 'The 24th Day' in Los Angeles with Peter Berg (where Noah played one of Peter's former tricks, but that's yet another story), one person called the theatre constantly trying to get Noah to 'hang out' with him. Noah knew this guy by reputation and didn't want to be another notch on the belt buckle of Kevin Spacey!"

Then came this item from *Filth*: "Whispers from the set of 'ER' report that on his recent down time Noah Wyle traveled to Israel with a close male friend and the network publicist. Nothing worth whispering about - 'cept that the publicist has been blabbing that Noah and his friend are *so* close – OK, everyone say it together - 'How close are they?' – so close that they didn't bother to get two beds when they shared a hotel room!"

Being in the public eye *is* difficult, especially with someone like Masters in lust with you! Wyle says, "You have to take a much more proactive stance in grabbing your life back. But once you put the ball in motion in saying, 'This is who I am; I've got a life that I don't want everyone to know about,' everyone sort of respects that."

The actor says he has his fun "where I can find it, but I know I'm not in the high life, because I know what I *think* that is, and I know I'm not part of that. There's certain things that go on and certain parties that happen, and I'm not invited to them."

At the Chase Lounge for an *ER* cast party, he behaved just as a young Hollywood star is supposed to: "I was so drunk.... I forced John Wells, our executive producer, to tango with me, and when the band went on a break, our first A.D. Babu and I jumped on their instruments and just started wailing – he was playing the saxophone and I was playing the drums."

"He's hardly the skunk at any tea party," says Dale Brasel in *Detour*.

"In person," *US* magazine said, "Wyle is an unusual combination of both Hollywood kid and Midwestern farm boy just off the bus. He's genuinely stunned by his sudden success, yet downright shrewd in the way he's handling it." While many of the *ER* residents spent their hiatuses reaping the benefits of being No. 1, Wyle worked on an indie film called "The Myth of Fingerprints."

"I want to be really savvy about the way I construct what I do coming off of this show," says Wyle. "Behind every decision I make is the concern of wanting to do this for the rest of my life. I'm drawn to the smaller, human stories where you can really track emotional lines between families and friends, or fathers, sons and brothers. Sometimes the little misunderstandings can cause the most hurt."

Noah has acquired a potentially indelible nice-guy image. And because he's young (he can still get carded when he buys cigarettes), most of his fans seem to be teenage girls. "I'm sweet, wholesome, dependable, and apparently not like any guy in their high school," Noah says with a shrug. As Noah's mom cruelly puts it, "George gets racy pictures; Noah gets 'Here's me and my hamster.' "

"Me-and-my-hamster is fine for TV," Larissa MacFarquhar said in *Details*. "Useful, even. Someone you let into your living room once a week should be appealing in a comfy, low-key sort of way. Mean, dangerous hormone gods are for the movies."

"I wouldn't pay money to see me as an action hero," Noah says. "I'm not a leaping-tall-buildings, swinging-from-ropes, shoot-'em-up kind of guy. I wouldn't pay to see me kicking anybody's ass." Still, he was quoted as saying, "I want to be extremely focused. And I want to get in shape. I've been skinny and built like Abe Lincoln all my life." Can an action hero really be far behind?

"Noah doesn't want to stay in TV forever (he is, after all, a Serious Actor)," MacFarquhar says. "It's a weird feeling to be *in*. It's nice, but it's all relative. You can't put too much stock into it, and you can't belittle it – you can just maintain it. Sometimes you can feel like you're conning your way through the whole time."

How in Wyle is was demonstrated when he was named to *Entertainment Weekly's* 100 Most Creative People List. The magazine's editors reported that when Noah's on the set, his goofiness puts castmates at ease. "He made fun of the film's deep emotion," says the director of Wyle's film "The Myth of Fingerprints," "so people didn't feel like they had to tiptoe around."

The creative one's parents were divorced and he was sent to boarding school. "Except for all the acting he did, Noah seems to have had all the usual symptoms of a boarding school coming-of-age," MacFarquhar says. "He tooled around in a long black overcoat. He read William Burroughs, Jack Kerouac, and Allen Ginsberg. On the baseball field his coach says he was known as 'the Quaalude Kid' for being slow. He was awkward with girls."

Wyle was hardly known as a cocksman; he does recall that he was pretty good at putting his notebook over his lap – hiding his teenage erections from the world. "Of course, I do have vague memories of that moment of panic – of having one and realizing that the class is about to end and I have to walk across campus. You start trying to shuffle your feet really furiously so the blood will flow to other parts of your body." He had his first sex when he was 13, when he was on vacation with his family. The girl was 18. "It was terrifying. Completely unromantic. It was at a party. I think she was drunk and thought I was somebody else. But of course I fell madly in love with her. And then she went home. That was one of the reasons I was so awkward in high school: I'd done something that not many other guys in my class had done, even though they all said they had. And it had been so terrible for me that I didn't see the point in doing it again. But I did. And now I enjoy it." Now Noah's seeing a makeup artist named Tracy Warbin, who's three years older. They met on the set of "The Myth of

Fingerprints."

"Noah is a good stage actor," MacFarquhar says. "In front of the camera, though, his seriousness tends to manifest itself in a series of irritating, actorish tics that make him seem bland and uptight. He's always pursing his lips and flaring his nostrils like he's trying to be John Gielgud. These tics bleach out a lot of what's charming and sexy about Noah in real life – qualities that were apparently obvious to his high-school drama teacher, Tim Regan. When I ask Regan what Noah would be if he were a piece of clothing, he says, without hesitation, 'a leopardskin Speedo bathing suit.'

"Noah gets a little freaked out when he thinks about his *ER* contract. He's signed on for five years, and after three, he is only just beginning to figure out what it means to be a TV star. It means being famous and being recognized everywhere he goes, but it also means that he could be known as John Carter, the medical student who cares too much, for the rest of his life."

For his part, Wyle says that, "If all else fails, I can always jet on over to Lithuania, where they love me. Did I tell you I'm a household name in the Baltics?"

No, but we don't doubt it – not a bit!

*George Clooney and Noah Wyle
joke around at a movie premiere
(at least, we think they were just joking!)*

The stunning David Charvet, photographed by the incomparable David LaChapelle

David Charvet

*"In school, I wasn't even close to being cool. I never fit in.
I didn't party. I wasn't a hang-out kind of guy –
I was definitely a loner."*
– David Charvet

"I am majorly psyched by David Charvet," a fan in Oklahoma wrote y/m magazine after they ran a cover story on the TV star. "The boy is way beyond babeness! What a gorgeous, talented, sentimental guy. I love his shows 'cause that sexy voice of his helps me clear my mind of any worries. If I ever meet him, I'll faint at his feet." Well, so would we, sweetie! This boy is the yummiest of the yummy on TV! What makes him so fanastic is the knowledge that, as he says,
"Craig's a lot meaner than I am." Yes, the 25-year-old actor who's played the trouble-making throb on *Melrose Place* for a season after leaving *Baywatch* in 1992, says his character is "out for money and power, which is very different from how I am. He'll do whatever it takes, even if it means getting rid of whoever's in his way. But I think it's important to be a gentleman. I don't want to hurt anyone."

Billy Masters in *Filth* doesn't want to hurt anyone either, but he couldn't let David pass to *Melrose* without notice:"D a v i d Charvet, better known for his Speedos on 'Baywatch' than his acting ability, is determined to make it as a legit actor. After quitting 'Baywatch' his first step was to do a made-for-TV movie with Susan Lucci. Yeah, that was a smart choice. Then, in his pursuit of an acting challenge, he's joined the cast of 'Melrose Place,' saying in a TV interview that it was 'real acting.' 'Melrose Place?' I think someone's been in the sun too long. My spies also tell me he had a 'no swimsuit' clause put in his 'Melrose' contract. Don't worry, Davey, they'll just shoot you skinny dipping!" Sadly, we are still waiting for *that* episode!

Later, Masters noted, "A pal of mine was recently at the home of *Melrose Place* hunk David Charvet. Davey gave my pal the grand tour and made a point of saying that he decorated the entire thing himself. This guest, who's no slouch when it comes to *object d'arts*, says that Charvet's was perhaps the most impeccabiy furnished house he's ever been in, and with nary a female in sight. Tastefully elegant in a way that only a gay man could appreciate. Draw your own conclusions."

Later, Masters was at it again! "...Charvet was recently spotted at two different private parties in the Hollywood Hills - engaged in a close encounter of the male-to-male kind. One was simply a lot of making out, but the other has him and said young man retreating to the privacy of the bedroom, only to emerge an hour later somewhat rumpled, but happy. What did they do in there? My source did sneak a peak (you know he HAD to) and, let's just say, they weren't playing Paarcheesi!"

One thing for sure, hazel-eyed Charvet *is* a sensitive boy, especially when it comes to love. He told *y/m*'s Chuck Arnold, "Sometimes guys are so worried about being macho, about being real men, that they don't know how to be with a girl," he says in his soft-spoken voice. "My mother always taught me to treat women nicely. She raised me to be more understanding and more caring toward them.

"I've always had serious relationships. I need intimacy in my life - it's very important," he says. "One-night stands aren't really happening for me." The search for a honey in Hollywood can be pretty brutal, he says. "I went through a period of about two-and-a-half years where I didn't have a girlfriend. I dated and stuff, but it's just so difficult to tell if a girl is into who you are or what you do. It's tough to trust people. I take my time, because I'm looking for somebody who's really down-to-earth.

"I really don't know how to approach girls. I don't have any pick-up lines." And don't expect him to hook up with any actresses - period. "I stay away from them now," says David, whose former flame is his ex-costar Pamela Lee. "I need someone in my life who's nurturing and giving and caring. And it's really hard to get those qualities from an actress, because she's got her own agenda and her own career to worry about. It can make the relationship competitive, and I don't want to deal with that."

"I had a great relationship with Pamela," he says. "I wish her the best. And I'm her friend if she ever needs one."

Things used to be very different between David and Pamela - she even once called him "the love of my life." But the two haven't spoken in more than a year, and David admits that her marriage to wild rocker Tommy Lee in 1995 had something to do with the communication meltdown.

But Charvet had nothing to say to the press about his ex-flame. Even if he had any dirt to dish on Pamela and Tommy, he wouldn't go there. He absolutely hates gossip. After all, he's been the subject of a few (untrue) romance rumors before, mostly when he was on *Baywatch* stud patrol. "People think that I went out with Nicole Eggert and Yasmine Bleeth and all that, but it's not true," he reveals. "Pamela Lee is the only *Baywatch* girl I was ever involved with."

Of his new castmates on *Melrose*, he says he's closest to Andrew Shue and especially tight with Heather Locklear, with whom he's been steaming up the screen lately. He isn't turned on by love scenes. "It's not very comfortable when you think your mom or girlfriend will be watching them. Plus, you've got 65 people looking at you on the set. And they're like, 'Uh, could you just move your nose a little? You're blocking our light.'"

Without any love in his life right now, the actor spends his free time playing his guitar, working out (weight lifting and playing basketball and volleyball), and chilling at his chalet-style house in Beverly Hills with his yellow Lab, Taylor Ann. He's also close with his family – his mom and stepdad, dad and stepmom, plus five sisters and one brother (he's the oldest). "I spend more time with my family than I do with anyone else," David says. "We all have dinner together on Friday nights. And we usually hang out on the weekends." Chances are, Charvet does the cooking: "I can cook practically everything. I make a great rack of lamb. And I love cooking pasta." I'll bring the wine, Davey!

Things weren't always so *Brady Bunch*-perfect in the family, though. David's dad, Sasson Jeans founder Paul Guez (David took his mom's maiden name), had a major drug problem from the time David was 8 until he was 16. When he finally hit rock-bottom, it was David who took him to detox. His dad's been clean ever since. "We have a great relationship now. He's my best friend," David says.

Still, his father's drug abuse hit him hard. Having to take care of his dad forced David to grow up more quickly, and it made him face the ugly truth about drugs and alcohol at an early age.

He was totally unpopular in high school. "I wasn't even close to being cool. I never fit in. I didn't party. I wasn't a hang-out kind of guy – I was definitely a loner." Charvet says he was never even tempted to do drugs or drink in high school, and to this day, he stays completely clean. "I'm not going to let booze and drugs affect me. I've seen so many people destroy themselves that way.

"I've had bad dreams about being 60 years old, sitting in a rocking chair and having all this fame and fortune and looking around and seeing nobody else there. That to me is the biggest nightmare of them all. I'm happy with my career and everything else that's going on in my life now. But if the right girl came along and wanted to share it with me, that would be really awesome."

What's pretty awesome is the Charvet since *Baywatch*. He's still buff, but now natural: He has hair on his chest – he used to have to shave it all off for *Baywatch*. And he's lost about 12 pounds since leaving the show. "I was working out to look big; now it's about working out to feel good and be healthy." And yummy!

Early Chad Allen publicity photo

Chad Allen

"I'm not saying be a slut, but let yourself be free."
— *Chad Allen*

"Jane Seymour's TV son has been caught snogging another man," *Gay Times* in London reported. "A picture in the *Daily Mirror* showed Chad Allen 'smooching in a swimming pool with a man.' A startled on-looker at a 'lavish Hollywood party' said: 'Chad suddenly put his arm around Jason and kissed him... (they) could not stop kissing and touching.' Chad will not be surprised he has been dumped by his girlfriend."

Chad Allen's outing on both sides of the Atlantic (*The Globe* broke the story first here in America) occurred shortly after *Playgirl* ran an interview with the actor. Examined in the light of subsequent events, the magazine's article becomes a model for how to obscure the truth to the media.

"Chad Allen looks tired and hungry this early afternoon," *Playgirl* magazine's Jenny Higgons reported. "His gorgeous blue-green eyes seem a bit weary, his slicked-back blond hair hasn't received a whole lot of attention and he's wearing an earring. On top of that, he's battling a cold and stuffy nose. This definitely does not look like 'Dr. Quinn, Medicine Woman's' Matthew Cooper, the 18-year-old frontiersman of 1870s Colorado Springs. But then again, Matthew has never indulged in Manhattan's frenetic nightlife and faced a busy, tightly scheduled publicity trip in the '90s. Also unlike Matthew, Chad, 21, is on his own in the big city, without the watchful eyes of adoptive parents Sully and Dr. Mike (Joe Lando and Jane Seymour) - although his publicist (who was also up much of the previous night) is hovering nearby. Invited to dig in to the lunch set in front of him and not worry about talking with his mouth full, he enthusiastically goes for it.

"'Going for it' is something Chad's done his whole life. An actor since he was little, Dr. Quinn is Chad's fourth series."

After discussing his character's love life over the four years the series has been on the air, *Playgirl* went on to state that "Chad's love life is also pretty free and clear, which suits him just fine. After all, what single Hollywood actor in his right mind wouldn't relish his romantic independence? He had a relationship for a while and doesn't want another one anytime soon, he says so emphatically that you just know he means it. 'When you're young, it's important to go places and try everything. Then, when something comes along, try it out. Learn. Meet different people. Have a good time. Being involved in a relationship inhibits all that. I'm not saying to be a slut, but let yourself be free.' So just how loose has Chad been? Well, there was that stage of, let's say, randiness, way back when....'I was all over the map.'"

The magazine went on to relate how Chad avoids the trendy clubs and goes to "unpretentious, lowkey" places in Hollywood to pick up his conquests. But most of his liaisons have come to him through the matchmaking efforts of his twin sister, who, despite her good intentions, hasn't exactly hooked him up with the woman of his dreams. Chad is quoted as saying, "Finally I told her not to set me up anymore. You'd think that somebody you know so well will probably have a good semblance of what you might like, and, no, it couldn't have been more off." You can say that again!

Chad was surprisingly forthcoming in the interview when he said he had been tested for HIV, twice, calling it "a frightening experience. Not everyone has been so lucky. I know guys my age who are HIV-positive. First you hear about people you don't know getting it, and then friends of friends, and then all of sudden it *is friends*." *Playgirl* went so far as to ask him how many "sexual encounters" he'd had: "Over 10, fewer than 1,500."

"When teen heartthrob Chad Allen showed up kissing another man in the *Globe*, his future as an actor came sharply into focus," *The Advocate's* Alan Frutkin said. "Although several prime-time performers have come out of the closet in recent years, no actor on a 'family values' show has ever revealed his or her homosexuality. And the prospects for such an actor seem far less secure than for those who appear on programs geared primarily for adults."

"The middle-American audience that Hollywood needs to attract is increasingly repulsed by these actors," says Robert Peters, president of Morality in Media, a New York City-based conservative watchdog organization. "But a family-oriented program like *Dr. Quinn* would suffer more from publicity that a principal actor is gay than would a program like *NYPD Blue*. If an actor flaunts or publicizes an off-screen lifestyle that is totally contradictory to his on-screen persona, that could detract from the believability of his on-screen character and completely turn off some viewers."

"Morals clauses are common in Hollywood," says entertainment attorney Pierce O'Donnell. "For example, Disney has a standard clause in its movie and television production contracts that says they can cancel a project if their view is that the material is contrary to Disney's standards or values. It's very vague and amorphous, so if a studio were going to move against somebody, they might purport to proceed under that morals clause."

A reader of the *Advocate* in Ohio wrote, "The editors at the *Globe* have proved once again that they have zero respect for their fellow man by outing Chad Allen. The tabloid press was wrong when they outed Chastity Bono, and they're wrong again to have done it to Allen. To be out to your friends is one thing, but to be outed against your will is another. It's a sad state of affairs when an unwanted outside source controls what the world knows about you."

Gay media, such as John Price in *4Front*, came to Allen's defense: "The fact is, there are tabloids and gay rags that will take away any privacy that people may think they deserve, without any regard for decency or respect. ...Some sneaky snake working for the *Globe* managed to snap a photo of Chad in a hot tub with another guy. A cute picture actually, and perfectly innocent by our standards. *Edge* was very critical of Chad, using the headline 'Closeted Celebrities: Won't They Ever Learn?' We'd like to know when the people at *Edge* and all the other invasive rags are going to learn that celebrities are not public property. They are human beings. You would think a gay publication would be at least slightly sympathetic to the 'coming out' problems of a young man. Supposedly it is the one thing we all have in common. Did it ever dawn on anyone that Chad has a family, too? Maybe he has personal issues he's dealing with in the best way he knows how. Chad Allen is a wonderful and decent person, regardless of sexual orientation. This is a young man who did volunteer work for Aid For AIDS years ago when people around him told him it was dangerous. This is a young man who has given of himself and his celebrity to do as much as he can for all sorts of fund-raisers and benefits. He rarely says 'no' to anyone's request and has helped to raise thousands and thousands of dollars for AIDS and HIV. I don't care what anyone's sexuality is. But when they're ready to discuss it, it is entirely up to them."

This won kudos from Hollywood figure R. Hunter Garcia (aka Gay Boy Ric): "I just wanted to say how thoughtful, touching and moving your defense of Chad Allen was. Particularly on target was pointing out that, at only 22, it would be very natural and hardly a scandal for Chad to be interested in 'younger men.' As for that picture in *The Globe*, I found it to be innocent, too. I was recently at a party in Benedict Canyon, where I had the pleasure of joining eight young men, all aged 19-22, in a Jacuzzi, and the entire experience was playful, light, and fun and had nothing to do with anything sordid as a lot of people in the gay community might wish to fantasize, and as a tabloid like *The Globe* might wish to blow out of proportion. The two young hosts of the party, for instance, supplied everyone with complementary guest Ralph Lauren swimsuits and freshly laundered towels for the move-to-the-Jacuzzi phase of the party. Everyone in the Jacuzzi had a wonderful time, but the emphasis was on frivolity and drinking champagne out of glasses, not on a pathetic attempt to duplicate some X-rated video from Catalina. The young hosts were even kind and thoughtful enough to supply limousine rides home for the careless, and as I was leaving, around 5 AM, Chad Allen was just arriving. If there's something wrong with young men having a party in Beverly Hills, I didn't see it there. Give back gay youth its innocence, damn it. As for the item on Chad in *Edge*, as the former editor of *Edge*, I hired and trained its current editor at a time when he was still afraid to interview Dan Butler alone because Butler was, gasp!, 'a celebrity.' As recently as the Reagan years, when he was in high school, this same editor was voting for Pat Robertson because he figured 'if he was religious, he was probably a safe bet.' It is easier to strike out at others than to simply look within, especially when wielding a twelve-pack after 2 AM. All of the gay media, including *4FRONT*, have been at fault in perpetuating a difficult environment for young gay men to grow up in feeling good about themselves and their sexual and emotional inclinations. Your defense of Chad was a step in the right direction... Chad's private life is his own...and that's that. As for Tom Cruise, his private life remained his private life until the night he showed up at my surfside bungalow in a red Porsche, begging to know who my favorite actor was. I was afraid to say it then, but I'm no longer afraid to say it now, 'Tom Cruise is my favorite actor.' There. I've said it."

Meanwhile, in New York, Michael Musto in the *Village Voice* broke the news that "Chad Allen (of Dr. Quinn and numerous hot tub parties in West Hollywood) attended a recent performance of 'Rent' on Broadway and was later seen having dinner with one of the stars, the 'out' Anthony Rapp. Don't read anything into this, however. Anthony and Chad are pals and they were accompanied by Chad's twin sister."

Last August, Allen joined such high-profile gays as Mitchell Anderson, Michael Jeter, Greg Louganis, and Bruce Vilanch in a special 30th Anniversary reading of the play "The Boys in the Band" at the Hudson Theater in Hollywood. Naturally, Allen played the character "Cowboy."

Meanwhile, Billy Masters reminded readers he'd been giving them the *straight* skinny, as it were, for months. "Y'know first I report that Chad was Brian Austin Green's boyfriend. Then I tell you he was at the Gay Erotic Film Awards. I even told you he was at the White Party in Palm Springs doing everyone in sight!" And that Allen's so-called "girlfriend" wasn't too heartbroken because she actually had a "girlfriend" of her own.

Masters added that Jason Padovan, the boy in the infamous *Globe* photo with Allen, was, sadly, "just a one-night stand."

SEX IN MUSIC

"While a lion is drinking at a river, a gorilla sneaks up from behind and slips him a Liberace. He then takes off, with the lion in hot pursuit. The ape jumps into a hunter's tent, puts on a safari outfit, dons a pith helmet, grabs the Johannesburg Star, and sits down to read. The lion follows the ape's scent to the tent, sticks his head in and asks: 'Did you see a gorilla come through here?' The ape replies: 'You mean the one that fucked the lion in the ass?' 'My God!' roars the lion, 'it's in the newspapers already?" - Famous old joke

"Undoubtedly the most flamboyant entertainer of the century," *Past Out* said, "Liberace was also one of the most fiercely closeted. On three separate occasions, the showman hired lawyers to help keep his homosexuality secret, each time defeating those who alleged that he was gay. The entertainer who absolutely reveled in gay stereotypes – from poodles to pink sequins – insisted on a heterosexual facade till the day he died of AIDS just over 10 years ago. The most noteworthy of these cases came when Scott Thorson, his former lover and chauffeur, sued him for 'palimony.' Thorson met Liberace in 1977 when he was 18. By 1982 the romance was over, and the legal wrangling started. In 1986, Liberace agreed to a final payment of $95,000. By that time, Liberace's health had begun to waver from AIDS. Despite an increasingly gaunt appearance, the entertainer played to sold out crowds in Radio City Music Hall, where he made a grand entrance by flying above the audience on cables. When questioned about Liberace's weight loss, his manager told the press that Liberace was on a 'watermelon diet' and was in generally good health. Not until Liberace's coroner held a nationally televised press conference was AIDS revealed as the cause of death. To this day, some of the devoted elderly women who conduct tours at the Liberace Museum in Las Vegas insist that Liberace's so called homosexuality and AIDS are nothing but cruel rumors about a talented bachelor."

Indeed, nowadays attracting some 250,000 visitors each year, the Liberace Museum is as much a phenomenon as the man himself. Full of flash and flamboyant fantasy, Liberace epitomizes Las Vegas. Myron Martin, executive director of the Liberace Foundation, which manages the shrine devoted to the extravagant excesses of the supreme showman, says the main attraction is a $750,000 cape that Liberace once bravely wore: "He liked to make an entrance." Even he is surprised that so many people get pleasure from laughing at the showman's mincing mannerisms and rhinestoned romanticism. Perhaps the fur-festooned Liberace's response to all the ridicule sums it up best: "I cry all the way to the bank."

"There's only one real museum in Vegas, and most everybody knows it's the Liberace," *Monk* magazine reported. "A bit too closeted for our tastes (even in death), Liberace ('Mr. Showmanship') did possess a certain tacky Baroque elan that is as hilarious as it is revolting. See the spoils of his ridiculously ornate pianos and his rhinestone-studded cars and wardrobe. Marvel at old homophobic retirees actually enjoying this stuff, even though they would have turned on the man had they known 'the truth.' Factoid: When Liberace began offering tours of his spread to the public, a local shopping mall complained about all the traffic. So Liberace bought the mall and lowered all the rents."

"The first gay person I saw on TV was a hero of mine, Liberace. He was what every straight person wants to think gay people are like – so camp, not at all threatening," Elton John says. But then he says, "I didn't have sex until I was about 23. And then I couldn't stop. Now, though, I'm very picket-fence."

In an October 1976 *Rolling Stone* interview, Elton admitted publicly that he enjoyed male companions. "The announcement did not surprise friends," reported the book *Rocket Man*, "but it made them worry for his popularity. By the time stardom arrived in 1971, Elton had been open with associates about his preferences. They need have looked no further than his manager John Reid, with whom Elton had a long relationship. Though Elton now downplays the price he paid for coming out, the revelation did impact his sales and airplay, especially in America. Despite the cost, he continued to talk openly about being gay. Two years later, as if to reinforce the point, he titled his new album *Single Man*. It included 'Big Dipper,' a campy, sexual song featuring his male soccer team on backing vocals.

His 1980 tour program offered a cover drawing of Elton in heavy makeup. *The Fox* album in 1981 featured 'Elton's Song,' written by gay activist Tom Robinson, about one boy's crush on another. Even in concert, Elton occasionally inserted the words 'young stud' in the slow love song 'Blue Eyes.'"

"The gay business really hurt me a lot," he said. "But I had to learn to take (it) well. If you take your seat at a football ground and 20,000 people are singing, 'Elton John is a homosexual,' you learn fairly quickly."

Entertainer Dolly Parton said she was out, in a manner of speaking. "I'm not gay but my best friend is. I have all these male friends, a lot of them gay; my manager's gay, and so I'm always out."

And speaking of being OUT, "George Michael can't bring himself to say one way or the other," *Gay Times* commented. "In an interview with *The Big Issue* magazine he comes over as a monstrously narcissistic and self regarding man. (Indeed 'George Michael singer' is an anagram for 'G: him sincere large ego.') However, the part of the interview that interested the tabloids was the bit about his sexuality. As *The Sunday Express* put it: 'To be gay or not to be gay? That is the question which George Michael cannot answer. Or will not.'

"'I think everything about me has always been ambiguous,' said the great artiste. 'Although my sexuality hasn't always been completely clear to me it was never a moral question. I've never thought of my sexuality as being right or wrong. To me it has always been about finding the right person. The only moral involved in sex is whether it's consenting or not. Anyway who really cares whether I'm gay or straight? Do they really think they've got a serious chance of shagging me or something?'

"Boy George, forever a thorn in Michael's apparently much-desired flesh, threw out this challenge to the great sex symbol in his column in *The Daily Express*: 'George says he has nothing to hide and that he has never considered his mysterious sexuality to be wrong. If that's the case then why can't he get it past his lips?'"

"Michael explains that his obfuscation about the gender of his preferred bed partners is really a career consideration. If he can maintain the ambiguity about his sexuality he can fascinate both men and women and then everybody is happy. Except those of us who find him absolutely repellent of course."

John Price in *4Front* said, "On a recent Friday night the stars were out in WeHo in full force. George Michael has become a regular at Cherry, on Fridays. Rumor has it that the pop superstar has even taken his turn in the DJ booth to advise on music. Many were surprised at the PDAs (public displays of affection) that Michael was dishing out to his boy-toy for the evening. You would think the young thing would be hanging all over him, but the opposite was true."

A survey showed Chris Isaak's video was the sexiest of the year. About him, Billy Masters reported in *Filth*, 'This week I've gotten conflicting reports on one of my favorites - poor, lonely Chris Isaak, he of the buff body and strange nose! Someone who worked with his tour manager said they have a tough time keeping him out of local bathhouses when he's on the road. That was particularly surprising in light of several San Francisco fans who told me that it was just announced that Chris is getting married to a woman. Go figure!'

"Call it what you will queercore, gay grunge, whatever – more lesbians and gays are popping up on the alternative rock scene than ever before," *The Advocate* said. In addition to the ones detailed here, others are waiting in the wings. For instance, The Bootlickers, a popular Philadlephia-based group performing country rock and harmonies, released their first CD in 1997, "Universal Nancy." *au courant* said, "Although lacking the excitement of live performance, 'Universal Nancy' features the good ol' boys at their acoustic best – with an emphasis on frank, openly gay lyrics and strong melodies. There are seven tracks included on the disc, among them are three fourtrack demos – including their ever-popular, hard-edged rendition of 'These Boots Are Made For Walkin'.'"

And then there's the good *new* boys: The Backstreet Boys, named after the shopping district in their hometown of Orlando. These kids have swiftly become teen idols, especially the blond Nick Carter (be still my heart!) Michael Musto had the opportunity to interview this hot new group for the *Village Voice*: "The Backstreet Boys are five slender studs from Orlando who sing...well, it doesn't matter what they sing, since it's always drowned out by teenage screaming anyway. They're the new New Kids, the old Menudo, the male Spice Girls, the white Boyz II Men, yet they're somehow *tres* fresh and original. And since they're on the cusp of explosive stardom, the Boys exude the kind of earnest gratitude that always seems to possess such types –until they become casualties living in the gutter or monsters living in Bel Air.

"At a frantic morning gala at the Official All-Star Cafe, I got to catch the quirky quintet in this transitory moment of lush contradiction. First, we were treated to the mixed signals of their videos, half of which have them shirtless and covered in what looks like salad dressing, and the other half of which present them in red, white, and blue sweaters frolicking wholesomely in the snow. Either way, they're pining for girls, girls, girls, who return the favor by touching the dressing and throwing snowballs. ('We date around' is all the Boys ended up telling us about their love lives.) Finally, the group quit playing games with my heart and emerged, as we took a few seconds to decode the lineup – there's a slick one, a Leonardo DiCaprio one, a nebulous one, an ethnic one, and a star – before firing away with dumb questions. Their answers reeked of a blank-faced, irony-free seriousness I haven't seen since New Kids, Menudo, Boyz II Men, etc.

"Why the wet bods in some of the videos? 'We thought it would be sort of artsy – something different,' said the slick one. (No one argued – you don't tell a cute fledgling pop star that gleaming semi-nudity is not all that novel.) Is it true that the Leonardo DiCaprio one had collapsed at one point in their rigorous schedule? 'First of all,' he said, 'I didn't collapse. It was very hot. The doctor told me to take a few days off and rest, so I did.'

"...Then the group moved on to a Virgin Megastore gig, where they signed a girl's boobs, fended off sexual offers, and sang a full set. And we all died happy. But then I had to retreat to a world without six-ways, a world where dressing's on salad."

Up and coming: The Backstreet Boys, left to right: Kevin Richardson, A.J. McLean, Howie Donough, Brian Littrell, and (sigh) Nick Carter.

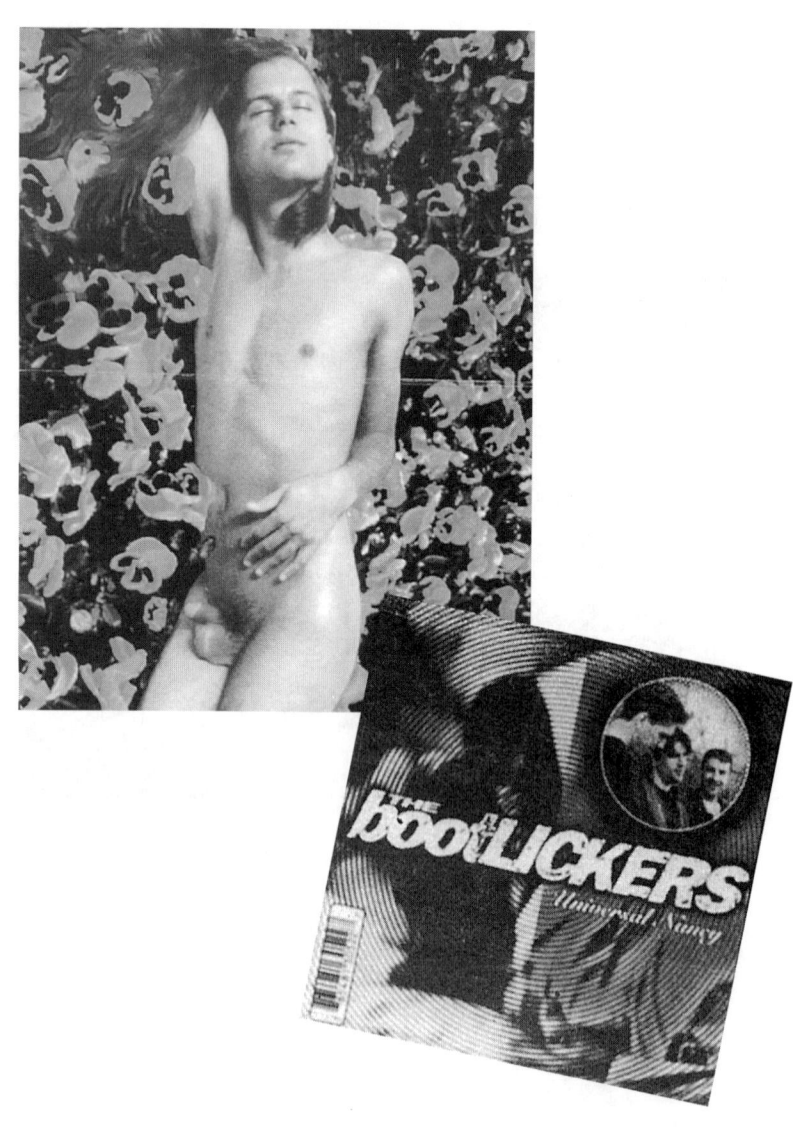

Hmmmm! Cover of Pansy Division's most infamous album, "Undressed," and the first CD from Bootlickers.

Pansy Division

First unleashed in 1991 with the idea of being an openly gay rock band, Pansy Division have most definitely found a niche to call their own. Since the release of "Wish I'd Taken Pictures" in 1996, they have been touring with all the vengeance of a plague, and working on a fifth album.

Next reported, "Wading against the water of shop-worn gay stereotypes and expectations, Pansy Division's kick-in-your face vocals and musical styling have attracted an audience of wide range; a combo platter of queers, straights, punks, indie kids, and all-out AlternaChicks. Pairing up with bands such as Tribe 8 and Team Dresch, they've paved the path for a succession of rock bands come to be known as Queer-core: openly gay, in-your-face-muthafucka, chock full of a blood-curdling sense of humor, and selling their soul for a stripped-down, loud rock format.

"Initially – and understandably – apprehensive of how straight venues might respond to them, Pansy Division now have hundreds of gigs underneath their belts, including a long stint as the opening band for Green Day. Other notches on their bedpost include venues all over the U. S. as well as Canada, Australia, New Zealand, and Europe.

"Recent articles about the band have boasted headlines such as 'Metallica Man on Gay CD' (*Kerrang Weekly*) describing the scandal that ensued when Metallica guitarist Kirk Hammett secretly teamed up with the band to record the B-side 'Headbanger,' which featured such lyrical highlights as "His fat boner bobbing up and down/playing air guitar as he danced around/he pounced on me and said, 'Let's do it'/ He knew what he wanted/ when he got down to it.' (Shocking!)

"Following their past endeavors – 1993's *Undressed*, 1994's *Deflowered* and 1995's compilation of B-sides and singles, *Wish I'd Taken Pictures* shows a marked evolution of the group's lyrical and musical style – one might even go so far as to say they've 'matured' (though it's a terrible word to use, it's one I choose to use anyway.) Even with that in mind, they're still fun, furious, and sure to be coming your way soon. *Duck!*"

"They're here," *Detour* said. "They're punk. Get used to it.

Thanks to former label mates Green Day taking them along on tour, Pansy Division was one of the first openly gay pop/punk bands to emerge from what is commonly referred to as the Homo-core scene (God is my Co-Pilot, Team Dresch, Extra Fancy, Tribe 8). The Homo-core tag is a bit misleading, though, because musically, they're closer to a horny or slightly perverted Sha Na Na than, say, the Sex Pistols. I'm sure even they have a hard time keeping a *straight* face on 'Dick of Death' and the ode to bathroom stage fright, 'Pee Shy.' Other songs, like 'The Ache' and 'Don't Be So Sure,' are wellcrafted pop without the slightest hint of penis envy."

"I think Pansy Division is the kind of band that saves people's lives. They're catchy, and they're really educational. They're honest about their sexuality, and that saves lives," said Green Day front man Billie Joe Armstrong about touring with the group.

"San Francisco's Pansy Division plays incredibly catchy punk-pop songs whose subversive hooks will have you humming about, say, fem boys or curved penises," raved *Interview* magazine's Evelyn McDonnell. "The Pansies' very out-queer lyrics pretty much guarantee that their three indie CDs and numerous singles will never get radio airplay. Fortunately, thanks to friends in high places, they've found other ways into the nation's ears."

"Too much fame too soon is deadly for a rock band, but a little success is nearly always a good thing," said Barry Walters in *The Advocate*. "Prior to its attention-grabbing tour with Green Day, Pansy Division was usually better in theory than in practice. The most infamous of 'queercore' punk bands, this San Francisco-based trio had lots of wit and daring but not enough experience to achieve something beyond being the gayest band in the land. Its first three albums have their moments but are often sloppy, silly, and one-dimensional. Pansy Division seemed as if it would forever remain one of those acts that leaves behind a lot of great T-shirts but no great records.

"But constant touring, a taste of mainstream recognition and a decent recording budget have allowed Jon Ginoli, who handles vocals and guitar and started the group in 1991, Chris Freeman (bass, guitar, vocals), and drummer Dustin Donaldson to make sounds slightly different from the last, and there's more attention devoted to proper instrumental mixes, tighter harmonies, hitting the notes. The result is much catchier and more accessible, particularly in this climate when punk bands go platinum.

"There's still enough straight-up gayosity in the lyric department to horrify your uptight parents/straight roommates/closety friends: Songs like 'Horny in the Morning' and 'Pee Shy' maintain the expected queer locker-room humor, but the serious love songs and overall professionalism negate the novelty aspects that limited the previous releases. Ginoli's tunes have progressed beyond the simple sex anthems of yore, and Freeman, whose writing and singing provide a fitting foil to Ginoli's, turns out a minor classic in 'Dick of Death.' This is the kind of their members. Instead of softening its punk-pop approach, Pansy Division now plays harder while refining songwriting and arrangements. The sameness that plagued the previous albums is gone."

In Touch magazine ran pictures of the collector cards and called them "America's most intense and completely unapologetic homosexual band...singing earnestly about the uniquely homosexual at a level which is often ignored in most popular media."

The magazine went on: "In concert, they are wild and unpredictable. Jon seems to maintain some sense of decorum even as Dustin cracks jokes and does 'drummer' impressions. The true wild card in the group is Christopher. Sometimes he throws on a dress, and sometimes he throws on nothing at all.

"Jon said, 'Most of the audience was accepting. The music helped the message go down.' Pansy Division's music, by its very nature, suggests an awareness of a political backdrop without being directly political. 'The goal of the band,' said Jon, 'was a certain kind of self expression.' Of course, what Pansy Division mostly expresses is sexual identity, as Jon pointed out, 'I think that people are really interested in sex. The interest in sex never really changes, and I wanted to write about the things people talk about. There is so much angst-ridden gay art out there, and I wanted music that was going to be enjoyed... Living the happy life is the best revenge.'"

The Pet Shop Boys on tour.

The Pet Shop Boys

"The Pet Shop Boys have never been about 'life's a party'. Maybe we're about that more now than we used to be but we certainly weren't 12 years ago," said Neil Tennant in *Gay Times*. He met Chris Lowe when he was 27, and had his first hit when he was 30. At that point he thought "behaving and presenting yourself if you made pop music in the mid-Eighties" was something he didn't want to do.

"...We wanted to do it in a way where we could still have a kind of dignity. We didn't want to make complete prats of ourselves, and by 1985 you had to make a bit of a prat of yourself to be a pop star.

"We never wanted to do the tabloids, and all those groups came up on the tabloids. It was Adam Ant that started that, his famous quote that he became successful because he was supported by the tabloids and *Smash Hits*. Chris and I wanted to do it without any of them, we certainly didn't do it with the tabloids or the *NUE*. We had *Smash Hits* on our side. We had television and radio I suppose.

"And ultimately we wanted to remain enigmatic. Because we knew it would make us appear more interesting than we considered ourselves to be. In fact, having said that, we used to talk to *Smash Hits* every bloody week at that point. And of course the whole of the enigma was being gay. It was one of those 'are they, aren't they' things you get in a mainstream pop artist - which is a great thing. It's a very powerful thing when everybody speculates about which is the gay one. Is it Robbie or Jason or Mark? Even though they're all straight in fact. Is Keanu Reeves gay? It gives it a resonance and interest that's otherwise lacking. And I can't help feeling that I am slightly less interesting a figure since I announced I was gay. In a way. Mind you, having said that, it's a bit pathetic when you're a certain age and you're not being honest about what you're about."

Tennant relates that at the time he "wasn't that bothered (about relationships) actually. I was very wrapped up in what we were doing in the Pet Shop Boys. But before that, in the Seventies, I used to go out with girls all the time - which I used to quite like but I knew it wasn't the whole story."

The group seems to be getting better with age. DJ Rob Eric in *Next* thought The Pet Shop Boys *Bilingual* was "Absolutely yummy. The best Pet Shop Boys album ever. Neil Tennant and Chris Lowe have managed to top themselves and create ridiculously charming synthpop tasty enough for anyone's menu. The album has more to offer than most of their former work combined. ...This is classic gay camp that has crossed the lines into a legendary music-making experience."

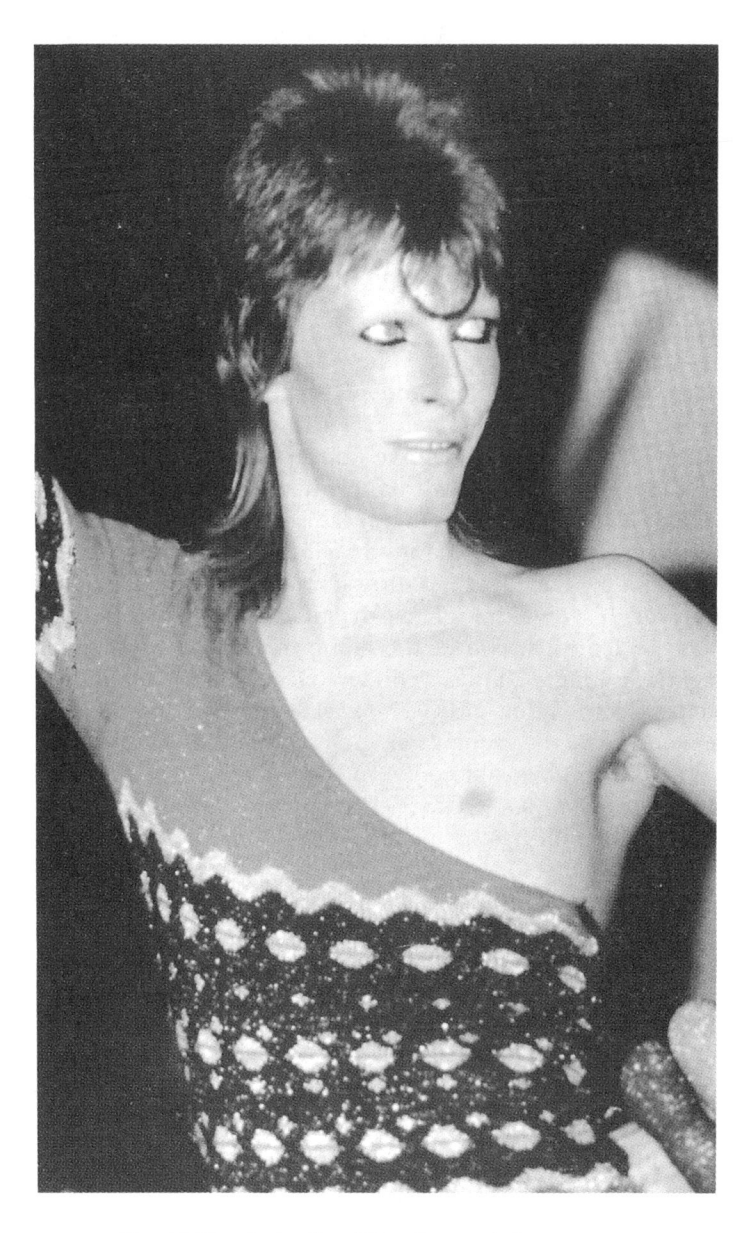

David Bowie in the '70s, dressed for success

David Bowie

"I've grown out of the dark aspect of performance and more into the irony of perverseness."
– David Bowie upon his 50th birthday.

In the early '70's, David Bowie was like, "Fuck it - artifice is the thing for me." Now, he says, the same feeling is evolving again. Yes, we are in the midst of a sort of David Bowie resurgence (everything old is new again?) that began with his appearance in "Basquiat" and on the "Basquiat" soundtrack, the Iggy Pop classics he helped write and produce on "Trainspotting's" soundtrack, his live appearances at recent benefits and the VH-1 Fashion Awards, his new album "Earthling" and his 50th birthday party bash at Madison Square Garden.

"How clever that the man who fell to Earth would name his latest album 'Earthling'," *Genre's* music critic wrote. "Bowie produced his own tracks for the first time in more than 20 years, and the balance of the album reveals a flirtation with breakneck jungle ('Little Wonder: Dead Man Walking') and intense electric guitar riffs ('The Last Thing You Should Do'). It even includes the punchy single 'Telling Lies,' which, until now, has been available only on the Internet. It's a decidedly different orgy of sonic experiences proving – earthling or not – that Bowie still has his head in the clouds. Just the way we like him."

And David continues to shine on screen as well. Now available on video from Miramax is "Basquiat," the story of the 19-year-old graffiti writer Jean-Michel Basquiat, who catapults from homelessness to superstar status in the opulent New York art world of the 1980s. Hobnobbing with the likes of Andy Warhol (played by Bowie), his fame grows as quickly as his inner torment, and he rapidly self-destructs. Some critics have said that it is possibly a too sympathetic portrait of a fascinating but difficult personality, "Basquiat" is highlighted by newcomer Jeffrey Wright's moving performance as the artist. In addition to a nice turn by Bowie there are interesting cameos by Christopher Walken, Willem Dafoe and Courtney Love.

Flame-haired David Bowie, the space oddity known as Ziggy

Stardust in the '70s, recently turned 50. But Bowie doesn't waste a whole lot of time reflecting on his golden years. "I'm not big on nostalgia," he says. "But I've still got everything – all the costumes, all the original Ziggy clothes – in storage in Switzerland. I've even got the miniature stages designed for each show I've ever done. I'm a real hoarder. Frankly, I don't quite know what to do with the stuff." He pauses, then adds, "I see theme restaurants."

When it comes to Bowie, we could believe almost anything at this point. He recently tapped the bond market for a $55 million issue of 10-year bonds. What's more they were priced about a percentage point higher than the U.S. government has to pay on 30-year bonds. The giant insurance company Prudential bought the entire issue, which is supposed to be paid by Bowie's future record royalties. One Wall Street wag suggested that Prudential policy holders could be forgiven if they'd prefer other uses for their money "than a bet that graying baby boomers will want to replenish their collections with new CDs of 'Ziggy Stardust.'"

Be that as it may, the deal allows Bowie to collect the full $55 million up front instead of waiting for royalty checks to trickle in over many years. No one has ever thought investors would be enticed by esoteric bonds tied to royalties, but leave it to Bowie to defy convention.

Back in January '97, Bowie finally got a star on the Hollywood Walk of Fame and celebrated his birthday in grand style with a party in the form of a concert at Madison Square Garden in Manhattan.

Liz Smith said, "David Bowie fans should check out the RCA Victor compilation album 'Another Crazy Cocktail Party!' which contains an early Bowie oddity titled 'Pancho,' about a leather-clad biker. This was written with lounge-music king Willi Albimoor, back when Bowie was still calling himself by his real name, David Jones."

Things are certainly looking up for the rock legend. Not that Bowie takes it all so seriously. "I've grown out of the dark, foreboding aspect of performance and more into just the irony of perverseness," Bowie told *Rolling Stone*. "For me, a lot of it is just funny."

Speaking of perverseness, the high point of the birthday bash came when Lou Reed traded verses with Bowie on the flamboyant "Queen Bitch," the Velvet Underground classics "Waiting for the Man" and "White Light/White Heat," and Reed's own "Dirty Boulevard." After a two-song encore for which Bowie donned a frilly Ziggy-period coat - the show ended with a guilty pleasure: Standing alone with an acoustic guitar, behind a huge translucent scrim, Bowie blasted into the ether on "Space Oddity."

"But," *Rolling Stone* reported, "that song wasn't the show's only moment of dramatic overkill. During 'The Voyeur of Utter Destruction (as Beauty),' from 1995's 'Outside' album, Bowie's face was projected onto a giant cocoon-like structure above the stage, making him look like a cross between Joan Crawford and the Wizard of Oz. And he gave embarrassing, melodramatic readings of 'Heroes' and 'Moonage Daydream.' But, hey, it was his birthday."

In the mid-'80s, Bowie says, he felt "sunk" and "musically threatened"; now, as he passes the half-century mark, Bowie is philosophical about that period. "It really pushed me into making decisions about why - or if - I wanted to continue as a musician," he says. "I came out of it really knowing how I wanted to spend the rest of my years as a creative force. It was a real freeing experience."

So is $55 million, up front!

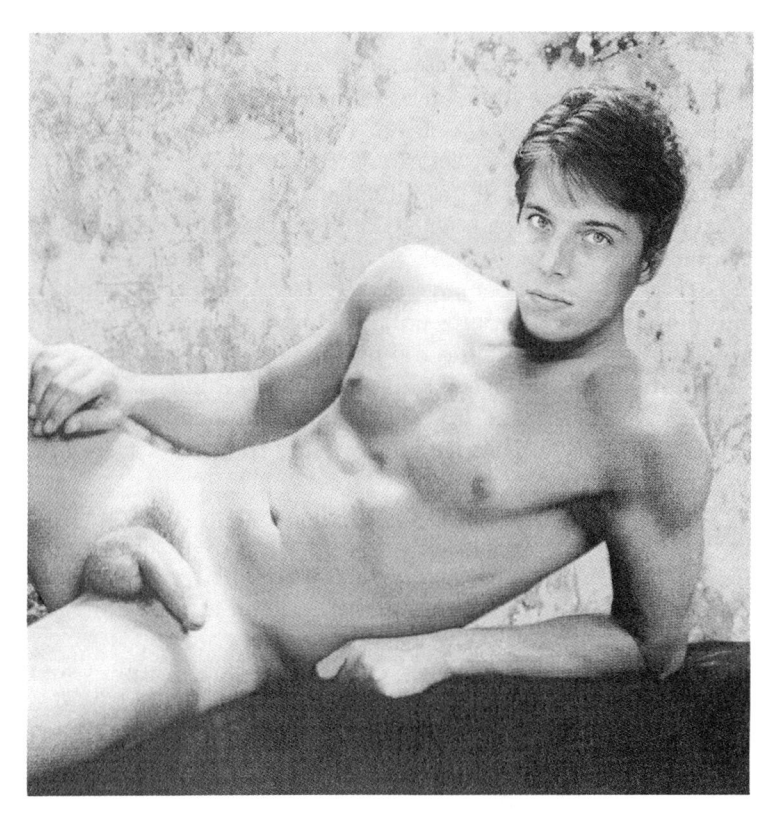

What Joshua Bell thinks of this exposure on the Internet is not known. We'd be delighted!

Joshua Bell

"Early in his career, Joshua Bell seemed to get as much attention for his virtuoso-next-door good looks and casual, jeans-and-a-T-shirt style as for his formidable talent as a violinist," said journalist Charlie Huisking.

"Screaming teen-aged girls lined up outside the stage door after his concerts, and *New York* magazine called him a matinee idol."

He has recently been the subject of great interest on the internet, where a computer-enhanced nude of him has men all over the world asking who the heck he is.

The answer is that Bell, now 28, is regarded as one the foremost musicians of his generation, a dynamic, sensitive performer who appears regularly with the world's leading orchestras and conductors.

"A native of Bloomington, Ind., Bell began playing the violin when he was 4 years old and made his professional debut at age 14. Not only has he successfully made the transition from child prodigy to mature artist, but he seems to have emerged with his head on straight."

In interviews, Bell comes across as a thoughtful, funny and easy-going guy. The violin may be his passion, but there's also room in his life for "too many" computer games, an occasional round of golf, his favorite TV show "Seinfeld," and a girl friend of long standing.

"I credit my parents for encouraging me to do normal things when I was growing up - playing lots of sports, things like that," Bell said. "It kept me from getting too narrowly focused, and I've continued to pursue lots of other interests."

Not that he has loads of free time. Bell performs more than 100 concerts annually – a punishing schedule. He said he judges how well his career is advancing by counting the number of concert dates "that are really exciting for me, that give me the opportunity to work with an orchestra or a conductor that I've been dying to play with. Thankfully, the percentage of those concerts keeps going up and up."

And Bell said he's continuing to grow as a musician. "Each year I feel I'm at another level, as far as understanding the music. And even technically, I think I'm still improving." Laughing, he added that, "Of course, I didn't practice a lot as a kid. So I left a lot of room to get better."

The critics don't seem to agree. *The Washington Post* said that Bell is "one of a blessed few for whom violin playing is an affair of the heart, not merely some arid study in technique . . . He has the gift of finding and communicating the emotional essence of almost everything he touches."

The New York Times praised Bell's flexibility of tempo and his "sweet, vibrato-rich tone." The *Times* also hailed him for what he is not: "Mr. Bell is not an exhibitionist, eager to soup up his interpretations with intrusive mannerisms. Nor is he any kind of hotshot, seeking to amaze an audience with his speed and volume. His Romanticism is tempered by an aristocratic elegance . . ."

Seeming almost embarrassed when those reviews were read back to him, Bell laughed. "Well, they only send the good ones in the press kit," he said. But, seriously, he credits his legendary teacher, Josef Gingold, with influencing his style. "Gingold's approach to music was personal, and very old-fashioned, in a way," Bell said. "He taught me the virtue of honesty and sincerity. He said that you should play in a way that seems natural, that comes directly from your heart."

After attending a Bell concert, music critic Richard Storm said, "Bell is everything we have been led to believe and much more.

"Advance publicity had prepared us for the youthful charm and good looks, for the technical virtuosity, for the aw-shucks, unassuming demeanor. What was not conveyed is the maturity of his art, the lack of the performance glitz that one might expect of this country's most famous former child prodigy, and the willingness – even determination – to put his talent and intelligence at the service of the music. So intense was this selfless concentration on content rather than surface that we in the audience sometimes felt as if we were witnessing a private act: just Joshua Bell and the music, alone in a large space. We held our breath, so as not to intrude, and were rewarded with exceptional music of different kinds from very different periods of time. ... The calm security of a great artist performing great art was all there was to it, after all. The room shrank, the audience vanished, there was only one young man using his skill and talent to make the music live again in all its miraculous complexity and paradoxical simplicity."

Separated at birth? Baby-faced comic David Spade became a long-lost brother of sibling rockers Hanson at the MTV Movie Awards

Hanson

"Hanson seems so perfect – very pretty boys with long blond hair and good family values – that they come off just plain eerie."
– Gay Music Critic John Stephen Dwyer

"Hanson, the three press-crowned little princes of bubblegum pop, are suddenly everywhere," music critic John Stephen Dwyer commented. And if they aren't there themselves, they are there in spirit. Not long ago, for instance, I found myself in the cluttered office of the manager of a gay club and there was a Hanson poster! This, in the trendiest club for miles around. It proved that beauty, especially young, fresh beauty, transcends all music genres.

Dwyer continued, "The sudden industry clout of the three musical boys, ages 16, 14 and 11, cannot be denied. They even stand at first place on the Billboard top 100. Ike, Taylor and Zac Hanson, three brothers from a strongly Christian family in Tulsa, Oklahoma, are a regular presence on MTV with their hit song "MMMBop" (from the album *Middle of Nowhere*). They performed and have been interviewed by CNN, Rosie O'Donnell, Jenny McCarthy, the Today Show, Regis & Kathy Lee, Letterman, and The Tonight Show.

"In the mold of kid groups of past decades, like the Jackson 5 or Osmonds, these juvenile celebrities are a big, big product. They have several web pages authorized by Mercury Records, each visited by thousands of people per day. Here young fans can read such fascinating information as the fact that middle brother (and frontman teen heartthrob) Taylor is left handed and 'shy but friendly,' blending 'The intelligence of Ike with the zaniness of Zac.' Can Hanson bath towels and umbrellas be far behind?"

"Whatever you do, don't call Hanson cute – at least not to their faces," said *Seventeen* magazine. At the magazine's photo shoot in New York City's Central Park, the band bristled at the idea of posing by a swing set. Their dad, Walker Hanson, says his sons also refused another photographer's request to pose with stuffed animals. Hanson does not see itself as just a kiddie show. "Listen to the music, it'll speak for itself," says Taylor. Zac has an even better suggestion: "Think of us as old people with high voices."

With the incredible sales of their music, Hanson has proven they are not "just a teen-girl thing," *Seventeen* said. "The fever has infected the entire country – this kind of hot family act hasn't been seen since the Jackson 5. After they were on his show, David Letterman said, "Someone should get these kids their own TV show," but the brothers don't want that. "We don't want to be the next Partridge Family," says Isaac. "Right now we're focusing on the music."

And not just music. Sex, maybe, as well. Michael Musto loved Kathy ("Suddenly Susan") Griffin's riff on "those NAMBLA faves, the whitebread sandwich known as Hanson. Upon meeting the group, Griffin – who claims to be a full-time Hanson gangsta bitch – nervily asked the oldest one, 'You guys must get a huge amount of pussy, right?' He said, 'What?',' related the comic, 'and like an idiot, I repeated it!' Worse, he then responded with a gesture that seemed to say, 'Yeah, a fair amount.' MMMBop!"

The boys have lived in Ecuador, Venezuela and Trinidad. Because the Hansons have always been on the move, they've been home-schooled by their mom and have never attended regular school. "We love home schooling," Ike says. "It lets you focus on things you enjoy." Adds Taylor, "We'll read about Notre Dame and then go to Paris to see it."

Despite all the time they spend living and working together, the brothers get along really well. "We're basically best friends," says the moody, introspective Taylor.

Maybe that's because they're so different. Ike is the goofy, sensitive brother who "is the kind of guy who thought he was gonna get married in the third grade," says Taylor.

As for the third Hanson, little Zac is just as hyper in person as he is in the "MMMBop" video. But he's also supercreative and quirky (he collects miniature shampoo bottles from hotels around the world). He's also a budding cartoonist, who's created characters called Superguys.

Entertainment Weekly went so far as to give us a rundown: "Hanson have 'MMMBop'-ed their way right into cyberspace. Images of the teenybopper trio, who have already conquered the music world, are currently the hottest download in America." Their website is getting over a million hits per month. "We've gone from getting five e-mails a week to more than 700," says Ike.

Dwyer continues: "The brothers supposedly started singing hymns around the dinner table, then picked up rhythm and blues influence and were a band before they knew it. They play their own instruments and write their own songs. However, Hanson seems so perfect – very pretty boys with long blond hair and good family values – that they come off just plain eerie.

"Labeled 'bubblegum' for their diabetic coma-inducing sweetness, the young fellows of Hanson are folkish in the current mode and aspire to be soulful in a mature way. Taylor, the clear favorite of the fans, occasionally sounds like a pubescent boy version of Janis Joplin. The oldest and youngest brother, unfortunately, can harmonize, but can't sing.

"Hanson is freaky. They might vanish instantly and completely. On the other hand, Taylor Hanson could end up bigger than Elvis. Who can say?"

"Christopher Sabec wasn't searching for the next pop phenomenon, just lunch," *People* said. "But as the music attorney munched barbecue at an Austin, Texas, music conference three years ago, he was interrupted by a youthful chorus: 'Excuse me, sir, may we perform for you?' Looking up, he saw three pint-size boys, each as blond as Macaulay Culkin and ranging in age from 8 to 13. Not wanting to crush their young psyches, he grudgingly agreed. Then, he recalls, he was 'blown away' by what he heard. 'I need to speak to your parents,' Sabec told them, as the last note faded."

Eventually Mercury Records talent hunter Steve Greenberg became interested. "Given the boys' ages and the quality of the demo," Greenberg says, "I assumed it was fake, that adults were playing the instruments (and) that the vocals had been electronically manipulated." But just to be sure, he went to hear the Hansons at a county fair in Kansas. "There was not an adult in sight," says Greenberg.

Now the group is a world-wide phenomenon, and Greenberg notes that the tune's catchy refrain – Mmmbop-baduba-dop – "means the same thing in every language. I'm sure that helps."

"These days," *People* reported, "between cracking wise on the MTV Movie Awards and filming a video for their next single, the Hansons have been touring Europe and making cultural discoveries: 'The nice thing about England,' notes guitarist Ike, 'is that they actually speak English.'"

The Village Voice was so impressed by the group they asked their esteemed culture columnists to comment. Here's a wrap-up: Scott Poulson-Bryant, "'MMMBop.' Mmm Mmm Good. Yummy to my tummy. Real chewy bubblegum in an era of self-important Everlasting Gobstoppers, with a fun-loving video to rival anything Bazooka Joe or Archie ever dreamed up. They don't make 'em like this anymore.

"I'm an old man when it comes to pop culture – 30 – so I should know.

"I was nobler than thou once, but now, nobility be damned. I wanna sing along, not be yelled at. I wanna love a single, not de-cypher it. ...(But) I'm not really looking forward to Hanson's inevitable TGIF-sitcom on ABC."

"Say this for Hanson," Robert Christgau said, "...What's not to like? The musical marketing. The claims of innocent spontaneity put forth for these ambitious young pros, most of whose wrote-their-owns are cosigned by chief producer Stephen Lironi, his studio henchmen, or song doctors including the notorious Desmond Child, are just image. ...No wonder Rodgers & Hammerstein liked Oklahoma..."

"More androgynous than Boy George," said Barry Walters, " more urgent than Sleater-Kinney, more godly than that scary Christian dad with the 'Butterfly Kisses' song about his daughter on her knees by the bed, Hanson is proof positive that the tune is right for boys with Breck Girl hair and cotton-candy tunes to infiltrate our oh-so-serious '90s rock consciousness. The real music news story of '97 has got to be the return of Young People's Pop, something the Hanson brothers generate with biological ease. ...A shockingly natural white soul aberration too impassioned to dismiss as merely pretty. He's the child Michael Jackson lost on the way to superfreakdom."

"Hanson is a teenybop band," Ann Powers commented, "no matter how high the concept. The sparkly new effects lure you in, but what matters is the familiar thrill. Michael's manboy voice pushed the confines of those sugary songs as his fleshy body strained his tight little pants, but his floppy hat and the boppy beat made the perversion cute. Years later, Kriss Kross did the same kiddiemack act with hiphop. In between, Debbie Gibson and Kylie Minogue turned Lolita back into a schoolgirl, the New Kids and New Edition made juvenile delinquency likable, Leif Garrett did disco without chest hair, and Boy George snuggled up to transvestism. And so the children (and the child-identified) turn our monsters into Puff the Magic Dragon.

"The scary pop energy Hanson channels is today's obsession with past ephemera (as if history has left us with a roomful of its trash), turning that fear into nostalgia on speed. *Middle of Nowhere* sounds like every single song on AM radio in the past quarter century – 'MMM Bop' alone starts with a Graceland-esque juju guitar riff, sticks a hair-metal rhythm guitar underneath, borrows rhythms from Gloria Estefan, and resolves it all in a chorus just waiting to become a Coke commercial. The humans in the midst of this giant jukebox have their own way of soothing current anxieties: they're Calvin Klein models who drink milk, perfect Aryan boys with long locks instead of Timothy McVeigh crewcuts. Not least, they seem built to survive their own fame. Home schooled and well-traveled, they come off as worldly, settled kids who get the game they're pawns in. Even little Zac knew enough to claim authorship of one song. As America feels more and more shame about eating its young, Hanson comes to us, well fed. That's a thrill in itself."

Speaking of thrills, Liz Smith reported that Ru Paul wanted the trio to appear on his VH-1 show, but the boys' parents said no. Said Smith, "Ru's too racy to hunker down with their impressionable blond babies. Yeah, like Hanson's suddenly going to want to wear miniskirts, bouffant wigs, and serious eyeliner after a few minutes with Ru." Well, gee, you never know!

ARTISTS & MODELS

"It was back to the male genital watch at men's fashion week," Michael Musto reported for the *Village Voice*. The event was highlighted by "parades of brooding models wearing – get this – shirts and pants! How did they even think of such a thing?"

While last year, the news was underwear, and the genitals were easy to view, this year everyone seemed to be covering up. But underwear or no underwear, you still have the models, 200 or so of 'em during fashion week, "enough rippling abs to give an average person cramps," Guy Trebay said, also reporting on the event for the *Village Voice*. Trebay said that John Barlett, the hot young American designer "with sharp instincts for the mood of the moment," explained that his look for today was "rugged yet ornamental." Trebay says, "By highlighting the model's facial and other features with gold powder, he aims to 'accentuate the positive attributes and make him as sexy as possible. To heighten this effect, he has instructed his staff to apply a narrow line of dark purple liner inside the model's lips, blended so they look a little bruised, like they've just been making out.

"One of the models, however, will be making just one change of clothing. That model is Ronaldo Rocha, a tree-tall, highly developed Brazilian with shelf-like pectorals, melon buttocks, arms the size of ham hocks and with five elaborate blue tattoos. Rocha exudes a confidence that might conceivably originate at the base of his stylized tattoo, whose tentacles twine around his bellybutton and down into the depths of the white jersey bathing suit that's all he's been given to wear. 'He'll probably get mauled,' Michelle Chillis, a dresser, observes of Rocha, who happens to dress left, as the saying goes – emphatically."

Trebay says the modeling profession's workers are alternately treated as though the sun rose each morning from their behinds or else "as if they had the collective brain power of a dead Eveready."

"There's a lot of big egos in this business" says Alex Manning, a striking Japanese-Irish model born in Paris and raised in Brooklyn. "You can't take it seriously and let yourself get dissipated. People eat up the hype. I try not to let anyone fuck with my mind because I want to make something out of my life."

"He can make something out of my life, too, if he wants to," a stylist whispers to a friend.

"Get over yourself, girl," the friend says. "He's a model!"

Back in the audience, before the John Barlett show started, one guy said, "I love how, when the models are walking down the runway, they give that penetrating look."

"Oh, yeah," replied his friend. "It's like they're told to give the penetrating look. You know, *penetrate!*"

And speaking of penetrating, one of our favorite male supermodels made some smooth career moves during the year. We speak of handsome hunk Michael Bergin, the boy who took over from Marky Mark as the CK underwear model. Bergin now wears skimpy Speedos as lifeguard Jack Darius on the TV show "Baywatch." This followed a small part on the failed soap "Central Park West." Now that he is acting instead of modeling, Bergin can bulk back up. He had to lose some of that muscle to model designer clothes, but now he says he's working hard on his body and is "pretty comfortable with it." So are we, Michael, so are we!

One of our favorite models, beautiful Michael Bergin, posed for Calvin Klein (inset), did runway (great bulge in those underpants), and now appears on "Baywatch"
(Photo by Michael O'Neill, Outline)

*John Wayne's sexy grandson,
photographed by L. Galud for Top Model magazine*

Anthony Wayne

Last year we featured Bruce Weber's Abercrombie & Fitch spread – eight pages of all-American homoerotica all the more piquant for featuring Patrick and Anthony Wayne, son and grandson of Big John.

It was this campaign that Michael Musto in *Village Voice* found to be quite startling on the party circuit. He called it "that weird new Abercrombie & Fitch campaign, with Patrick Wayne and his son sharing affection in ways that might not be allowed in Virginia." Said one Manthattan party-goer, "It's either father and son or older sugar daddy, younger fag. I guess their demographic is very Christopher Street."

Since then, Anthony has been making a name for himself as one of the sexiest of the male models. Philippe Tretiak said in *Top Model*, "Anthony, like John (and like Patrick, his own father) is photogenic by nature. In fact, Anthony looks exactly as his grandfather did in his prime years as the young hero of the silver screen – he has the same clean cowboy image and the same broad-shouldered charm. At twenty, the Los Angeles-born Anthony has already been on the cover of *Uomo Vogue*, and has been featured in a recent edition of *Rolling Stone*.

"He is nonetheless a quiet-living student, who takes economics classes, and keeps an eye on stock exchange activities (between photo shoots) with a near-professional interest. Anthony is not yet sure how he will use his degree: For the moment, modeling is both fun and lucrative enough to allow him to put off decisions about the future. He does, however, have a nose for business which he intends to pursue."

"If I get into the movies, I want to play the lead. I want to be like Tom Cruise, or, even better, Dustin Hoffman, who is, I think, really the greatest American actor."

In pursuit of these ambitions, Anthony has been taking acting classes, although he sometimes admits to moments when he dreams of signing a big contract with a cosmetics or clothing company. But it is work, being this gorgeous. "People don't realize that it takes real effort to go to classes and to take exams in between photo sessions," he says. "But then, I'm not unhappy at all."

In his spare time, Wayne doesn't ride horses, as you might expect, but he jogs and loves team games such as soccer and basketball. Growing up in Idaho with his mother, he had plenty of chances to ski, and has been an alternate member of the United States Junior Olympic team. "When asked about his positive qualities and his flaws, Anthony responds with an almost-British dry humor, and it's hard to be sure whether he's being entirely serious," Tretiak noted.

"First of all," Wayne says, "I'm intelligent. And then, of course, I'm handsome. I have a broad vocabulary. I speak well. In the modeling world, many people have no education at all, so that makes a big difference." His greatest flaw, he admits, is "not thinking enough about others. I'm somewhat self-centered, and I need to pay attention to that.

"I am popular," he admits candidly, "but that doesn't prevent me from being alone. I don't have a girlfriend. I want my partner to be as perfect as I am. I'd like her to be beautiful, gifted, and above all, educated. I want her to know who Shakespeare is. In the fashion world, I'm generally better educated than most of the other models, and I want to be able to talk to my wife; in short, I suppose that I want her to be like me."

While waiting for the woman of his dreams, he amuses himself with his dog Hondo (named after one of his grandfather's greatest films), drives his black jeep, plays the drums, and indulges his passion for doughnuts.

There are no cuter twins on the planet than the Brewers.

The Brewer Twins

"I don't know what the deal is with those Brewer Twins," Billy Masters said in *Filth*, "but would I like to find out! Now, for those of you who don't know, these are two very hot guys who live in Florida, incredible bodies, and they pose, they strip, they model, they surf, and they have their own web page! They also claim to be straight, which I would believe, 'cept I don't know any straight men, twins or otherwise, who would pose together in quite so provocative and homo-erotic a manner. Knowing of their huge gay appeal, they say they're flattered, and also added they don't have girlfriends. Me neither!"

That was *last* year. *This* year, this is what Masters was reporting (hold on your hat, or whatever): "...Who should be spotted looking particularly incognito but Keith Brewer, of those oh-so-terrific The Brewer Twins. He was not joined at the hip (or anywhere else for that matter) by his brother, and, did I mention this spotting took place in a gay bar? While Keith may have gone in alone, he definitely didn't leave alone. Although my source wouldn't kiss and tell too much, he let me know that Keith was very nice, soft spoken, polite, and likes guys with dark hair and blue eyes. I guess his brother is that exception which proves the rule!"

As you will recall, we first became aware of these luscious New York-based supermodels in *Joe's*, the $40-per-copy magazine issued by New York stylist Joe McKenna. The superb Bruce Weber photo layout of the kids spending a lovely weekend together at a cabin have ended up on the internet. The series includes shots of the boys taking each other's jeans off, the two of them wrapped in each other's arms among the ferns, kissing, and holding flashlights on each other's cocks. "We do have secrets from each other," Derrick says, "but never for long. The urge to tell always comes out."

In the book *Male Supermodels*, George Wayne gives us some vital statistics on the guys, who say they always wanted to just be surfers: height 6'; suit 40R; shirt 15 1/2; waist 31; inseam 32; shoe size 9; hair, brown, eyes, green. Derrick says the sexiest thing about him is his eyes; Keith says it's his smile. Derrick says the worst thing about being a mannequin is "never knowing when that next job is." Keith says the worst thing about being a model is "trying to hid a zit."

When you're these boys, it's hard to hide anything. Our spy in Manhattan was not aware of the phemonenon known as the Brewer Twins and one day he was walking with his friend in Chelsea and there they were. "Visions, actually," the spy says. "They were standing right in front us. My friend went ballistic: 'It's the Brewers! It's the Brewers!' Anyway, I saw them a couple of more times this summer, but they obviously don't live here permanently because they look far too healthy." We wouldn't want them any other way!

Last summer, the master photographer Reed Massengill stated in an interview that he would like to shoot, among others, Tony Ward, Antonio Sabato, Jr., and the Brewer twins. "They are so adorable," says Reed. We couldn't agree more, and can hardly wait to see if Reed gets his chance to immortalize these boys at their prime.

Tyson Beckford for Ralph Lauren

Tyson Beckford

It's easy to see why Tyson Beckford made *Playgirl* magazine's 10 Sexiest List: "Tyson Beckford's lithe, exquisitely proportioned body looks like all six feet and one inch of it was personally crafted by the Almighty himself to wear the defined, classic lines of Polo Ralph Lauren clothing (with whom he has an exclusive contract to the reported tune of $550,000)," the magazine reported. "Throw in a distinguished face – with its exotic Asian eyes (courtesy of a Chinese grandmother), full lips and silky skin – and you've got a killer combination that's brought him to a well-deserved level of celebrity unmatched by other male mannequins."

Ralph Lauren hires blacks for its shows, but Tyson was the first to snag an exclusive contract for print advertising. The industry observers always felt that black didn't sell, but Lauren has proven them wrong. He chose Tyson not because he was black, however. Says a spokesman, "Tyson has the spirit that Ralph envisioned."

But the spirited Tyson hasn't let his success go to his head: "My parents raised me to never get cocky and walk around like I'm better than anyone else," Beckford explains. "If I went broke tomorrow, I'd be the same person. You gotta be normal, because it's just a job – one that's a little bit more glamorous than the average person's."

Beckford has been studying the acting craft for two years, setting his current sights on snagging the male lead in the movie version of Terry McMillan's book "How Stella Got Her Groove Back," the story of a fortysomething African-American banker who finds love with a penniless Jamaican 20 years her junior. *Playgirl* comments, "If the film includes some of the book's explicit sex scenes, they probably wouldn't make him blush. He's constantly getting hit on by intrepid women asking for a date or his phone number, with one bold proposal sticking out in his mind: 'One girl said she wanted to give me oral sex:' he recounts with a laugh. 'I just want to have you, baby.' I said, 'Um, that's nice...very interesting... "

When he first saw himself in an ad, he said, "When it first dropped, I was skipping down the street like a little kid. I was pleased with it.

"That was a few years ago. Now I'm like, Damn, I was in good shape when I was young. I'm getting old. (He's twenty-six.) I try to get to the gym four, maybe five days a week, when I have the time. Sometimes work can be stressful. I'm traveling a lot. Sometimes I'll go a whole day and forget about eating. And that's not because I don't want to eat. There just isn't time. Now I understand how the girls get so skinny. They're just working so hard. I'm one of the biggest male models, physically, but I have a bodyguard here and in L.A. I kinda don't want to have one. But it's gotten to the point where it's not safe for me anymore. Let's put it this way, I can't go back to the old neighborhood and hang on the corner like I used to. And it's kinda sad, but that's part of the responsibility of moving on and being a, you know . . . like, someone people kinda, you know, look up to."

A model who doesn't like role models, he does enjoy meeting other celebrities: "I met Prince last night," he says. "He's so little. A little, little guy. I gave him one of these homeboy hugs and I didn't want to hurt him."

THE SEX SUPERSTARS

Top or bottom, year-in, year-out, the legendary Chad Knight never fails. Courtesy Vivid Video.

THE GAY-FOR-PAY STUDS

"I don't think there is such a thing as a precise sexual orientation. I think we're all ambiguous sexually."
– Tennessee Williams

The lure of a career in porn is understandable if you're a gay exhibitionist, perhaps down on your luck, dancing for tips in a gay bar and Chi Chi LaRue shows up. But what is it with "straight" guys anyhow? It seems for some of them just a taste of dick or the feel of it up their ass is what they've been looking for all their lives, yet they maintain they are "straight." In fact, some, such as Chad Knight and Chad Connors (and the late, lamented Christian Fox), come to Hollywood to get fucked, then, satisfied for awhile, go home to the wife (and maybe the kiddies too.)

One of the newer "straight" bottoms who has caused quite a stir is Falcon's "Hard Knocks"-star Troy Halston, a boy called by *Torso* "a professional hole." "Troy is one of the cutest and most natural bottoms in the biz despite being a confirmed bi offscreen," said the magazine. "His lust for women is nowhere to be seen as he receives a long, sloppy-wet rimjob from handsome Damien Ford (great hair!), who then plows blond, vocal Troy with his long, thick tool. These two really had sex that day, if you know what we mean – no acting involved."

While some of these "straight" or "bi" actors play bottom, most are tradey tops, some of whom can't get it up for their partners. One who doesn't seem to have any trouble in any situation is Mike Lamas, whose magnificent scene with Kevin Dean in "Rawhide" from Studio 2000 is one of our favorites. "Some people don't believe in bisexuality," Lamas told *Manshots*. "But I think I'm bisexual, because I like to play with men and I like to play with girls, too."

He says his first time with another guy, "just happened," back when he was 15: "We started looking at each other, and then, just like that, we just go to the river and start like..." Lamas admitted. After this touching scene of youthful mutual masturbation, Lamas didn't have any contact with other boys until he moved to California. One of his friends was leaving the state and gave him his gym membership. "I didn't know there were any gay people inside, so I was in the shower, and I saw all these guys looking at me. And I think, 'What is this?' And I think maybe there's something wrong. I'm like kind of a pervert person... I start to meet the people, especially the boys. So, they look at my *pito* (cock) and they want some. 'Okay. C'mere. C'mere, man. I will give you some.'" And they've been coming and coming ever since.

"The boundaries of homosexuality and heterosexuality are different (in Latin America)," states filmmaker Kristen Bjorn, who estimates that 95% of the models who appear in his videos are straight-identified. "In the States, any man who allows another man to touch him or even look at him is suspected of being homosexual. In Latin America, men can – and do – have sex with other men without considering themselves homosexual. Most Brazilians believe that for a sexual act to take place between two males, one of them has to be the 'man' and the other has to be a 'fag' – that's how they would say it. They would consider it impossible for two homosexuals to have sex together. So the act of posing for me in no way compromises their masculinity. They're very proud of their bodies. It's a different way of thinking about sexuality."

"Basically, my objective is to shoot the video and not psychoanalize the models or change their minds," he says. "If they don't accept themselves, that's up to them and really none of my business."

Ferenc Botos, star of Bjorn's "Hungary for Men" and "The Anchor Hotel," told *Manshots* that it's harder to be a bottom than a top. "You have to use muscles that you don't normally use." In his second film, it was easier because he knew what was coming. "I felt more comfortable. I could relax more. Relaxation is important. When you're relaxed, penetration is easier to do and it speeds up the filming. The guys are important, too. One had experience, and that also made it easier. Fucking is easier. It's a normal movement. When you are getting fucked, you can't think about your usual way of having sex. Active, you can."

Botos says he is straight and that during gay sex he focuses on something erotic, "like my girlfriend's breast, but when I'm getting fucked, the fucking makes me lose my trend of thought.

(To be able to do it) shows that a model is a good performer."

In a change of pace, Bjorn's video "A World of Men" features studs from his travels in five countries. One cutie, Jozeph Polgar, was called by *Stars* the kind of boy you could "take home to meet the parents." Polgar tells an interesting story about a supposedly-straight guy he met while filming: "I love men and love to have them in me," the magazine quotes the boy as saying. *Stars* said that Polgar heard about Bjorn from his friends and he was determined to meet the man who made the biggest impression on him since he decided he was gay. "I remember first seeing one of Bjorn's videos at a party and seeing for the first time a guy I had made love with there in the video. I remember laughing out loud all of a sudden and everyone in the room turned and looked at me like I was crazy. I was laughing because this guy had told me he was a top and never got fucked. I sat there counting one after another of these dudes spreading this guy's ass and fucking him right there on the scene. I'm talking every guy in the video fucked this queen. And he had the fucking nerve to tell me he never got fucked. Well, if he never got it, he sure made up for it in that movie."

"I don't like working with straight guys," Eric ("Hot Cops 3") York says. "Let's face it, they're in it for the money. They go in the bathroom with a *Playboy* to jerk off to, and what am I going to do, stare at the ceiling fan and try to get a hard-on? It's just boring. If I had a choice, I would never do another movie with a straight guy, because it's just a waste of time. I don't know why, if you say you're straight, that some fucking directors and producers look up to you. That's wrong. If you're gay and are man enough to say that you're gay, then more power to you. Many times on the set, I'm with a guy who is supposed to be straight, but he's way more feminine than I or my friends will ever be. I look at that little nelly thing, and he's just lying in the bed like a little princess, reading a Playboy, saying he's straight, and I'm like, 'Please, get a life! Go home!'"

In an interview with *Manshots*, Tom Katt said, unlike his straight pals at school, Katt's first experience was with another boy, "which is kind of weird. I don't really meet too many people who are like that. But I'm not much into the whole definition thing, the whole labeling thing. I don't really give a crap what anyone's into. It's funny – in my position, I experience both sides of the prejudice: my gay friends who resent that I like women and my straight friends who resent that I like men. So I've got to put up with twice the shit from people now."

He says that first being in videos was a little nerve-wracking, "having a room full of people around you, and if you're not into the other person. It's something that's just so much more mechanical than people realize. Sometimes it was difficult, but I don't really feel any set I've ever been on has ever posed any kind of problem. I've heard horror stories and I'm just glad I was never a part of them.

"I guess you would say part of me was a little worried, because it wasn't till afterward that I realized I'd crossed that line that you can never go back over again. I knew I'd permanently become part of a world that, in a way, there is no way out of. I mean, I could retire forever, and the general population will never let you forget what you've done. At the same time, I was almost a little excited about it, wondering how I'd be reacted to, whether or not I would be successful.

"In a way, part of me wishes that I had paced myself a little bit more from the beginning. I feel that I did too many movies in the beginning. Luckily I feel like I slowed down in time to not do the old over-exposure thing. I don't feel that there was anything too horribly wrong with the path of things.

"I would tell anyone interested in porn to think very hard about it – and really imagine that in years to come, if he can deal with that being the foremost thought in other people's heads about him, that that's what he wants his reputation to be. If he wants to cross that line, he can never go back over again. To be honest, I would tend to always advise people *not* to get into it. Therefore, if they do anyway, it's really something that they want to do. But I would never pull somebody into it. I don't think it's really for everybody. I think there are a lot of people who get into it, they make a few quick bucks, and then they really hate it and they really regret it. I know so many people who just hate that they've done this. And I can understand it, because of the way the traditional common folks look down upon the whole thing. Sometimes that's the one thing that makes me feel a little resentful about it – the way that people will treat you, once they know."

Straight or gay, Gino Colbert, a former performer who now makes his living directing adult videos, cautions: "This is a good hobby, not a career, for a model. They should keep their day jobs." What many of these young porn hopefuls don't realize is that in addition to the "superstars," there is an actors' B-list, C-list, and so on. "Some of these D-list models," Forest says, "are working for $200 to $300." Colbert offers an even bleaker picture for those who get hooked up with one of the low-budget producers: "They pay actors a mere $100 per scene." Still the lure persists.

If a guy *is* lured into porn, could he leave porn and achieve success in another field or in a "more legitimate" form of entertainment? The answer is a qualified *maybe*. "Now that American society routinely forgives divorce, adultery, alcoholism, even criminal acts (think Oliver North or Marion Barry, for example), has gay porn become the latest taboo of polite society to become normalized?" Eric Gutierrez asked in *OUT*. "The short answer, as former physical education teacher and coach Jeffrey Dion Bruton can tell you, is, not really. Also known as porn star Ty Fox, the Virginia middle school teacher lost his teaching credentials and his job over his X-rated moonlighting. But Bruton's story is no longer the only possible future for porn actors who go legit. Depending on the field they choose and how they spin their past, a triple-X resume is no longer the kiss of death for an A-plus career. Not surprisingly, the apparent rules for evading or even building on a porn background resemble the rules for achieving mainstream success as a gay entertainer: 1) Pick a field that's relatively immune to puritan morality – music is excellent, acting variable; highly skilled behind-the-scenes professions are good, supervising kids not. 2) Pick a place where homosexuality is more generally accepted – sinful cities are great, Virginia not. And 3) Always be one step ahead of your press – if you're open about your past (or at least don't try to hide from it), people are less likely to use it against you."

Gutierrez reports that one young man determined to break some barriers is Adam Wilde, Gay Erotic Video Award winner in 1996 as Best Bottom, who has a 3.5 GPA at Ohio State University, where he's pursuing a master's degree and his dream of becoming a high school or college coach and PE teacher. "Insisting he's unfazed by Ty Fox's experience, Wilde's withholding his real name from print is his sole concession for the sake of his future career."

"I don't worry about it at all," Wilde claims. "Having been in the military, I know how to separate my professional from my personal life. I know what's appropriate around high school kids and what society accepts. If someone wants to be evil and get me fired, I'll deal with it then. That's why there's a legal system, to fight discrimination, and I'm one of those types who would sue if I was fired for no other reason than having been a porn star."

"In America more than any other nation, you are what you do, and you can always expect someone to ask or find out about it," Gutierrez asserts. "But maybe Americans are starting to grow up when it comes to distinguishing between personal or past behavior and professional performance. The people we've made our presidents and our movie stars say a lot on that count. And the post-porn success stories believe that now that they have their foot in the door to respectability it won't ever be entirely shut again."

Porn legend Brett Winters wants to be a singer. "I've been working on my music for two years. Popular music, like pop. I also have some ballads I've written and a couple of dance songs. Right now I'm in the process of finishing my demo. The next step will be performing live." One of Brett's pluses is that he's easy-going and he doesn't let us porn past bother him. He just has a good time. "I can pretty much work with anyone. Anytime I do a movie with Gino Colbert, it's good. He's the greatest. And Max Grand ...For a while I was kind of goo-goo on him. I liked him a lot. I topped him in a video, and we warmed up beforehand. We went into another room, and he was supposed to bottom and wasn't ready for it, so we got ready. It was actually very nice. And then we dated." Yes, one of the great benefits of working in porn, you meet such hot sex partners!

If you don't aspire to a career mainstream entertainment, you have the opportunity to go behind-the-camera in porn. Ryan Block told *Manshots* that he's found a solid career through his pal Colbert: "He's a great person. He's down to earth, he doesn't play games, he doesn't lie to you. He's not like the others. You know, they sweet talk you to get you to the set, and once you're there, boom, they're like total shit. Gino is straightforward and honest. He has his style, and I can always tell what he likes and how he gets it. He'd make the models relax by asking them, 'What do you need? How can I help you?' Sometimes, when he's not getting what he wants, he roams about the set and you gotta let him. You gotta let him be that way. I learned a lot from him. I wish I had met him sooner. I wouldn't have been so naive about the biz. I worked as a grip for him, I've been his cameraman...which is a great honor, because he has a great cameraman. But I guess Max Ferrari wasn't around, and he knew I could shoot a bit, and he gave me the opportunity, and I loved it. Every time I work for him, I learn something new."

"Look at the number of gay professionals who've come out in the past 10 years," says West Hollywood political figure Steve Schulte, who appeared as Colt's Nick Chase in 1978-79. "Just 10 or 15 years ago, being gay was the kiss of death professionally, just like porn is thought to be today. Times have changed. Lots of people aren't so quick to typecast anyone who ever took off their clothes in front of a camera."

Another encouraging thought – not everybody pays attention. We were amused to read in Matthew Rettenmund's interview with novelist Scott Heim (of *Mysterious Skin* fame) in *Torso* that the author is into pre-AIDS porn, but he did have a "soft spot" in his heart for "one porn star...I can't remember his name. Ken Ryker, I think?"

*Ty Fox,
courtesy SX Films*

Ty Fox

"I didn't look at it as cheating. I looked at it as a job."
– Ty Fox in OUT magazine about his porn career

While Ty Fox was appearing at a Washington, D.C. club, Charles Winecoff interviewed him for *OUT* and filed this report: "He's huge and glowing like a cartoon superhero come to life," the reporter said, "but his strength failed him after the *Washington Post* article and his divorce. He fell into a deep, five-month depression."

"All I did was sleep and think about taking pills or shooting myself or hanging myself," Fox said, without self-pity. He surrendered his state teaching license and left town. "I just wanted it all to go away."

For the first time, Bruton talked about what propelled him to become Ty Fox in the first place. "I was discovered by my agent in Virginia. I was in a mall shopping and he came up to me and said that I had a good physique, a good build and a good look and handed me his business card and asked me if I was interested in doing some modeling. So I called him the next day and went and met with him. I did some still photos, like in swimsuits and G-strings, stuff like that. Some of it was for postcards, calendars and other stuff like that for gay companies, which didn't bother me at all. It escalated, and he took it one step further and asked me if I was interested in doing a jack-off video. I'd always been intrigued about it. I've always liked to be a performer. I love to perform, even though I'm kind of shy. But I enjoyed it, and I liked thinking that I am something on the TV that everyone was getting excited over. It had always been kind of a fantasy of mine."

Making his first full-sex video, "Ty Me Up," was the first time he had sex with another guy. "It didn't bug me at all. I just did whatever I normally do, and when it came time, I went to the set and did my job. It's not realistic, really. A lot of starting and stopping. But it was exciting, and exhilarating and was a lot of fun. It was a great experience and it made me want to keep going further and further into the business."

This all happened during his last six months at Georgia

Southern University in 1992 when, he says, "I had a little credit card problem"; he did "about three videos" while still a student, engaged to be married. But Bruton concedes that doing gay porn offered him a more personal gain as well: "The movies allowed me to explore that part of my life and to fulfill some of my fantasies," he says – fantasies he'd suppressed while growing up in Falls Church, Virginia. "It would have been much harder (coming out) without them."

"If Ty Fox had lived in L.A., I don't think the school board would have responded the way it did," speculated Sabin, publisher of *The Gay Video Guide*. "But in any profession dealing with children, you're asking for trouble. In regular professions it doesn't matter as much. I know mortgage bankers and realtors who are known to have done porn, and it's not a problem."

After Fox's marriage, he explained to *OUT*, "I didn't look at it as cheating. I looked at it as a job." Most of Fox's films were shot during the summer break, but Bruton would occasionally take a day off and fly to the West Coast on a Friday for what he told Melanie were weekend "modeling" assignments. Like many American men with scant emotional options open to them, Bruton had compartmentalized his life to a dangerous degree. "I guess to my wife that was cheating," he reflects in retrospect. "My mistake was being dishonest with her. But, you know, I did it for my satisfaction. I just couldn't let her in."

Actually, the video was first spotted by another teacher, Bruton now recalls. "It was a man, who was also married. So I'm like, 'What was he doing in the gay section?' I was naive. I didn't think the people I knew or worked with were the kinds who went into porn video stores and I was wrong. And here I am getting condemned for being in them, but nobody else is getting condemned for going in and watching them.

"(The media) portrayed me as being a bad person. They implied that I was a animal for doing the movies, but that's not how it was at all. They never talked about how my coworkers and students thought highly about me. Some people said that from what they knew of me, I was a great teacher, very enthusiastic and they liked me."

A year after the clash of his two lives, Bruton – who answers to either "Dion" or "Ty" – says he's on good terms with his ex-wife and happy to live close to Loudoun County to watch his year-old daughter grow up. He now considers himself "gay to bisexual" and hopes one day to return to teaching. "If I had to do it all again, I think I might try to fight back. Nothing I did broke the law. I mean, it's OK for another teacher to go in there and get videos to watch with his wife or lover or whatever, but I get blamed for being in them and having 'bad morals.' Teaching and helping kids was very important to me. It was the one job I had where I felt like I mattered as a person.

"Well, my life was turned completely upside down, and for a few months I was very suicidal. I couldn't deal with it all. The one thing that kept me motivated was finding a gym to train at. I was keeping to myself and my family pulled together to be there for me. They kept insinuating that there was nothing wrong with what I was doing. I wasn't a criminal, I did nothing illegal. They told me to keep my head up and say I didn't care. That process took me a little time."

By December, Ty was ready, making personal appearances, making "Fox Tale" for All Worlds. It had been a long wait for his fans.

"How I pined for Fox during his absence," John F. Karr admitted in the *Bay Area Reporter*. "To those of us unable to cope with the boorishness of Blue Blake, Ty Fox had been the epitome of patrician muscle. Although built like a refrigerator – neither taller, less square, or more yielding to the touch than your basic Frigidaire – Fox isn't merely big. He's also beautiful, with watery blue eyes and unblemished skin that burns from within with the warmth of the sun. His hair is Nordic blond; his eyelashes are translucent butter creme. His ample asshole hums a mystic blond tune, basking in a hairless, honeyed glow between globes of mountainous maximus. The heavy girth of his cock juts from the sleek half dome of his abdomen, with hardly a pubic hair in sight to mar the molten flow of skin down its pile-driving length. All this, and muscles, too, though it's misleading to speak of Fox's muscles in the plural, because he is a muscle, singular. One big and solid muscle. Though it's the sort of body that strikes me dumb, a friend of mine who seems impervious to majesty quibbled, 'Oh, he's so stiff.'

"'When stiff hits this big a scale,' I snapped, 'just lay it down on top of me and let it press out my wrinkles.' What I like about a body like this is its lack of doubt. Ty Fox is convincing in the extreme. His arms are armaments, his ass doesn't jiggle when poked, and each of his thighs is thicker than my entire body, and that's the reason I love him."

Karr was disappointed in "Fox's Tale" because "it undercuts Fox's salient qualities. With Dirk Yates as producer, it's nearly budget free, and with Fox himself as co-writer it's almost literacy-free, too. After all, few Phys. Ed. teachers are noted for their literary moonlighting. With Eddie Douglas directing, the video is nearly incoherent, and the videography, sets, and editing are the usual vague attempts of LA's second-string porn machine. Fox looks okay, but neither the director nor videographer expend much artistry on him. The video's story focuses on a subsidiary character, further lessening Fox's impact. And the script treats him like a dummy. It doesn't mention his double life, his deception, his amazingly naive employment combo of high school teacher slash porn star. After incredulously showing Fox lying to his wife, and calling her a bitch, it tries to portray Fox as the wronged party, an innocent bystander whose world is brought down after an unrequited fan exposes him to the press."

Karr did like the finale, however, during which "Fox beds a seductive youth named Troy Halston, an attractive combination of Christian Bale and Matthew Modine."

Fox himself liked it as well. Said he, "I worked with Troy Halston for the first time. He's a very good performer, I enjoyed working with him. I met him a year ago at the Adult Video News awards in Las Vegas. And Hodge Armstrong, Jake Cannon and I did a three-way together that was a lot of fun! Hodge is a very good actor, and a great-looking guy, and I think it went really well."

At least it went as well as Fox's scene with Derek Thomas in our favorite Fox video, "White Hot," about which *Manshots* said, "The last scene is the best of the lot. Thomas plays with his ass in a white easy chair, wearing a white jockstrap, and thus entices voyeur Ty Fox to plug his ass. (This was the last scene Fox filmed before *The Washington Post* revealed his double life as both gym teacher and porn star.) As usual, Thomas is here an insatiable bottom and Fox a tireless top. The major problem is the predictability of the sex – we've seen both men play their respective roles too many times before to get too excited by the professionalism of the coupling."

In Touch liked the scene as well, commenting, "Derek warms up by working on his own ass with his fingers. It's amazing to see the lasciviousness with which Derek licks his fingers before pushing them deep into his hungry hole. And, once Ty starts fucking him, you can tell that his ass is feeling good. Ty's cumshot is spectacular, falling like rain all over Derek's raised ass and crunched up chest and stomach."

Fox does not rule out bottoming himself at some point: "Oh yeah, I'm not excluding anything." He did stress, however, that he has never bottomed, ever. But, he adds, "If I say I'm going to do it, I'll deliver!" He said he would even consider bottoming for Jeff Stryker: "It would probably kill me, but I think I could take it!"

Jeff Stryker played Santa for Jock magazine's readers and starred in a solo video, "Santa's Cummin." He can slide down our chimney anytime!

Jeff Stryker

"My dad is where it comes from – he has a huge dick...
When I was a little kid, it used to scare me:
'Whoa, Dad, put that thing away!"
– Jeff Stryker

Miss Poubelle in *The Guide* says he doesn't usually pay much attention to the dialogue in a porn video: "It's generally of a quite mindless quality. Occasionally, it serves to advance the plot – 'Well, you're gonna have to pay for that pizza!' or 'Gosh, I sure am horny' – but by and large it is a very predictable sort of non-talk. Jeff Stryker, for example, keeps up a mechanical dirty-talk in many of his videos, of the 'Suck that dick!' 'Tighten that asshole!' variety. (But) as far as Miss Poubelle is concerned, men with dicks big enough to be citizens of many countries can talk any way they want..."

Yes, the mystique of Stryker continues, despite many problems for the superstar. During the summer, Mark Adams at *Video View* was reporting, "It seems that little Jeffy Stryker was recently incarcerated, and not just to do research for a new video. It seeems the endowed one had fathered a child. The mother retained custody of Jeffy's offspring, and this just didn't please the lad, so he kidnapped the little one." Well, we knew about that child. A couple of years ago, Jeff agreed to take Jim McClellan, from the British magazine *The Face*, on a tour of the headquarters of Stryker Productions in Hollywood (he works out of his home): "...an unassuming bungalow on a very swanky street in L.A. As soon as we arrive, Jeff insists on showing us round the warren of guyishly cluttered rooms. The things you might expect to find in a porn star's home – the kind of weird sex toys needed to stimulate a jaded sexual palate, the sad, soiled left-overs of last night's orgy – are nowhere to be seen. Instead there are telephones and TV's everywhere. In one of the bedrooms there's an arcade video game titled *Astron Belt*. In another there's a makeshift video edit suite. Across the hall is a nursery, piled high with toys for Jeff's three-year-old son, Little Joe. Out back, there's a pool and a set of weights (he works out for an hour every day.)

"At the center of the house is the living room, which is packed with kitschy stuff – two wooden horses from a merry-go-round, two mushroom dummies, a glass-topped coffee table whose base is a crouching black panther, some very bad abstract art, a life-size cardboard cut-out of Jeff doing karate (he's done an hour a day for the last eight years), a real zebra skin on the wall, a big-screen TV which plays daytime soaps continually while we're there. The stone wall is covered with flashing fairy lights. I ask Jeff if it's a deliberate design detail. He grins and says that he put them up three Christmases ago and it took so long he couldn't be bothered to take them down.

"Tanned, heavily pumped, sporting tight black jeans, white singlet and cowboy boots, Jeff looks almost too healthy. The boyish looks he had when he first started have mellowed into a kind of soap-opera handsomeness."

To McClellan Jeff revealed publicly for the first time how he came to be a father. It seems a few years ago Jeff was pursued by a woman claiming to be an actress who was "desperate" to do a movie with him. He "met" with her for about three days and then she disappeared, only to turn up a few weeks later saying she was pregnant. "At first I said it couldn't be possible. But it was premeditated."

When Little Joe was born, Stryker was there with his attorney." "It was a nightmare," Jeff says. "The mother was trying to get outrageous sums of money from me to visit the child." The paternity was proved and after a court battle that dragged on for over a year, Jeff won custody. The mother is now in a drug rehabilitation center. "He's definitely a terrorist, but I love it," Jeff says of Little Joe. "It's like the ultimate dream – having a child, but not having to deal with that crazy woman."

We could never confirm whether he went to jail or not, but anything is possible.

Further, Jeff's troubles didn't end there. As Rod Skyler in *Nightlife* reported, "An electrical fire in March gutted Jeff Stryker's office in the NoHo BofA shootout district. The star was unharmed and is back in business in a temporary office. This is the superstar's second major setback in the past year. On July 19, 1996, Stryker was rear-ended by a drunken driver. A confrontation ensued and Stryker was run over. He suffered a collapsed lung and was kept alive with a breathing tube. The driver got away."

Adams went on to report, "Meanwhile, it seems that the fire that recently destroyed Jeff Stryker's digs – but not the masters of his videos – was determined as arson. Surprise, surprise. The insurance company is refusing to pay. He may just have to appear in Ryan Idol's finale video if only to pay those mounting bills."

If not with Idol, at least with *somebody* – and, hopefully sucking dick.

"Jeff Stryker as Cocksucker. Was it good for you, too?" *Manshots* asked Alex Stone, now retired from the porn industry. "Yeah," Stone replied. "It's my claim to fame. Fun. It was the high point time. But I don't think I was the one he wanted. It just happened. It was gonna be a threeway, and it didn't happen in the movie. So, it worked out that way. But it seemed every time I got up on my knees, my dick got really hard. Cause to lie down – I don't like that position, and as soon as I got up it was tough. They cut that stuff out. Standing up, my dick was hard – anything where I was taller than him, they cut that stuff out."   So now you know.

"It was a live performance by Stryker, rather than a video, that drew a capacity crowd to the Crew Club one Saturday night early in 1997," Lou Chibbaro Jr. reported. "Several hundred men packed into the Crew Club's lower floor room, where employees had constructed a stage and elevated runway enclosed inside a five-foot high chain-link fence."

The performance lived up to all of Chibbaro's expectations, and then some. "Stryker fans, including some of those who flocked to see him at the Crew Club, say Stryker's appeal goes far beyond physical attributes. 'Anyone who says pornography is just a matter of the mechanics of the sex act has never seen Jeff Stryker,' said one patron.

"Afterward, Stryker returned to the lounge to sign autographs for nearly two hours on both paper and undergarments. Several men wearing white jockey shorts turned their backs to Stryker, leaned forward, and asked him to sign their seats. He happily obliged."

Before the performance, Chibbaro found the handsome stud sitting quietly on a sofa in a parlor off the main lounge at the

Crew Club, Washington, D.C.'s gay male gym and nudist club. With nude and towel-clad patrons peering through a glass window separating the parlor from the lounge, Stryker, dressed neatly in sweat pants and a light wind-breaker, spoke softly and deliberately about his 10-year career in porn: "I dedicated my life to it. When I do something I try to do it the best that I can. And I put my whole life into it, dedicated my life."

When asked if he considers himself gay, straight or bisexual, Stryker says, "I always leave that a mystery. I'm open to all things and I respect all people."

His explanation: "Well, it's keeping up a mystique, a suspense, holding people's interest."

As for fans who want to know whether they can ask him for a date, he says: "Well, I'm single."

Before his retirement, Hal Rockland posed for an All-Man magazine photo shoot with photographer Anneli Adolfsson

The Brothers Rockland

*"...the Rocklands were fast becoming
the Gabor Sisters of porn."
– Gossip Dottie LeFay*

We first heard that Ken Ryker had "saved" Hal and Vince Rockland from porn hell from our pal Gino Colbert, who had the great misfortune of being in the middle of making a video starring the boys and their brother Shane, who reportedly has *not* been saved. What Colbert told us was confirmed by Mickey Skee in *AVN*. During the Colbert's shoot of "Three Brothers," a groundbreaking release since it would mark the very first time in history that three biological brothers appear in the same video, a so-called street evangelist was ranting and raving outside the building (did he know what was happening inside?) and even though Colbert told the boys to stay inside, they went out anyway. The guy preached to them and followed them around relentlessly, calling them sinners. Then Ryker happened along and off they all went. Next thing you know, Ryker and the Rocklands are cleaning old paint off school buses for a church. That almost sounds like the starting off point for an intriguing sequence in a porn film, but we swear it's true.

Unfortunately, in what may very well be the Rocklands' (Hal and Vince) last appearance in porn, the brothers don't fuck each other. Originally, Southwest Management of Las Vegas announced a two-video deal with Colbert to produce and direct the Rockland brothers in "Three Brothers," and the second title was to have been called "Porn Fiction." Now, it turns out, as the old saw goes, truth really is stranger than fiction.

Gino later let us know the one who was hurt most emotionally by all this Jesus-freak business was the bottom boy in the scene with the Rocklands Three, none other than cutie Derek Cameron, who also appears in Gino's "Just Guys." Said Gino, "Derek told me he cried for days after the shoot, falling in love with both Hal and Shane. (Vince didn't seem to hit him that hard.) Then lucky Derek was able to take his mind off his misery by jetting off for Italy with Lucas Kazan to film 'Journey to Italy.'"

Earlier, porn industry gossip Dottie LeFay said that the Rocklands were fast becoming "the Gabor Sisters of porn." He was commenting about Shane's debut for producer/director Sam Abdul in "Military Issue #3," in which brother Vince also appears. "I guess you'd call Shane's role a cameo, as all he does is walk on and get blown by Derek Bishop. You've heard the phrase 'There are no small roles, only small actors?' Well, Shane Rockland certainly doesn't fall into the small actor category either temperamentally or genitally. What a honker! I know you can spot the family facial resemblance, but Dottie also insists there's another, more fascinating similarity. Am I wrong, or is there a 'Rockland cock?' And while I'm on the subject (of Rocklands, not cocks), I heard that Hal, after being pussy-whipped out of gay porn by his wife (which is one of the reasons you haven't seen him lately), is that close to being signed as a Calvin Klein model. The rumor is that CK knows about his porn background and plans to use it as a publicity tool if *(when)* Hal is 'exposed.' Well, whether or not he lands this gig, it's a cinch probably no one in the world looks better wearing Mr. Klein's undies than Hal."

Hal got his chance to exhibit just how true that statement is in an exclusive, multi-page photo spread in *All Man*. The magazine commissioned their top lensman, Anneli Adolfsson, to shoot Hal (as a fireman, no less). They heralded the spread with the headline, "Hal Is Back!" The pussy-whipped Hal was flown to Manhattan in December of 1996 and *All Man's* editor gushed, "He breezed into our offices and had friendly words and an affable personality to offer our delighted co-workers who were uniformly shocked to discover that the man wasn't only gorgeous and buffed, but he has a sweet, easy-going personality as well. More than one of our staff members could be seen shuffling through file cabinets soon thereafter, no doubt searching out a Hal Rockland video to bring home to see him in action. Thanks to his consummate professionalism, the photo shoot went on without a hitch. The concept of Hal as a hunky fireman worked even better than we'd hoped. And believe us, guys, this man can get hard faster than anyone you've ever seen before! He's a natural performer who belongs in front of the cameras."

But not in a theater, if our spy in San Francisco can be

believed. As we reported last year, this fan was disappointed when he saw Hal and Vince together: "I had seen Vince do a solo show a year and a half ago, so believe me it was Hal who I was going to see. Hal Rockland is truly, absolutely, fucking gorgeous. He has a beautiful body, a beautiful face, a beautiful ass – I wish I could say a beautiful dick right now, because I've seen it in the movies and I know it's true – but it couldn't have been more flaccid that night. The boys come out partially clad and walked around collecting tips, slowly stripping. Once naked (except for shoes and socks), they continued to stroll the crowd for 15 minutes and then exited the stage, waving goodbye. I have to give Vince his due – he tries to be friendly. He actually looks you in the eye and tries to make a little small talk over the loud music. I remember from the time before and also from a bondage type video that he made that he hates having his nipples played with – which makes me want to do it all the more. Technically it's against the rules to touch the dancer's dick, nuts or ass, but people sneak a grope here and there and the place basically leaves it up to the dancer's discretion. If they have a problem with having their nipples played with they do indeed have a problem since the majority will probably go for them. So it was fun to get a rise out of him in this way.

"But I don't think Vince's dick showed a single sign of life either. Both boys were yanking and yanking on totally soft dicks. I guess there's a lot to think about – performance anxiety, being groped by strangers, the exhibitionism complex – but, hell, I always try to make the dancer comfortable about being naked. I wear running shorts with the sides totally ripped up to the waistband so that I can have my dick and nuts out completely. I've been grabbed by many a Campus Meatpacker in my day. I guess I just figure that if they are going to sign on, take the money and say they'll do it, then they should at least be into it and not act totally aloof and bored.

"At this live show, consummate top Hal was much busier putting his ass in the audience members' faces than his dick. Maybe he felt bad about his limpness. I don't know if his ass is shaved but it appeared to be beautifully hairless and it has a unbelievably gorgeous complexion. Full and fleshy but not starting to show those little flabby creases like Vince's ass. Hal an ass that gorgeous not being used to its full potential.

"I hung around for the next show hoping that this time we would see hard dick, maybe even jism fly. But I was wrong. They had the same boring, aloof look on their faces and the same limp dicks.

"For the second show, I did notice Hal's hair. It was great too. Real long bangs down to his eyes. Jesus, if he needed someone to help get that dick hard a few minutes before the show there would be about 100 volunteers. It makes me think of Whoopi Goldberg's comment at the Oscars about the parade of models: 'Jesus, these people are getting $500 an hour and they still look pissed off!'"

So far, it appears Shane, for his part, is hardly pissed off about being in gay porn. For a ripe view Shane, don't miss "Sure Thing," " a loose montage of unconnected sex scenes starring a cast of attractive white twentysomething males. (How unusual!)," Real Men reported in *HX*. "It features Shane Rockland (brother of Hal and Vince), who, by the way, is hung like a fire hose. 'Sure Thing' delivers raw sex with no bullshit and no plot worth mentioning. These guys do it in the dorm, on the stairs, in the garage and even in a doctor's office. And the best part is, they hardly utter a word!"

Although certainly not as beautiful as his brothers, Shane definitely has a cock to die for and a special rough trade appeal. In a recent issue of *Advocate Men*, Shane revealed he packs 9 1/4 inches. Brother Vince interjected, "And, baby, it's loaded." We'd have to agree, and for foreskin fanciers, Shane's is a real treat. Says Shane, "A lot of people are obsessed with foreskin, and I've never understood it. I've had it since I was a kid, so I guess it's not a novelty to me anymore." Novelty or not, Shane let it be known that he loves stroking his nearly ten-inch long, uncut meat: "I love masturbating. I get a kick out of it because you don't have to worry about pleasing your partner. I guess I'm a little bit selfish in that regard. I like to blow my load and get on with my life."

Adam Hart always delights his many fans with a good feel.

Adam Hart

*"Trust me, that boy likes his vittles.
No wonder he's the size of the Statue of Liberty."*
– Gossip Jack Francis about Adam Hart

In his review of Ronnie Larsen's documentary "Shooting Porn," Elloitt Stein in the *Village Voice* seems surprised that heterosexual men do gay porn. "An interesting polemic erupts briefly about 'gay-for-pay' performers. Apparently some of the biggest queer porn stars are heterosexual. But just how het can they be?" He quoted Gino Colbert's line in the movie, 'The straight guys do the best cock sucking.'"

For proof of that statement, rent Adam Hart in "Hart Attack," and watch him devour the smooth young blond Kris Moss's very pleasant penis. This, of course, as prelude to his fucking the kid's ass, of course, always proof as to who is the real man! *Skinflicks* agreed, saying the noteworthy highlights of the video, Adam's first for his new company, was the performer going down on Kris and finger-fucking himself.

And Hart can't seem to get enough queer cock. Gossip maven Jack Francis at *The Advocate Classifieds* was "intrigued and horrified all at once" by Chi Chi LaRue's invitation to play a sleazy agent in "Hardcore," the filmed in New York release for All Worlds: "It didn't help any when Jordan Young, the author of the script for and not incidentally, one of its stars, called to emphasize the dire need for me to accept this plum offer. Only I, Jack Francis, could do justice to the role of the embittered, sleazy, alcoholic porn agent whose star client, played by the bodacious (but unfortunately straight) Adam Hart wanted to leave the business. Huh. Sleazy? Alcoholic? Embittered? Me? I thought long and hard for about 36 seconds..."

Typically, the hotel in New York got the merry band's reservations screwed up but eventually Jack got to his room. "Eventually our band of not-so-merry travelers was joined by star Adam Hart, followed soon thereafter by genius cinematographer Bruce Cam and lighting whiz Brian Mills. By the time ultrasexy Cliff Parker sauntered into our midst, things had gotten fairly well sorted out, so we repaired to our respective rooms, all of us clustered together on the third floor. My room was next to Adam's, so I was privy to a lot of banging and slamming and swearing as I unpacked. Great, I thought. One of those high-strung, temperamental straight boys, bursting with 'tude. Feh!

"After I heard Adam stomp out of his room (he's a big 'un, you know), I crept down to the room Chi Chi and Jordan were sharing and proceeded to alarm the director over what I perceived to be the state of our star's nerves. 'He's gonna be trouble,' I predicted. 'I don't know about him.'

"Well as a matter of fact, I didn't know about him. Adam showed up at Chi Chi's room moments later, exasperated but hardly in a rage, explaining that he'd been unsuccessful at using the telephone in his room. Since I had already had several such misadventures myself trying in vain to call both my boyfriend in Los Angeles and my brother in New York, I could vouch for the screwed-up nature of the telecommunications system...

At dinner, Adam ordered a steak and Jack watched in awe "as he devoured a meal fit for the Tasmanian devil, awe that turned to shock when, in a deli immediately after dinner as we bought sodas and nibbly things (no room service, no ice machine, no nuttin' in our hotel), Adam turned to the counter person and ordered a mountainous pastrami sandwich. Unless you've eaten in a New York deli you really don't know what I mean. Trust me, that boy likes his vittles. No wonder he's the size of the Statue of Liberty. Chi Chi read his beads about the amount of food he was consuming (after all LaRue was footing the bill), but Adam just chuckled good-naturedly. Even when we all started to mock him, he just laughed. I began to think of him as the Pauly Shore of porn. I was falling in love. Hell, I needed to. You know, for my character's motivation." As the shooting of the video began, Jack lost his heart completely. "I couldn't help being transfixed by Adam's natural beauty and aw-shucks charm. Especially when that charm started snaking out of the leg of his red silk boxers and pointing straight at my face. At my mouth, it seemed to me. I was sweating buckets." Later, in a very crowded minivan, going to dinner, Jack was sitting next to Hart. "I turned to him and said, 'You know, I expected to hate you.' He just burst out laughing, and I thought what a lucky bastard am to do what I do.

"The next day I was leaving, but not till that evening, so I hung out on the set watching Jordan and Adam have sex. Golly, what a waste of my day. I must be sick or something. I particularly enjoyed watching Adam jack off over porn magazines – you know, things like *Hustler* and *Cherry* – with his butt facing me as he...worked. The thoughts I had! I confess to feeling a touch of resentment as I watched and listened to Jordan slurping on Adam's big piece o' meat, almost as much resentment as I felt because Jim Buck, another of the video's stars, wouldn't be arriving till after my departure. And that I'd be missing out on the filming of all the big sex scenes where Cliff Parker would top Jim Buck and where all manner of unspeakable acts of perversion would take place with any number of delectable, willing, eager-to-please, and massively hung young porn stars..."

Back when Adam Hart was just a John Travis/Studio 2000 contract player (four big videos) we got to know him a bit, especially when we photographed his Florida-based dance troupe for a story in *Encounter* magazine. Adam impressed us, but on video he just doesn't exude the same heat he does in the flesh.

An exception is the scene contained in one of his own Hart Productions releases, "Deep Desires," and it features Hart all by himself. This scene provides us an opportunity to dwell on that miraculous member, so hard and playful in the finale.

"There's a joke about straight men that goes: add alcohol and you have an instant bisexual," commented Jordan Day in *Stars* magazine. "The guys in 'Deep Desires' don't drink but they are able to get a little heavenly help from angel Adam Hart. In this video, Hart swoops down upon unsuspecting heterosexuals and convincves them sexual fufillment is theirs if they just try turning on to each other. Your ability to suspend belief is really tested in this video (to think any of these guys is straight).

"...Hart, who also directed, finally makes himself visible, unwinding from a tough day of converting straight men by beating off in a bathtub..." But not before teasing us unmercifully with that heavenly hard-on!

*Johan Paulik loving Ion Davidov
in George Duroy's foreskin-feast "Frisky Summer"*

A FEAST OF FORESKIN

The recent popularity of the videos from Eastern Europe by masters such as Kristen Bjorn and George Duroy (through Falcon and his own Bel Ami company), as well as assorted books and calendars featuring the stars of these technically superior sexfests, has sparked new interest in the fetish for foreskin. Men of Odyssey traveled overseas for the first gay adult video shot in the countryside of Northern and Central Italy. The only cast member being shipped across the seas was the hunky, blue-eyed blond Derek Cameron. Mark Adams in *Video View* commented, "The story, like we care, is about an American art student who searches the countryside looking for models and yadda – yadda."

"Romance is what we're shooting for," says director Lucas Kazan, himself a native Italian who came to the U.S. six years ago. "We wanted to taken advantage of Americans' fascination with uncut penises, and we looked forward to introducing Cameron to 'the wonders of foreskin.'"

Adams commented, "Kazan found the Italians were a lot like the Bel Ami models - totally unaware of their sexuality and think of themselves as straight, but just love to suck cock. I couldn't make this stuff up if I tried."

"I've had sex with over one thousand men in my life," the writer Tumbleweed admitted in *The Lavender Reader*. "I've cruised guys all over the world, and that's how I discovered my prime fetish. See, the sex doesn't vary that much from place to place except for one thing: foreskin.

"I love foreskin, the feel and taste and smell of what's under the hood. To me, prepuce makes the man. It's an added erotic turn-on. Strange, that a piece of skin the size of an eyelid makes so much difference. But imagine if eyelids, or lips, were cut off at birth. Then some of us might get an erotic attachment for those few fortunates left with uncut lips or 'lace curtain' eyelids.

"Getting fucked by someone with a foreskin is an altogether different experience. No friction. The dick inside you slides in and out of its own skin, not chafing the inside of your rectum. Soft, unobtrusive, almost there, yet not. Of course, condoms changed all of that, now it's latex in your butt, one way or the other, and there's not really much difference, the latex rubs against the inside. But, I get a secret pleasure, anyway, just knowing that I'm getting fucked with an uncut dick."

In "Forced Service," Sticky Remote in *HX* loved the scene with Anthony Gallo, who "sports a fine Italian sausage if ever there was one," working over Billy Dare, who together deliver the three best moments: Dare sucking and chewing on Gallo's foreskin; Gallo's prepping of Dare's asshole with his tongue and fingers; and the beautiful sight of Gallo's big fat cock stretching and pounding Dare's pretty-boy butt."

Gallo was also properly showcased in the final vignette of "Toolbox," where director Wash West's genius really shows, *In Touch* claimed: "Lumberjack Anthony Gallo pulls his truck over to pick up a hunky jogger, Kurt Stefano. In the middle of their conversation, they're transferred into a cheesy old porno from the seventies. The film quality changes, and they're suddenly clad in vintage clothing. The scene quickly turns nasty and highly stylized as the two of them fuck right out in the open like they used to do in the old days. Edited by Dan-o-rama, the scene nostalgically simulates porno that's been done on film. It even includes occasional flaws and breaks in the celluloid, becoming an unbelievable tribute to the pornos of the past."

One of the most popular foreskinned studs is Max Grand. One fan in Ohio rates him as the best of the best! Max was the best thing about a high-budget Chi Chi LaRue epic, "Hung Riders II," from Catalina featuring most of LaRue's resident stock company, including that screenwriter/actor/bestboy/grip and god-knows-what-else Jordan Young, Chris Green, Sharon Kane, Mr. Ed (as Trigger) and even Chi Chi him/herself, all in non-sexual roles. It doesn't hurt to rent the original "Hung Riders" (a campy porn parody of a Hollywood western) to refresh your memory, but to spare you that, here's a recap provided by Rick & Dave at *Frontiers* magazine: "The town drunk is able to get the local Indian to reveal the location of the gold. But not before all the men in town have sex with each other. Somehow the stranger finds out where the gold is and starts to make off with it. He is stopped by Daryl Brock and Jake Tanner. Before they can get out of town they are ambushed by a 'beautiful, petite and kindhearted little filly (Chi

Chi),' who steals away with the gold."

In the sequel, Deputy Drew Andrews has been left in charge since the sheriff has run off with the stranger who started all the commotion. Drew is organizing a posse to track down Miss Clitty (Chi Chi). Somehow, the "plot" leads us to a jailhouse, a favorite porn location (many horny men there!), where we find Max Grand behind bars, playing harmonica like he's never played before.

"In fact," joke Rick & Dave, "we're SURE he's never played before. Max hints to Deputy Anthony Mengetti that he may know where Miss Clitty is. Anthony wants the gold as badly as anyone else in the town and is willing to do anything to get it – even suck off a prisoner. And that's exactly what he does. To be fair, Max also dives onto Anthony's cock and eats Anthony's butt before humping him like a wild stallion. Max explodes passionately and so does Anthony, but we could have done without the Godzilla-movie-style sex-groans that didn't match the movements of Anthony's mouth. Afterward, Max refuses to turn over on Miss Clitty." No Chad Connors that Max!

Then we cut to Miss Clitty and her shockingly stereotypical Chinese manservant Hip Swing (played by Young). Miss Clitty is upset because her horse just keeled over and she has to make it to the border by sundown. So Jordan takes over for the horse and carries Miss Clitty on his own back. We can imagine Jordan needed to see his chiropractor after this filming. He would have been FAR better off bottoming for Max! Indeed, anybody would – and that includes many a porn star. For instance, when Jamoo (who is also uncut, you know) asked Bryan Kidd ("Law of Desire" from Minotaur) who his favorite co-star was, Kidd replied, "That's a tough one, but I'd have to say Max Grand. He's really attractive and has a great dick. And he's uncut. I like big uncut dicks, like Max Grand's and Blue Blake's. They just feel good in my butt. An uncut dick feels better in my butt." Enough said!

They can't get enough of each other and we can't get enough of them: Lukas and Johan, courtesy of Bel Ami

Lukas Ridgeston and Johan Paulik

"Bisexuals, I've come to realize as an adult, are troublesome because they can leave you for twice as many people."
– Frank DeCaro in "A Boy Named Phyliss"

A reader of the porn film review *Manshots* wrote them asking for help: "Please help me! I am so in lust with a porn star. I am counting on you to put me in touch with him. Enclosed you will find an envelope. Inside that envelope is a letter to the object of my wet dreams! His name is Johan Paulik. I pray you will forward my letter to him. Great googly noogly! Ever since I purchased *Frisky Summer*, Johan has been in my every fantasy. Some will disagree, but in my opinion, he has surpassed even Lukas Ridgeston as Bel Ami's top model. Perfect body, perfect face, perfect dick, and oh, what an ass! The stuff dreams are made of. Signed, Heartsick in Harrisburg."

Take heart, Harrisburg, you have a great deal of company, not only in the U.S. but in the U.K. and most of the free world we would imagine. Johan Paulik has become the hottest international "youthful" property in porn since, well, since Lukas Ridgeston.

A poll in London's *Gay Times* showed Johan come in a respectable number two to Hollywood's own Oscar-nominated heartthrob Leonardo DiCaprio in the "young but legal category" of gay icon. Last year, in an interview in London's *Vulcan* magazine, Mike Esser of Pride Video was quoted as saying that all you had to do was put Johan on the boxcover and you were assured of an instant best-seller.

In June, the German company known for the best nude male photography, Bruno-Gmunder, released *Euros 8*, a book of nothing but photos of Johan. (Later in the year, the company released a book of nothing but photos of Lukas, to even the score we would guess.)

Still, some fans were fuming. A *Manshots* reader in the wilds of New Jersey said that after reading Jerry Douglas' interview with Johan, all he had to say was "Is he kidding?"

Said the reader, "What is it with all these gay porn stars,

much less with movie stars? Why is it that they must so fervently hide their gayness that they continually lie in interviews about their sexual preferences? I've seen Johan Paulik in a couple of George Duroy's films, and I must say that I have never seen a porn star who seemed to more enjoy what he was doing in a scene than Johan. The expression on his face when he performs is one of absolute joy and happiness at what he is doing, not nearly the expression of someone who is acting in any way. Never have I seen someone who seemed to enjoy his work more than Johan! Never have I seen someone who knew better what to do to please another man sexually, in all ways!

"If Johan is not a real gayboy, then he must be the best actor in the world, and he should go to Hollywood to try his luck. But then we read in your interview that he says he prefers girls, doesn't really like taking it up the ass, and other statements seemingly designed to convince his family that he is really not gay, when all that can be seen in his work is that he is one of the happiest gayboys that the screen has ever seen, and seemingly enjoys being a 'bottom' as much as anyone ever has! How is it possible that this boy does not fully enjoy what he is doing? He seems to just love his work!

"And if I am right, didn't Dano Sulik say in an interview in a previous edition of your magazine that Johan was living with him and that they are lovers? And wasn't that a 'D' I saw hanging from a string around Johan's neck in the movie 'Frisky Summer?'

"Well, I just can't believe what Johan says. I must write it off as an attempt at prolecting his reputation from his family, and to the possibility that he will go to Hollywood someday and try his luck. Once again, if he is not gay, he really should go to Hollywood, because from the way he performs in his porn films, he looks gayer than a pink hairnet to me, and if he is not gay, then he is the best actor in the world."

Manshots' editors shot back: "First, the likelihood of Paulik's family ever discovering his film work is negligible, since George Duroy's films are not available in the country in which they live. Perhaps, therefore, Paulik is not trying to convince his family that he is straight half so much as he is trying to convince himself. Second, Europeans (even more than Americans) tend to make a distinction between homosexual activity and homosexual preference. He has been hired to do a job, and financial considerations being even more powerful in Europe than in the States, he has a very definite incentive to do the best job he can. Third, perhaps he is the greatest actor in the world – he has a theatrical background of performing. Fourth, check the Dano Sulik interview again – he never said that he and Paulik were lovers. Besides, Sulik's real name is not Dano, and as for the 'D' pendant around his neck, 'D' is the first letter of Johan's real name. Now that we have offered all these explanations for his behavior, we would also like to add that we agree with you wholeheartedly: Johan Paulik seems as comfortable with gay sex as anyone we have ever seen perform in adult films, and we can only hope that in time he will come to terms with those impulses that obviously make him so happy onscreen."

From what we hear, Johan simply loves sex. In an interview with *Vulcan* Matthew Anders, who co-starred with Johan in "Summer, the First Time," says, "Johan is gorgeous! I don't normally go for younger guys or even guys my age, but Johan was certainly hot, and the sex didn't stop when the cameras stopped rolling. I was quite surprised that Johan, with that sweet, innocent look, liked to fuck, and he's a very good top! He's got a gorgeous dick - you know, just right. For a young guy he certainly knew what he was doing and what he wanted out of sex. It was romantic and sensual. He liked me to suck on his balls while he wanked off and came all over my face.

"And everybody on the film got to know him! Johan certainly put it around a bit. He tended to go for the older guys, but he needed to cum about three times a day to keep satisfied, so we all got a look in. The whole filming of 'Summer, The First Time' was a party - well, to be honest more of a fuck-fest than a party."

When asked who his favorite male partners were, Johan listed Lukas first, Dano Sulik second. "Because," he explained, "they are my very good friends." Johan says that it is easy to do the sex scenes with these boys and, indeed, he can do it with anybody; all he does is think of his "boyfriend." Yes, he did say *boy*-friend. He says that he likes both boys and girls, that it didn't matter to him what sex the person was. What was important was the personality.

From what we've seen, Lukas has the perfect personality to bring out the best in Johan. For proof, you need to look no further than "Lukas' Story." Johan says, "When I was filming with Lukas, Lukas was in the same mood as me. He wasn't any more reserved and shy. It was very easy to work with him, so I wouldn't say that Lukas was overly reserved with me."

Duroy said the boys met at his house. He told Douglas, "There was trouble because Lukas had troubles with his hard-on, which was sort of upsetting for all of us, because we didn't know if we were going to have that trouble on the set."

Johan added, "It's very, very rare for him to have an erection problem. He had this kind of problem only when he is sick, gets cold or something."

Johan was fucked for the first time by Lukas during the actual filming of "Lukas' Story." "Yes," Paulik explains, "because the date didn't work and we didn't have more time for preparation. So we went on with start of filming, and on the set it worked perfectly."

For Johan, the best part of the scene was when Lukas was blowing him. Johan said he always thought the best cocksucker in the world was his girlfriend, "but I was very impressed by Lukas because he did very good job too. The worst thing about Lukas sucking me was it gave me a lot of worry that I'd come too early."

Coming too early is probably what most of us would do if we were ever fortunate enough to get Lukas alone. But we can dream, can't we? Indeed, in his review of the video "Moments with Johan," Ian Bloomfield in *Vulcan* speaks for many of us when he says, "This really is for serious Johan lovers only. Personally I think Lukas Ridgeston is ten times more sexy. I hope and pray that one day I'll get a moment or two with him. Well, a man has to have a dream, doesn't he?"

Sticky Remote in *HX* reviewed the complete Lukas trilogy and commented, "These young men certainly suck and fuck with adolescent abandon. But they could use some of the professional sex-pig finesse that comes with age and experience. There's not much creative juice flowing when these boys are handed a big, fat, hard uncut dick to play with and explore. Then again, there's plenty of creamy man-juice flowing, even if it is vanilla.

"...The guys are all great-looking – handsome, smooth and naturally muscled. They're all kind of the same type, which is great if you're into that type. They don't sport designer pubic hair or steroidal water retention. What they do sport is an abundance of thick meat, tasty foreskin and prime bubble butt. We gave up trying to match the names with the bodies, but because you won't find these guys in the classified escort ads, it doesn't really matter.

"Lukas comes of sexual age by discovering that literally every other young man he knows or sees is into the joys of man-sex. *Wow!* Who would have thought this would be the *fin-de-siecle* outcome of a half-century of repressive Communism? We're moving to Bratislava!

"The erections are in a class by themselves. Not since the glory days of William Higgins have we seen so many of the young, the hung and the hard in one flick. Kudos to the 'casting director' for finding this flock.

"Genre-defining Lukas leads the way, with gusher after gusher after gusher. Many of the guys cum more than once per scene (ah, sweet youth) and not a scene ends without a chest, face, back or butt covered with creamy white jizz.

"George Duroy's camera crew really loves these boys and captures the action up close and well lit. How they stay focused when only inches away from a lip-covered shaft or an ass-stretching entry shot is a mystery to us, but it's fun to watch!"

In his review of Duroy's "Frisky Summer 2," *Manshots'* Preston Richie calls Lukas "the last great face of the Twentieth Century. With his ever-changing iridescent eyes, his smile which promises everything and delivers more, his ripely buffed body, and his endlessly erupting wang of wonder, he remains the once and future prince of most gay men's deepest, most primal dreams." Wow, we couldn't have said it better ourselves!

Richie also expressed our reaction after seeing Lukas' partner in "Frisky Summer 2," blondish newcomer Sebastian Bonnet, when he said the boy "moved to the top echelon of the Bel Ami stable" with his video. Their first encounter as an all-oral scene on the beach and Sebastian "treats Lukas to a blowjob of such deliberate force that by the time he reaches his multi-squirt, fountain-like finish, his whole body is trembling with pleasure. Seldom in the history of male erotica have two objects of such pure, unadultered beauty embraced with such simple, yet exquisite perfection." Since Lukas was last with Johan, of course.

Back at the hotel, Lukas and Sebastian (and the other two performers) are naked and in bed together and one thing leads to another. As Lukas fucks Bonnet doggie style, the other two go at it in the missionary position. The screen can hardly contain it all.

But Bonnet cannot be satisfied with just having sex with Lukas. He has to have Dano Sulik, and Dano has him in every conceivable position. Bonnet must have liked it; he comes five times during this sequence. (Note: Bonnet is also featured in Duroy's Falcon release, "Wide Open," getting his brains fucked out by cute, dark-haired Jiri Lubov. Then, showing great versatility, Bonnet fucks Jiri. This is a boy to watch!)

Robert Sumners in *Mondo Porno* thought that Lukas was cuter in his previous entries: "Bonnet and Dano are more my speed," he admitted. "The second sequence is very hot with Lukas, Sebastian, Julian Armanis and Eric Kovac kissing and sucking on the beach and then fucking in the bedroom. They still dub the sex noises, though, and that's a turn-off. While Lukas' first orgasm is surprisingly bland, his second and third more than makes up for it. Pretty fun!"

The mail order version of "Frisky Summer 2" is the one to get, of course, containing as it does the interview with Lukas and some superb footage of the making of the segment in South Portugal. As the camera rolls, we see the cast, lead by Lukas, leaving for the airport, and the van is driven by, Lukas says, "My friend Johan." We glimpse a smiling (as usual) Johan and you can't do anything but laugh that the boy whose fame has quite possibly eclipsed Lukas' is really nothing but a handy chauffeur! Remember, Johan was the one who picked up Jerry Douglas at the airport in Vienna and took him to Duroy's studio. This certainly says something about having a studio system in the porn industry. Jerry writes, "Paulik speaks very little English, but we manage to communicate clumsily throughout the trip. It is not until several days later that he, Duroy, and I settle down with the tape recorder in the upstairs studio where I have interviewed Dano Sulik the day before. Paulik is much more cautious than the laid-back Sulik, and much more thoughtful about his answers, which Duroy translates. But the twinkle never leaves his eyes."

Johan revealed to Douglas that everybody told him that he was a very sweet little kid. "When I was really small, the real trouble was they mistook me for a little girl quite often, till I was five or six. Later on, it didn't happen again. So I suppose I was good-looking – contrary to Lukas, who was fat and ugly. *(Laughs)*" As cute as he is, he would like to have a better body: "I have to go to the gym because I would like to be more muscular. I couldn't afford it while I was dancer. As far as other people, I think they like most my eyes. And I think that's funny, (but) I would like to have lot bigger dick. That's true – at least thirty centimeters, which is twelve inches."

Duroy first saw Johan, who is a dancer, among other things, when he was still working as a producer for a major theater. "I took notice of him, so later on, I needed somebody for one show to sing, 'Lollipop,' with three other boys. I needed somebody who would dance and sing it, and I remembered him from these competitions. I went there and asked him if he would like to do it. Then I was not doing porn; I was still in regular show business. That's how we met and we were in touch then, basically, all the time, and later, when I started to shoot porno, I asked him to do stills."

Johan said, "After the first photo session, he claimed that I was too thin and childlike, that I looked too young, so he couldn't shoot me. Later on, basically, George asked me about filming, about doing a solo, but I didn't want to do that much."

Finally, Johan agreed. "The primary reason, of course, was the money, but there was also curiosity of how it looks, because I'd never seen a shoot like this. So there was this state of new experience and sort of adventure in it. So that was the second reason why I did it. Same as Lukas, I didn't think about it too much. (After awhile) I was watching boys do it all the time, so it wasn't so strange to me anymore. The first person to suck my dick was either Dano Sulik or Daniel Valent, one of them, and it was on the set of 'Sauna Paradiso.' I never did it with boy before that. Since they were doing it, I was determined to do it. As they did it, I was trying to imagine how the girl would do it. He would do it the same way. (But) I was not really thinking about sensations like that. It was basically a job, and I was supposed to do the best I could. I was just thinking about how to do it so that it would look best. It was not pleasant or unpleasant – maybe a little bit awkward because it was the first time.

"The reason I like the pleasure to work with Dano is because he's employed with the company and goes on the shoots with us and comes to the office. He's closer than other boys who come to the office, because we are quite close to George, and so we would go out. But I don't think I'm closer to Dano than the other boys."

Earlier in *Manshots*, Dano spoke for himself regarding his experience with Johan. Sulik told *Manshots*, "It was marvelous place (where we filmed 'Sauna Paradiso') and I loved it. The main thing is that I met Johan there, who is my main friend and competitor in this company. So I was the one who was teaching Johan the ropes, how to do certain things. So that's why it was very good."

Duroy said, "You know, it might be the reason why Johan decided to shoot hard core, because he had seen a lot of other people were doing it, and he was just supposed to jack off in 'Sauna Paradiso.' That was the only thing he agreed to do before the shooting. After the first day's shooting, he agreed to do the rest of it. So, after the shoot, Dano taught Johan how to do the rest of it.

"So it would be easier for Johan," Dano said, "Johan would fuck me first, and second time, I would fuck Johan. Johan made it clear that he likes it as much as I do. Because we are very similar in our attitude toward sex."

Johan said he has no trouble with anal sex, but prefers to be top. When asked by Douglas what the difference between fucking a boy or a girl might be, Johan said, "The answer is very basic: one is girl, one is boy." When filming was over, Johan said he was looking for somebody to fuck him again, but Duroy said Johan was just being sarcastic: "The truth is that what caused major problem (and still does a little bit) is that Johan has some kind of trouble with his prostate, and it hurt him. So that's where the problem was, but on the other hand, from what I can see now, he's handling it very well."

About Johan's performance in "Chain Reaction," Douglas says, "Particular praise must be heaped upon the performance of Johan, who proves himself far more than a pretty face and a hard dick in the demanding role of the panicky youth, desperate to find himself, terrified that he will. As he races through his long night of self-discovery, weaving the various scenes together, his expressive face and body language reveal the instincts of a born actor. He creates one magic moment after another, but perhaps his most affecting is that instant toward the end of the film when he stands facing the barman, drops his pants, and tensely waits to experience his destiny, his soul as naked as his body. The moment, like the rest of his performance, is shattering."

Vulcan agreed, with good words for Johan: "A very sexy young lad - known to millions as the very talented Johan, or even as Daniel in 'Boy Oh Boy' - hell, it must be so hard being this busy, you even forget your name – who is having a little trouble coming to terms with his sexuality. Now, when you're that age there's no point telling someone that you just can't hurry love (but) actually I think it's more to do with the fact he hasn't had a hot and sticky boy-on-boy sex session that's the real problem.

"Johan, in my opinion, deserves an Oscar, as he plays the part of a desperate virgin so well I actually believed it... The quality of production is exceptional and takes a fresh, new, and welcome approach at a time when soft core videos were becoming boringly predictable.

"The narrative is at times a tad corny and unrealistic but the excellent music more than compensates. It's not often I say that about music on videos, which usually sounds like it's put together in a music lesson at play school. To sum up, 'Chain Reaction' is a well-made and downright ball-busting package."

As a measure of the incredible popularity of sweet-faced Johan, late in the year Pride Video in London rushed to market a compilation tape of scenes from the star's videos. In America, we would call this, "The Best of Johan," but in the U.K., it is called, simply, "Moments with Johan" and provides an interview with the star as well as outtakes from past videos never before seen. This "homage" to Johan is yet another tribute to the youth's incredible popularity. The video, which finally made it to the U.S. market last June, is a delight, featuring scenes of Johan in bed, eating a banana (oh, that boy loves to suck!), and just being a boy. Tony Claffey, executive editor of London's *QX* magazine, got to do the interview and he found sitting beside "Bel Ami's most popular stud starlet" wasn't the most relaxing position he'd ever been in. Tony says, "Every time he looked at me with those drop dead gorgeous green eyes I lost the plot and forgot what I was going to ask him. I'm not normally a chicken fancier, but there's always the exception."

Johan told Tony that he "loved" making porn. "It gets me to visit places that I'd otherwise never see and I make more money doing one film than I could earn in a month back home."

Johan said his favorite films so far were "Chain Reaction" and "Summer: The First Time," filmed in Portugal. Johan said he loves to travel and has been to New York and London. London was his "very favorite place." "I have many friends there," he said, flashing that incomparable smile. The cut on his chin from an in-line skating accident was evident in the interview and he commented that he has had "many accidents."

When asked why he thought he was popular, Johan suggested that perhaps it was his smile, which he says is "interesting," or his eyes. Well, two good points, but with this boy, it's the whole package. Mike Esser of Pride Video agrees, saying that "apart from being stunningly beautiful and having the most fabulous personality, Johan's a dream to work with. He kisses beautifully – I could watch him kiss for hours, he gets a hard-on in a second, he doesn't need much direction and he instinctively knows how to look amazing on screen. It's hard, if not impossible, to shoot him badly, which is why he's so hard to edit - every shot of him is beautiful. I've worked with some of the world's most beautiful specimens - but never with anyone as perfect as Johan Paulik."

Duroy says, "I prefer Johan now that he's filled out a bit and is more mature, he still has a lot to offer and I think that he's even more attractive than when he started, so he'll be around for some time to come."

In fact, he is listed as a "production assistant" in the credits for George Duroys' "Souvenirs" video. Knowing Johan, we would imagine his "duties" are far-ranging indeed!

Meanwhile, last July, Lukas won a Probe ("Men in Video") award for having the most seductive eyes in gay video. More to the point, "Lukas' Story 3" was voted a Probe as "The Video That Gets You Off."

Aiden Shaw, by Pierre et Gilles, on a postcard to announce Shaw's book of poetry

Aiden Shaw

*"If exploiting my big dick gets someone to listen to what I have to say, I'm willing. It's not about the fact I've done porn or been a prostitute or even written a book.
It's about saying as much as I can, being as much as I can, feeling as much as I can." – Aiden Shaw*

It took a while but at last there is a Doc Johnson replica dildo molded directly from the cock and balls of Aiden Shaw. The Brit's famed, curved manhood joins the ranks of such long-donged heroes as Kris Lord, Brad Stone, and Ken Ryker. Falcon says it is "the first member of the Realistic collection to be molded from an UNCUT penis. From the realistically retracted foreskin to the distinctive arc of the shaft, every detail of Aiden's incredible equipment has been captured."

And speaking of this incomparable dildo, Robert Sumners in *Mondo Porno* reported that on a recent venture to San Francisco, *Skinflicks* editor Gary Philipp was given the Aiden Shaw dildo as a lovely parting gift from the folks at Falcon. (Note: it makes a wonderful sexual aid or doorstop.) Having only brought carry on bags with him, Gary innocently went to the airport and put his luggage on the conveyor belt to be X-rayed. Apparently, however, the replica of the British porn star's immense member showed up on the monitor (Gary suspected perhaps a metal rod to keep the object at attention drew attention) so they requested that the bag be opened. Philipp proceeded to turn a shade of red usually only seen when one is sporting clown make-up as a woman unsheathed the sex toy from its flannel pouch. According to Philipp, she looked at it and said, 'Oh.' Then, as if wrapping a piece of delicate China, she put the dildo pack into its pouch and returned the bag to Philipp. 'She did a really good job of keeping a straight face I have to admit,' Gary adds. They don't call it the friendly skies for nothing."

You undoubtedly know Shaw best as one of the most consummate, uncut tops in the history of gay porn. One of my all-time favorite scenes finds Danny Sommers, the legendary bottom, servicing and being royally serviced by Shaw in a real barroom setting in Catalina's "Night Force." About this scene, a fan wrote, "I know it's your job to make it look like you're enjoying yourself, but when your cum spilled all over his buttocks...that was not acting!" And, of course, Aiden won considerable press, if not praise, by being the one who took flavor-of-the-month Derek Cruise's cherry in "Lovers, Tricks, and One-Night Stands." Both of these scenes can be found in Catalina's compilation tape, "The Best of Aiden Shaw."

And the studly Shaw also has done many dance gigs over the years, especially in the Miami area. But lately Shaw has branched out, becoming widely known in literary and music circles as well, thanks to the success of his first novel, "Brutal," and his band, Whatever, which released its first single in London last August.

"Brutal" is a 131-page, first-person account of London's swinging club scene. The narrator, a stud named Paul, is a hustler who we realize early on is out of control, living in a near-constant state of hallucinations brought on by addictions to drugs and drink. He takes very little pleasure from the abusive sex scenes he's dragged into, and is left trying to deal with being HIV-positive after his best friend Marcus succumbs to AIDS.

New Yorker Matthew Rettenmund, a novelist himself (his very funny "Boy Culture" is finally now available in paperback), found that the novel "not sunny," but "remarkably raw, and the ending will likely shock most readers. It's hard to believe so bleak a premise came from Shaw, who is soft-spoken, polite and quietly charming when he's not screwing someone's brains out in a video. But ultimately, Shaw hopes readers will find his challenging novel's message to be uplifting and life-affirming."

Dale Reynolds, in *Frontiers*, raved about the book: "Aiden Shaw is a prolific, if that's the word, pornstar, most often associated with the avant-garde work of the late Brad Braverman. His first novel, 'Brutal,' reads very much like a grainy-hued, black-and-white porn film from the late '60s: grotty apartments in slummy London, drug-dealing-and-taking, sex with wildly inappropriate men and women. His book is grim, indeed, but full of vivid honesty and Brit Gen X aphorisms. Paul is a hustler (or rent-boy as they more colorfully say in

Britain) who hangs in the underground club scene. He falls in love-need often, tries to care for his HIV-condition, and also to care for those worse off than he. Shaw's novel is a difficult, but ultimately inspiring, read. Shaw himself is a hooker, as bespeaks good porn modeling, and Paul is clearly a self-portrait, layered however with an understanding of his needs and failures. It's also a testament to how resilient the human body can be under the stress of LSD, speed, pot, barbies, and other colored drugs. Paul and his friends have become chemical waste disposals and yet they eventually get up (not all of them, however) and go off to do it again. That this malaise infects much of Paul's 20-something compatriots is never explored socially or psychologically, which is a pity, but the political implications are there. This is a powerful and disturbing read."

In his interview with Rettenmund, Shaw said it took about three months to get down the rough draft for his book, then about a year of thinking it over, rewriting and editing. Millivres – an English publisher – is using a distributor in the U.S.A. to circulate the book. Said he, "I was very lucky that a friend of mine showed it to that publishing house – we had the contract signed within a week." He chose the title "Brutal" because he believes this is how many of us treat ourselves as gay men: "While 'Brutal' is not autobiographical, it is based on things I have seen, heard and experienced. I think gay men spend too much time looking for sex but not enough having it."

Unlike the hustler Paul in his book, Aiden says, "I do not have an addictive personality. If anything, I suffer from too much self-restraint. But I do love extremes, within sex, with drugs, with people and lifestyle in general. I don't think gay people have addictive personalities any more than other people. Some people don't take sex addiction seriously at all. Why do you think that is? I would guess they scoff at it because they can't express themselves well."

Aiden's hustler alter ego says: "If I could live my life again, would I have been a prostitute? Would I have taken the drugs I did? Would I have had the sex I had? My answer to all of these questions is no, but that's only if I was able to keep everything I've learnt from them. Otherwise I would go through everything again."

Aiden last appeared in "Boot Black II: Spit Shine," filmed in

1995. *All-Man* commented, "Supertop Aiden Shaw and Alex Kincaid have a suck/fuckfest with some terrific foreskin work, and you gotta see Alex licking his own load off Aiden's chin!"

Currently, Shaw says he is looking for shy, sweet, button-bum, milky-white, natural, boyish, ruddy-lipped, honest-eyed, pretty puppies who like to kiss and kiss and kiss and get screwed. Says he, "No, I love these young men, but I guess they're not making films. If anyone fits this description and is interested in working with me, call Titan Media at (800) 360-7204."

Of his many partners, Shaw said that he enjoyed topping Sean Diamond, Rob Cryston and Christian Fox the most,"...but I would have enjoyed it more in private. I get on very well with Rob Cryston. He's a very sweet man. My favorite videos are 'Roll in the Hay (1994),' 'On the Mark (1993)' and 'Grease Guns (1993).'" Shaw admits to having had sex with fans: "As long as they're cool about it and don't get intimidated, it's great. But I'm not working as a prostitute at the moment."

What he *is* doing at the moment is looking for an American distributor for his new book of poetry. Aiden says, "(The photographers) Pierre and Gilles are lovely men. It's hard to know more because of the language barrier – I don't speak French. I spent a day with them in Paris at their kitsch apartment and studio and will probably do the same again soon. I am using their picture of me for my hardback edition of poetry called 'If Language at the Same Time Shapes and Distorts Our Ideas and Emotions, How Do We Communicate Love?'" Hope springs eternal. For all of us.

*Marcello Reeves starred as the "Matador"
directed by the always-interesting Michael Zen*

Marcello Reeves

"I have to admit that I was a bit nervous walking on to the set of Michael Zen's 'Matador,'" Robert Sumners said in *Mondo Porno*. "Never having met the director, I wasn't sure of what to expect. Luckily, the day's scenes were being shot at the home of Chi Chi LaRue so while the people would be new to me, the surroundings were familiar.

"I was a bit surprised when the first thing I saw, walking through the door, was Marcello Reeves humping a wig-wearing Sharon Kane on Jordan Young's bed. 'Si! Si!' she shouted with her best Spanish accent. 'Have I wandered into the wrong movie?' I wondered."

No, just a set on which the star is bisexual!

Chuck Edwards of *Stars* also visited the set and said that he had never heard of Reeves before so he was anxious to find out why this was the man they chose from the many they thought about using. "He is dream of a man. Sensitive, handsome, uncut and hung (he was naked when I met him in the dressing room), soft spoken unless excited, not very tall but rather muscular, olive skin you want to touch immediately, a bubble butt you want to take a bite out of, a penchant for perfection, a man of many languages, including Spanish needed for the film, a man you want to hug as soon as you meet him, and he will let you. I watched him rehearse his lines. The thick Spanish accent could have been a problem for the English lines but instead he carried it off so well you fall for the accent and want to hear him say more. His eyes are definitely bedroom eyes. He told me that he is bisexual but has two or three male lovers about the planet and sees them when he can. The Matador costume fit him like a condom and it showed that all important basket we love to gaze upon when we see a bull fighter. I saw a Polaroid of him in the costume and it looked like he was wearing a dildo. Once you see the Matador's cock hard and ready to penetrate you are convinced the man's meat is all his own. In fact, you will wish you had it in your mouth, your ass, your armpit and your ear for that matter."

Meanwhile, Sumners was busy on the set: "Quickly my eyes caught a familiar face - Sam Dixon, porn boy... (who) introduced me around and had soon met Zen himself who filled me in on the...er...action.

"'Matador' is the tale of a (surprise!) matador who is questioning his own sexuality. When he seeks solace in a church, the priest in the confessional tells him that he must find a virgin and then he will be happy. Of course the priest probably didn't expect Mr. Matador (Reeves) to find love with a male virgin in the form of a young artist visiting Mexico. 'I like all of my movies to have conflict at all times,' Zen explains as the boys take a breather. 'So I thought I would do a movie where each person is in love with the wrong person.' Therefore, the limo driver (Hodge Armstrong) is in love with the manservant (Eduardo) who's in love with the matador who's in love with the artist who eventually falls in love with the canvas of the matador he is painting.

"After Zen has given me the low down, it's time for Marcello to take a pee. Now this is not just any pee - it's the mother of all pees. I am shocked when he is actually able to let it flow for well over two minutes! In fact, the entire crew drops their jaws in a thunderous unison as we stare at the monitors watching it keep on going. When he's finished, I had to ask him how he does it (drinks a lot of water) and how he can pee in front of a camera when I have trouble urinating in a public rest room. 'I was prepared,' the very sweet Marcello says with his delicious accent while kicking back, wrapped in a white towel. 'Normally I'm pee shy but because I felt myself as the character in the scene, it was easier.' Wow, method acting in the porn world!"

Manshots' Ethan Clarke was another one of the lucky journalists who visited the "Matador" set. He commented, "Reeves is a true perfectionist. The discriminating nuances he brings to each scene reflect not only his acting skills, but the incredible amount of work he has done on his own. It reminds me that if people weren't dropping their clothing and fucking, this would be like being on the set of a fine Hollywood film production."

Meanwhile, back on earth, *HX* magazine's reporter visited Reeves in Manhattan. Here is their report: "He is padding around his immaculate Midtown apartment, proudly showing off the souvenirs of his career. Casually dressed in jeans and a T-shirt, the unassuming performer has made a big splash in the porn world. In the past two years, he has appeared in more than a dozen films and has steadily built a devoted following for his live shows. But his rapid rise as a screen stud was anything but planned.

"Born in Brazil, Reeves is the youngest of seven brothers and sisters. As a child, he spent his time working for his father's bakery and playing soccer. At age 18, he enlisted in the army."

"It was wonderful," says the Portuguese/Spanish actor in his still-thick accent. "That's why I'm so organized now. It is where I learned discipline."

After getting out of the service, Reeves went to college and eventually moved to Rio, where he worked as an interior designer for six years. In the summer of 1991, he came to New York City on vacation. "I never went back," he says of Brazil. "I always had a big imagination. People always said I should come to New York. It was just so exciting to be here. I called the company I worked for and said, 'I'm sorry, but I can't come back.'"

"But that was only the beginning of Reeves' journey," HX says. "He found himself in a country where he didn't know the language and had no working papers. He took a crash course in English, and within three months was speaking perfectly. He then applied for a work visa, and a friend got him a job at an art gallery as a custodian. It was there that he was spotted by a photographer who asked whether he'd ever considered modeling."

"I went to his studio, and he took some Polaroids," Reeves recalls. "Two days later, he called. He had a job for me. The next thing I knew, my picture was on the cover of a trade magazine."

"More modeling jobs followed," HX reported. Soon, Reeves decided to audition for a spot as a go-go boy at a local nightspot. He got that job, too, and started dancing four nights a week at some of New York's hottest clubs, including Palladium, Tunnel and Roxy."

"In two months, I was the busiest dancer in the city," he says, "and I was making more money than at the art gallery. At first it was strange, but then I saw other guys like me, and they were supportive and friendly."

Then the movie offers started rolling in. After turning down scripts from such major studios as Falcon and Catalina, Reeves took a fateful trip to Florida. "I was performing in South Beach," he says, "and a man introduced himself. He said that he had a movie company, and he wanted me to be in one of his movies. I thought he was joking, so I asked for a huge amount of money that I never thought he'd pay. But he said okay. I couldn't believe it! Then, I thought, Oh God, now I have to do it!"

Within a week, he was in Los Angeles shooting his film debut, "For Your Pleasure." "In my first movie, I didn't know what was going on," Reeves says, "but I just did my best. I got lucky because Karl Thomas, my scene partner, was very supportive."

The movie got a good response, and more offers came pouring in. Reeves was chosen to star in the first gay porn CD-ROM, "Men in Motion." He started doing photo layouts for major gay magazines and even appeared in *Playgirl* magazine. He also posed for the late photographer Bill Costa's best-selling calendar.

Marcello's screen appearances have been delightfully varied. In addition to his stellar casting in "Matador," he has scored big in "Hung Riders II" from Catalina, Titan's smash "Island Guardian," and "The Road Home."

Frontiers' Rick & Dave described the scene in "Hung Riders II" that should not be missed: "David Thompson has wandered into a saloon in a neighboring town. He meets Marcello Reeves at the bar. Marcello offers him a drink, but David just wants to play poker. He starts a friendly game with the town drunk (Sharon Kane in man-drag). As they play, David pulls a card out of his pocket. Marcello sees him and busts him. Marcello takes David over to the bar and makes him strip. At gunpoint Marcello makes David suck him and rim him. Marcello spits wine into David's butt and then fucks him right there on the bar. David shoots a load onto his stomach and Marcello washes David's face with his load. Marcello sends David running out of the saloon totally naked."

Even in a minor role, such as in "The Road Home," Reeves makes a lasting impression. His part was saved for last, a four-way with Todd Gibbs topping Nino Bracchi and Reeves topping Dan Brewer.

Reeves was one of major visual delights of Titan's "Island Guardian." "See the beautiful boys on the beautiful beaches," Joe Phillips said in *The Guide*. "The boys run. The boys splash in the water. The boys screw. 'Island Guardian' is, indeed, a visual treat. Titan Media wins hands down in the category of best location for an outdoor shoot. The tropical paradise in this video is spectacular. Unfortunately, for us (though perhaps fortunately for those who live here), the producers don't let us know exactly where this video was shot. In addition to the amazing scenery, 'Island Guardian' features several stunning young men for our viewing pleasure. ...Adriano Marquez and two other terrific bottoms steal the show. Rick Matthews is just a cute as he can be and delivers another excellent performance for Titan. Will Clark is simply wonderful. Even covered with mud (as he is for most of his scene), Clark is gorgeous, and the mud just confirms what we already knew. He's a sex pig."

Frontiers' Rick & Dave describe Marcello's scene: "At the waterfall, Rick Matthews drops to his knees and starts sucking on Marcello's spigot. Marcello does the same to Rick and gives Rick a bonus rim job. Then Marcello humps Rick..."

"Talk about your natives being restless," Shante Skinflix raved. "In another part of the island we find Rick Matthews and Marcello Reeves bobbing for cock. Matthews serves up some fierce, tight, pink hole so fresh that Marcello has to shove all nine fat inches of his fat hung cock up it. The friction gets so hot they have to part and go to separate rocks to beat their cocks, after which they both kiss and call it quits."

Fred Goss in *Advocate Men*, called the scene "an ode to manly beauty. Marcello Reeves and Rick Matthews have it in abundance, and their scene at the waterfall is juicy, sexy, and sensuous."

Reeves's busy work schedule leaves little time for a personal life, he says, and his career choice has made it even more difficult at times. "I'm so busy traveling that I have no time for a relationship," he says. "But when I did have a lover, he was jealous of my work. He wanted me to choose – him or my career. I said, 'This is my job.' Besides, I don't want a man supporting me. It's that whole macho thing; I like to pay my own bills, even if I have to work hard." And he has worked hard. But for now, the diminutive star is enjoying his time at home before setting out on a month-long tour. Reeves breathes a contented sigh and smiles. "I'm happy with my life," he says. "I'm saving up my money, and I'd like to open my own business. Maybe a coffee bar or restaurant. It would be hard for me to give up on the porn business now. I can't just blow it off. This is my big chance."

HOT COUPLES

It takes two to tango, they say, and when the chemistry is right, a coupling between two actors can set the screen ablaze. Think of Bogart and Bergman, Gable and Leigh, even Hanks and Banderas!

In gay porn, each year brings forth a dozen or so truly memorable pairings. Some do not even translate to the screen and we only hear about them later. Consider Steve Marks in Falcon's quickie "Face Down," co-starring with Danny Sommers and Chad Connors. Steve said later that Danny was "incredible sex," but you'd never know it from the video, wherein Danny fucks Chad while Chad sucks Steve and then Steve fucks Chad while sucking Danny, with the fucking of Danny by Marks as the finale. It's all rather lukewarm, but there are some great close-ups of the entry. Perhaps the mistake was having Connors there at all. *In Touch*: "We can't get enough of Danny Sommers and his beautiful compact body and semingly inexhaustible innocence. It amazes us that he can fuck like a wild mustang and still be as adorable as a puppy on Christmas day." *In Touch* didn't even mind Chad in "Face Down:" "That gorgeous, stocky little stud was so damn nasty, we had to use our drool as lube. Every time he shouted out, 'Fuck that ass!' we felt our lust boil and boil to the point of eruption."

During the year we were treated to many such "damn nasty" scenes. One of the hottest scenes involved newcummer Jake Cannon and Sam Dixon, who is, at this writing, in reality Jordan Young's lover. The video is Falcon's "The Player," and Dixon crowed about it in an interview with Jamoo for *Freshmen*: "He's really cute...just his look and his personality. He's got that kind of straight jock-boy attitude that's really cute."

So cute, in fact, that Sam seems to devour every inch of Cannon, first his prick, then his ass. Here we have one of the most convincing ass-eating scenes ever. Jake tells Sam to "eat my ass." It seems to be music to Sam's ears because he dives right then, then sticks his fingers in, followed by his cock. This is perfect. What we hate more than anything is a bottom boy eating out a top and then having the director cut directly to the top fucking the bottom. You want to say, Wait a second! But not in the case of Sam and Jake. So it is with HOT couples.

*The luscious Todd Stevens,
courtesy Huge Video*

*Matt Bradshaw,
courtesy Hot House Video*

Todd Stevens and Matt Bradshaw

One of our favorite scenes of all time involves Matt Bradshaw and Todd Stevens, along with sexy Kevin Wolf as an added bonus. This is what Falcon's copywriter had to say about this scene in "Renegade": "Sexy Matt Bradshaw squirms with pleasure as he wriggles his cute bubblebutt over Kevin Wolf's face, feeling the blond's talented tongue probe his tight hole. Todd Stevens groans lustfully as the velvety muscles of Matt's cocksucking throat ripple up and down his meaty rock-hard cockshaft. As Kevin shoves a fat buttplug into Matt's freshly spit-lubed hole, the asslips stretch wide to accommodate the plunging sextool. The huge and powerful intrusion turns into rhythmic pleasure as Matt fucks himself with the buttplug, sucking it deep into his hungry hole. Todd and Kevin take turns slamming their big cocks into Matt's sex-starved holes, filling him at both ends. They take on one another's sweat-glistened bodies in every combination, fucking and sucking themselves into multiple cum-drenched orgasms."

This was Bradshaw's first video and he's never been better. He brought out the best in young Stevens, and our favorite moment comes when, after many minutes of butt-plugging Bradshaw, the tables turn and Stevens slides a condom on Bradshaw's unusually bent tool and begs him, "Fuck me," and you know he means it – and gets it! Boy, does he ever, coming copiously while Bradshaw bangs away. Whew! They also lit up the screen in "Chained Desires," from Vivid. Now we anxiously await another teaming of these two sexy guys.

Meanwhile, Todd joined in on the most unforgettable sequence in "Download." Fred Goss in *The Advocate* said, "And an all-star wonderland it is, for right away Johnny Hanson espies Glenn McAllister and Todd Stevens indulging in some very juicy oral exercises as Kevin Dean, Cole Youngblood, and Marco Calles look on and abuse themselves. Things quickly progress to full-scale Falcon-flavored spicy raunch dressing, and before long Calles's asshole has played host to all present, at one point accommodating Dean and Youngblood at the same time! Calles has a big talent, no question. How he spews the copious load he tosses with Dean's big Louisville Slugger parked way up inside him is something to ponder. But while Calles's come shot is impressive, Youngblood's is truly spectacular (8 1/2 very seismic jets of jizz)."

Why Stevens is not a major star we'll never know. He's cute as can be, has a decent body by porn standards and has a cock that can only be described as luscious.

Stevens told *Manshots* he first became aware of sex when he was about five: "I remember my parents saying I'd have to take a shower or something after gym, and it just upset me so much. I don't know why, 'cause now I would love it. I don't know. I guess I was really self-conscious. I'm still self-conscious. I was sort of a normal-looking kid. I can't really explain it."

Stevens said he was molested when he was seven. It wasn't traumatic, but it definitely sort of altered his outlook. "I didn't think it was horrible, and I didn't think too much at the time. He was a pedophile, a guy in his late thirties, I guess. I used to play pipe organ in the theatre, and my parents belonged to the organ society. We'd go on Sunday mornings and play the pipe organ and putz around. And the guy that molested me used to run the theatre. So, he sort of got me alone and did the 'do you want to play a game?' routine. And then as I was doing chin-ups, my pants came down, and he sort of sucked me off. No ejaculation, but I was ejaculating by the time I was nine. I had kicked into overdrive or something. (Now I think) it would be interesting to, like, see him. I'm sure if I really wanted to, I could. I mean, it wasn't violent, it wasn't anything that was painful in any way. But looking back, I definitely wonder if it helped me or hurt me. I knew I was gay probably even before that happened. So it sort of didn't really faze me. It never was a big issue with me. When I was in high school, I knew that wasn't exactly the time to come out. So I dated, and as soon as I got into college, I met gay people. I knew that I was gay, and it was no big deal."

What *was* a big deal, to Stevens, was meeting Kurt Young. Stevens was Kurt Young's body double in the twins scene of "Flesh and Blood" and remembers Stevens, "Oh, he's gorgeous! I thought he was great to work with. He's adorable. He's one of those people who gets up in the morning and looks good. The kind you just want to douse with lighter fluid and set on fire. But he's a very nice person. We got along really well. When Jerry Douglas called me up, he said, 'It's a thankless role.' I realized that going into it, but of course, I wanted to work with Jerry because everything I had heard about him was just outstanding. And it was a thrill to me to get to work with someone who's been in the industry and putting out really good work for so long. Because, let's face it, you can be in the industry a long time and still not do really outstanding work. So, I thought, 'Well, since I'm on a roll, and since I've already had Matt Sterling and Falcon, worked with the legends, and then later on, Chi Chi and Jim Steel, this is my opportunity.' Knowing that Jerry only does one movie a year – you don't turn down something that comes along once in a lifetime.

"I thought everyone in the cast was good-looking. But that's just me. Almost everyone in that movie, like, nine-tenths were my type in one way or another.

Stevens is known for his ability at auto-fellatio. "I actually knew that I was capable of doing it when I was in high school, but when I was with my lover, it didn't really occur to me that I should actually do it. I did it when I was in high school, and when I got to college. I got drunk one time and was having phone sex with someone and just did it. The first one I did it in was 'Men Matter Most' or 'Pushing the Limit.' Then there's 'Auto-fellatio 2.' And I can be seen doing it in 'All You Can Eat,' which is the Chi Chi LaRue movie, and I did it, or came close to it, in 'Tradewinds.'

"If I'm really turned on, it's a little bit more than nine inches. I've been cast for a Doc Johnson dildo."

In Touch reviewed "Titan Men" and said it was "a new jack-off video with style, with Todd Stevens' sensuous stroking of his beautiful piece in a beautiful setting and a number of hot come shots..."

When it comes to coming, few can match Matt Bradshaw, and he can give it and take it with equal vigor. Says he, "I'm the type of person that when I do something I dive into it."

One of the hottest scenes he has done in a video, says Bradshaw, was with Kyle McKenna in Centaur Films' "Hot Cops 3," directed by Chip Daniels. "I was a police officer and Kyle was a bartender. He was totally submissive to me, calling me, 'Sir' and 'Officer.' He was a nasty, little pig bottom, and I was a butch top man who told the little boy what to do. We both got into the scene and it was genuinely hot. Sometimes I've been in scenes where I've been fucking someone and it's like fucking a piece of furniture. They just sit there and they don't even moan; the director has to remind them that they're being fucked and to enjoy themselves. But Kyle and I didn't need to be reminded! We both totally got into the roles, the role-playing, and it was very hot."

Bradshaw told Ed Karvoski, Jr. in *The Guide* that he enjoys playing "both sides," both in real life and in videos. "In Falcon's 'Ripe for Harvest,' Bradshaw and Ricky Price portrayed brothers who live on a farm and bully their young farm-hand, played by Ryan Wagner," Karvoski said. "Bradshaw recalls a scene that involved roughhousing among the three guys, a scene that summoned his acting skills to portray the terrorizing menace. 'Ryan was carrying this big pail of water, and Ricky and I were running from around the barn. We were directed to come running around the corner quietly, so that we'd surprise Ryan, then push him down in the mud. The first take we did seemed to go fine, we pushed him into the mud went flying everywhere. But then we heard, 'Cut, cut, cut!' The director, John Rutherford, looked at me and said, 'Everything was fine. Except, Matt, next time, could you run a little bit more *butch?*'"

Rutherford replayed the scene and Bradshaw was amazed when he saw himself. "There I was, creeping quietly around the corner with my hands down at my side, my fingers fanned out, and I was just kinda like *prancing!* I looked like I was patting down a tutu!" Take two: "Next time, I ran with my fists clenched, down by my side."

"There have already been a small number of pornos that give audiences a glimpse of what it's like behind the scenes of a porno shoot," *In Touch* said after visiting a taping at Hot House. "However, none of them have been as intriguing or as complete as 'Take One: Guys Like Us.' Director Steven Scarsborough combines candid footage, on the spot interviews, behind the camera hijinks and excellent pornographic filming to create a video like no other.

"The video stars Matt Bradshaw, and the director could not

have made a better choice. Matt is one of the most easy going, friendly and likable porn stars in the business. He's charismatic, charming and fun to watch whether he's naked, sucking cock, or just watering the plants. Having hung out with Matt, we've found him to be incredibly well adjusted as a porn star, and that aspect of his persona really shows as he interacts with the camera. Of course, what really matters is how he fucks, right? Well, he's an all around pro as he fucks Aaron Brandt. In this first scene, both Matt and Aaron send the VCR into meltdown, making this porno one to be remembered.

"Matt also shows up in the second sex scene with the adorable Kyle Hunter and the very sexy redhead Will Clark. After a brief candid discussion about sex and their profession, the three of them get into a hot and nasty fuckfest on and above a plush stairway."

About Bradshaw's appearance in "Take One: Guys Like Us," Jim D'Entremont said in *The Guide*, "...These models have great bodies, but their expressive faces may be their most erotic assets. The video hits the stratosphere in the second of five sequences, with Matt Bradshaw, Will Clark, and Kyle Hunter in a long, spectacular three-way in and around a stairwell. (This scene alone makes 'Take One' worth owning.)

"'Take One' is presented in artily modulated, bleached-out color. Sometimes this recalls the burnished, monochromatic early prints of John Huston's 'Reflections in a Golden Eye'; sometimes everything just looks light-struck. This cooling and distancing effect detracts from some sequences. Fortunately, the color warms up during most of the best scenes, as if heat from the performers affected the processing. During the masterfully directed Bradshaw-Clark-Hunter segment, the muted tones look just right."

In "Shooting Stars: MEN Magazine Live!" Bradshaw plays the photographer, a shutterbug who also just happens to get nude himself. Jack Francis jokes, "Now, who would we want Matt to 'photograph?' I guess I'm not revealing too much if I admit that there was no film in his camera. Hey, this is showbiz. ...I'll say this much: Matt Bradshaw was happy with our casting! And from what I witnessed, I'd say the feeling was entirely mutual."

"Aside from the luxurious homes and fast cars, the most

attractive scenery in 'Dynastud 3' is Clay Maverick," raved *HX*'s Real Men. "The black-haired, blue-eyed, baby-faced stud muffin plays it cool in his debut porn performance. Thankfully, the plot is so thin that it falls apart, leaving the cast to do what it does best – fuck! Everyone gets a piece of the action, even the chauffeurs. International muscleman Alexi Ferrera and his all-American counterpart Matt Bradshaw will surely keep you hard with their filthy-rich antics. An abundance of group sex and one-on-one WASP action guarantees a good time for Circuit queens, while the rest of you might actually be inspired to visit West Hollywood for a taste of the good life."

About "Matador's" orgy/gang bang scene, Chuck Edwards in *STARS* said, "The scene ties into the film story rather nicely and it is a hot piece of the film. The devils actually have little horns but their cocks are nowhere near little. I didn't know until the make-up came off that one of the devils was Matthew Bradshaw. I should have known when I saw that monstrous cock stretch from one side of the villa to the other. So often production companies dread the thought of there being an orgy because it means more than a couple of guys having to cum. Not a problem in this film. They all cum buckets but I shall not spoil it for you."

Bradshaw certainly didn't spoil it for his cock-hungry fans when he appeared at New York's Champs bar recently. According to *Torso* magazine's spy, Matt "wowed" the crowd by working his dick from under baggy overalls, "then stripped naked to flash his killer ass and stroke his tall tool to full attention. Carried away by the response, Matt shocked everyone in attendance (including himself) by losing control and shooting a load, right there in public, a wall of video screens behind him showing every spurt. His fans went wild and the management was moved to put 'slippery when wet' signs all around the stage."

Bradshaw sat down with Jordan Young for an interview in *Skinflicks* and said that he didn't expect making porn would be a lot of fun. "It's not like being put in a room with a *really* hot guy and having hot *sex*. I didn't *expect* that. I think a lot might *dream* of that but I knew it would be work. I guess it is a lot harder than I expected. The mental capacity to maintain and control your thoughts is the hardest part.

"I had a great time with Buck Phillips. We didn't hang around on the down time, but then there wasn't a lot of it anyway. Just lots of sex. As far as techniques go, no, I don't have any. I just try to keep my mind focused on what's going on. He's very quiet. Very reserved but very sweet. When it came time to do business, he did it. He didn't sit around and complain, 'Oh, my God it's been two years since I've been fucked. It's gonna hurt!' Quit thinking that! Your hole's just gonna get tighter and tighter if you think that. I mean, if you know you're gonna get fucked today, be prepared for it mentally and physically. Buck wasn't like that. He didn't complain. So that's what's good about him. I also enjoyed working with Adriano Marquez, just because he's so hot. Sometimes I wanna be a pig bottom. (As in my first film 'The Renegade' from Falcon and VCA's 'Dynastud 3.') I'd be a pig bottom for Ken Ryker any day! But I'd like to fuck Dax Kelly. He's kind of hot and I think it would be fun. He's a bottom and I work mostly as a top. I mean I have bottomed but I prefer to top. I think he'd be a good bottom. I haven't seen any of his work but I've met him.

"I like the doggy position best. I like a nice beautiful round butt pointed up at me. I know a lot of bottoms though who like to be on their back so they can look at you but, I'm like what if I don't want to look at you? Turn over and stick your butt in the air!

"I like smooth skin. Nice features. A pretty dick. Versatile men in shape not someone pumped out on steroids or tweaked out of their mind. Definitely no attitude. Attitude encompasses a lot. Having a sensuality about them. I like someone who's confident and aggressive. Someone who will play with my nipples and talk dirty to me. That's what I love!" The line forms at the right, guys. No pushing or shoving, please.

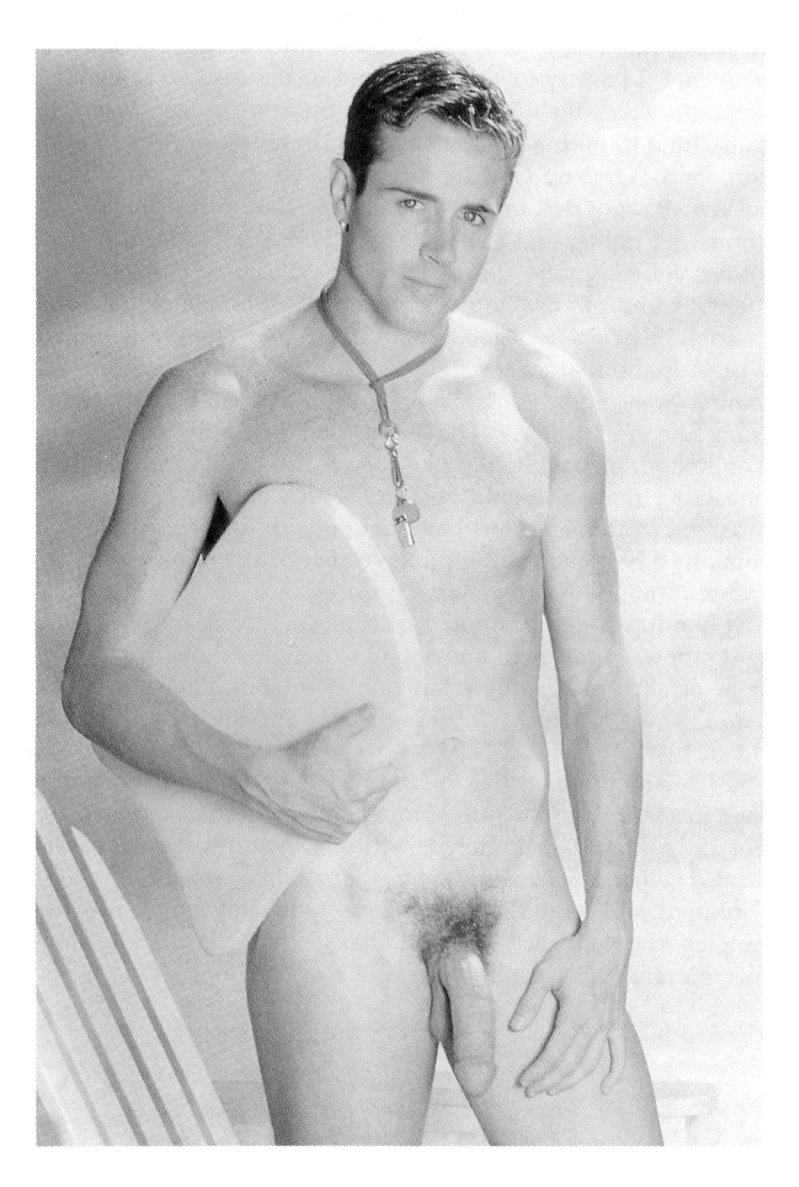

*Kurt Young,
courtesy Studio 1435*

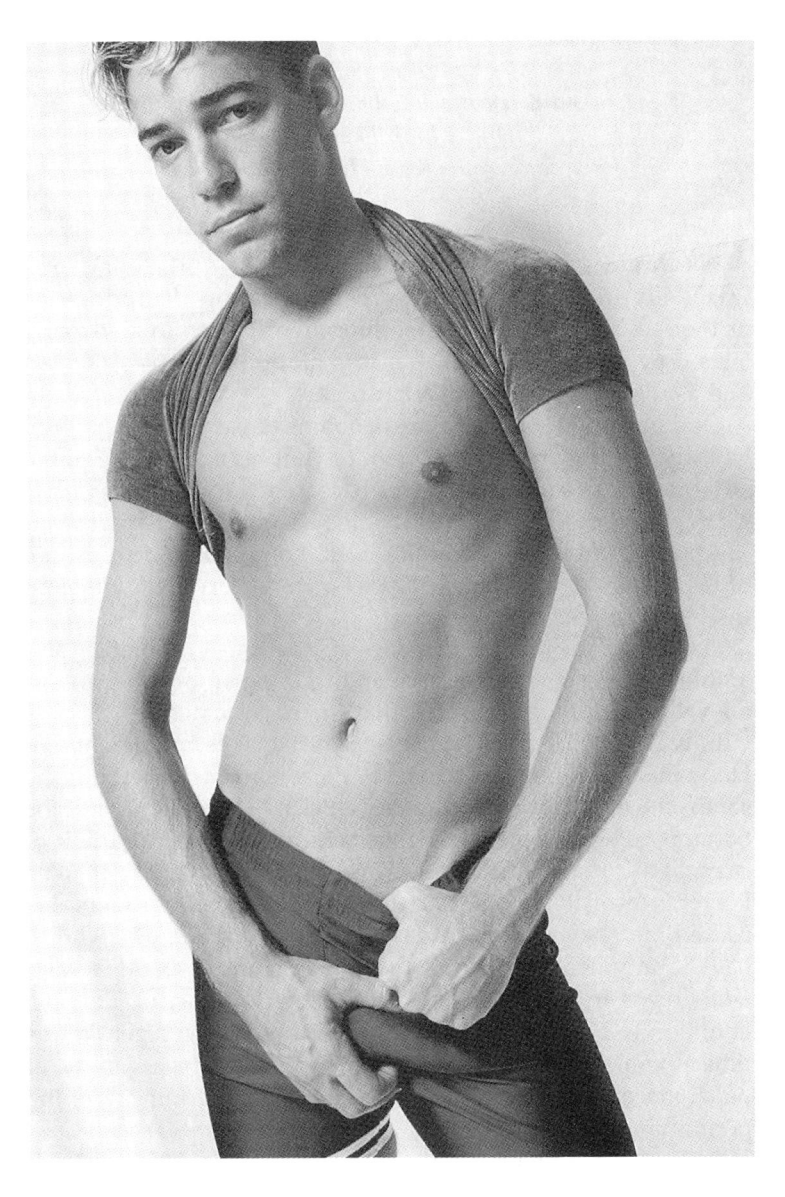

K.C. Hart,
coverboy for Freshmen, courtesy Matson Jones

Kurt Young and K.C. Hart

"I get called a tease a lot, because I'm not a bottom but I look like one."
– K.C. Hart

We thrilled to the teaming of K. C. Hart, Kurt Young, and Dax Kelly in "Extreme Measures" from Falcon, featuring one of the few DP's (double penetration) we've seen in a while. It lasts only a few moments, but it is glorious because it's Hart and Young. What a team! What cocks!

Orange County native Hart is one of those performers who looks better in person than on video, but his cock is one of the current wonders of porn, always hard, ready to afford us many, many views of it as it penetrates the assholes of his partners.

And Hart's former roommate Kurt Young, of course, is one of today's great beauties of porn who won every award in sight in 1997.

Hart is, *Playguy* says, "one of the most adorable and ambitious young performers working in porn today. (He has) a level-headed, healthy spirit that's hard to match."

In real life, Hart says he is bisexual. He likes his men butch. He wants a "workout partner," not a romance. Apparently he saves the relationship stuff for chicks. So you know if he bottoms, it's got to be for a good reason, and we can think of none better than Jeff Palmer. They appeared together in "The Player," for Falcon, and Hart says: "He's really rough! He fucked me six ways to Sunday!" We know! We know! And to have it on video – wow! As John Erich in *Advocate Men* said, "Hart turns in his usual delectable blow job, paying devoted attention to Palmer's balls and ass, and Jeff is even gentle this time – well, *gentler*. Palmer then fucks Hart in a variety of positions on his couch, giving another outstanding topping performance."

In Touch commented, "Naturally, K.C. is in love, and Jeff takes complete advantage of K.C.'s feelings. Jeff starts off gently, but he gets increasingly rougher as he makes K.C. work his body over with his mouth and tongue. By the time Jeff gets his hot cock up K.C.'s beautiful asshole, K.C. is totally convinced that this man is 'The One!' But, we all know better than that, don't we, boys? Once fountains of cum gush out from their cocks, Jeff does exactly what we expect him to do, being of course, the utter pig that he is."

Hart also bottomed for Chad Donovan in "Hot Cops 3" from Centaur: "I don't know why but when they ask me to bottom it's always with these guys with huge, huge dicks! But I got paid, so I guess I can't complain."

Hart's admiration for Donovan didn't go unnoticed by critics the world over. "Wow!" John Erich said in *Advocate Men*. "'Hot Cops 3' is one rowdy, ribald ripsnorter of a fuck flick. Daniels has outdone himself in terms of sex-piggishness. Just the fucks, ma'am, and who says crime doesn't spray? With four hot films under his belt (including one Hot Firemen), Daniels is fast establishing some trademarks: long, athletic fuck scenes, lots of ass play; and packed-butt come shots. This 110-minute opus, which follows the adventures of Officer Steve O'Donnell and his new partner, Matt Bradshaw, has all that and plenty more. We initially join the cock-hungry crusaders on a routine domestic-violence call, where they find lovers K.C. Hart and Chad Donovan brawling over Hart's drug use and promiscuity. The combatants are separated for questioning, and Hart tells O'Donnell that he can't help his whoredom, he's just so horny, and do you want a demonstration? You got it, sarge, in the form of a savory blow job. Meanwhile, Donovan convinces Bradshaw that he and Hart can work things out, and the cops move along. The squabbling couple then make up in one of the most frantic lovemaking scenes seen on video in a long while. If there was no genuine chemistry here, then give these guys Oscars, because this scene is wild."

Hart's own masterful topping technique has been described by J. Keil in *Mandate* as "fucking like a bunny-rabbit, punching holes left and right with quick little thrusts that set my teeth on edge." Hart says that he has to do that in videos because the sex has to be visually demonstrative, but when he's fucking in real life, he has more energy yet he moves more slowly and with greater care. Just so you know. For a good example of Hart's visually thrilling fucking, you need look no further than "Malibu Beach Hunks," during which Hart comes, then fucks Steve O'Donnell and comes again.

In "Showboys," written, directed and starring David Thompson, Hart was again paired with Young and in this one K.C. bottoms for his pal! *In Touch* commented, "K.C. looks really hot as his big cock explodes while Kurt continues to pump his ass. Then, Kurt's beautiful dick shoots loads of spunk all over K.C.'s eager face. Seems untoppable, doesn't it? Well, it does get topped in the next scene when David (as director) gives Kurt, Adam and Dino the break they've been looking for. The sex immediately begins with David's mouth being fed two cocks while another mouth works on his prick. From there, David gets to have fun with Kurt while Dino and Adam fuck for his entertainment, and eventually, Kurt plows his award-winning cock into David's hot ass. Clearly, in this scene, David is the one having all the fun."

The Guide also raved: "Showboys Entertainment has made an exceptional little tribute to gay male strippers. They dance, they prance, and they service the customers. A little reality thrown in makes this a gritty drama that lets you know what a dancer's life in the business can be like. No overly beefed physiques molded at the gym the boys in this film are *au naturel* types in their original wrapping. Very hot."

And speaking of hot, there is another Hart favorite, Adam Wilde. In their review of Jocks' "Hardline," *Manshots* says, "...Ever-popular Wilde wants to seduce the pizza boy (K.C. Hart) and does so by lying in bed naked with a sizable buttplug up his asshole. The boyish and versatile Hart does indeed make a delivery, but the action is both predictable and static. The buttplug bit goes on for an eternity, followed by Wilde sucking Hart and Hart topping Wilde. Long before Hart blasts his batter on Wilde's face, one is more likely than not to be reaching for the fast forward button."

"We love a man in a uniform," gushed Sticky Remote in *HX*. "And we love men having sex in and out of their uniforms even more!" Sticky was reviewing three Centaur Films: "Forced Service," "Raw Recruits" and "Marine Crucible," and had high praise of Hart. "With a few exceptions, most of those uniforms are camouflage fatigues and T-shirts, which are referred to in one scene as 'utility blouses!' We don't know how much of the military jargon is realistic, never having served personally (well, not in the military sense), but we were impressed that K.C. Hart actually wrote some of it (well, not that impressed), expanding his career horizons beyond porn (well beyond, as 'Forced Service' reveals).

"Kudos to the director for letting us hear all of the action, though we're hardly dealing with the most expressive guys in the service here. Horse-hung Mike Nichols is fun and especially verbal in his superextended topping of Chris Rock in 'Marine Crucible.' Anthony Gallo, who sports a fine Italian sausage if ever there was one. With a sometimes disappointing lack of enthusiasm, the tops could be reading their lines off cue cards. And most of the bottoms wince through a repertoire of 'ungh, ooh, aahhh, ughhh, uhhh, ahh, aghh, owooo,' except for Chris Rock, who actually seems to improvise, with a lot of variations on 'fuck my Sergeant ass.' And the fact that you get to hear all the 'dialogue' is a plus. ...Most of the bottoms seemed (and sounded) pained, and a few of the tops seemed reluctant ... It seems all the recruits are pansies, and they all get made. K.C. Hart tops Sergeant Chris Rock in 'Forced Service' and calls it sexual harassment because he's a bottom! Here's a boy who knows how to maximize his assets."

In Touch commented: "The interrogations – conducted by Lieutenant Shawn London – begin when Private K.C. Hart accuses his sergeant, Chris Rock, of sexually harassing him. As it turns out, everyone in the barracks is getting it on with one guy or another, and the qualifications for sexual harassment become a little unclear. The video features an impressive cast of smooth young men, including Hart, of course, as well as Ethan-Michael Ayers and boyish newcomer Billy Dare. Shawn London is stunning from beginning to end. He's an awesome actor, a beautiful young man, and a nasty, foul-mouthed, big dicked top. We were also taken aback by Matthew Easton's convincing performance, hot body, and wonderful sexual intensity.

"Rock is amazing as the sergeant that every private loves to hate. In his volcanic scene with K.C. and Ethan, he steals the show by barking one vindictive order after another at the helpless pair. Chris is quite a stud. He's extremely sexy and handsome, but his shouting of commands even as he's getting fucked makes him the ultimate turn-on. Like a man on a mission, he gets exactly what he wants: two fresh young cocks right up his eager ass. Unfortunately, K.C. feels a bit used after the experience, but then, who ever said serving your country was easy."

In "Summer of '44," from Catalina, K.C. is again in uniform. Jim D'Entremont in *The Guide* comments, "In a prologue staged in a Pacific island foxhole resembling the set of a '5Os *Physique Pictorial* shoot, Drew Nolan, a pouty GI with slicked-back out-of-period longish blond hair, has sex with horny fellow soldier Bruno Bianchi. No sooner has Nolan spurted his way to fulfillment than we hear the ominous drone of a Japanese plane. The scene then switches to California, where Nolan's kid brother (K.C. Hart) and his buddies are debating the relative sexual merits of the soldiers, sailors, and marines they pick up at the local USO. None of these guys has any particular concern about World War II, but they're grateful for the availability of men in uniform. In the sexual episodes that follow, Hart sucks and fucks Private Cole Reece, Ryan Wagner gets blown and rimmed by Seaman Marc Pierce, and, in perhaps the best scene, Ethan Ayers has a nice, dirty field day with married Marine Ty Davenport. (At the end of all this, it's clear why they're called servicemen.) Since the premise has potential and most of the cast is worth watching, it's too bad this video often feels dumb, cheesy, and slow. This is a period piece where almost every element is out of period. Nothing looks right for 1944 and the gay culture depicted belongs to the '90s. Since the uniform fantasies are handled without any zest or imagination, it's hard to know what, if anything director Bill Hunter had in mind."

For "The Real Freshmen World," an *Advocate* promotional video, Jack Francis reports the publisher was lucky enough to get Hart and Young to appear for them, along with Falcon exclusive Brian Cruise, "whose cock is a sexy twin to K.C. Hart's. Though K.C. is a veteran of many videos and Brian (at the time) was an untried novice from the Carolinas, I'm able to report in all honesty that both K.C. and Brian were equally up for everything.

"The perfect complement to wild-ass K.C. and Brian was the handsome Kurt Young... Coming from the same neck of the woods as Kurt does, I recognize a homegrown beauty when I see one, and Kurt's the genuine article – a real star. We were lucky to get him. All I can add is that if you aren't as enthralled watching Kurt take a shower in 'his' pink granite bathroom as we were, you must be dead down there."

Chris Ramsay of "Hot Summer of Sex" fame found Young "was real personable. He'd just talk with me and help me with anything I needed. He'd just say, 'How did it go with this? Am I doing this all right?' He was really nice. I really didn't get to know Kurt Young on that scene. I got to know him more after. I thought, at first, that he was straight. But his (then) boyfriend, Matt Easton, he's really a nice guy, too. He always worked with us, and they're both real nice. Kurt was really fun to work with, and I would work with him again."

Everybody seems to love Kurt. Dino Phillips says, "(While making "Showboys!") I just really fell for Kurt Young. He is the perfect boy, as far as I'm concerned. He is so cute, and he has a nine-inch dick, beautiful piercing eyes...but he has a boyfriend. His boyfriend is Matthew Easton, also in the business, and also a dream, too. I would love to watch them have sex sometime. I would love to bottom for him. He is the quintessential boy. He's very shy. His hair is like a California surfer dude, and he's just my type."

About "Flesh and Blood," Robert Sumners in *Mondo Porno* raved, "Kurt Young can actually act! He's gorgeous and although he's in every scene you NEVER get bored. Kurt has an endless supply of semen which he sprays intensely every scene. Using Hollywood technology and a body double, Jerry Douglas was able to create the illusion of the twins having sex with each other. Fierce!"

One of our favorite Kurt Young scenes is to be found in "Beverly Hills Hustlers." Forgive us but we love the hyperbole in Club M's description of the video featuring Tony Cummings. Said the copywriter: "Street prostitute Tony Cummings is walking down Santa Monica Blvd. He is picked up by detective Kurt Young and Kurt wants a hot ass, so Tony tells him, 'Yeah, for a price.'" That should have gotten him taken to the slammer but instead a deal is struck and "off they go." Tony starts to suck Kurt's cock and Kurt slaps on the handcuffs. Tony begs not to be taken to jail. Pleading with the hung cop that he'll do anything... well, Kurt was getting turned on by the way Tony was sucking on his rock-hard, cum-filled cock and tells Tony that if he makes him feel real good maybe he can look the other way. Tony now knows that he must suck cock better than he's ever sucked before, so he first licks the head of it, then goes all the way down until it's firmly lodged down his throat. Kurt loves the feeling of his dick down the tight warm throat of this hot submissive street whore, and is almost ready to pop his load, but knows that Tony has to give him some of his hot ass. When Kurt's big cock is rammed inside Tony's asshole without lube (cops have no mercy), Tony revels with both pain and pleasure. Kurt takes delight in fucking the street boy, stretching and stretching the hot pink asshole until it's raw. ...Finally after fucking Tony in every position, the tightness of Tony's asshole and his whimpering cries for mercy are too much for the hardened cop so he pulls out and shoots his load all over Tony's face."

Nightlife gossip maven Rod Skylar found Victoria Paris' Dragville the place to find Kurt Young in West Hollywood. During a typical evening, Rod found a "spectacularly dressed" Chi Chi LaRue, "fresh from Berlin...made a grand entrance minus her usual entourage missing the first 90 minutes of the show and left too quickly for the time she surely spent doing herself up. I cannot believe how many hours a drag queen will spend in hair and makeup just to make a 20 second entrance. And she calls Karen Dior a 'greedy media slut.'

"A far less gaudy entrance was made by gay video's favorite son Kurt Young and his fiance David Thompson. The couple flew in from Seattle, where they reprise their roles in 'Making Porn.' Both were witness to Ryan Idol punching co-star Blue Blake in the face in the NY production forcing the departure of Blake from the cast. What an incredible complexion Kurt has! Thompson is much hotter in person than in videos. Anyone for a three-way?"

Skylar was the first to report that Thompson and Young, who dumped Best Bottom nominee Matthew Easton for Thompson, have set the date for the most anticipated wedding of the season: "All Worlds Video's Ivy League intellectual and directing virtuoso Jerry Douglas will give Young away. The couple is perhaps best known for their appearance (or non-appearance) at the '96 GVG awards, where Young blurted out something about how people were being 'mistreated.' Their scheduled stage number was cut at the last minute by the show's director Gender, Chi Chi LaRue's estranged 'make-up and motivation' person, for time considerations. Although he later apologized, most in attendance mistakenly thought Young had a beef against the entire industry.

"The lovebirds produced a T-Dance at Long Beach's Gay Pride festivities and choreography, producing/directing the Probe 'Men In Video' awards.

"Young and Thompson were in Washington, D.C., appearing in 'Making Porn' when combative producer Ronnie Larsen checked out the production and found everyone in the cast not quite up to par. It was after this that Thompson retired from porn to run his own production company with Young, whom he now also manages." What the couple is producing are videos for children. Go figure!

Derek Thomas (aka Brent Sawyer), courtesy Falcon Studios

Logan Reed,
courtesy Studio 1435

Derek Thomas and Logan Reed

"Derek Thomas is a terrific bottom with a beautiful ass," Christopher Hogan, in *The Guide* in his review of "Why Marines Don't Kiss" from All Worlds. Hogan didn't think much of the video itself, however: "It could just as easily have been titled 'Why Marines Can't Act.' While there is plenty of great sex in this video, writer/director Stan Cross has given his cast an inordinate amount of lines to deliver. The plot follows a complex – perhaps even convoluted – series of flashbacks and flash-forwards centering on, not surprisingly, gay sex in the Marine Corps.

"As if all this wasn't strange enough, the cast is small, and therefore some double and triple casting is necessary. For example, Sam Crockett plays three roles, and it makes things really confusing. This could have been done for artistic reasons, but it seems more likely that economics and efficiency were the motivations.

"The overly complex and somewhat silly story telling does not, fortunately, detract from the top-notch sex scenes...Thomas's partner is Hodge Armstrong, dark-haired and handsome, with classic leading man good looks like Andrew Shue. (Armstrong doesn't act much better than Shue, but he's twice as good looking.) There's a lot of sexual electricity between Thomas and Armstrong. The only problem is that they are both bottoms which poses some problems for their scene together. The resolution of this problem could have been handled better, but is nice to see these two babes get fucked."

About Thomas's appearance "Hardline," *In Touch* said,"...Hunky Mike Branson spices up his love life with his boyfriend Brent Sawyer (aka Derek Thomas) with a blindfold, a banana, and a lot of whipped cream.

"...Brent/Derek has really changed his look. His buffer body and spiked blond hair makes him seem quite different than the boyish bottom we've come to love. But, there is definitely something extremely sexy about his new look and new persona, and his incredible performance as Brent makes the transformation more than worth it."

And upon seeing Thomas (and company) in Falcon's

"Manhandlers," *In Touch's* reviewer started having orgasms and couldn't stop! "Mike Branson. His dark hair, rugged good looks and unbelievable body make him the perfect porn star. And then there's his cock. Oh...my...God! It's amazingly big and juicy!

"The runner up in the cock department is Jeff Palmer. He's got an awesome body and cock, complimented by a pair of alluring and mysterious eyes. And man, is he mean! He shows up in three scenes. First, he teases Mike Branson just enough to make Mike go after his lover, Tony Manchester. Second, he gives in to the seductions of Derek Cameron, but then, if you watched Derek shove an ice cube into his own ass, you'd give in, too. But, Jeff shows us what he's really made of in the last scene, pounding the asses of both Derek Thomas (billed here as Brent Sawyer) and Jordan West, after, of course, grabbing them both by the hair and sadistically pulling their mouths down onto his monstrous prick. Overall, we were extremely impressed with his performance. He got our attention with the way he wields his cock like a weapon: cruelly, but with passion.

"Naturally, we can't leave out Thomas. For the past year he has consistently been one of our favorite bottoms. In 'Manhandlers,' he gives yet another stunning and fully committed performance. With Jordan West as his partner in crime, Thomas manages to take on three very horny men just like a pro."

Thomas probably grinned from ear to ear when he read that. He *has* become a pro in a very short time, especially for a straight boy! German-born Texan Thomas told *Manshots* how it all started: "I was in Venice Beach, California, with my parents, walking down the beach. And a man gave me a business card, and he told me that they modeled swimwear, gymwear, and beachwear. And he told me later on about the nudity and stuff, what it consisted of. And I tried it, and there really wasn't much to it. Once I tried one, I found out that I could make the films and be good at it, so I decided to stick with it. Once I found out that nobody else cared – I know that all those photographers see good stuff everyday – I just...it's kind of fun when you can just walk around naked and no one really cares. Everyone's very cool." Meanwhile, when he isn't stripping for the camera, Thomas returns to Texas and continues his college studies and even waits on tables part-time.

Thomas said he had no homosexual experiences whatsoever before he showed up on Jim Steel's set at Vivid Video. He and his video partner began fondling each other. "It was probably better than I thought it was gonna be," he recalled. "I told myself I'd try everything. My agent told me what to expect, so I had a pretty good idea. I didn't regret anything. I didn't feel bad about anything. I couldn't wait to make the next one."

When asked how he prepared for a scene, Thomas replied, "Since I'm a bottom, I always get loosened up. And I'm always nervous before a scene, until we get started. And once we get started, I'm like, 'Yeah, I'm havin' fun now! I thought it was gonna be really painful, but it wasn't a bad feeling. Right now, it's just fine with me, unless the guy's got a *really* huge dick.

"I think certain directors have made me look really good. Like Chi Chi LaRue. 'White Hot.' Logan Reed's in it. I really like him. I did a scene with him in 'Brother to Brother' that Chi Chi directed. His scene with me was really wild. Like Chi Chi turned me upside down. And she had Ty Fox fuck me like that too, which is kind of great."

As much as Derek loves getting fucked by guys, he insists he's straight. He tells his girlfriend he's modeling clothes like swimwear, gymwear.

When asked what he liked best about his clandestine career he responded, "I guess popularity. I like being an actor."

And many of us, watching him going crazy with a big dick up his ass, would say he's a damn good one!

About Derek's appearance with Logan Reed, Christopher Hogan comments on "Brother to Brother" in *The Guide*, "Never has the subject of incest been treated so lightly. While there's nothing wrong with two consenting brothers having 'relations,' 'Brother To Brother' does not address anything other than the sex, perhaps because to do so would stretch the acting abilities of 'brothers' Derek Thomas and Shane Thomas far beyond their limits.

"Interestingly, the film does grapple a bit with the issues around the attraction a gay uncle (played by Drew Andrews) feels towards his nephews (the 'Brothers Thomas?'). Writer Jordan Young (who also penned 'Like Father, Like Son') seems to have quite an interest in incest. Perhaps he should either work through these issues elsewhere or throw caution to the wind and write a script that really embraces the fascinating sexual tensions among family members. Despite their inability to deliver lines and the fact that they are not convincing for one minute as brothers (they look about as much alike as Beau and Luke Duke – who, come to think of it, may have been cousins, not brothers), the two Thomas boys come through where it counts, in the sex scenes. Their scene together is wonderful. They both have terrific bodies and clearly enjoying rubbing them together. Derek is one of the best new bottoms in the business, and it really shows as Shane fucks him.

"Derek also has a great scene with super-cute and super-hung Logan Reed. None of the rest of the sex quite lives up to Derek's two scenes, but it is all well above average porn fare."

Hogan also liked "The Last Taboo" from Studio 2000, finding Reed "terrific" in a solo scene in which he dildo-fucks himself. "Later, Reed and Mark Montana fuck each other in the best scene of the video."

"Mark Montana thinks he's straight," Reed said. "Mark represents everything that I'm not. Harsh and crass and loud and hard – although I was really attracted to that. I've always been probably most attracted to that. He's the kind of person who goes against everything that I represent. I was so intrigued by him, though. He's very large, very tall. Very large. I knew it's all an act. It's all an act and...there's a good person there. That's why I had a good time. That was all part of the game. It was just very erotic off the set. I know that some actors have had problems with that kind of stuff – not liking each other, or liking each other too much. I think it's a matter of professionalism. This is a job and you have to do it. The chemistry I think is better – for me, it works better to get to know them. Not sexually, not intimately. If you don't know each other and you're just suddenly in this room, then there's no game and there's no excitement. I try to be professional. I don't want to be a diva. I don't want to be high maintenance. For the most part, I'm not in the business to be a celebrity. 1 don't want to be a celebrity – or act like a celebrity. I'm doing this because I like doing this. I like the people I've met doing this, and like I said, I miss it when I'm not doing it. Eventually I'd like to do something behind the scenes. I don't want to direct. I don't want to do that. I give a lot of respect to the people who do the work. It's an industry I don't want to get out of."

Hogan said, "'Cock Fight' from All Worlds, may be the first porn video based on a work by Herman Melville. The story is an adaptation of Billy Budd – honest to goodness, it is. The homoerotic subtext of Melville's sea tale is simply brought to the surface in this story of Marines at an isolated base. Just like when The Simpsons co-opts a film classic such as Lifeboat or Citizen Kane, the adaptation is done in a totally appropriate way. For a porn video, the script and acting are great. Most of the sex, with one very notable exception, is completely justified by the story. In fact, it's all necessary for the story to move forward. Don't let any of this scare you away from 'Cock Fight.' All of its pretensions of being a 'real' movie don't get in the way of this being a first-class jack-off video.

"The all-star cast insure great action in every scene. In addition to Reed, we have a three-way featuring Blue Blake, Max Grand, and Paul Carrigan... Blake plays an officer who barks orders at Grand and Carrigan. Each of them is at their best. Blake as the tough top and Grand and Carrigan as the butch bottoms. Reed and Bryan Kidd are also terrific in the leading roles in this story of gay military intrigue. Kidd was born to play the quintessential boy, Billy. His youthful, blond looks and superb skill as a bottom are perfect for the role."

In his review of "One Hot Summer" from John Travis's factory, Chris Pomiecko in *The Guide* found "especially appealing" the rimming by Mike Lofton, "a lickable puffy-titted studpuppy who's paired with hairy humpy gardener Logan Reed, in a scene highlighted by some hard-tongued rimming of Lofton's hairy, rosey-sphinctered butthole. Lofton shows up again in the concluding six-man orgy scene, where he's paired with star (and 'Studio 2000 Exclusive') Rick Chase, a dark-haired demi-god. While their action is limited to mutual masturbation, Lofton's guilty hang-dog look and constant looks offscreen (a sure giveaway that the actor's straight), gives this scene a perverse kick. Also noteworthy in this scene are craggy blonds Bobby Golden and Jon Davis with some savage butt-pumping.

"In 'Dark Side of the Moon,' Sonny Markham and Jordan West play a pair of archaeologists in search of relics from a lost Native American tribe," *In Touch* commented. "Interestingly, the relics are large stone phallic symbols and phallic pendants. Apparently, they have some connection to an ancient ritual which is presently invading the lives and dreams of this archaeological team. Markham begins this adventure by having a vision of one of the lost tribesmen, Kurt Stefano. Kurt makes for an extremely hot phantom, and it doesn't take much for him to seduce Sonny into fucking the hell out of his ghostly ass. As Sonny starts to cum all over the warrior's back, the vision disappears, leaving Sonny to erupt all over his empty bed. Of course, Sonny is left with a memento: a perfectly intact stone phallus. Unfortunately, no one believes his vision, but soon, the energy of the archaeological site begins to have an affect on everyone involved in the dig. The new recruit, Logan Reed, finds himself engaging in some rather erotic rituals with fellow assistant Matt Bradshaw in an outdoor shower. It's a hot scene, with awesome fucking and a beautiful switching of roles."

In his review of "My Secret Collection," Jim D'Entremont said in *The Guide*: "Logan Reed, who lit up 'Lost in Vegas' and has appeared memorably elsewhere, moves through this one with proficiency, but not much more. The efforts of porn stalwarts like Matt Bradshaw are largely wasted. Rappalo tries too hard. The director, Derek Kent, doesn't try hard enough."

In Touch loved "Dirty White Guys" from All Worlds: "Fifteen porn stars are mixed and matched with such fluidity that the entire video seems almost chaotic or random – a lot like the real thing. Eventually, a massive orgy develops, involving eleven guys (we think). Stud lovers will be impressed by Jake Andrews, Matt Bradshaw and Logan Reed. They really put themselves into this one, and the effect is cum- splattering. Boy watchers will be captivated by Jay Anthony and Rod Barry. Jay is a total dream. He's beautiful, sucks cock with passion, and lives to bounce up and down on Matt's massive cock. Rod is a bit different. He's a slender ex-Marine who's too sexy for words.

"After an insane amount of rimming and fucking take place, the orgy transforms into a rather big daisy chain which circles around the room. All that's left after that is the cumshot, and, damn, you'll be impressed. Cum cascades, plummets and explodes from one cock after another, all of it falling on the two guys lucky enough to be lying in the center."

In "My Secret Collection" Reed plays a young man with a bit of a problem. He's a hopeless voyeur armed with a video camera and a lack of inhibitions. *In Touch* describes what happens: "Logan's first victim is his next door neighbor Rappalo. Through a hole in the wall, Logan captures the erotic images of Rappalo masturbating in the privacy of his own bedroom.

"After that triumph, Logan packs his camera into his gym bag and heads off to college where he catches English professor Matt Bradshaw taking some intense interest in one of his students, Rainey Foster. Matt and Rainey are especially hot as Matt pounds Rainey's mouth and ass right on top of his desk while Logan, fortunately, captures every bit of it on tape.

"From there, Logan heads off to a recruiting center 'just for fun.' Apparently his idea of a good time is to almost sign up for service in one of the armed forces. Pretty twisted, huh? Luckily, another future recruit shows up, and Logan is once again given the opportunity to immortalize two hot and horny men. Recruiter (and porno veteran) Brett Winters really tears up little boy Austin Reeves, never suspecting that Logan is close by, giving 'Don't ask, don't tell' a whole new twist.

"What could Logan possibly do next to feed his deviant desires? Well, there's always the back room of a gay bar. When inside, Logan spots two really incredible guys going at it in the darkness. Before Logan's eyes – and lens – Derek Bishop enjoys the fuck out of Danny West's mouth and ass. Derek hammers his cock into Danny's ass with intense passion while they constantly switch positions until Derek shoots all over Danny's chest.

"The next day, Logan starts setting up his camera in the locker room of his local gym. Unexpectantly, he gets caught by his next door neighbor Rappalo.

"(Before long) the oral sex is definitely steamy as the two work each other's cock until Rappalo finally lifts his ass in the air. Logan gives him a spirited fucking, causing himself to eventually blast his cum all over one of the lockers. In the end, the two of them both get into watching others and themselves.

Apparently, there's a certain comfort in knowing that you're not the only one."

Reed said his first visit to a gay bar was the Hide and Seek, "and my first gay night was when Jeff Stryker was there. And I met him and was just overwhelmed and awed.

"I had the girlfriend and I had the female friends, so that it appeared to everyone...well, let them assume what they wanted to. I did the prom and all that, but never sexually. Well, sort of, very light petting. And it didn't do it for me. I moved to Denver when I was nineteen. I've always been very much an exhibitionist, I guess. Also, I'm a voyeur. I stripped for a little contest at the bar when I was nineteen. It was 'Mr. Colorado, Mr. Right' or something like that. I ran for that and did a little strip routine."

Reed enjoys going to the gym, for many reasons. "I learned long ago to watch people watch other people, and that's when you learn most about them. And that's what the mirrors are for. Mirrors are in the gym, they're all over the place, and you can get away with things and you can watch other people. And whether it be homoerotic or just jealousy or intrigue or whatever it is, it's a guy thing. It is truly an addiction.

"And then I met who every other actor meets. I met Miss Chi Chi LaRue. I was a video jockey in a video bar in Denver, where all the Denver boys used to dance before they became skin stars, porn stars, or whatever you want to call them. I think 'porn' is okay. I hate the word, 'porno,' but I think the word, 'porn' is okay. Then I got an agent. I knew who he was, because of working in the video bar. And all of the boys from Denver – there are a lot – Bo Summers, Cort Stevens, all those boys. I knew them, sort of, when they were just starting out. So I knew who he was – and one day, we just kind of met and started talking. And he actually asked me out. I had a boyfriend at the time, and we really kind of became friends. He's a very nice person, very giving, everything. I can't say anything bad about him. And then, I finally said, 'How come you never asked me to do this?' And it was because he liked me in a different way than them. So, it never happened. He knew that I wanted to do it. Chi Chi came to Denver quite often, and it all just kind of worked out. I didn't do the dancing, the magazines. I skipped all that and went right to 'Men Only' for Chi Chi.

"Steve O'Donnell ('Cockfight') is insane. We had a great time together. He's a raunchy boy. We had great sex, and we gave LaRue a helluva scene. And we knew it and they knew it. I think directors are very good – for the most part – usually very good about casting. I don't know how they figure this out, finding two people – or two or three or whatever – who work well together."

He didn't mind his three-way with Steve O'Donnell and Derek Cameron; there wasn't a problem because he had worked with each of them before. "I don't really care for that, because no matter what happens when there are three people – unless they are three people who don't know each other at all, then it's a little more balanced. But it's usually not. It's usually a couple and a single, and there's always an imbalance. Always one is attracted to another more than the other. It never works.

"I think Kurt Young is great. The scene went very well. He's a great actor – you know that. He's one of the ones I couldn't say more than enough about – good things about. We danced together in New York and had a great time. And I like him on a personal level, as a person and as a co-star."

Logan says, "I've had several boyfriends, but I've never really had a long-term. I've dated some incredible people, and it's not that I'm being self-centered, but it's just that I like to do what I want to do, and that'll change as I get older. For now, I enjoy being alone. As much as I've been working, I don't have sex socially at all. Maybe someday, that person will come into my life, but I just don't see it happening right away."

One of Logan's ex-boyfriends is Jordan Young, who has also dated Tom Katt and current beau Sam Dixon, an ex-police officer who has since gotten into the business.

Originally from Montana, Jordan Young moved to Wyoming with his family when he was in fourth grade, *HX* reported. He says that he loves the Midwest, but always felt suffocated by the small-town atmosphere there: "It's a wonderful place to raise your children if you want them to grow up to be bigoted, hateful people," he says. Born to a Korean mother and a Greek father, Young's unique looks gained the attention of casting directors when he was a teenager. At 14, he began modeling for Banana Republic and Calvin Klein. "Modeling is just a higher form of pornography," he says, "because they are sending the same message, only in a much more glossy way."

After graduating from high school, Young relocated to Denver, where he got an agent and started dancing. He also sent some pictures to director John Rutherford at Falcon. It was through Rutherford that director Chi Chi LaRue became aware of Young: "I saw his picture and thought he was cute," LaRue recalls. "I thought, there are no Asian boys who are considered stars. So I decided that I was going to make him a star. We hit it off immediately. I think it was fate that brought us together."

Young soon moved to Los Angeles and became LaRue's housemate. He was cast in his first film, "Nightwatch 2," shortly after that. "The night before," Young says, "all I could think about was, once I step in front of that camera, I can't take it back. I can't buy back the film. There was nothing I could do. It was scary, but I knew that I would never be president," he laughs, "so I did it."

He also began writing scripts. "Lost in Vegas," "The Taking of Jake" and "Striptease" were noteworthy.

"When you find someone you're comfortable with," Young says, "it's a fine line you walk. You don't want to mess it up, but you don't want to sacrifice who you are. I didn't tell Sam about my work until our third date because people have preconceived notions about the way people are in the porno industry – that they're slutty or trashy or stupid, and it does have its share of that, but so does every other job there is. I'd like to 'go legit,' although I don't consider what I'm doing not legit. I don't deny it. I'm comfortable with it. It's a form of media that's out there; it's just not as widely accepted.

"I told my mother that I'm a model, but I think she knows what I'm actually doing and she doesn't care. I think she knows that I'm happy. And I am happy where I am. But the bad thing about me is that I want everything, and I want it now. And that causes lots of problems because I'm not taking the time to be a kid. 'Cause I am a kid. I just can't imagine what my life would be if I hadn't done this." Neither can we!

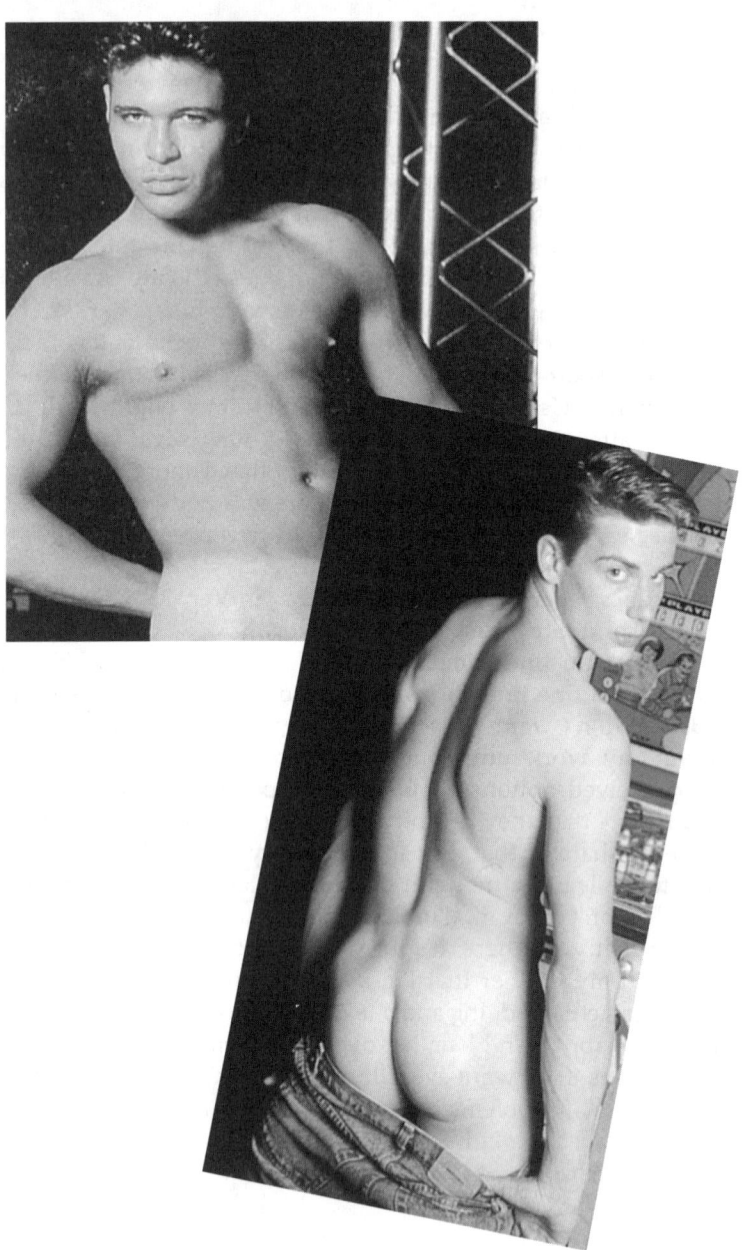

Chad Knight and Cole Youngblood,
courtesy All Worlds Video

Chad Knight & Cole Youngblood

"How can the lovely Cole Youngblood pout for so long without moving a facial muscle?" asked Video View

In Chi Chi LaRue's "Striptease," the best thing in it isn't even a scene, only a snippet: In one of the continuous short-cuts we see Knight topping a cutie who is kneeling on the bar. Knight's fucking as only he can, but we aren't allowed to linger. A stud stands over Chad Knight jacking off and comes, with Chad, meanwhile, giving it his all, which is considerable as his fans know. But how did this start? And, more to the point, why don't we stay on this? No, we are given more of the boring "plot" of two quarreling lovers, and then more cross-cutting to the point of distraction. Even Cole Youngblood's long-awaited, at least by us, plugging of all-time superbottom Knight is spoiled by all this cross-cutting. You can't work up a sweat (or anything else). And of course the mistress Chi Chi LaRue herself has to make an appearance, to announce Chad and Cole. Ugh!

One can only hope that some enterprising producer will team Chad and Cole again.

Knight seems to go on forever. Thank goodness. In his other major appearance in 1997, in Chip Daniels' "Marine Crucible," Sticky Remote in *HX* agreed with us about the scene that found "blond, buff and hot Bo Summers getting Jeep-side service from Chad Knight, before bending Knight over the roll bar and topping him."

The video is especially memorable because of its great close-ups of Summers's heroic meat entering Chad's willing hole. Bo stays hard throughout and shows no mercy with his frequent penetrations. Chad, of course, comes after Bo does, completing the sequence. Rad in *STARS* loved it too: "When you see Bo Summers pull out that long hot cock for his buddy to play with, suck, lick, stroke, and back into, you will just be envious of the Marine he fucks. Knight is so convincing with moans of ecstasy you wish you could have gotten at least one moan from Summers so you don't get the impression he is doing it in a jeep just for the money. 'Ho-hum' tops are gorgeous and hung but hey, we want to know they love shoving that big cock up our asses. But let's face it, Knight loved it, and I'm sure the director and the cameraman loved it too."

K. Y. Gellie in *Next* agreed: "'Perfect-dicked Summers penetrates Chad from a variety of different angles, now on the hood; now in the back-seat; now in the front-seat; the hood again. Knight, they say, is a porn legend. Watching the aplomb with which he takes Bo's tool shows why. He is not merely a talented bottom – some might say his skills border on genius. This film marks his best performance to date. How can he top it?"

Speaking of topping, Knight is one of the few performers we enjoy watching giving as well as taking. We enjoy this probably because we know how great he is at both, at least according to everyone who has ever worked with him. There are even occasions when he surprises us and tops a stud we never thought would be topped, such as Blade Thompson in "Score 10." Granted, he's only in there for a few moments, but he does it – after he's come with Blade fucking him! This from one of the greatest bottoms the industry has ever produced. He is also glimpsed fucking a woman in a sequence of "Oh, Brother!" while some frat boys are getting turned on by watching a het video.

Yes, Knight can top, man or woman. And the number of people who can have the privilege is increasing by the day! Interestingly, we noticed Chad was, for the first time, listed in Southwest Management's ad in *The Advocate Classifieds*. This aroused our curiosity since we had just seen a notice that Chad had danced at the Park-Miller in San Francisco. We called the agent, who informed us that yes, Chad had danced, but he did no private shows during his engagement. The agent told us that Chad and his family had moved to Atlanta and he was trying to put together a down payment on a house. Thus, we has begun doing "private shows." However, his rate is three times that of other stars on the agent's roster. His day rate is $4500. His hourly rate in Atlanta is $1500. The agent says they get more calls for Chad than for anybody else (he didn't say how many takers) and that Chad is "a very sweet guy." Also, you have to give three alternate dates since Chad is "so busy" what with filming, his family, etc. "Ye gods! Maybe someday, when

I win the lottery!" was one fan's reaction when I told him about this latest development in the career of Chad Knight. Hell, maybe we wouldn't be happy with the real thing at any cost. Perhaps it's an illusion, that Chad is one of those who looks better on film than in person. As Falcon's videographer Todd Montgomery says, "Knight is not my type personally, but he photographs beautifully."

To see Chad in his topping mode, check out Michael Zen's "Bullseye," Chad tops a sailor (played by Danny Orlis) in a surprising turn-about. One gets the idea that Orlis couldn't get it hard enough to fuck so Chad came through – again. In "My Dick Is Bigger," he seduces a young black, first by sucking his cock with incredible finesse, then shoving the lovely meat up his ass. Then, just for fun, Chad tops the black!

In its review of "Cram Course: Sex Ed. 3" from Minotaur, *Fig Leaf*, in its usual hyperbolic style, notes, "Knight takes a recess from teaching class to get a moment's mental relaxation via a hardy blowjob in the college men's room. Mason Walker portrays a young, highly determined student whose brains seem to be concentrated in his penis, and who understands the advantages of scoring brownie points when it comes to receiving a passing grade. Mason is an expert cocksucker and seems to welcome as much extracurricular gaysex as possible. After being brought to the brink of orgasm Chad returns the spine-tingling favor and adulates Mason's stalwart cockmuscle. Before the bell rings, Mason manages to score an A+ by filling Chad's analytical stud anus with his steely sextool."

Last year, Knight stunned us with his "comeback" after staying home with the wife and kiddies for a few months – resting up – or whatever it is he does. Chad once told an interviewer that as much as he likes gay sex, he would never consider a relationship with a gay man. He much prefers being a hubby and a daddy. Some might think he has the best of both worlds. You can't help but envy him, considering the studs he has entertained over the years. Some might say he has entertained *too many* studs. Gianfranco says, "I did it with Chad Knight, and my god, he was so loose! I just slid in and out of him like there was no tomorrow."

Maybe the incredible ease with which Chad gets fucked finds him so frequently paired with the newer fellows, to sorta break 'em in right, we suppose. In John Travis' "Ultimate Reality," Knight enters a booth at a video store and is transported to a misty white bedroom with hot newcomer Steve O'Donnell, who turns out to be a young Dracula. *Manshots* commented: "With his masculine face, hairy chest, long lean body, and beer-can boner, O'Donnell is the treasure of this video. Never mind that he looks more like the Boy Wonder than the Transylvania Count, he is a find by any name. O'Donnell and Knight kiss, then sixty-nine. Knight sucks the Count's huge, fat joystick, then opens his ass for a thrilling screw that is played out with a passionate surrender Anne Rice might have envisioned. O'Donnell comes in eight magnificent spurts before devouring his prey. What a way to go!" Unfortunately, Chad doesn't get hard during this fuck.

Over the years, Chad has learned to act, or perhaps that is stretching it a bit. Suffice to say he can be "natural" while being taped, which does take some skill. He exhibited this ability in David Babbitt's "Bad Moon Rising" from All Worlds. Stan Ward, in *Manshots*, says, "For the most dramatic role, he has chosen Knight, a familiar but never unwelcome face. Knight's long-lasting popularity – among viewers and directors alike – is due to his unique combination of all-American good looks and a truly superior ability to handle dialogue. Knight is also sexually versatile, but Babbitt makes the mistake of having him bottom in all three of his scenes. The reason, one suspects, is the lack of versatility in the other two actors." Be that as it may, Chad won the Gay Video Award for his three-way with Luc Russell and Brad Hunt. His oral scene with Luc Russell in the same video tied for best honors with Chris Green, Joe Romero and Jeff Jagger in "Courting Libido."

Chad's topping ability is supremely in evidence in "Tales from the Backlot" (from All-Worlds) and we recommend it to you. Chad tops Kevin Kramer, who told us that Chad is one of his favorite sex partners. Kramer noted, "We did that scene all in one take, without stopping. Chad is simply a wonderful lover!" Ah, yes, if you need a good top, use a great bottom.

When Jamoo interviewed Cole Youngblood for *Freshmen*, the first question was, naturally, "How big is it?" The performer answered, "It's really big. I never really measured, but I think about ten." Youngblood is cut, but he's got a lot of skin, and a lot of people think he's uncut. Youngblood says he loves what he does: "I'm a dirty boy, I can't lie." And he loves to eat butt more than anything. "Just give me a good, juicy butt, and I'm in heaven. I could sit there for hours munching away. Before I do my come shot, I have to eat somebody's ass. Just pop a big, juicy ass in my face, and I'm ready to go in two seconds." His favorites? "I enjoyed fucking Marco Calles, the guy in the sling in 'Download.' That was the best fuck. 'Cause he was a hot, juicy ass and a dirty boy, and the dirtier, the better. And the more he screamed 'Fuck me!' the harder I did. And loved it. That was great. That was about the best ass I've fucked on film. All of the rest have been very, very good, but he sticks in my memory the most. Every time I go out to San Francisco, we hook up."

Cole satisfies a lot of tastes, thanks to his heritage: half white, one quarter black, and one quarter American Indian. "Everybody guesses I'm Spanish." He also says he's "gay as a daisy." He tried fucking girls but, "I'm sorry, it was good, and I really enjoyed it, it was just that... I like boys. Absolutely. But tiny dicks are no fun. Big dicks are fun to suck. I'm a homosexual, so of course I like big dicks. As long as the ass is bigger than the dick, I'm happy. I love big asses."

"Jockstrapped," from Falcon, is quintessential Youngblood, yet the video stars Dave Russell. Preston Richie in *Manshots* said "the complex, carnal choreography is quite astounding. The opening moments find Russell in his bedroom sniffing a jock and remembering a school encounter with Kyle Hunter. Before putting on his jock, Hunter slowly strips to reveal his smooth, succulent ass for Russell's inspection and approval. They kiss, Hunter pulls Russell's prick out of his jock, and begins blowing him. Russell also pays a good deal of attention to eating Hunter's hungry hole. The mirrored ceiling above the bed allows great views of the action as these two brunet beauties meld into a sixty-nine punctuated by deep-throat action and ball play. Russell fucks Hunter doggie, then missionary, which leads to two splashy loads that leave the jockstraps as sticky as the men.

"Next, Russell dreams of a locker room threesome including towel boy Chad Donovan and football players Joshua Sterling and Sky Thompson. While inhaling the aroma of a, dirty jockstrap, Donovan pulls out his jumbo joint and sucks on his own dickhead. Jockstrapped Sterling and Thompson arrive and drop to their knees to service Donovan's shaft as he continues his self-suck. Three mouths on one dick is a clear testament to the size of the Donovan dong. Ultimately, Donovan eats both men's asses and screws them both to exhaustive climax. One never tires of watching the horse-hung Donovan, and here he is just about perfect, driving the entire scene with manic delight. A grease monkey threeway with Youngblood, Kyle Brandon, and Tony Tarango appears to be performed by rote, but still manages to percolate, thanks to Youngblood's role as super-schlonged ringmaster. Jockstraps are snapped, cocks are sucked, and the highlight of the event finds Youngblood rolling his pals over on their backs until they are asshole to asshole and rimming them both. In time, they fuck around a Jeep in the garage, and as we have come to expect, the Youngblood emission is atomic.

"The final scene brings us full circle back to Russell and his boyfriend Mac Reynolds. We know before the action begins that Russell will suck cock, eat ass, and get fucked, while Reynolds will stoically stand at tradey attention. To his credit Reynolds is handsome, and his rockhard rod more than fills any space it invades; however his sexual repertoire is predictable and severely limited. Thanks to Russell's expertise and versatility, this exercise still manages to fly."

In his review of Catalina's "Cat Men Do," Dana Wells in *AVN* says, "...A truly well made fuck flick full of inventive camera angles and editing make this one hard to resist. Some interesting aside shots about how videos get made add to the enjoyment. Cole Youngblood is a stand-out performer..."

"Youngblood is the focus for much of the movie," *Adam Gay Video* said. "His big dick is unleashed on (and in) Steve Rambo, Michael Cody and Steve O'Donnell after some very inspiring butt-licking."

Rick & Dave at *Frontiers* describe the action: "Cole Youngblood is asleep on the beach in his bikini. Two guys walk by and tuck a note into his waistband. It is an invitation to a Catalina Video model search party. Cut to: Steve Rambo and boyfriend Michael Cody waking up together. Steve finds Cole

Youngblood's business card from the night before. Cole had expressed an interest in getting into the porn industry and invited Steve to contact him should Steve see potential in Cole. So Steve and Michael decide to go to Cole's house. They find Cole in the Jacuzzi stroking his big potential. They all get naked and get down. Michael takes Cole's massive manmeat in his mouth. Then Steve does the same. They orally share Cole's pole. They get into some three-way suck action and all three studs explode in close-ups. Cut to the living room where the action continues. Cole pumps Michael's hole as Michael kisses Steve. Then it's Steve's turn to take Cole's pole in his hole. They all shoot glorious amounts of manstuff. So they all agree that Cole has what it takes."

One of last year's prime new-cummers, Tony Cummings, told us he loved getting fucked by Youngblood, and Rob Erickson of *HX* would volunteer anytime. Erickson went to see Cole in his dressing room backstage at the Eros Theatre in New York City and says: "Youngblood has just steamed his way through a sensuous dance number on stage, wearing an American flag, military cap and nothing else. His ease with the audience belies the fact that he's only been dancing and acting in skin flicks for less than two years. As he sits his hunky self down, Youngblood admits that he's more than a bit nervous. So, how is this paramedic from Harrisburg, Pennsylvania, enjoying his foray into adult video?"

"It's a lot of fun, but it's work,' Youngblood told Erickson. "It's a lot more work than it seems. You know when you're shooting a movie, you've got to get this angle, that angle, stop, start, do this, do that. It's hard."

"He's an incredible performer," director Chi Chi LaRue says. "He's got a big dick, and he loves to eat ass, which makes for a good porn star." Youngblood had sent LaRue some photographs two years earlier that she says were "blurry, weird shots and didn't make him look good, so I never pursued it. Now, he's a big star and I turned him down!" The drag superstar recalls that the first time she and Youngblood actually worked together, he was very nervous at first, but "all he needed to do was stick his face in someone's butt in order to get hard."

Though he has appeared in such films as "Studio Tricks"

(Chatelaine) and "Black Muscle Machine (Brick House)," Youngblood says Falcon's masterpiece "'Download" is his personal favorite: "It was my first. I felt a lot more comfortable than I thought I would. And there's one scene with Marco Calles and Kevin Dean that was very hot." But he admits that he's not a big fan of his own videos. "I never really watch them," he says. "I'm too critical of myself."

In the Ross Cannon-directed "Ultimate Reality," Cole plays a manufactured monster to Nic Collins as Dr. Frankenstein. *Manshots* comments: "In a decent mock-up of that infamous laboratory, Collins kisses and unstraps his beefy creation for a feast of sexual experiments. Youngblood is hung just as a monster should be, impossibly long and thick with a bulbous head. The blowjob, of course, revitalizes the monster. The doctor straddles his creation, and Youngblood forces his hefty prick into Collins' willing hole. Hip to hip, they fuck hard until both unload, and the scene ends with a kiss."

The second episode of "Cram Course: Sex Ed. 3" Youngblood and Ryan Wagner are auditioning for a campus play and *Manshots* describes the scene: "Wagner persuades Youngblood to improvise a scene that was barely suggested in 'Boys in the Band.' Wagner will play Michael, and Youngblood will play the Birthday Present – alone in Michael's bedroom. After a prolonged kiss, Youngblood blows the birthday boy, who soon returns the favor. After a well-photographed sixty-nine, Youngblood fucks Wagner – energetically, passionately, and without once losing his hard-on."

Jocks' "Family Secrets" requires the simplest of acting skills, said Sticky Remote in *HX*, "and it's a good thing because these boys didn't study with Lee Strasberg. Sam Crockett 'acts' like a closeted sex addict. Jake Taylor 'acts' like he loves being serviced by three guys at once. Cole Youngblood 'acts' like a sex pig. And Steve Cannon 'acts' like he enjoys getting the Ken Ryker Supercock dildo shoved up his butt. (It's all) a bit on the detached, mechanical side, but generally very hot. The bathroom scene sizzles with sexual acrobatics at their best.

"Dax Kelly stands with one foot in each of two urinals, grabs the water pipes and makes use of at least three principles of modern physics to fully impale himself on Youngblood's massive tool. The final 'fourgy' is a real winner, with Sam

Crockett munching on a triple-decker butt sandwich and, another triple treat, three studs using two fingers each to open up Steve Cannon's butt for the Supercock dildo."

But *HX* had the highest praise for Youngblood. "This guy just loves getting dirty, whether fucking, rimming or sucking. This is the second video we've seen in which Youngblood shoots eight (count 'em eight!) times. Too much! And worth the price of admission. Every other gusher pales in comparison."

One of the "Studio Tricks" in Catalina's video is Dane Tarsen, caught on the casting couch by Youngblood. Says Floyd Johnson in *Advocate Men*: "If you want to work for Youngblood's company, you have to be able to take his prodigious length up the old wazoo. Tarsen manages nicely, but does he ever wail and moan in the process. Neighbors must call the police when he comes; certainly video reviewers turn down their TVs. The sex...is pretty good: ten performers, an equal assortment of daddies (Paul Carrigan, Tarsen, Eduardo, Sam Crockett, Jake Taylor) and boys (Youngblood, Adam Rom, Matt Easton, Adam Wilde, Chaz Carlton), and some very enthusiastic sucking *(very* enthusiastic) and fucking."

In its review of "Studio Tricks," *HX* says the video served up "a few hot moments mostly featuring the nasty mind and massive cock of Cole Youngblood. His pairing with Tarsen (a sexy, shaved-headed pig) is terrific. Youngblood, a 'Beverly Hills 90210' look-alike, has a big, always-hard dick that he uses like a true pro. Tarsen is reduced to screaming like a pig – or like he's being murdered or disemboweled (hmm, how attractive)."

Erickson revealed that Youngblood still makes his home in Pennsylvania and flies out to Los Angeles about once a month to make a movie or do a photo shoot. He remains close to his family, and says that his parents and sister have come to see him perform on stage. "It was strange," he recalls, "but they said, 'We want to know exactly what you're doing,' so they came one time. I think that was enough for them."

As for his personal life, Youngblood claims that at the moment he's single. "It's tough to have a boyfriend in this business," he says. And though he hopes to continue his education at some point in the future, for now, his career comes first: "I figure I better do it while I can."

Two great bottoms, Steve O'Donnell and Kyle Brandon, get together in "Raw Material," from Hot House.

THE BEST OF THE BOTTOMS

Ryan Wagner says he loves to play "the little victim, the innocent, little boy-next-door who gets picked on, then willingly gives up his butt."

Ed Karvoski, Jr., in *The Guide* said, "In a scene in 'Like Father, Like Son,' Wagner found himself in the center of a circle, surrounded by nine of the most handsome hunks in the adult entertainment industry, including Hank Hightower, Drew Andrews, Ace Hardon, Mark West, Shawn Justin, and others. 'I had to give all nine guys a blowjob,' explains Wagner. 'It was nine on one, and I was the one giving them the attention. It was wonderfully hot. I love giving another guy a blowjob and I love all kinds of shapes and sizes of dicks, and it seemed like they were all right there in front of me. I had to be with one guy for about four seconds, then move to the next one for about four seconds, and so on. I had to keep everyone in the group going. Some guys were really squirmy, some guys were rock-hard, some guys were just moaning. It was really a turn-on to me, knowing that I was satisfying nine different people at the same time, and that everyone was responding differently.'

"Also in the group of sexy studs was Bryan Kidd. For Wagner, it was love at first sight. 'I loved his charisma,' says Wagner. 'He had this wonderful smile on his face and he was so friendly with everybody.' Did Wagner give Kidd extra-special attention in the ten-way scene? 'No, 'cause I didn't want anybody to know I had this crush on him,' says Wagner. 'I was trying to play it cool, but I was always gawking at him, between the takes and even in the scene. I'd wink at him every once in a while to get him to laugh.'"

Kidd also met with Karvoski and he commented, "My first day on a porn set was very nervewracking. I was so nervous because I knew I was going to be taking Mike Nichols's big, big dick."

"In my personal relationships, I hadn't been much of a bottom," Kidd continues. "At the time, I hadn't bottomed in about a year, and certainly not for anything that big. So I was really nervous."

So his director, LaRue, gave him "this really big dildo to take home with me and to work on, to make sure I could do it," explains Kidd. "So I came back the next day and I said, 'Yup, no problem.'

"It was such a great introduction, 'cause I found out that I just love playing with dildos. From that point on, I've loved playing with any little toys I've tried – dildos, butt plugs, anal beads, all that stuff. I was totally shocked. I surprised myself to find out just how much of a bottom I actually am.

"My asshole, that's the hot spot! When I want to be aroused, I love the feel of somebody touching me. I love for a guy to play with my ass and give me a lot of attention, so I can just lay there and be in ecstasy."

Of all his co-stars, Kidd says, "Max Grand was really good at giving me the attention I like. He's Latino and really hot. He has a great dick, it's nice and big and uncut. I love that! And he's the sweetest guy, too, which helps."

Kidd's appreciation for dildos is captured in a CloseUp video, "Michael's Leather Dream," starring Michael White.

The sexy scene also features Kidd's one-time real-life boyfriend, Ryan Wagner. "Ryan and I were side by side and Michael fucked both of us with dildos.

"Ryan has shown me so many different things and broadened my horizons sexually. So anything I've done in videos since I've met Ryan, I've already done at home. Also, Ryan introduced me to some of the companies that do fetish videos. I don't think I would have done any of the bondage videos that I've done if it wasn't for Ryan.

"I've become much more open-minded about sex in general. Before I got into the industry, I used to be very vanilla. Sex for me was always so cut-and-dry. It used to be: pick someone up, suck dick, fuck, and that's it. But now I've changed a lot because I realize that there are so many facets of sex to explore and have fun with. Now it's much more adventurous.

"I've tried some SM, spanking, ball torture. I've learned to really love bondage. Since my eyes have been opened to this stuff, sex has been all that much more exciting."

Sean Dickson, in an interview with Jamoo for *Freshmen*, said that he really liked the video "All Night Long" because Jeff Hammond "is really hot; he's a good top, and I think it turned out to be a really hot, sexual scene. I was a bottom in that, and he has a great dick. ...I used to consider myself only a top, but that was years ago. Then I tried bottoming and found that I really liked that too, so now I don't have a preference. I enjoy being versatile. (My dick is) nice; it's a very good-size dick: 8 inches by 6 inches. But the head is a little larger than six because it's a big mushroom head. That's the most memorable part of me. It's my best locker-room feature, as I like to say. I can be noticed during a workout, and guys will be checking me out and following me around, but as soon as my jockstrap comes off, then all eyes are focused on that. I just get used to it.

"If I'm a bottom, I like a top who's really big, well-built, and taller than I am, with a really big dick and possibly some body hair.

"I'm always horny; I have a really high testosterone level. I like to come three to five times a day; otherwise I get cranky. I like to cruise guys at the gym and check out their dicks. I like sweaty guys, hot, naked guys in the showers with soapsuds running down their bodies. I like a guy who's turned on to my dick, and if he's a bottom, he'll bend over and show me that he wants it. I get cruised really often, so I'm used to being bad. I work on my body almost every day. I stay really lean and defined and trim, and that's a turn-on to guys, especially when you have a big, fat dick hanging off it. I enjoy beautiful men and sex. If you're versatile, you can experience the best of both worlds.

"I prefer looking for a bottom rather than a top. A guy about my height or shorter, young, cute, and smooth, especially if he has a smooth butt. I like guys, when they're bottoms, to be like that and to be strong and muscular. I don't really find skinny guys to be my choice in men. I like meaty, young, smooth bubble butts and cute, boyish, college-jock looks. Like the kid who bottomed for me in 'The Company We Keep.'

"(And) as long as a bottom relaxes and gets used to it and takes the head in, then I'll go from there. As long as he realizes it'll take a while to get used to it."

"Sometimes I wish I were a top," Kyle Brandon told *Skinflicks*, "so I would get a little more of the respect that I am looking for, but to me, you need one with the other. If more of the respect that I am looking for, but to me, you need one with the other. If everyone were a top, then nothing would happen. It just so happens that it's harder to be a top, so there are more bottoms. I go through it and come the twelfth time I'm being penetrated, it's very uncomfortable and you just grin and bear it. And the top has to get hard over and over and you have to endure all the pain. And it's not the kind of pain that I like! Another problem for me is that bottoms are treated differently. There's a scale, and tops are higher paid and bottoms are lower paid. I guess it's easier to bottom. The reason I don't top on film is because it's very difficult. You've got to put on condoms, stay hard for hours. I mean, if it were a video about leather or S&M obviously I wouldn't have any trouble staying hard, but this is vanilla sex, and I can just as easily be fucked and have other things going through my mind and I don't have to stay hard.

"It's always my luck that I get paired with a top who's straight or bisexual, who has to look at girlie magazines to get hard. I'm here to do a job and hopefully have some good sex, but there's got to be some chemistry and if he's looking at some picture of tits, it just doesn't do much to turn me on."

Skinflicks commented upon meeting the porn star: "Kyle Brandon, apologetic because he hasn't showered or shaved, still looks awesome – his muscled chest and butt stretch out the knit material of his T-shirt and sweats. A Milwaukee native, he moved to the City of Angels almost a year ago to pursue a burgeoning porn career, go to college, and 'hopefully find a boyfriend.' In under a year, Kyle has worked with many of the major studios, as well as performing in his own line of S&M videos."

Brandon said he worked at Trax in D.C. and was sitting at the front desk, and going through *The Blade* (D.C.'s gay newspaper) andwhen he saw an advertisement for bondage videos. "And obviously I was into that so I said, 'Wow!' and this was when I was really coming out strong and I saw the videos were made in D.C. That was right here! So I sent Bob some pictures and he called me back the day after he got them and that was my start. I've probably done 12 to 15 videos for him. One of his most popular ones is called 'Caught in the Act' and I'm in it! I had lots of fun. Bob Jones showed me that the industry was a really nice industry, it would be additional money, and I'd get my own little prestige, my little spotlight. So yeah, I wanted to take it a little further, see where else I could go with it. ...And finding Mr. Right was a main reason for moving here."

One potential Mr. Right appeared with Kyle in "Hard As Marble." "Definitely," Brandon says. "I had a very good time with Jake Andrews. We had this connection where, if he needed to get hard, he'd get this big smile on his face and call me over. For my no hands cumshot, he was doing it all and just when I was about to cum he jumped out of the way. The night before we even slept together so it was very much of a bonding thing, on and off the set. I had a very good time with him.

"While I was living in Philadelphia, I topped all the time. When I first came out here, I did a lot of bottoming. So I haven't put my equipment to use much since I got out here. But I've met a couple of people lately who've pulled that top back out of me! It's nice knowing I have two sides to me. I know I'm more of a bottom than a top. But even if I'm 55 percent bottom, there's still 45 percent of me that's a top! It depends on what mode I'm in."

"Before doing 'Flesh and Blood,' I had never taken bananas up my ass," another of our favorite bottoms, Steve O'Donnell, told *The Guide*. "Kurt Young and Ace Hardon were the ones who were giving the bananas. Steve Pierce and I were on the receiving end. It was odd, just really odd. But, in porno, I don't know if there is anything that's too weird. Between the bananas and having peanut butter licked off my ass... In 'Street Smarts,' I kind of smeared peanut butter all over my ass and a guy licked it off. It was a really long shoot because we had a lot of dialogue. It was very messy. By the time we were done, there was peanut butter everywhere – all over my butt and my hands. Then I'd try to lick it off my hands and it would get all over my face. I had never done anything sexually with food before I started doing videos. And it was never my idea when I started off in porn that I would do – a whole bunch of videos with food. I just kind of got cast that way."

O'Donnell debuted in Falcon's "Download" in a scene that

he describes as the "wildest" he's ever done in a video. "It was like an adrenaline rush for me because of the size of the butt plugs I was giving to the guy," he says. "I was having the time of my life. I just couldn't believe the size of the things he was taking. I had done smaller dildos on people before, but these were considerably larger. It was something I'd always wanted to do, and on top of that, I was getting a chance to do it and it was all being recorded on film." And in Centaur Films's "Hot Cops 3," O'Donnell gets to play with a nightstick and a flashlight. Stay tuned.

Another hot bottom, star of "Hot Cops 3," Swedish-born, Finland-bred Eric York, told Jamoo he started doing porn in 1994. "I was at Revolver in West Hollywood or one of those twinkie bars, and this one guy came up to me and said he was an agent for porn stars. At the time I didn't know anything about this business, and I thought he was just another sleazy old man. He gave me his card, and two weeks later I called, and he gave me a lot of work."

Eric first moved to Miami and met a lot of locals. "Then I came to Hollywood. I like the money, and I like the freedom.

"When I lived in Sweden, I had a girlfriend, but I haven't been with a girl for years, and I don't miss it. I like boys because you can be as rough as you want to be. I did a movie called 'Bullseye' for All Worlds, and it was fun because the story line was so hysterical and weird and fucked-up. I mean, J.T. Sloan in drag! Scary! One of my favorites to work with was Jake Andrews. He's a nice guy, no attitude. Joe Romero is the fastest man in porn; he's so professional. In and out, you know. He's good.

"Usually, I guess, I like to be on top, but if somebody is bigger and older than I am, then I'll bottom. It depends on who I'm with. I like guys with good looks, and a thick wallet is a plus! No, really, just guys who aren't pretentious. Regular guys, no princesses. Guys who don't take themselves too seriously.

"When I go out for fun, I'll usually go to Miami or New York and go barhopping, just doing the club thing. The clubs in L.A. aren't as good. For a date I'll usually just pick some nice restaurant where we can go, have a few drinks and just spend a nice, quiet evening.

"I like rough sex. I like to play with guys' butts. First I like to eat it, lick it, put my finger in it, then two, three, and then my dick. I could eat a nice butt for hours. And I like big dicks because they're more flexible. The smaller ones are pointy, and they can hurt. A big dick feels good, like a massage. I like toys, but I have to be real fuckin' horny to play with them myself or let somebody else play with them with my butt. I don't like a hairy butt, because I want to see the hole. I like a few hairs to play with but not a jungle.

"I like real, normal guys with hot mouths and nice round bubble butts and nice chubby dicks with big, juicy balls. A nice man's body."

"I love getting a blowjob, but one of my least favorite things to do is give a blowjob. And when it comes to getting fucked, I like uncut cocks. You get to feel the foreskin sliding back and forth inside the condom, and that's a big turn-on to me.

"The first time I did a three-way was hot. Everybody was out of control, fucking and sucking. I was fucking and getting fucked all at the same time. God, it felt so good!"

BEST NEW-CUMMERS

"Imagine that nothing else mattered but your penis," Chris Heath, researching the porn industry for *Details*, says. "You are a male porn star. You probably lived in some remote backwater, but you will have moved to Los Angeles. Either a girlfriend or a male buddy from the business brought you in, or you went to one of the few agencies. You find that, even though about 75 percent of would-be studs can't even get it up in the agent's back room when they are given a magazine and left alone for a few minutes, you can. You make a few films, and you realize that it's more difficult than you ever imagined. You struggle. Erections come, but they also go. Then, if you prosper, one day it clicks. You can work, for now.

"You will be paid by the scene. By the orgasm, so to speak. Most men can only do one scene in a day. You may get anywhere from $200 to between $500 and $700 if you are a reliable, well-known specimen.

"...It may be you who has the most difficult job (the girl can fake everything, but there is one thing you may not fake), yet you are only important in one respect: You are the penis. You must stay hard and have sex, whenever it is required, no matter how long the wait or how cold the room or how unattractive you find the other person.

"...You will learn to use any method you discover to keep yourself aroused. Your methods may be banal, or they may be as sick as your imagination allows. But you're just doing the job. You are probably not the kind of person to think too much about it, or to speculate on what your erection supplying fantasies reveal about the darker recesses of human sexuality."

Steven Minuk, the publisher of *Icon*, visited Chi Chi LaRue in Hollywood and was treated to a revealing look behind-the-scenes at the filming of Scene One of "Coach's Boys II," which starred new-cummers Brad Eliot (well-endowed Tom Chase's partner in real life) and Kevin Myles, who was featured as a centerfold in *Advocate Men*.

The scene started slowly but eventually the boys got cooking. "After several more attempts," Minuk reported, "the chemistry between Eliot and Myles becomes definitely exothermic: they begin kissing without any prompting from

LaRue, and Myles starts to massage Eliot's crotch with his hand, and then with his tongue. 'Let's undo that zipper Brad. Reveal that prick for me. Let me see that cock. Suck it up, Eric, baby!' Eliot undoes his zipper and Myles begins to fellate him. LaRue is glued to the TV screen, clenching his fist. The camera crew hovers around Myles and Eliot, at different angles and from different heights, to get close ups of the action. Five or six minutes into the scene, Eliot sports a hard-on though Myles, the coach, is unable to get aroused. Chi Chi shrieks 'cut,' but the two models continue jerking off, kissing and sucking each other, even though the camera has stopped rolling. Considering that they could stop for a break, this burst of libido strikes me as odd: the passion seems genuine, not prefabricated, and the fact that there are about seven *other* people in the studio watching, irrelevant.

"...After Myles gets hard, Chi Chi begins rolling the camera again and both models are now excited as they kiss and perform oral sex. Losing an erection is a common problem in porno movies, where many models can be unable to relax enough to become aroused. In the final version of an adult video, it will seem that our two models were continuously aroused from the moment they began kissing till the moment they had intercourse. In fact, this scene, say fifteen minutes in the movie, will normally take up to six hours to film. (Sometimes, when an actor really can't get it up, the director will call in a "stunt dick" to perform the final honors.)

"After we break for lunch, Eliot and Myles take turns fucking each other gleefully, while LaRue cheerleads them on in front of the TV screen. 'Yes. Brad! Now fuck him!' He crows, as the two bend each other into shapes that would put gymnasts to shame.

"When shooting is complete, and both models have done the *de rigueur* cum scene, Chi Chi calls it a day and marvels at the good chemistry between the two models. More often than not, there's a lack of sexual tension and the production becomes all uphill.

"I ask for a copy of the script and he searches for one on his desk: it turns out to be only *four* pages long. Chi Chi tells me that his assistant is the one who wrote it. Each scene consists of about ten lines of dialogue and stage direction. This makes sense, since the purpose of most adult videos is to get you off, not to stage Oscar-winning performances, at least not for dramatic acting."

LaRue told Minuk, "The average budget for a movie I produce now is about $20,000. And I'm doing about twenty movies a year. At this point I'm making enough money to live comfortably, but I never seem to have any money. It's like I have a huge rent at the house. I have this car payment. I love to travel. I'm out of town all the time. I'm able to pay my bills and able to buy the things I want. A lot of people think that I'm filthy rich and that I have boys laying around my house naked in various special positions. But it's not true. It's actually kind of hectic and stressful and sometimes pretty boring."

Another reason you might want to think long and hard about becoming a porn star is that relationships are made difficult if not impossible. It's like LaRue told Matt Bradshaw, "You don't need a boyfriend. You moved out here to become Matt Bradshaw, so be Matt Bradshaw for a while. Fuck having a boyfriend!"

But you never know where being a slut might lead. A porn star could become tomorrow's print ad superstar. Grind, Buried Undz and Fresh Jive have all started using porn stars (female variety only at this point, sorry). One, Jasmin St. Claire, star of "World's Greatest Gang Bang 2," has also worked as an ESPN commentator. St. Claire said, "People can't say we're just whores anymore. I *am* a whore, but I'm also an entertainer." But we knew that all along!

Freshmen coverboy Jim Buck, photographed by Matson Jones

Jim Buck

"Although he may have had 'star' written all over him, Jim Buck is anything but your typical porn boy," Joseph Manghise wrote in *HX* magazine. "This hazel-eyed Leo has two Master's degrees – the most recent in arts administration – and is just as likely to quote Nietzsche or Camus in conversation as he is to casually reference 'the theory of hybridity' or 'Kinsey's continuum of human sexuality.' But on a visit to New York to film a new movie, Buck arrives looking more like a Chelsea boy than a farm boy. The strands of hair that used to dangle sexily in his eyes have been unceremoniously chopped in favor of a short military-style do. 'My hair kept getting in the way,' he explains. 'So I went home and took out my clippers and began cutting away. I cut off a big clump in the front by mistake, so it all had to come off. The hair was just an aesthetic of Jim Buck, anyway.'

"...Born and raised in Laurel, Mississippi, Buck was always interested in the arts. 'I'm an actor at heart,' he says. In high school, he even appeared in plays with indie film queen Parker Posey. But Buck left the small Southern town to pursue his education in New Orleans in the early '90s.

"It was as an undergrad that he made his first steps toward porn stardom. At a local bar, Buck met a man who was the roommate of drag-superstar-waiting-to-happen Varla Jean Merman. Vidkid Timo, the writer and director of 'Mardi Gras Cowboy,' was a friend of Merman's and an aspiring pornographer with an eye for talent. He and Buck became friends, and seven years later, Timo offered Buck his first part.

"'I love him deeply,' Timo says of Buck. 'He's as smart as he is sexy, and I wouldn't think of doing a porn movie without him.'

"But did the brainy schoolboy have any qualms about making the leap to screen stud? 'I've found the best way to do things in life is to always say yes and never look back,' Buck says. 'Don't think about the consequences, just do it. Timo walked into the gym one day and said, 'They want to do 'Mardi Gras Cowboy.' Do you want to be in it?' Sure, I've never done porno before. Why the hell not?'

"'..Jim Buck is just another name for me attached to my

presence on video. I'm playing a role, so it's not completely me, but it's definitely a part of me.'

"And Buck claims a part of him is actually shy: 'I've not got the best body and I know that,' he says, 'but I'm not really insecure with it. Although standing next to some of those boys, I should be. But I'm shy in other situations. In certain social situations, I'm not outgoing at all. I'm most comfortable with my friends and in situations where there's intimacy, which may explain why I'm so comfortable on a porn set. It's completely intimate; I mean, how much more intimate can you get than having someone's tongue up your butt? That's pretty intimate."

"Buck's trademark Prince Albert-clad cock is the product of an intimate relationship – a lasting token of 'the man who broke my heart.' He says that his now ex-boyfriend thought piercings were sexy. 'It stuck in my mind, so when he dumped me and I was delirious, I went to a local piercing salon and said, 'I'd like a Prince Albert.' I'm still not sure if it was to get back at him or to get him back,' Buck shrugs.

"But it has certainly provided him with a memorable gimmick and makes him stand out in the sometimes cookie-cutter world of porn. 'There's a formula out there, and everyone tries to follow it,' he says. 'But there are a lot of us who are tired of the formula...

"When he's not busy making porn, Buck can be found tooling around New Orleans in his pickup truck or spending time with his dog, Gaston. Although he claims that Jim Buck doesn't get asked out on many dates, the actor hints that he's recently met a special someone whom he's been 'bewitched, bothered and bewildered by.'

"'I've reached a point in my life where I refuse to wake up when I'm 70 or 80 or 90 and say, 'Why the fuck didn't I do that?' Life is way too short. I've had nothing but fun doing porn ...It's a way of getting up and entertaining people and being kooky and letting it out, whatever it is.'"

Rico de la Playa, director of "Mardi Gras Cowboy," wrote *The Guide* to thank them for a favorable review of the video. He also thought it "refreshing" that the reviewer knew the film "Midnight Cowboy." "I'm surprised by how many people don't know this film (mainly 18 to 30-year-olds," de la Playa said. "As porn, 'Mardi Gras Cowboy' is problematic. I've got it all worked out now, though. (Director) Wash West was the guy that got me started in porn. I owe it to him. After seeing 'Mardi Gras Cowboy,' he gave a lecture (Porn 101) on the proper way to shoot sex scenes. So my next film will be a very big improvement. I really hope porn continues to go in a new direction. It seems to be moving too slowly, though. I plan to continue to make porn with lots of humor. I think it's really the only way to go. And of course, most importantly, hot sex."

"Jim Buck is an amazing actor," *In Touch* raved after seeing him in "Mardi Gras Cowboy." "In fact, he's so good, one wonders why he's actually in porno. But, what the hell. We're more than lucky to have him. He's a bit more natural looking than most porn stars, but he's unsurpassingly sexy and undeniably charming. And, if that isn't enough, he has a beautiful, big cock that's strikingly pierced with a Prince Albert."

In Buck's second video, "Dr. Jerkoff and Mr. Hard," he plays Dr. Stephen Jerkoff, who has "'Brady Bunch' hair, a mustache like a stillborn shih tzu, and dorky glasses," *The Guide* said. "We first see him dribbling out of UCLA's Plasma Physics Building and meandering across campus to his olive-drab nerd-mobile. He moves with the grace of a penguin tormented by piles. His voice oozes out of his sinuses. Fellow faculty members shun him; insolent students take advantage of his willingness to let them turn their work in late. His mother (Lola Cornfeld) is a nag. Venturing into a gay bar, he's scorned and rebuffed. 'I haven't had sex since the last Star Trek convention,' he laments, 'and that was with a Klingon.' Desperation drives him to consult a vaguely Santerian spiritualist, Madame Guadeloupe (Carmen), who sells him a potion 'that will unchain the wild man inside of you.' The mixture looks suspiciously like Pepto-Bismol. Jerkoff samples it anyway, and in a flash he morphs into Mr. Hard, a clean-shaven, hard-bodied stud with club-rat hair, dropdead attitude, and Buck's trademark Prince Albert. Entranced by his new appearance, Jerkoff/Hard makes love to his reflection in a floor-to ceiling mirror, brushing his lips and cock against the glass until he spurts. Limited by the four-hour duration of his transformations, he goes on the prowl for sex and finds it in an alley with an unsuspecting student and in the backroom of his local bar. We've all seen a few too many versions of the

Jekyll-Hyde scenario' but British director Wash West infuses the material with new comic life. This is the skillfully shot, masterfully edited video project of a wryly intelligent artist who loves sex and loves film (and should be working in that riskier and more expensive medium). Dr. Jerkoff is full of good jokes, bad jokes, quotable lines, good performances, film-maker's riffs, and homages to '70s porn and movies like 'My Own Private Idaho.' All this only enhances the erotic passages that start with a fire-lit encounter between Matt Easton and buddy Mason Walker and conclude with happy, spontaneous sex between Easton and Buck. As a homeless drifter who piques Jerkoff's interest, Matt Easton, in a fine, understated performance, provides Buck with a perfect foil. There are flaws. You may wish, for example, that Jack Simmons wasn't sidelined halfway through his hot backroom three-way with Buck and Dax Kelly, and you may find the visually complex but overlong dream sequence a bit arty – here the expert pacing flags, and West appears to be showing off. Quibbles aside, Dr. Jerkoff is several cuts above the average gay video.

"Jim Buck, whose appearance as Jerkoff follows a remarkable debut in 'Mardi Gras Cowboy,' is developing one of the most likable personae in the history of gay porn. He takes infectious delight in having sex on camera, and his studly Mr. Hard is as funny as his dweeby Jerkoff. Attractive in a fresh, accessible way, he's a real actor whose career should expand into crossover roles. (John Waters, please take note.) Meanwhile, in West's capable hands, he shines. Here is a director who knows how to raise the sexual temperature through character..."

Jerry Douglas in *Manshots* said, "'Dr. Jerkoff and Mr. Hard' is not so much about the battle of good and evil that is explored in Stevenson's novella as it is about the ugly duckling who becomes a swan. The new variation by director Wash West is an ambitious achievement that succeeds more often than not, and reminds us once again what a promising talent he is. It also features a notable newcomer, Jim Buck. ...(He) is either one hell of a narcissist or one hell of an actor, probably both. ...He engineers a high-energy threeway with Dax Kelly and Jack Simmons, in which he calls all the shots and proves himself to be quite a pricktease before he gets around to giving head, fucking both of them, and delivering a hailstorm money shot.

...(In his scene with Easton) Buck proves that he has learned one can be both gorgeous and giving. And his final money shot, right into the camera, is absolutely atomic!

"Keep your eye out for director West's next project, and your fly unzipped for Mr. Buck, in case you happen to run into him."

In Wash West's "Toolbox," Buck stars in the first of four vignettes, aptly named "Dumb As Paint." It stars, *In Touch* gushed, "the incredible Jim Buck and Hank Monahan as two painters who take some time off to get off. As always, Jim is amazing, especially as he's getting fucked by the remarkably tall and lanky Hank. Wash West's style is equally interesting, with lots of movement, quick cuts, and unnatural angles."

Real Men in *HX* called All-Worlds' "Gold Diggers" "another campy cruisefest from our favorite wigged-out flesh peddler, Chi Chi LaRue. The drag demon has taken overnight porn sensation Jim Buck under her wing and cast him as a swishy bitch – a far cry from his bad boy debut in 'Mardi Gras Cowboy.' Sporting a Chelsea do and less body hair than the good Lord gave him, Buck joins Jay Anthony, Sam Dixon, Kevin Gold and others in this tale of lust, power and greed. The movie opens at the reading of a sugar daddy's will. (The poor executor of the estate has to put up with all kinds of shade from the harem of twinkies who've come to soak up the inheritance.) Naturally, the old geezer couldn't croak without sticking it to his boys one last time: The will states that they must live under the same roof and have sex with one another before they can inherit all of his riches. Needless to say, the gold diggers put aside their petty rivalries and waste no time getting down to business.

"In one incredibly hot scene, the houseboy takes a break from polishing the limo and sucks off four guys at once. One by one they jam their cocks down his throat and shoot loads on his chest.

"After the gang-bangers drain their veins, Buck and Anthony get into a flap over who was daddy's favorite slut. But their wrestling match soon turns into a spirited round of French kisses, blowjobs and intense butt sex."

Speaking of butts, Joe McKenna in *Inches*, in his review of Mike Donner's "A Tale of Two Brothers," comments that in the very first scene, "there's an intense close-up of Jim Buck's hairy ass and balls. Taken from behind, the shot records Buck's dick sliding in and out of Josh Conners' tight, hairless hole. But it wasn't the cock I found myself staring at. No, it was the hair on his nuts, scrotum and upper thighs – a mat of masculinity. In an industry where rock-solid men are often de-pubed before they get in front of the camera, although thankfully this annoying trend is changing), Jim Buck's ass hair is a badge of honor. The only thing better than seeing it would be tasting it."

In the video, Buck plays "a well-heeled (and very well-hung) Los Angeles restaurateur who's being urged by his lawyer to track down his long-lost brother, who was given up for adoption when he and Buck were infants," Fred Goss explained in *Advocate Men*. "Actually, both brothers were adopted, but apparently not as a package deal. As an incentive for the reluctant Buck, there's a lot of dough to be inherited if the missing bro is found. Why Buck would inherit the cash instead of his sibling isn't clear, but if it wouldn't end up in our star's pockets, then I fail to see why he should give a fuck. Or a Buck. Except, well, there would go the plot. All this *tsuris* about the brother follows a very tasty scene in which Buck administers a formidable fuck to street hustler Josh Conners. Buck treats Conners like trash, though he's rather appealing. Buck, however, is just not a happy camper, though camp it up he does from time to time. There's no camping in this fuck scene, though, and to say it gets things off with a bang is to use an unavoidable but perfectly apt pun. I like to think of him as Jim Fuck."

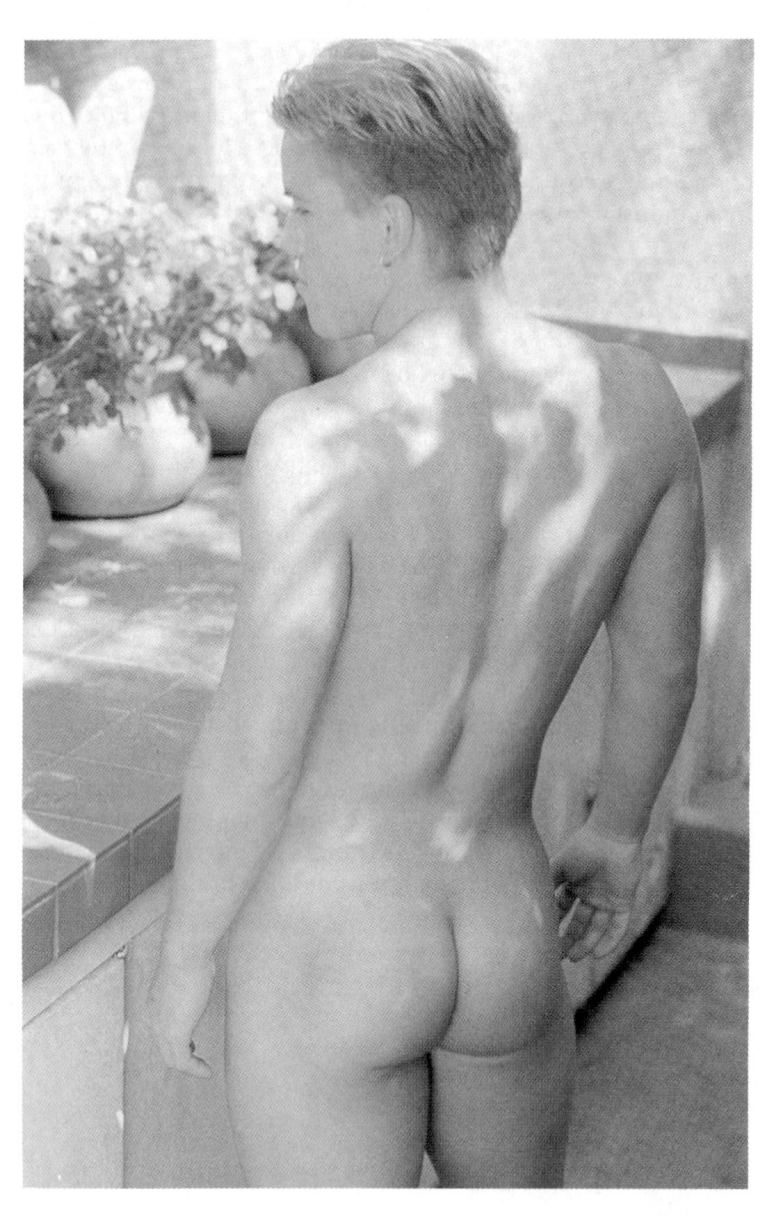

Jake Cannon, another great Chi Chi LaRue discovery, courtesy All Worlds

Jake Cannon

A reader in Montreal wrote *The Guide* after they featured Jake Cannon on their cover in a still from "Beached:" "Cannon is very hot and it made me go out and rent his video. Thanks again! I now have to go and jerk off to Jake!"

Jerking off to visions of Jake apparently became a national epidemic during most of 1997.

"In 'The Taking of Jake, Jake Cannon looks like jailbait," Robert Sumners in *Mondo Porno* said. "This is a good thing. But, alas, he is awful. I thought I was watching Night of the Living Dead when he delivered his lines. He may be cute but when he talked dirty, he couldn't have seemed less genuine. 'Oh fuck me. Please.' Whatever. But it does have a great cum shot, with hot-n-horny criminal Derrick Baldwin blowing his wad with verve over Cannon's young, pretty (and empty) head."

In Centaur's "Raw Recruits," Jake Cannon appears with porn vet Brett Winters. *In Touch* noted, "...Stocky blond Jake Cannon shares a fantasy with Brett Winters. The two of them are transported to a place where they can enjoy each other unrushed and uninterrupted. With nothing by black surrounding them, the two boys fuck almost poetically to create a visually stunning scene."

Rick & Dave in *Frontiers* described this hot scene: "'Recruit' Winters is out jogging and twists his ankle. He shows up in the infirmary and is assisted by chunky 'medic' Cannon. As Jake kneels over to help Brett, they stare into each other's eyes. There, in the darkness of Brett's imagination, Jake is naked and stroking Brett's rock hard cock. Jake goes down on Brett and licks his chest and stomach. Brett boinks Jake and we notice that Brett has a tan line, even though Kyle did not. (Reviewer Dave gets bored and his mind wanders. He asks whether anyone has ever attained more popularity in porn for having a tanline.) Brett shoots a huge load and Jake shoots a load."

In the end, say Rick & Dave, "the moral of the story is: Don't ask. Don't tell. Don't let 'em find your dildo."

In "White Hot," Cannon is involved in a threeway in a white-tiled steamroom with Bryan Kidd, and Ethan-Michael

Ayers. Ayers, as the only top in the group, fucks both Cannon and Kidd, and all three men come and kiss. *Manshots* says, "Unfortunately, Ayers does not look good as a bleached blond – it is too obviously fake."

In their review of "Beached," *In Touch* said, "Every actor in this porno is young, boyish and golden-skinned. The video stars Jake Cannon in the role of a down-and-out beach kid who gets kicked out by his disenchanted boyfriend Troy Halston. Despite Jake's love for Troy and the awesome sex they have, Troy becomes discontented and starts cheating on Jake with platinum haired Ethan-Michael Ayers.

"After being kicked out, Jake wanders the beach in search of a new place to start. He comes across Drew Nolan, who, even though he's 'straight', is curious enough to take Jake home, and live happily ever after with him.

"In two scenes, Troy demonstrates what a good fuck he is with two distinct, butt-ramming performances. Jake is also impressive in his two scenes, showing off his full ass and getting fucked with the fever of a true pig bottom. It absolutely must be seen."

Floyd Johnson in *Freshmen* commented, "Nolan and Cannon are immediately joined at the face, then Cannon's face to Nolan's dick, then Nolan's dick to Cannon's ass. An undying love is born, and Cannon has a new home. OK, it's a bit formulaic. But seeing Cannon perform is worth the price of admission."

And speaking of admissions, when interviewed by Jamoo for *Freshmen*, Sam Dixon said his favorite on-screen sex partner was Cannon (in Falcon's "The Player"): "He's really cute...just his look and his personality. He's got that kind of straight jock-boy attitude that's really cute."

Speaking of Winters, he told *Urge* magazine's Hank Ferguson that he was aroused in "pretty much every scene" he has ever done! Said Winters, "You get to a certain point where your body is like 'Okay, it's time to cum' and you have to tell your body, 'No, it's not.' And you have to start thinking about... pussy or something. Anything, so I don't come.

"I have a good friend, Hank Hightower, who is definitely the best guy to work with. He is professional. He knows the ingredients to a movie. It's easy. Basically, I like more masculine, dark-haired, hairy guys. They don't have to be hairy. But they tend to be more masculine. I don't like to be dominated or to dominate. I like it to be an equal situation."

Winters is famous for his incredibly thick prick, and he's never had any complaints, except once. "One model did tell me that I hurt him a little bit. I do feel bad about that. But, he didn't tell me at the time (we were doing it), so I didn't know." Winters says he is very sensitive himself and would never bottom: "I just think that the bottom's image is more vulnerable. I wouldn't be a 'proud bottom' because I would be in pain and everyone would see that."

We mention Winters here, among these profiles of newcummers, because of this observation on the biz he made to Ferguson: "It is very hard to be a porn star in public because you have to put up with a lot of shit. I have people coming up to me all the time. People follow me home. I have a lot of jealous, bitchy queens talking about me constantly, pointing at me. They are very hypocritical. They'll watch (my movies), jack off and they'll cum. And yet when they see me (in person), they talk about me like I'm this evil thing. That's because a lot of people who watch my movies are mainstream, middle-class people.

"I know some of the other porn stars that do the leather movies – some of the more avant garde, San Francisco type movies – and their fans are great. They are very open minded and when they see them, it' s like 'Hi, it's nice to meet you.' When they see me, it's almost like they watch me (on film) yet they'll tell everybody they don't. It's like they 'accidentally saw me,' like a picture of me or a video of me fell out of the sky and landed and they were forced to see that I did movies. It's almost like they think they know something about me that's bad."

BONUS BOOK:
LEGENDARY SEX PIGS
& THE BIG HUSTLE

*It Pays to Advertise: A hairy Tom Katt,
photographed by Anneli Adolfsson for All Man*

Introduction

"A porn star's take-home pay is dramatically increased by his off-screen work," Scott Seomin noted in *Icon* magazine. "...a lot of men will pay big bucks to have sex with a porn star. It is this fact that makes a gay porn video simply an infomercial for a hustler."

"The vast majority of actors - or models, as I prefer to call them - supplement their incomes by hustling," Gino Colbert told Seomin. "Any model who denies prostituting himself at one time or another is simply lying. One cannot survive on videos alone, because the career of a gay porn model is extremely short. Consumers want to see new faces all the time and get tired of the old ones after two or three years. If they're smart and have a marquee name, there's a lot of money to be made for a porn star."

Mark Adams in *Video View* noted, "Cougar Cash is now doing what he does best on stage in San Francisco, performing live sex acts while his partner reads poetry. Obviously, a class act all the way." A class act who also advertises his services regularly the *Bay Area Reporter*.

"I'm much more marketable because of my film work," Jake Andrews told Seomin. "I took out an ad in the 'models and escorts' section of the *Bay Area Reporter* in '92. I had made a couple of videos, but they weren't out yet, so that first ad was not lucrative because I didn't have name recognition." Once his first two videos hit the stores, Andrews found himself in big demand at $300 to $400 an hour. "The next ad I took out said, 'Jake Andrews, star of *The Swallowers* and *Jaw Breakers* at the top of it. My pager went off constantly. And it was a lot easier to get the price *I* wanted. It came down to my film work - that's the only reason I get escort requests, even with my high prices."

Seomin notes that in addition to their high fees, most porn-stars-for-hire enjoy the high life: "Case in point: versatile model Rob Cryston, who has appeared in over 90 videos and retired after just five years in the business. "With my clients, I got to travel most of the world, including South America, most of Europe and the West Indies. One guy took me on the

QE2 to England. Coming from a small middle-class family that didn't have too much money, I got to do and see so many different things that most people will never see or do." Capitalizing on his porn-star status, the 5'8" Cryston commanded handsome fees. "Basically, I charged $2,500 for a two-day weekend, plus expenses. Longer trips were more and my by-the-hour fee started at about $300."

Hustling on the side does have its drawbacks, Seomin acknowledges, such as sexually unappealing - or even repulsive - customers. "It's true," says Blue Blake, a favorite star of Colbert's. "The men who pay for sex are usually, but not always, the older, overweight and balding stereotype. So basically, you just lay back and let them suck your dick. It's not totally awful. I mean, how bad can a bad blow job be?"

And although Andrews admitted to Seomin that he has worked for up to three customers a day, the work is not something he ever really enjoys. "It's just odd to go to someone's house or hotel and do a sex act," he notes. "Some of the guys can be pretty gross. I'm not real comfortable with it - I don't like that kind of work." Fortunately for Andrews and other gay porn stars, there is another way to cash in: dancing in gay clubs around the world and doing "the circuit." *Circuit Noize* magazine defines "The Circuit" as "a series of queer parties that gives gay men the chance to escape the pressures of day-to-day existence and to enter the altered world where man-to-man sex is not only accepted, but is celebrated." The Florida-based publication, which boasts the sub-title "A Rag Custom Designed For Crazed Party Boys," covers such legendary circuit parties as Montreal's Black and Blue Party, Miami's White Party, London's Red Heart Party, and Fire Island's Morning Party. "A well-timed, advertised appearance by a porn star can elevate a circuit party from a no-interest event to something special that everyone just has to go to," says *Circuit Noize* publisher Gary Steinberg. "Hiring porn actors as a draw is smart business. After all, they can be considered the stars. of our community. We spend many private, intimate moments with them." How a model is utilized at a circuit party - and how he is compensated - varies. "I have seen porn stars do everything from simply dancing on a speaker and signing autographs," notes Steinberg, "to modeling live in a condom fashion show."

"A porn star can make a fortune doing the dance circuit," Blake told Seomin. "I've made more money than God by dancing for $2,500 for a 15-minute set." It's an expense, he says, the clubs can easily afford. "Club managers and promoters will hire a porn star to dance or strip on a given night and then heavily advertise the model's appearance at the club. It's simple but it works in packing in the crowds. And since my name got out there through gay videos, I've been in demand for in-person appearances." Blake has danced from London to Paris to Budapest to Berlin as well as all over the U.S. and Canada, which reveals just how far and wide his video work is appreciated.

"Since the dance circuit has become hugely popular, I've seen many guys do porn just to build up a name so they can go out and dance," Colbert told Seomin. "A video career makes an immense difference. Male strippers who have been at it for years cannot make the kind of money that they later make once they do a couple of porn movies."

Seomin notes that if a A-list porn star earns $1,000 per sex scene and completes two scenes for a video, he's earned two grand. "Multiply that by, say 20 videos a year, and said porn star takes in $40,000 for his camera work in a single year. However, if the same actor/model works privately for just four clients a week at the average marquee-name rate of $350 per hour, his yearly income will increase by over $72,800. Additional income should be considered, of course, such as the $2000 to $3000 circuit party appearance fees as well as those $1000-for-an-overnight stay customers and $2500 weekend clients. Complete the math and it is apparent that although he may not carry a briefcase, a porn star can be a smart businessman as he supplements his on-camera earnings."

Fans of Rob Cryston will be disappointed to learn that he has made his last video, now lives with his boyfriend in a monogamous relationship and works full-time as an office manager. Cryston was one of the more industrious porn stars, according to Seomin. Cryston said, "I sold clothing, personalized videos and locks of hair. You know, guys would ask me to wear the same underwear for a week and then send it to them."

"As far as I'm concerned, I'm retired from porn," Cryston told Seomin. "I'm happy with my life where it is now. The industry allowed me to make a load of money, most of which is now in Mobil stock. Some of that will go to my little brother's college education. When I got into porn, I was curious and got what I wanted out of it: money. And I'm grateful for that."

Writer Robert Sellers recalls how "handsome men of slender means" paid the rent when he was coming out.

"For many, the stereotype of the hustler is that of a skinny, streetwise kid driven to prostitution out of desperation. He may or may not be homosexual. He may or may not enjoy the sexual contact he has with his clients. But he lets the 'faggots' take his meat into their mouths, palms the cash they offer him and has lots of tough-talkin' girlfriends to remind him of his basic 'masculinity.'

"(In) the 1970s, this image began to change. The era ushered in the new age of sexual permissiveness, and the prostitute was less and less viewed as a low-life. Young hustlers were now classy, well-fed, and well-bred. They were 'call boys,' sophisticated, sharply-dressed men on the make who, far from being desperate, willingly chose a career in prostitution and made hundreds of dollars a week in their profession. These were gay gigolos. Educated, cultured, a far cry from the gutter-tramps of the past.

"Both types of male whores, of course, are still in abundance – still the average hustler falls somewhere between the street and the service – the call boy service, that is. That was the midway category that I fell into during my period as a hustler in the early seventies. I was in my early 20s then, just out of the closet, with a BA in English from a New England college that was virtually useless in getting me any kind of job more prestigious than filing documents or stuffing envelopes. I won't say I was 'forced' into prostitution. Actually, I was kind of intrigued into it. The notion of selling my body for cash held a powerful excitement for me. And it made sense. Making a living through such pleasurable activity was preferable to working in an office for an insubstantial salary.

"Many hustlers, despite their good looks, are actually insecure about their appearance. They need the constant reaffirmation that such a career can give. This was true for me, as I arrived in N.Y.C. Also I was interested in renting out my dick because it seemed daring, unconventional, 'outlaw.' Like many people who were unpopular as children, I looked upon being 'outcast' as a rather romantic state. Hustling was thus the perfect anti-hero profession."

Anti-hero or not, hustlers have always fascinated me. Being with them, you sense an exhilarating release of positive energy. They are viscerally exciting. They have the requisite beauty, the requisite body, but most also have the brains to set them apart from the others who are also attractive. They know what to do with their gifts.

Porn stars especially light my fire. When I am with them, I feel intense flashes of power. Yet, knowing their abusive lifestyles and the sybaritic abandon they put into their performances, I know my allotted time with them is perversely short. That's why the fact that I possess them still, on video, is so appealing. I'll never forget the time I visited Kevin Kramer in Hollywood and one morning he took a friend to the airport so I was alone in his apartment. He had several videos starring himself I had never seen. I slipped one in and in moments I was hard and coming. The fact that I was watching this incredible performance in the comfort of the star's own apartment was a new experience that sent me flying.

For your edification, we present a group of legendary stars who have impressed me over the years, followed by a group working today who have sent me flying, in one way or another.

*The legendary Rick Donovan,
photographed at the height of his fame by Bo Tate*

Rick Donovan

We are taught by mass media to admire bigness. The greatest, the grandest, the most beautiful. It makes sense that we should include cocks as an object of our esteem. The downside is that the person with whom you become obsessed can be reduced to a statistic. This was the opinion of Nick Jerrett, whom I chanced to meet after he appeared in "Summer of Scott Noll," wherein he fucked Leo Ford with that incredibly thick, long rod of his.

Nick said, "Psychologically, I don't think anyone minds having a big cock, but along with the benefits come the problems, like people looking at you just for that."

Dr. Charles Silverstein, in his book *Man to Man*, agrees, noting that "in the gay world of today, the penis is revered. The big cock is the prize, adorned and adored, the possessor enormously attractive to the hungry hunter who wants to engulf it or be overpowered by it, with minimal regard for other physical characteristics, and none whatsoever for emotional or social ones." I understood Nick's position completely, that's why I preferred "dates" with the objects of my desire rather than quickie sessions.

While I thought Nick's cock was grand, and he knew how to use it better than almost anyone I've ever met, I was totally bowled over by Rick Donovan's a year later, revealed in a scene lodged in the middle of yet another William Higgins travelogue, this one called "Sailor in the Wild." It was yet another poolside sequence that could have played in almost any other film. Sunbather Leo Ford, Higgins' blond utility bottom, was suddenly coming on to a hunky dude with wide-set eyes, a thick neck and a laconic manner. Once Leo got the man out of his pants, he started hungrily working on the stud's cock and, as if by magic, one of the biggest cocks anybody had ever seen in porn was springing to life. And another porn legend was born.

While the reactions to his endowment amuse him now, in fact, he never realized what he had until he was in his late teens: "Of course, I went through high school having sex with cheerleaders who always said, 'My God, you're SO big!' But my theory was, 'Well, how many cocks has she seen? One? Two? Five tops!' Secondly, girls are taught to think dicks are the size of a thumb, and anybody's is big compared to a thumb. And when I was in the military, there were prostitutes telling me how big I was. But I discounted that, too, because they're paid to tell you how big you are. My first lover was the one that convinced me I was big."

Unlike Roger, another horsehung performer I fancied years earlier who had the biggest basket I'd ever seen, Rick showed nothing - and he loved it. "When I'm soft I don't show a basket," he revealed. "It's the biggest deceiver in the world. It's great because I know people are attracted to me, not my dick because they can't see it." (Can't you just hear echoes of the poor little rich girl's lament, "I want a man whose interested in me, not my money?")

When I saw Rick he played a super-macho role, which was fine with me. That's part of the fantasy in adoring a super-hung stud. Doug Richards of *Manshots* agrees: "The myth perpetuated by the on-screen persona of a mega-endowed star is that a man with a big cock is the quintessential man, and as such, never, assumes what has become known as 'the female role.' The message that a big cock equals control, control means power and power is potency, sexual potency."

So potent is the vision of Rick fucking it is recalled with great joy many years later. When L.A. club promoter Billy Limbo began his series of weekly happenings in Beverly Hills, he called it Club 1984. Dirk Festive, writing in *The Advocate*, said: "But we choose to remember 1984 not by breaking out our preppy handbooks, gravity-defying collars, and skinny ties but by bending over a schoolroom desk and taking Rick 'Humongous' Donovan's dick up our ass. The scene in question is the boffo opening from Matt Sterling's 'The Bigger the Better,' and the man facedown in the inkwell was the adorable Matt Ramsey."

Indeed, Rick Donovan was responsible for more "boffo openings" than anybody I can think of. But as he proceeded from one hot video to another, Rick was dogged with the reputation that he couldn't get it up. The truth was, it took a long time for the monster to rise. He joked, "Sure, it does take me ten minutes to get a hard-on, but, Jesus, give me a break. It takes a half-pint of blood to get this thing up!"

He defended himself by reciting a litany of his finest on-screen performances, where he undoubtedly had the biggest hard-on most people had ever seen. He considered Matt Sterling's "The Bigger the Better" his best, and he liked "The Arousers," "The Biggest One I Ever Saw," and his debut film, "Sailor in the Wild." John Rowberry comments on "The Bigger the Better:" "The high-quality production values, mixed with a cast of ever-erect actors, and some ball-churning sex (like Matt Ramsey getting plowed by his student, super-hung Rick Donovan), set the standard for a new generation of gayporn video. The sex never lets up."

Rick's theory was that he had to be a star with his first outing. "The first thing you do sets the standard for good. I lucked out with William Higgins. He's a good filmmaker and he said I could choose who I wanted to work with and they would also want to work with me. And he offered me a lot of money. As it turned out, Leo Ford (his co-star) was a great guy to work with. Everything clicked."

Rick was not to have the same success with every video. In "Boys of Company F" he does a credible job of playing a hard-nosed sergeant but he doesn't have sex until the end and gets lost in the shuffle of the orgy. In the appropriately titled "King Size," Rick is paired with Jesse Koehler. Bijou said, "The sight of Donovan's whang buried deep in Koehler's ass is lusciously lewd, but much of the action fails to rise above mediocrity."

Off-screen, Rick said he preferred the company of transvestites and lived with Nicole Murray, a regular at the Brass Rail in San Diego, for many years. He made only one video with a TV, however: "She's A He," with a pre-op Lelani.

Dave Kinnick, in his excellent book *Sorry I Asked*, recalls the time he worked with Rick in 1986 on "Stick Shift:" "We were in the little studio in North Hollywood that was next door to The Compound bathhouse. We had a car pulled into the room and the background draped with black cloth. Rick was going to fuck Michael Vincent, but first he had to get that huge thing of his hard. With Rick, it was always a challenge. One can't blame him, not with *that* thing hanging between his legs.

"But we worked Rick that day. First off, you have to know what Rick is into. Rick likes to look at pictures of transsexuals. That's what gets him hard. So, we have these TV mags spread out on the floor in front of him. Michael Vincent waits in the wings drinking Diet Cokes. As Rick gets closer to being hard, stroking for close to an hour, the director signals us into position. My job was running and monitoring the two decks. The two cameramen start to stalk the subject, jockeying into position, trying not to break Rick's concentration.

"It was supposed to be one of those fantasy scenes that directors like to fall back on and it soon came time to bring out the old rented fog-making machine and squirt some white puffy stuff around the set to make it pretty. Of course, these machines work on the principle of very hot oil ejected forcibly out of a nozzle, theoretically making white smoke in the process. One of these production assistants grabbed the machine as instructed and began to make clouds down close to the floor, all around and behind Rick. Just as things started to look promising, a big glob of very hot oil that had failed to turn into smoke shot out of the nozzle and hit Rick around his knees. Rick yelped. The production assistant jumped about a foot in the air. All hell broke loose. Rick's erection ran down the flag. There was a good deal of sadness in the air. It wasn't serious, though; the oil didn't burn and we were back in business a few minutes later. I think some of the oil got on the she-male pictures, however. I don't know if the ink smeared on them or not, but Rick didn't seem to have any more erection problems for the rest of the day."

In "Bi and Beyond II," starring hermaphrodite cult figurehead Delilah, big Rick's a sad sight trying to get an erection with a rubber slipped over his humongous equipment. "The closing orgy is silliness personified," John Rowberry says, "but note that Rick Donovan finally found a condom that fits." Rick manages to get it in and there are a few brief glimpses of him plowing the field, but, again, he's lost in the shuffle.

After that video, Rick retired to teach scuba diving, then bounced back in Jerry Douglas' award-winning "More of a Man," in which he gets it on with Joey Stefano, although he doesn't fuck the infamous ass.

In Falcon's "The Big Ones" Rick demonstrates the reason he's legendary in porn circles. There he is, in 1991, still sporting a macho mustache, looking better than ever, reading lines with aplomb and fucking grandly. He even kisses his bedmate goodbye. It's a short peck on the lips but it's better than nothing. The only thing we found fault with was the fact that there was a noticeable lack of latex in his scene, odd for a star who has appeared in several "safe sex" entries in his lengthy, in more ways than one, career.

In 1994 he returned briefly to the video cameras playing, of all things, a john, who picks up, of all people, Danny Sommers, for some quick sex in "Club Sex-A-Holics" for Fox Studio, directed by William Hunter. "Unfortunately," Hank R. Chief said in *AVN*, "these guys failed to eat their Wheaties, so their huge wienies spend much of the time half-cocked." Especially Donovan, who continues to suffer from an inability to get fully hard, even when tended to by a sexualist as fine as Danny Sommers. (They must not have had any pictures of transvestites around – that's the only thing that sparks Rick's interest.) "Yes," Hank says, "Rick Donovan, otherwise known as the donkey dick of the '80s, displays a temperamental hard-on through all of the oral and anal festivities. I got a good sense of what Hunter was trying to accomplish. In the good old days, having a generous endowment seemed to be a prerequisite for being a top. You don't have to be a size queen to appreciate the hot ass-stretching action. Unfortunately, these performers don't always deliver..."

Danny saves the scene, however, with his marvelous on-screen charisma and his sweet gesture of giving Rick back his money after he gets off but Rick doesn't.

One of Rick's more memorable performances late in his video career was in the sequel to the popular "Dynastud," "Dynastud 2: Powerhouse." Kinnick summed up Rick's appeal when he commented, "Rick Donovan is just one of the all-time best tops and it is a pleasure to watch him work over Tanner Reeves."

Amazing as it may seem, even today Rick is listed occasionally in the classified sections of gay magazines as being available for escort. Bigger, it seems, is *always* better.

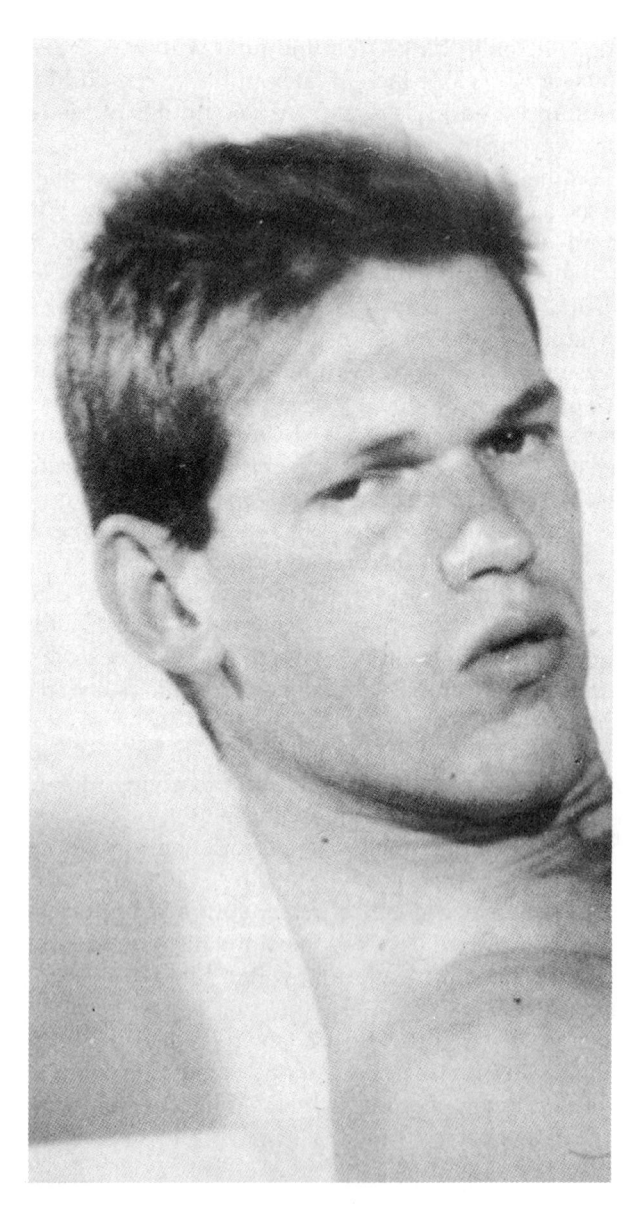

Scott O'Hara in his heyday

Scott O'Hara

"August 11, 1985: won Greasy Jockstrap Contest at Powerhouse San Francisco; met Al Parker. September 2, 1985: fucked by Al Parker."
– *The Journal of Scott O'Hara*

The above entry is significant because it is the *only* journal entry in his autobiography, called *Autopornography*, that Scott O'Hara makes note of any overt sexual activity. It may well be that this was *the* fuck of O'Hara's young life. One can well imagine it was. Or maybe it was second to his sex with Jon King. Or Chris Burns. Or maybe David Ashfield, or maybe...well, you get the picture.

O'Hara's book was met with almost universal praise – and good sales. In his review of *Autopornography*, Lawrence Butler, in *Lambda Book Report*, says, "He starts off light, with anecdotes about his childhood as a sexual rebel. Always open-minded, he cheerfully advises that readers 'who couldn't care less about my formative years should now 'skip to the good parts.' The good parts begin on page 55, but really, you shouldn't skip the rest. Part of the fun of this book lies in recognizing yourself in his quirky but basically normal adolescence. The difference: 'I was a boy who knew what he wanted.' Young Scott moves easily from jailbait to happy pro: 'Why, it seemed perfectly natural to me.' Mightn't anyone, possessed of a clear head and 'The Biggest Dick in San Francisco,' have taken the same path? Just as naturally, we are led through the growing consciousness of the plague in the early 1980s, its effect on the porn industry, the deaths of friends, and the sexual defiance for which he has become more recently notorious. Through it all, O'Hara takes notes, fills diaries, compulsively keeps lists...

"Names are named, members measured, kinks explored – foreskin, fist, piss and John (sic) King fans take note... It's hard not to like him, and he does speak with a certain authority. We are convinced of his honesty ('two inches' or 'two fists,' I believe him), charmed by his unlikely modesty ('I think a whopper is a nuisance, whether on oneself or on one's sex partners'), and somehow grateful for his missionary generosity ('...everyone has a sex life, even those who seem totally unsuited for it')."

O'Hara is at his most poignant when he is recalling how it all began with Parker: "I didn't go in for these contests as a general rule, especially in bars it didn't seem like my arena. I mean, you can't show your dick in a bar, and god knows my chest is nothing special to look at. I don't have rippling abs or dazzling deltoids. But hey, a jockstrap contest is crotch-oriented enough that I figured I could win it. I also wanted to meet Drew (Al Parker), and hopefully be in one of his videos. (He'd already established a reputation as a foreskin lover, even before his own foreskin restoration; I figured that if I were in an Al Parker video, I could count on some uncut dick, at the very least.) As the Saturday night approached, I realized I needed that $100 prize to buy groceries for the weekend, having dreadfully mismanaged my checking account the previous week. So I showed up, still somewhat uncertain about actually entering; no one else wanted to enter, either, so they upped the prize to $150 and got (I think) three contestants. Maybe it was four. I think two of the contestants were twins. Mr. Marcus, the perpetual emcee at these events, poured motor oil all over our jockstraps, and we got to be as lewd and lascivious as we felt comfortable with, which meant that my dick did get exposed (surprise, surprise), and yes, I won. Drew and I made the connection, he made the inevitable offer, and we scheduled the shoot for early September. He even hinted that I might be paired with Jon King – which made my dick jump to attention right away. I'd never met King, at that point, but I'd always wanted to. Unfortunately, it didn't happen: Jon got arrested, or disappeared, or something.

"The week before the shoot, Drew and his lover invited me down to spend the weekend at their house in Hermosa Beach. Oh, it was an official audition, too, I suppose, but I was just enjoying myself. It's the only real 'casting couch' interview I've ever had: I spent the night sandwiched between the two of them. I've always liked sandwiches. I fucked Steve, Drew did his pretzel number with his dick and my dick, and eventually fucked me. A good time was had by all. And I was officially hired. The next weekend, it was frantic and laid-back, simultaneously. Drew, having been a performer himself, knew how to make performers perform: don't tell them how to do their job, just turn them loose on each other and let them go to town. I was in three scenes in that video, all shot over the course of the weekend. Only one of them was really difficult for me, partly because I was asked to fuck someone standing up. That's never been an easy position for me to work from and my partner, a lovely blond, although quite turned on and enthusiastic, with a wonderfully muscular bubble-butt, just didn't inspire me the way one of the Italian boys in the other scenes might have. Still, I think all the scenes worked out adequately. I have only one complaint, and I can't decide if it was deliberate sadism or accidental bad luck.

"Drew, in his original interview, had asked me what sort of partner I'd be most turned on by. I had a pretty good stock description of my ideal type: dark-haired, dark-skinned, foreskinned, with a last name like Lopez or Rodriguez or Alfaro or Dal Porto. He got the picture. He and I shared similar tastes, in fact, and he assured me that he had several such men on line for the production.

"So he did. Two of 'em. He even put them in a scene with me: the final scene, when I was supposed to be standing at a washbasin shaving, watching this scene unfolding in the showers. I got to jerk off, watching – but never joining in. To this day, when I watch that scene, I get hungry...and angry. A foreskin I was *that* close to, but never tasted. A set of tattoos I saw, but never licked. A pair of hairy calves that I would've loved to worship, but didn't get the chance. God, that man knew how to tease."

O'Hara's memoir was an instant smash with his long-time admirers and he made many new friends as well. As Robert Friedman notes in the *Bay Area Reporter*: "Unusually for a porn star, he also has a first-rate mind, a well-developed philosophy of life, and a seductive way with words. His (memoir) is a new take on the autobiography genre, containing extended ruminations on the pleasures of foreskin, a treatise on the drawbacks of committed relationships, even some introspective verse between chapters.

"...His is a San Francisco sort of story. Not only does he keep returning here at key points in his life, but the themes of his life – sexual and spiritual growth, freedom from attachment – are just the sort of bohemian concerns that have always typified the Barbary Coast.

"...We learn that this exhibitionist extraordinaire developed a taste for orgasm in the great outdoors from boyhood sessions milking the snake outside in the wilds of Southern Oregon. It's an aesthetic which has paid off plenty in his travels and back home in the Bay Area.

"....He does very well at establishing his own personal myth, required of all SF celebrities. He is most inspiring in his approach to living with AIDS. If first in denial about his symptoms (passing off a KS lesion as a motorcycle exhaust pipe burn), O'Hara eventually owned up to his serostatus in a big way, even tattooing HIV+ on his bicep. His account of surviving lymphoma is brave and honest. More than a juicy piece of meat, O'Hara is a gifted survivor with a tale to tell."

Jon King

And what a tale O'Hara tells about one of our favorite bottom boys, the insatiable Jon King. "There were lots of pornstars who did scenes with me in private that never made it to the screen. Some of them really should have," O'Hara says. "The most stellar of these was Jon King, aka John Gaines. No, I never made an on-screen appearance with him (it might have happened in 'Oversize Load,' but didn't). I never even got to meet him until 1986, when I went to see his performance at the Campus Theater – hot stuff. He recognized me in the audience, sought me out afterward, and made sure we got together. Nothing subtle about that boy: when he wanted something, he went for it. I like that in a man. We got together: I vividly remember meeting him at a motorcycle dealership to pick up his bike, which had been in for repairs, and riding home with him on the back of it. Jon enjoyed taking risks. But once home, this changed: it was Rubbertime. I'm not sure, at this point, whether or not to be happy about this. He claimed, at the time, that he was still negative – despite having been fucked, condomless, by a lot of men over the years. Well ... I gather that, sometime in the next nine years, his luck ran out. I could take satisfaction in knowing that it wasn't me who infected him; or I could, wistfully, wish that we'd fucked unprotected, since in the long run, it wouldn't have mattered.

I guess I have a love/hate relationship with my virus; if someone like Jon King was determined to get himself infected, I kind of wish he'd chosen mine.

"Yes, our sex was truly stunning, right up there with the all-time best fucks of my life. That boy knew how to work his butt in a way that no one else could. He was hungry, and demanding. (It's nice to know that even a megabottom like Jon King can occasionally be manipulated into a top role – which he performed with great panache.) He only fucked me once, in all the times we played . . . and I found myself wishing, as he shot inside me, that I could keep his cum up my butt as a souvenir.

"I remember a quiet, romantic sushi dinner with Jon in Japantown; and another dinner, somewhat less quiet, that he made at his apanment on Liberty Street. He claimed, at the time, that he was signing up for chef's school. (He may have signed up, but I doubt he attended more than two classes. While he was certainly one of the most charming men I've ever met, he was also one of the most unreliable and capricious.)

"Then there were the times we ran into each other in New York. He spent a couple of nights with me at the Colonial House Inn, when I was performing at the Black Party. I think he was drugged out of his mind; I know he was impossible to wake. But the most poignant of our encounters – not the last, but certainly the most painful – was at a pal's apartment in San Francisco. I'd already moved out of the City, I guess this was 1989. I was back visiting, and somehow I got a call from Jon. He sounded very dispirited. Bill wasn't there, so I invited Jon over. We sat on the futon and talked. Jon poured himself out to me; most of what came out was 'people only want me for sex.' I could sympathize, but at the same time, his body language was sending out a strong 'hold me' message. I did; and guess what, before you know it, we were having sex – foreplay, at any rate. I didn't understand, but it seemed like it was what he wanted. Comfort. But after just a few minutes, he got even more depressed, and withdrew, huddled up like a kid who's just been hit. He left soon afler, leaving me truly distraught. Somehow I'd failed him: I'd confirmed his worst fears about the animal natures of gay men."

According to Ed Wiley, Jon was pretty animalistic himself. The awesomely long-dicked Wiley, Golden Age of Porn star of

"Head Trips" and "Someone Is Watching," told *Manshots* that King had gotten his number and come over to his apartment for sex. "It was fun to just do it without camera people being around. Jon was very nice, very sensual, very animalish, very hungry. He was fun. He was a nice looking man. He was very *1-2-3-now!*"

"The thing about pornstars which the general public forgets (and even I forget it, obviously) is that no matter how sexually insatiable the public persona, there are also times in their lives when they'd like to be...nonsexual," O'Hara says. "Jon was, in a sense, a victim of his own irresistibility: no one could see him without thinking 'SEX.' Being able to provoke this response is exciting, at first. Being unable to turn it off gets very depressing. This episode was never brought up between us; I never saw him in that sort of funk again. But I've always regretted not being able to give him what he needed at the moment. I think he brought out a very maternal response in just about everyone he met, just because he was so immature. Everyone wanted to take care of him. Me, too. I kept wishing he'd call me up and ask me for ... something. He never did, of course.

"I understand he made several more films, in the early 1990s including a sequel to one of my all-time favorite flicks, 'These Bases are Loaded.' I haven't seen any of them, and I'm not sure I want to. I kept hearing occasional mentions of his name, which I took as a good sign; then, in 1995, I heard a rumor that he was HIV-positive. I greeted this news with ... well, with eagerness, mostly. When there's a man in my sights who I've been lusting after, it makes him twice as attractive to learn that he's HIV-positive.

"Suddenly, I *really* wanted to see Jon again. Ironically, by the time I heard that rumor, it was already too late. I didn't get the news until June 1996, but he'd died early the year before. I don't know anything about his death. Everyone always wanted to take care of him when he was vital and healthy; I wonder if there was anyone to take care of him at the end. I didn't get the impression that he was someone who had cultivnted any deep friendships. There are drawbacks, you might say, to being the most sexually appealing being on the face of the earth."

Legendary bottom Chris Burns in his heyday, with the super-sexy stud Tim Kramer, and friend, during the filming of the classic "Men of the Midway."

Derrick Stanton

A star who *did* appear on screen with Jon King, in one of his most famous scenes, the double penetration in "Brothers Should Do It!," was Derrick Stanton. Recently, Stanton talked with *Skinflicks*, fondly remebering Jon and his years in the limelight.

Stanton started making porn in 1977. "I was 24," he told *Skinflicks*. "I was a longtime friend of Barry Knight who was a photographer for Jaguar Productions and one day he asked me on a whim if I wanted to be in a movie. It was called 'Hard Hat.' I said yes and I enjoyed it. I'd occasionally see some straight porno with guys in it and I'd be checking out the guys, but you have to remember back in the '70s they didn't really show full frontals.

"We were shooting at some house up in the Hollywood Hills. It was about some straight construction worker who leaves his wife for me. Unfortunately, in most of my films I bottom, but on my first film the guy was so messed up on drugs and his sugar daddy was hanging around the set so he couldn't get hard, so I had to top. I'm pretty proud of the cum shot I did for that. I actually challenge anyone to try and beat that one!

"...Shortly thereafter, I met William Higgins and I did 'The Boys Of Venice.' I got to rollerskate and it had a neat story. Sexually speaking, I'd have to say 'Brothers Should Do It' was my favorite. I always had this fantasy about being in a double-penetration. I always had a crush on Jon King but I wasn't really his type. He liked the clone type (big guys with moustaches) and I didn't fit that. In the scene from 'Brothers' Jon is sitting on top of this guy getting fucked and I come in from behind. It was so erotic. Jon was enjoying it so much that they missed his cumshot because he came without touching himself!"

It's much harder to become a star today, Stanton says, "because there's so many more people in the business than there were back then."

Stanton says he was always able to get a hard-on. "A good example of that was I was in this director's office who wanted me to work for him but he had to make sure I could get a hard-on. He handed me some straight porn and some gay porno but I told him I didn't need it. I took down my pants and got hard without touching myself and he said, 'You're hired!'

"I'd enjoy working again. What I'd really like to do is to go to Czechoslovakia and do a film with William Higgins. A lot of people would probably say he was a pain in the ass to work with but he and I really got along and I would call him a friend.

"But now I'm a labor activist. I'm involved with getting gay rights in the workplace. I'm involved with a national gay labor group called Pride At Work. I'm also becoming quite a computer junkie, thanks to my lover Quan. I enjoy running and playing tennis, and working out."

In Chi Chi LaRue's "Hardcore," Stanton appears as Adam Hart's biggest, most obsessed fan. *Advocate Classified's* very own Jack Francis, who has a non-sexual role in the video, says, "Trivia buffs among you may already know that in the classic Joe Gage film 'L.A. Tool and Die' in the scene in which the late, great Casey Donovan is handcuffed to a tree and left by a car thief, Derrick was the faceless man who came up behind him and fucked him as he was thus immobilized."

Chris Burns and David Ashfield

"The first pornstar I ever met was Chris Burns ('Danny' to his family, but Chris to everyone else)," O'Hara reveals. "It was October 1, 1993, the day I moved into my Hayes Street apartment. I'd gone down to Safeway, yes, THAT Safeway, the one at Church and Market, where 'you can get anything you want' twenty-four hours a day – to stock the kitchen. Of course, I walked out with about six bags.

"As I was exiting, I noticed a hunky dude in loose sweatpants and a tank top, a cocky little rooster of a guy who looked vaguely familiar. He gave me a very blatant come-hither look, and followed me out to the bus stop. We both got on. When the bus got up to Hayes, he got off the bus with me. He started following me up the hill. I assume he started the conversation, since I've never been any good at that. I invited him home, and he accepted. When he told his name was Chris, I suddenly realized who he was. I'd just seen 'Men of fhe Midway' at the Century Theater a few weeks before, in which he tries to pretend he's an innocent youth. (I'm not sure Chris was *ever* innocent. Certainly not by the time I met him.) H e invited me to go to his place.

"We talked some; I was very impressed by his collection of 78s, which took up two whole walls of his living room. But he wasn't interested in socializing. That much was clear. He wanted to fuck me; I was agreeable. So we went into his bedroom, and he fucked me for about an hour. He came, got up, and implied that it was over, thanks very much. I'm not complaining; I enjoyed myself. It was just a little more abrupt than I'm used to. I think I called him the next time I was down south, but I don't believe we got together. I was saddened, a couple years later, to read of his death.

"If I meet a fan who starts waxing rhapsodic about one of my scenes, at least half the time it's a scene from 'Below the Belt' (1985)," Scott O'Hara says in his memoir. Well, we have always listed this scene among the greatest of all-time and it's interesting to read O'Hara's take on this incredible event. "Surprisingly, I enjoyed myself immensely. The director, Philip, was a rather fussy little queen who was nevertheless quite endearing . . . except for his extremely tightfisted attitude toward money. I don't remember how he contacted me originally, but he had a list of credits that included several grade B mainstream Hollywood movies, which I found impressive at the time. He also had done one pornflick, the year before, which had gotten a lot of attention . . . so I was eager. Yippee! I'm about to break into the Big Time! The locations Phil had chosen for shooting: a suburban house in the San Fernando Valley, a nearby bathhouse, and a warehouse next door to the bathhouse where most of the karate class sequences were filmed. Actually, I don't think we did any shooting at the bathhouse, but it was where we all cleaned up before and after filming. It was also where Burns and I did most of our extracurricular fooling around while we were waiting for scenes to get underway. Burns, old friend and pornstar extraordinaire, provided the technical expertise that made the karate sequences in the film possible. I don't know his training background, but he was capable of some very impressive moves, and he taught Chad Douglas how to appear dangerous. He also filled in for one of our more delicate cast members when the boy proved unable to accommodate everything Phil wanted him to take in his virginal butthole. Chris was known for his capacity, which he just loved to demonstrate – anywhere, anytime.

"I think we shot three scenes indoors on Saturday. They kind of fade together. There was the dream sequence, where a bunch of phantoms move in on a helplessly bound Asian boy and shoot their loads all over him (very spooky and surreal, and still quite sexy – and I produced one of the best cumshots of my career); then the locker room scene, which sandwiches the dream sequence; then the orgy grand finale, in which I had the dubious honor of deepthroating Chad Douglas (who has all the delicacy and finesse of a jackhammer). So that was my second orgasm of the day, and then we all got to hang around while we waited for the last scene to finish (the romantic conclusion to the orgy, between Chad and Jim Steele). I got turned on again, and actually moved in on the scene and shot another load all over Jim's tits. Don't know whether it improves the video or not, but it did move him to finally cum. (Can we go home now?) On Sunday, we moved on to the Valley Ranchette for two more scenes. One was the straight boy seduction scene, which I, thank god, did not have any part in. The other was the infamous Wussie (sometimes spelled 'woosie,' sometimes 'woozy,' in the hilarious script) Scene, in which David Ashfield and I double-dick (a faintly protesting) Michael Cummings.

"This was Burns' opportunity to jump into the action as a stunt-butt. I was given the chance, for once in my career, to essay Real Acting, heaping verbal abuse upon the 'wussie' bottom; for this reason alone, it's the movie I have the most difficulty watching. To whatever extent I was successful, I find it unsexy: I don't like watching scenes of brutal meanies taking out their frustration on wussies. I was a wussie when I was in high school, and lots of brutal meanies took out their frustrations on me (never sexually, alas), and it was never any fun. But hey, I wasn't writing the script, and I don't dictate the fantasies of Gay America. My fans tell me it's a hot scene. It's the one time I've double-dicked someone on film, which gives it a certain status in my mind, since that's one of my all-time most effective sexual fantasies.

"But the reality never lives up to the fantasy. I had, I'm sorry to say, difficulty keeping a hard-on. Fortunately, David had no such problems. He never does."

"Possibly nobody in the history of the gay x-industry has done more videos than David Ashfield," said William Spencer in *Manshots*. "He has over 200 titles to his count. He has been in countless gay, bi, straight, and she-male films, and his famous ever-hard cock has been in even more videos than the rest of him as the premier 'stunt dick' of his time."

Retired now (his last video, in 1989, was "The Rites of Spring"), Ashfield told Spencer that he was "glad the door's closed. It served its purpose at that point of my life. I'm too old for that, and life goes on."

It all started when Ashfield was a kid and read a book about a hustler boy in Houston. "The author told all about his life. By fourteen years old, I knew what a hustler was, and I knew that was something I would probably do some day. Oh, yeah. I knew as young as fourteen, fifteen years old that someday I'd be selling dick. I knew that Houston was the place. Houston was the town in the story. It kept gnawing at me. There was supposed to be a wild street strip where you just walk out there and it just happens to you. *America's Runaways*. The first time I ran away, my stepmother's dad sent it to her, and when she was done reading it, she gave it to me to read. Stoo-pid! Gimme all the case histories of all these different runaways and let me study their M.O. I was like, 'Hey, this is a Bible. This is a blueprint here. Oh, yeah!'"

Eventually Ashfield ended up in Houston. He managed to find the gay bar and got pretty seriously drunk. "Pretty soon, I had to go to the bathroom. Ooooh! Nobody told little boys, 'Careful when you go to the bathroom.' (Laughs) I went into the bathroom, and I remember being kind of drunk and kind of wobbly. And I walked in the door, and the next thing I know, I'm against the wall and people are taking my clothes off. And there are tons of hands all over me. And I'm just sucked up into this bathroom orgy. This goes on, I don't know, probably ten, fifteen minutes or whatever. And I guess enough people got off or whatever. Pretty soon I reach down and I pull my pants up. They're completely soaked with water and piss from the floor – and I'm just an absolute wreck. So, very embarrassed, I stumble out into the bar, get into my car, lock the door, and go home and wash up. I'm just absolutely devastated by the experience. The following week, I go to the area, looking for a place to eat. I see a pizza joint, so I park the car and I go in. Now, this is a nice, clean, friendly atmosphere, not a bar or anything, and there's some big, ol' fat man sittin' there with all these cute boys around him. And I go, 'Click! Ding!' So, I go sit in the corner and eat my pizza all alone. And sure enough, he sends the minion boys over: 'Dude, why don't you come over and sit with us?' 'Oh, okay.' We all sat there and talked for awhile, and I'm doing lots of listening and smilin' from ear to ear. They ask me if I've ever hustled before, and I'm like, 'No, but I've read about it.' And they go, 'Oh, dude, it's no problem. We'll show you the different bars and everything. ... You'll make thirty bucks plus ten more just to lie there and get your dick sucked.' ...He calls the guy, the guy comes right on down. We go back to his place, and the other boy gets so drunk he passes out. So this man pays all his attention to me, sucks me off, and I get my forty bucks. And it's a really cool experience. I'm like, 'Oh, wow!' My first serious blowjob. I'd had a blowjob before, but not like that one. I came my brains out. I was like, 'Wow!' It felt good and I got forty bucks! I went to work the next day thinking about this. I worked all week. Friday night comes, and I go back to the hustler bar. I'm in there probably an hour or so, and some guy comes in and starts making small talk with me. And I'm, 'Oh, wow. This is really getting close to the moment. Is this for real?' We sit there and talk, and he invites me out to his house. So I follow him all the way out to his house in my car. And I spend the whole night there and he gives me like, fifty bucks. And the next morning, I just get into my car and drive home. 'Oh, wow! This is really bitchin'.

"I thought, 'Gee, that'd be kinda neat, getting paid to go to bed with these older guys.' So they fed me to a few men, taught me what to do, what to charge, and before I knew it, I had a job – one I could pick my hours at.

"...I stayed in Houston two and a half years, about. Toward the end, the boom was crashing and business was going away. And just like always, I meet one boy named Paul – hot little kid with a big, long dick – he starts hanging out every once in awhile, and eventually he brings over another boy named Randy. He starts telling us this story that his dad wants him to come home to California. And finally, we all say, 'Let's go there. You can go to L.A. and make a hundred bucks a trick. The hell with this thirty bucks a trick, fifteen bucks a trick, whatever you get down here. You can make good money there and you can drive a truck anywhere, right?'

"So, I saved up a thousand dollars in the next couple of weeks, bailed out of my apartment, and drove out there in my car. Got an apartment the first day, got my first job, driving a truck, started going to the hustler bars, and things were going kind of well. I was at the hustler bar one night. A man walks up to me and starts yacking about pictures, films, and stuff. He's like, 'I work for this company. I'm a photographer, blah-blah-blah, dirty movies. Here's my card. Nova Studios. ...I made their movie, 'Lockerroom Fever.' This is the beginning of me putting my dick in somewhere for money on film. There were three people. It was a locker room scene, snapping towels and all of a sudden, doing it. I was willing to do anything except get fucked. I wouldn't get fucked. I got paid. I was happy. Wishing I could do more. They said, 'You can only get used one or two times. Otherwise, you're overexposed.' So I believed him, and then, standing in the same bar, late one night, a producer picks me up – Mark Reynolds – takes me home, finds out what I've got, and says, 'Okay, I'm gonna put you in a movie, blah-blah-blah,' and puts me in 'One Size Fits All.' That was the beginning of David Ashfield.

"I met Daniel Holt on my second shoot, and after that, he really started pumping a lot of stuff my way for awhile. Daniel Holt was an agent, and a porno star. He was a hustler's hustler, constantly hustling those bucks. 'Thank you very much. Next!' (It was all) very crisp, very businesslike.

"I worked for William Higgins just on a few movies at first, and then I did lots and lots of work for him as a stunt dick. Bill was very good to me. I went up there and tricked with him and got a hundred bucks. After he got into my dick and everything, he's like, 'I think I really can put you into a movie.'"

"The Pizza Boy, He Delivers" and "Delivery Boys" were Ashfield's first films for Higgins. "Everybody who's seen porno movies has seen 'Pizza Boy,' it seems like," says he. "It's everywhere. We're talking now, oh, over ten years later and people are still talkin' about 'Pizza Boy.' It's like one of my best flicks. Bill had a certain magic. At least it worked on me and all the boys in the flicks I was in. ...Bill Higgins was the only man who was a good director. Part of being a good director is understanding how to take two boys, let them get turned on, and be able to follow correctly with a camera. That is Bill's attribute. That is any really good director or cameraman's attribute. 'Cause you're trying to see real sex. If you put up fake sex, it's gonna look like fake sex. I got my claim to fame because I always went in there with the idea of making it look like real sex."

Ashfield made many straight porn films as well and says he can psyche himself up to fuck women: "Like fucking a fish, man. Understand, when I'm on a porno set, it's all about performance. It's a skill. It's as if I were there like someone else going to play their professional game or something. You do a professional job."

Speaking of being professional, Ashfield was also one of the most successful stage performers. Of course, he hustled on the side when doing these gigs. Once when he was dancing at the Show Palace in New York, I arranged to have him stop by my hotel for a little fun. He warned me right off: "I do five shows a day and I have to pop for every one of them. I owe it to them, the audience."

I told him it didn't matter to me; I could catch one of the shows to see his "pop."

"But I'm a horny dog," he gleefully admitted as I played with his cock, which began swelling immediately. "Always have been. I did my experimenting at ten and eleven with other boys and their sisters. But I learned the female of the species is no fun. They like to play their games, they like to be bitches and that wasn't for me. I could tell. Already.

"Yeah," he boasted as his hard-on slid into my mouth, "Directors know they can count on me to be on time and be up on time. I guess I'm a nasty boy with a big hard cock."

"Oh, yes," I said, kissing it, then running my tongue along the full length of it. It was a magnificent cock.

"Yeah," he went on, holding my head as I sucked. "That's the most important thing, being able to produce a good hard-on. Who wants to see a limp-dicked boy?"

"Not me," I confessed, removing his splendid cock from my mouth to keep from gagging on it while I came.

Zipping up, Ashfield passed along this advice to potential

porn players: "I would tell him that if he really wants to do it, go ahead and try it once. Be careful of the other people around you, because it is an environment, not only just a job. It's more like what I tell anybody if they say they want to hustle. It's there, if you have a strong enough mind to deal with it, if you can deal with it like a job and keep your mind together, keep your shit together. It's the kind of thing that psychologically can tear you apart, if you can't deal with it. It is a brilliant financial opportunity set up by human nature. It's always been here and always will be here. But, it's a personal decision. You gotta be nasty enough to do it, and strong enough to get past it."

Jon King, photographed by one of his hottest on-screen partners, Kristen Bjorn

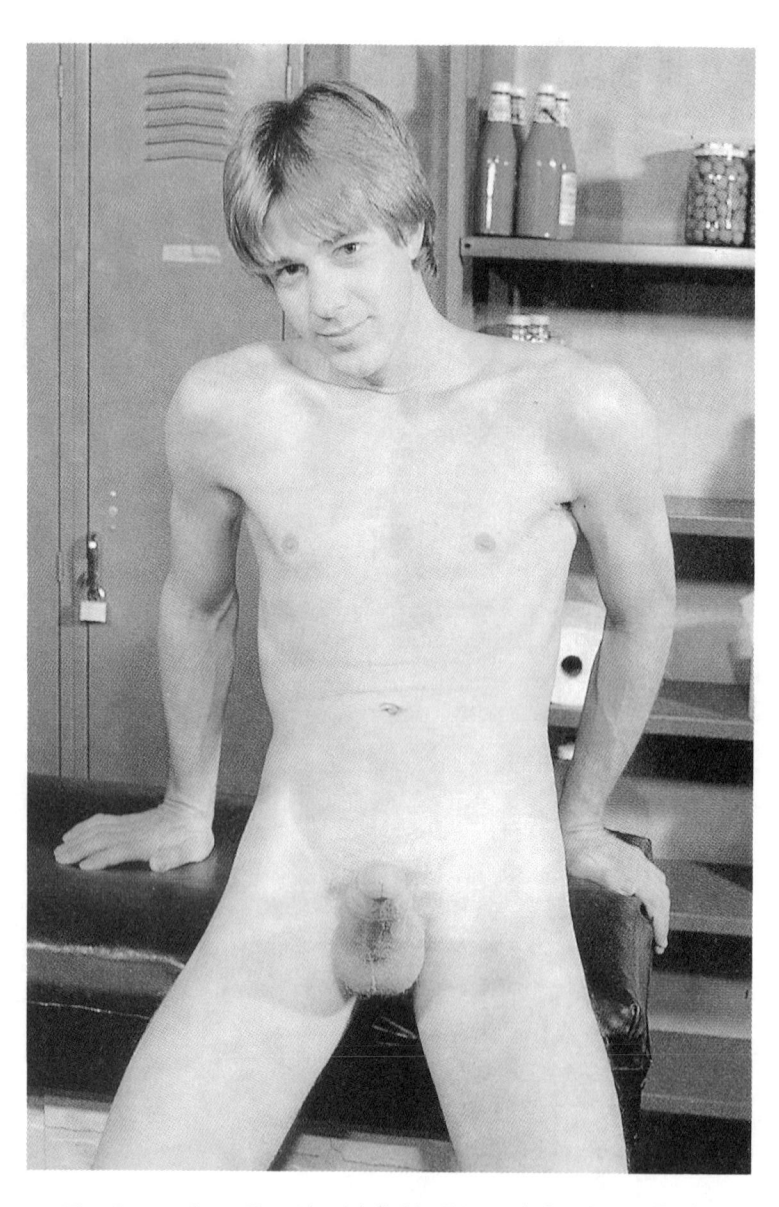

The Legendary David Ashfield, King of the Stunt Dicks, in "Delivery Boys," courtesy Catalina Video

Marc Stevens

"I was the kid in the doorway at Third and Fifty-third, looking a punk eighteen, looking you straight in the eye, looking to score," Marc Stevens said in his autobiography, *Making It Big*. "All the johns ever cared about was that fat bulge in my pants, anyway – all the rest was style. My father was dead and I was living to fuck, and Third Avenue was the hottest place in the city to cash in on my kind of pain."

He quickly discovered that his pain could be alleviated by popping Seconals, Tuinals, or Nembutals, and – driven by his need for money – he graduated from $20 car tricks to $100 dates with men who wanted to taste a few of his ten-and-a-half inches.

But it was with his appearances in porn films that he was able to command top dollar. Because of his incredible penis, he was in great demand in straight porn and appeared in the classic "The Devil in Miss Jones," among dozens of others. He was sometimes billed as, not surprisingly, Mick Allman. His one classic gay film from the '70s was "Michael, Angelo and David." Bijou describes what happens: "A rather naive Italian boy visits his uncle in the Big Apple. Upon his arrival in New York, somebody steals his pet chicken. On his way to his uncle's, he stops to gawk at the skyscrapers and his waylaid by Marc Stevens, who shows him the tall structure in his pants..."

With his fame, Stevens joined a "celebrity service" called Adam's Athletes, and knew he'd made the big time. In his memoir, he recalls a very old classical pianist who paid handsomely for the actor to come on his elegant fingers and then lick off his own semen. A famous rock star (the implication is that it was Cat Stevens) watched as two homosexuals sucked and fondled Marc from both ends. A famous black singer paid him to fuck her.

Self-loathing struck Stevens rarely. Unlike other sex stars present and past, Stevens was not tormented by the guilt feelings that disturb so many prostitutes. He records only a few episodes when he felt degraded. Once a man spat in his face. Another time a woman wanted to shit upon him. Stevens tells funny stories about some of the women in his life (one who became a regular with a group of Hasidic Jews) but with a few exceptions, *Making It Big* is better in its descriptions of the hustler milieu than in its descriptions of sex.

Stevens died of complications from AIDS in 1989.

Leo Ford

Leo Ford

"I guess my real first experience with sex was camping out in the back yard with one of my neighbors and playing around with each other. You know. Going down on each other and trying it out. That's when I started to feel like it was okay to like another man," Leo Ford related to *HOT Male Review* in 1985.

"I once ended up getting in a fight with this guy just so I could get near him," he went on, "And then when I got near him, I kissed him on the cheek. He turned me around and started fighting me and kissed me back on the cheek. It totally blew me away because we were both very young at the time. I always thought he was a bad ass in the school, so I never really fucked around with his whole scene or his friends or anything. But it was really cute, because it was sort of affectionate in its own way.

"But until Jamie (Wingo), really, I didn't have any outwardly open, gay relationship. I really fell in love with Jamie. It was like the end of the world when we broke up. The end of the world. In fact, I was still helping him and throwing him money and gifts and everything months after we broke up. I was still crazy about him. All he had to do was wave a little bit.

"I still think about him, but I don't think about him in the same way. I feel we've both come a long way. I've come up to him in nightclubs in San Francisco and New York, but I haven't had the nerve to try and make it happen again, but I'm sure the same magic would exist with him if we ever did. I'm sure of it. But I'm not ready for it; I think I've grown out of past relationships.

"A lot of people think I like to get fucked a lot. And movies sort of depict it that way; but, that's really what the filmmaker wants it to be. It's just like Larry Ginsburg who would give you a big dick to sit on and then splice out all the going down on the dick. Just show you starting to go down on the dick, and all of a sudden, plump, you're down on the damned dick. He's notorious for shit like that.

"In 'Spokes' I got fucked by Dick Fisk, Lee Ryder, then the next guy and the next. And that was very difficult. It was the most difficult shoot I have ever done in my life. Because they had a straight Mexican boy from San Diego; they had Lee Ryder and his lover, who were only willing to touch each other, which is just like the craziest thing I've heard in the world, because they're notorious. But that's all they would do. The two lovers. You'd go near them and they'd both get upset that you're near their lover, you know, and all that kind of crap. Jamie and I didn't have that. Jamie and I weren't insecure with our relationship. I could even watch him being with someone, but it would just increase the fantasy for me. And I think the same thing with him. The fear that most relationships have is when you start not getting along and all of that, you just don't really know how to work it out, to where it would work for you in your kind of situation.

"Jamie and I were pretty wild. When our relationship started not to work, we decided to involve other people and have three ways. And after a while when that wasn't working, we decided to see how it was just to sleep with other people on our own. And when that drew us further apart then one thing led to another. We moved out of Laguna, where we were fine and happy. I was working at Buffum's. I really didn't know what hustling was, because I wasn't exposed to it really, yet, and I didn't know what it was at all until I went to San Francisco. The first thing I did after I'd made a *FALCON* film was to run an ad saying, 'Falcon Model, Leo Ford for sale.' And it was good. I made a great deal of money. We moved to Los Angeles, like I said, and Jamie and I moved into a sleazy hotel.

"One day when I got home and found him in bed with some young stud, it blew my mind and I just took off. I moved in with this friend of mine who had an apartment there and I kept running that ad. And after a while I was making about $1,000 a week with no overhead. I flew back home to Florida. Then I came back to L.A. and Jamie came back and started living with me again.

"As you get older you realize how you have to make a relationship work. I've learned a lot about relationships. It's hard for me to like people that I'm around all the time. To be with them. To be able to accept where they're at all the time, and them me the same way. It's too hard for me, at least right now. I'm very vulnerable. Lots of kids can suck me in. But then the time comes when I have to sit at my desk and work. But a lot of the kids just like to fool around and play all day, and I've got to work."

Part of Leo's work was doing live shows. As might be expected, he put on one helluva show. Said he, "While I'm on stage, before I get into being extremely explicit, I have the chance to associate with the audience, to pick certain individuals out of the audience. Then I get into it with them. And myself. Mostly myself."

Another part of Leo's work was the making of videos. After his stint at Falcon, he made videos for a number of different producers. One of our favorites is "Blonds Do It Best," in which he co-starred with the legendary Lance. Bijou said, "In a lakefront cabin in the woods, golden-haired fuck machines realize that they can't keep their hands off of each other and decide that lip-locking is much preferable to bird watching and camp fires! Superstars Leo Ford and Lance simultaneously ram their greased, hard cocks into *Playgirl*-cover-boy Philip Anderson. Lance rims and fucks baby-faced Ty Cashe's peach-fuzzed buns. Lance and Mark Sheldon roll around by the fire – Lance flashes his famous smile, and Leo Ford shows up just in time to plow into Mark's ass. Leo and Shawn Michaels attract the twinkle-eyed attention of Ty, and they delight him with cumloads landing on his face. A Richard Morgan film, his first shot directly on film and then transferred to video."

Jock magazine also raved, ".. An impressive array of graphic zoom-in asshole penetrations with piston-like butt-fuckings and cock sucking..."

Leo remembered the experience: "On the 'Blonds Do It Best,' we spent hours trying to fuck people. I tried to fuck these guys, and they were so difficult to fuck. Philip (Mark Sheldon) was the only one who could really take it good. He had a Lance fetish, but it was interesting. It was a good shoot. I got off on it. I was really into my fantasy in that movie.

"...I'd rather do a guy with a big dick, like anyone else. The size of the dick *is* important when you're getting fucked. I like big dicks. But I really like fucking a guy and looking down and seeing a big dick because it's like, wow, you're fucking this guy who's got a big dick. And there's a little bit of a fantasy there. But for some reason, I've worked my mind to the point where I really like to fuck. I want a guy to be as loose as I can get him! I'll fuck the shit out of him and really get him loose. And the looser the better. It doesn't even matter if I can feel myself. It's like the mental thing. A perfect example is if someone cringes with me and gets real fidgety about getting fucked, I'll just walk out of the room sometimes and say, Fuck! Because I just won't take any fidgetiness. And that's why I was having a problem with 'Blonds Do It Best' because if someone can't sit there and really get it from me, it's going to be hard for me to get into it, because I really am a powerful fucker. Phil (Mark Sheldon) was pretty loose but very enjoyably loose to me. I mean I truly enjoyed being with him, even though he is really loose. I realized he looked a little rough and everything, so I *started* thinking, well, you *little street bitch, I'm gonna start. . . I'm gonna fuck your ass, I'm gonna fuck you good.*

"And all of a sudden I started getting really, really excited. Because when I start to one-pointedly think about something like that, I can really center my mind down on a single thought and, whoosh, everything starts to react. A lot of people like tight asses. To me, it's a total turn-off. All I have to do sometimes is rub someone's butt or just look down at someone's bun and, boom. I'm excited, ready to go. Jamie was good for me that way. But then he started realizing how to work me and then he wouldn't give it to me at certain times – things like that. Sometimes I feel more when I'm getting fucked. If the person and I have a real kinetic tie, if we're really turned-on to each other, I feel really good about being fucked by them. But otherwise forget it. I'll stick to fucking. At least in my personal life.

"I like them mostly on their stomach, so I can look at the butt and the back and the torso. I like to fuck on the side, too. It's easy that way. More comfortable. But the thing of holding someone's legs up and fucking – it's okay – I can get off that way, but it's distracting.

"How I really like it is when some one kneels and really accents their ass and then you come in from the back and maybe grab them by the shoulders and really fuck them. That's the way I like it and I like to feel that sort of giving. I like the other person to be in a very good mood.

"I don't like to be thought of, especially now, as being a hustler. I don't think I'd be in my mail order business today without that Falcon model ad. But that was then and this is now.

"The repeats were more gross. But there were a lot of one-time super hot guys who would call. I'd get three or four guys a week who were really hot, who would call me, and they don't normally call ads. I guess they were people with a fetish for Leo Ford or just calling on a onetime shot. I'm not going to say I don't hustle anymore, but I may not see even one person a week. I've seen one person in three weeks as it is right now. It's not the way it was before. Now I have just about everything I want. I'm set up in my business."

Other memorable Ford appearances included William Higgins' production of "Leo and Lance," wherein the pair concentrate on each other's pleasure in a lush outdoor setting. Bijou describes this action: "After jacking off in the woods, Leo joins Lance for blowjobs. Foreskinned Lance rims Leo and then fucks him till he's sweaty. Both hunks come on each other's face. In a later scene, Leo gets involved in a three-way with buddy Bobby Madison (aka Brian Michaels) and hitchhiker Aaron Gage. Leo's as good a top as a bottom – as he proves by fucking Aaron with tireless strokes in a long-dicking fashion. Gage, then, takes Bobby's boner too."

In another Higgins' other classic, "Sailor in the Wild," Brian Thompson spends the night with Dave Sommers and Leo Ford, who rape his tight, sweet ass. Bijou noted, "In another scene, Rick Donovan screws Leo Ford relentlessly, and Leo grimaces in real pain."

Speaking of real pain, one of our favorite Ford videos has to be "Style," from Falcon, featuring Ford with Todd Baron and then again with sleek black Art Williams and the insatiable Tim Kramer. In the three-way, Leo takes the other guys' cocks at the same up his backside. "You know," he said, "it's funny, I didn't like it very much when it was happening. I must say that. And it hurt. But I would have gotten into it and it wouldn't have hurt as bad, or I probably would have liked it a bit more or enjoyed it if there was a more positive group of people around.

"I always thought it would be fun, but I never really concentrated on it or thought about it as being one of my fantasies. Just like before I got into this whole movie thing, I didn't even know about tit-pinching, believe it or not. But I made that movie and then, along down the line, I went with a friend of mine to a sex club and he was a pretty hot guy. And we saw this really hot stud and I thought, *Oh my God! I don't believe this! There's someone really super-hot.* And we took him in our room and I got it on with these guys and they fucked me. Both of 'em at the same time. But this time it was a totally different kind of experience. What happened was I sat on one and I bent over and the other guy came in from above. And it really worked. But when I did it in the movie I was really freaked out. The one guy's lying down and they're saying, *You sit on this* and then the other guy comes over... I just couldn't get into it with them.

"At the sex club, though, what was really funny was I was expecting maybe to go ahead and do this and it would work, but I didn't expect to really get a good fuck out of it. But we did get a really good fuck out of it. Both guys got off and they were able to go in and out and get really crazy, and it was really fun. I really had a great time. Everybody got off on it, and it was such an experience. But, I'm telling you, making that one movie was not *the* experience. It may have looked like it, but it wasn't." Could have fooled us!

Regarding Todd Baron, one fan reports that he treasures some lewd photos (now tattered) of the model when he was living in Philadelphia in the early '80s. The happy fan remembers, "Oh, what a dream come true! Cute, dark, and so, so hot!"

Several legendary sex pigs are featured in "Stiff Sentence," in which Ford has torrid sex with Justin Rhodes (a/k/a Geoffrey Spears), a fresh-faced newcomer at the time. Rhodes, in the words of Ted Underwood in *Manshots*, "proved to be a versatile strawberry blond with an impressive intensity and a scruffily handsome demeanor. Instead of going to jail, Rhodes is sent to a rehabilitation home peopled by a band of delinquents (Blake Cass, Michael Cummings, Kevin Wiles, and David Ashfield), and a horny warden (Chris Burns, who was beginning to make the shift from baby bottom to a new look and attitude that were much tougher). Two group scenes, one in which Cummings is gangbanged, and the other in which Burns is serviced, are both violently lusty. Sandwiched between them is a long masturbatory solo by Rhodes, during which he fantasizes of better times gone by – those spent with Ford. Their flashback coupling before a roaring fireplace shows both off to great advantage, most particularly Rhodes' ample endowment. Ford's untrammeled frenzy is not nearly as spontaneous, however, as it was in his earlier films. Still, he is something to see in action."

Interesting, Jamie Wingo, Leo's great love, resumed advertising his services nationally in 1997. His ad reads, "Legendary Porn Star Jamie Wingo; Bld/Blu Eyed; 5 ft 10; 160 lbs; 45 chest, 29 wst, cut Escort; plays hard; all scenes; Call 24 hrs." One of Wingo's most famous scenes is found in William Higgins masterpiece, "Brothers Should Do It," wherein he engages in a most stimulating fuck of Jon King. The scene is also on the compilation "The Best of Jon King." Wingo and Ford appear together in "J. Brian's Flashbacks," in which contestants tell of their sexual exploits during a jockstrap contest in San Francisco. Wingo and Ford get together poolside and, as Bijou says, "Wingo explains exactly how the two best cocks of the show get healthy, hard and mouth-wateringly meaty."

THE BIG HUSTLE

Tom Chase, courtesy Falcon Studios

Tom Chase

"Are you ready for this?" Robert W. Richards exclaimed in *HX*, "Tom Chase is a top. And he's *gay*. And he *admits* it! Not gay-for-pay, but really deep-down, from-the-gut, from-the-heart gay!"

"It's really interesting," Chase told Richards. "The industry has almost convinced itself that straight guys are the only real tops, that they're what the audience wants to see. And then someone like me comes along. A top with a totally gay sensibility. I think, at least I hope, I'm making a lot of people rethink their biases and consider new possibilities. Falcon has begun to change my screen character, to make me a little less one-dimensional, more interesting as a person – something more than just a big cock." It is ten inches long and six inches around – and it hangs five inches soft, according to Chase.

Although Chase is not *constantly* aware of his cock, he never forgets that it's there. "I'm not as aware of it as others seem to be. People have always told me it was huge, but I really didn't think it was much different than other guys...well, maybe a little bigger. When I was in college at Boston University, I think there were only about five tops in the whole city and I was certainly among the top three, so all the sex I wanted was always available, but I thought it was all about my aggression and preferences, not size. Not until I saw myself in film did I see what others see. In real life you're always looking down at your own cock, so the perspective is completely different, even if you're looking straight ahead into a mirror. So the first time I saw myself standing sideways in a video, I thought, Whoa – that really is big! I couldn't believe it!"

While some may call Chase an escort, Richards chose to call him a "personal trainer," and, boy is he busy! You can see why when you see his ad in *Frontiers*, in which Chase advertises himself as "10.5 X 6 CUT," and lists an 800 number." (His lover, Brad Eliot, advertises himself as an Ivy League model with "huge low hangers." Presumably they'll rent out as a pair – if you could stand it.)

Richards says he pursued Chase relentlessly for a month determined to arrange a meeting, leaving endless telephone messages in various cities until they finally connected. Even then, all he could spare was less than an hour, having just returned from an appearance in St. Louis the night before to film a ground-breaking segment for RuPaul's talk show.

"I'm very realistic," he says. "I know my time in this business – like everyone else's – is finite, and I want to grab onto everything there is to grab onto before the party's over."

"Despite, or in addition to, all the above," Richards comments, "Chase manages to sustain a live-in relationship with fellow porn actor Brad Elliot. When I ask him whether their relationship – other than their acting – is monogamous, Chase seems surprised at the very idea. 'Oh no, no, and we both understand that completely. We even have sex with our friends. We have great friends, and that's just our way of expressing emotion and affection, of bonding. Sex is a very natural thing for both of us – and playing with others doesn't affect how we feel about each other. When we first met, before Brad was in the business, I took him to a porn set of a film I wasn't in to give him an idea of what my work was all about. We stood quietly on the sidelines just watching a group of beautiful blond boys really going at it. That's all we'd planned to do, but the scene got so hot and out of control that we just jumped in and volunteered our services as fluffers – and had a great time. There's never been a problem since."

Except, perhaps, getting someone to bottom for him. "You know the bottoms get to choose their tops," he says. "And there's always the problem of who can accommodate me."

If you think *you* could accommodate Chase, you'll be glad to know he can get it up. Mark Adams at *Video View* says, "it's reported by my usually reliable source (aren't they all...) that Chase is quite effective and receives high grades as an escort by one who knows, and exhibited none of the...er, problems, he was reportedly having during the filming of one of his epics."

Speaking of problems, Falcon's John Rutherford, talking with Jack Francis of *The Advocate*, said that Chase's cock, despite it's bigness, is easy to swallow. John was comparing it to the tool of Falcon's other man-of-the-moment, Mike Branson: "Branson's cock is so wide and stiff and very, very straight," thus making it harder to deep-throat than Chase's. No wonder Chase is such a popular escort, averaging five to six clients a day! Yummy!

Chad Connors

Last year, David Widmer in *4-Front* was the first to break the news that "everybody's talking about the latest legal problems for agent and one-time producer David Forest. According to my source, Forest, who plea-bargained a pandering charge about a year ago, has been formally charged similarly again. Two telephone calls to a friend of this column are revealing that Chad Connors, who worked for Forest's escort service, says he was caught in an LAPD vice sting while on a call arranged by Forest. Connors is cooperating with the police and plans to testify against Forest. Not surprisingly, he admits his motivation is to get the law off his own back. Forest has long been a controversial figure attached to the gay porn biz. He blames Connors for his current legal problems and tells my friend that he hopes Connors ultimately chooses not to testify against him. I'm sure this will be an interesting drama as it plays out."

The drama played out all right, with Forest doing time and Connors slipping away for awhile. Eventually, he was back, in a string of low-budget videos and announcing his return in the classified sections: "Superstar Is Back; call now for your rendesvous (sic)."

While A-list producers were reluctant to use Connors, the performer was able to find work. Interestingly, he shows up as, of all things, a top in the otherwise undistinguished "Malibu Beach Hunks," which also featured the talents of K.C. Hart in the best scene, a three-way in a boat that was obviously filmed "on location." Chad's scene with Ken Griffin has the advantage of atmosphere as well, with Chad fucking Griffin amid the splendid rock formations of the Pacific seacoast. Chad shoots his load while Griffin licks his balls.

It would seem that with all the posing the newly-buffed Connors does while he is fucking, perhaps he's seeking a new career as a second-rate Ty Fox.

We'd rather see Connors spreading it on the back of a pick-up the way he did for Sonny Markham in "Mavericks."

Chad even said he enjoyed bottoming in "Mavericks," by Studio 2000, but he told Jerry Douglas in *Manshots* that he does tend to be more of a top. "I don't care who it is – you take 'em home and you pull out your dick, and their legs fly up in the skies as fast as they can! It's not something that I prefer, it's just that it's a rare occurrence for me to get fucked.

"Studio 2000 had been calling and calling and calling, wanting me to bottom, and I was refusing. The thing that John Travis had in his mind was he wanted to put Kevin Dean and me in a scene together. And have us turn back to back and me fuck him at the same time as he's fucking me. Which, I guess it could have worked. I can point my dick backwards and so can Kevin."

It wasn't to be Kevin Dean, of course. Chad tells it: "I was fucking Robbie Cryston at the same time that Bo Garrett was fucking me. It wasn't anything like I have sex at home. It hurt! I almost squealed. And Robbie Cryston's saying, 'Breathe. Breathe.' I love Robbie. He's great. He is really great! Besides being a great performer with a lot of energy on set, he was also one of the first people I worked with when I did 'Super Sex, Part Two: The Sex Radicals.' And he showed me more of the ropes. And if it wasn't for him - I've worked with him four times now - a lot of the times, I would have flipped out on the set. Because it gets nerve-wracking. And Robbie has a way of calming me down. He's beautiful - and if he'd have me, I'd marry him! (Laughs) I would. But there have been several times when I was cast with people where there was no attraction whatsoever. You become less human and more of a machine at that point."

MODELS / ESCORTS

TOM CHASE
FALCON EXCLUSIVE
10.5X6 CUT
1-800-985-0561
(3ACS0506) P01756

IVY LEAGUE FALCON MODEL
BRAD ELIOT
HUGE LOW HANGERS
Page me (888) 358-2948.
(3ACS0607) P01479

CHANCE CALDWELL
Hm: (714) 841-0811 Pager: (213) 878-3497, www.chance-caldwell.com (3ACS0505) P00243

MODELS / ESCORTS

Tom Katt
Hairy Body Builder
5'7", 205lb. 6% body fat
Very personable. Always in shape
$250 hr. Overnight Rates Available
800-605-9605

MAX GRAND
NO DRUGS
NO ATTITUDE
1-310-298-3951
(3ACS0506) P01441

MODELS / ESCORTS

Colt Model
BOYD HANSON
Pager: 800/605-3639

Tom Chase and his lover, Brad Eliot, both advertise their personal services, as do Tom Katt, Chance Caldwell and Max Grand. Even the studly Colt models advertise, leaving little to the imagination – except their faces!

SUPER STAR CHAD CONNERS IS BACK
CALL NOW FOR YOUR RENDESVOUS
888-341-3793
DAY OR NIGHT
[3ACS0104] P01707

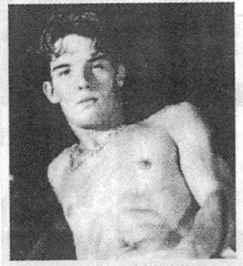

PORN STAR RICHIE FINE
Fine from head to toe. Hot, hung, young and horny. Masculine, 20yo, 5'8", 140lbs, 8½x6 cut. $200.00 & up. Pager # (213) 390-5506. 24hrs. Outcalls only. [3ACS0404]

Super Star Marco Rossi
714-602-2346

Yes, it pays to advertise! Richie Fine is one of newer faces to take advantage of his immediate porn "star" status by offering his services, alongside such established favorites as Marco Rossi. And, incredible as it might seem, Chad Connors was back, newly buffed and topping in low budget sexvids, as well as offering a private "rendesvous!"
(So where was he? We have no idea, but we do know he wasn't in jail – he co-operated – and was boycotted by most major studios. There must be a demand for his personal services – but will he really let you fuck him?)

Richie Fine

In its review of "So Fine" *In Touch* says, "Eventually, Richie gets together with Chaz Carlton and it looks like love. They couple furiously, ripping up underwear and eventually settling into a nice 69 position. Chaz finally offers Richie his ass, and Richie takes it, ramming his handsome cock into the boy with a great deal of passion."

"'Hustler Blue' is a footloose tale of pimps, pushers and police. Everyone is on the take, especially Richie Fine. Never afraid of a little checkbook romance, the aptly sur-named star does what he must to satisfy his dark desires," raved *HX*'s Real Men. "The action begins with two horrendous actors negotiating an affair somewhere indoors. (At least we don't see any scenes of Santa Monica Boulevard – yet!) In what has to be the worst performance ever recorded, a blond hustler explains to his mate that he must call his boyfriend to assure him that he's okay. Then the two get busy while their goatees scrape each other's faces like sandpaper. Later, the sexy Fine bags a trick in a hotel room. Most of the time our hero takes top billing, but in this arresting scene he finds himself bent over a billy club taking orders from a civilian. (He later fucks the same trick with the same nightstick, making us cringe at the thought of where that thing has been.)"

Fine seems to enjoy being on both sides of the law. He played a cop in "Hustler Blue" and in "So Fine," he plays the hustler role. In their review of "So Fine," *Manshots* says, "Three scenes of this production actually try to tell an interesting story about a hustler (Richie Fine) with no family, his current boyfriend (Eric Hamilton), and a cop (Sam Dixon) who murders hustlers with no family and then investigates their disappearance. How he manages to get himself assigned to such cases poses a challenge to verisimilitude, but we'll let that pass. The bigger problem is that the first two scenes are so tenuously related to the main story as to be virtually irrelevant. First up are Austin Black and David Cline. One is a hustler and one is a john, but from looking at the two, it is impossible to tell which is which. Black and Cline exchange blowjobs, and then Black fucks Cline. Cline actually delivers two money shots, which gives the scene something of a kick."

Fine comes in on the third episode. After Fine agrees to stop hustling, he and his lover (Eric Hamilton) make love, with Fine fucking Hamilton. Then Fine's beeper goes off and off he goes. This time, he fucks Sam Dixon. Then Dixon stabs him! Turns out Dixon is a cop and he gets assigned to answer Hamilton's complaint that his lover is missing. Of course, Dixon ends up fucking Hamilton but, since Hamilton isn't a hustler, Dixon doesn't kill him, only tells him to go home to mother!

Pagan Prince first hit it big as a rancher in Studio 2000's "Mavericks"

Pagan Prince

"You have to enjoy sex...that's the secret."
– Pagan Prince

"I first met Pagan Prince in Las Vegas," Mickey Skee said, "and he told me that soon he was *leaving* Las Vegas and coming out to do porn with the adult A-listers. He got there quickly, gaining nominations at the *Adult Video News* awards, and impressing super-director John Travis." Skee hung out with Prince on the set of Studio 2000's "Seaman First Class," and found that director Travis was "totally enthralled with Pagan." Travis told Skee, "He's a total professional on the set, and is otherwise very comfortable. He's another Christian Fox, physically, and has a great sexual personality."

Prince says he's very critical when watching one of his videos. "I like to tear it apart. I know which angles I'm better shot, what makes me look heavier, and what makes me look awkward."

Prince says he was discovered by the famous model photographer Dean Keefer, who sent a spread to *Blueboy* magazine which was quickly published. "Then, I got to do the fantasy sex scenes I'd always dreamed about, I was cast in movies where I got to play an Air Force commander and things like that."

In his private life, Prince likes older guys. "I like intelligence," he says, "people who are full of life. He may be average looking, but has to be fun."

What's fun is watching Prince fuck. In their review of Prince's performance in "Mavericks," *Manshots* said, "Prince's spherical ass and mega-thighs fill the screen as he throws a serious fuck into Beau Saxon, who shoots a blue ribbon load."

There was *more* serious fucking in Studio 2000's "Seaman First Class," in which Prince played a horny sailor looking for adventure; he heads to the desert where he hopes to find trade and finds Danny Sommers! While *Manshots* thought this scene had more sweat than lust, *Fig Leaf* loved it: "Prince encounters sexy Sommers at a truck stop. Danny is a muscular Adonis with an insatiable appetite for steely-hard peters. Without vacillating, the two over-heated hunks go to Danny's homesteader's castle where the hungry gas pump jockey (Danny) sucks Pagan dry. After coming, Pagan gets aroused rimming Danny's quivering pink pucker-hole then rams his meaty cock repeatedly in and out of Danny's clutching anus until both men are ready to off-load again."

In addition to his stellar debut in "Mavericks" and lusty fuck of the legendary Sommers in "Seaman First Class," Prince appeared in "Playing to Win," again paired with a notable bottom, Kevin Kramer. Joe McKenna in *Inches* said, "If you like guppie comedy, you'll love the following scene, in which a group of smugly gorgeous, married, closeted gay men sit around in a group therapy session talking about what's wrong with their pathetically perfect lives. If you don't like that kind of thing, you can turn the soundtrack off and just gaze at the images, because this particular group operates in the nude. I've long held the assumption that men who look as good as these guys really have nothing wrong with them no matter how fucked up they are, and they seem to agree; they quickly forget about the therapy, pair off, and fuck with abandon. My favorite in the group is porn veteran Kevin Kramer, whose almond eyes and blond hair have never looked better. Watching him suck off hairy-assed Pagan Prince is a real delight – better than any group therapy I've ever been part of. When he pulls Prince's cock back between his legs and sucks him from behind, it's a marvel of human engineering: two furry, muscular orbs, a stiff prong, and a cute blond stud's face, all in the same small space."

Rick & Dave in *Frontiers* describe Prince's scene in Minotaur's "Cop Out" with Blake Kennedy: "...Pagan pulls out Blake's big suckable boner for a little lick. Then Blake goes down on Pagan. A lot. Finally, Pagan boinks Blake. They both blow their loads and kiss. Even after all that sex, Pagan is still worried about his lover, Gregg Rockwell. Blake is a little jealous because his man Pagan is consumed with thoughts of his partner...But all does not go well because Pagan is killed in a shoot out but his death makes Gregg confront his sexuality, so..."

And speaking of shooting, Prince also jacked off in both of Bruce Stanton's "Wacky Wack-Offs" videos.

Prince's advice to guys who want to get into the porn business: "Don't make hasty decisions. Seek advice from friends or agents and don't dive in to the first offer that you get. If you want to be treated well, look for the better companies, and they'll treat you with respect." Also, he says, "You have to enjoy sex, that's important. You have to enjoy sex with the guy next door, or a big hunk, or anyone they put you with. That's the secret."

Prince is one of the few who takes full advatange of his fame. He advertises regularly, offering his services: "Sculpted body; European Educated & Refined; for companionship as well as great fun! Will travel. Photos available."

Vince submits!

Vince Cobretti

Our spy in New York reported that Vince Cobretti is alive and well – and still in business! This was good news to us, since we were so fascinated by the little Italian stud that in 1990 we even wrote a book about him: *A Charmed Life*.

Our spy reported that a pal of his, whomwe'll call Pete, was in the landmark bar called Julius on West 10th in the Village when in walks "this hot looking guy whom he thought looked familiar. Pete ordered another drink near the guy so he could get a closer look. Indeed, it was Vince – looking a bit older but still buff and gorgeous.

"After carrying a torch for Vince for seven years, this was the second time in all those years that he had seen the stud in Manhattan. Cobretti began talking to a gentleman and apparently they made a deal because Vince got up and Pete overhead him say he would see his new benefactor at six.

"Cobretti went out into the street and Pete went after him, right into the mob scene of the Gay Pride Parade. Losing sight, he wasn't about to give up and he started circling the block, returning to Julius when one of hustlers near there called out 'Vinnie,' and there he was again! The chase commenced once more, reminiscent of the Keystone Kops, with Cobretti managing to slip away again. Maybe in another seven years?"

We relate this story because it reminded us of our "meetings" with Vince over the years. Every time we went to New York, we'd try to meet him and something always happened to thwart our attempts. Most of the time, the phone number Vince gave us was disconnected when we finally got around to calling. Then he'd call, and the thing would start all over again.

While porn stars spend thousands on advertising every year, they remain incredibly elusive. A few months back, we saw an ad for Marco Rossi in New York, listing an 800 number. If you called, you found it was disconnected. Then the ad re-surfaced in Los Angeles, with a local number, but if you called it you found it had been disconnected.

"Like bad pennies," we noted in our 1992 edition of the Superstars series, "hustlers always have a habit of turning up, so it didn't surprise me that shortly after Easter, out of the blue, Vince called one of my associates saying he'd lost my phone number. (I recalled that the last time he was with me he was conducting a desperate, futile search for his appointment book which he had left in a lounge at one of the innumerable airports he was always passing through)."

We had kept up with his checkered career, a series of mostly dismal videos for the low-rent end of the business, going for the cheap shot, occasionally hitting it right with such as "Lust Boys" or "Houseboys," but mostly in bilge such as "Hard Moves," during which he can't even keep it up to fuck Joey Stefano! We decided his renewed interest in me at Easter stemmed from his having seen one of the ads promoting *A Charmed Life*. Later he told a club owner he found out about it because his sister had walked into a bookstore in Los Angeles and seen it, saying what a coincidence it was there was someone named Vince Cobretti that looked so much like him! I had heard another version of this "Vince's greatest fears" story before, in connection with his porn video career. This was a more plausible scenario since the star has made bisexual videos and his sister could conceivably venture into a video store to rent a tape and there he would be. But it strains credulity to think she'd even find the bookstores, A Different Light or Circus of Books, the outlets in the city that carry my books, and just by chance spy the book stacked somewhere in the back of the store, most likely in the "Sex" section.

Just how the star finally realized, after a year, the book was published didn't really matter. What did matter was his demand to my associate that "it's about time" he start "making some money out of this thing."

When he called me, I was out of town and he was forced to leave his number on the machine. Arriving home, I was told that he was coming to Florida and would be dancing at the Carousel Club in Tampa. I juggled schedules to attend.

Normally, three "porn stars" constitute the entertainment fare on Thursday nights but the boys were being held over for a special appearance on Saturday in honor of emcee and gad-about-town transvestite Esme Russell's 30th birthday. There were three "stars" on the bill and because of Vince's last-minute plea to his friend, the club owner Alfredo, one of them had to go, but not entirely, as it turned out. Vince told Al he "usually" got $800 to dance but when the owner balked they ended up agreeing on $100 per show. When my Tampan friends and I arrived at the club a little after ten, the word was "Vinnie" was coming by limo from Orlando and had left at 9:45. This meant he might miss the first show. This permitted the original threesome to go on as scheduled. The motley crew consisted of Lance, not the uncut blond star of early porn but a true dancer who Esme nonetheless introduced as a "porn star." The dark-haired little trooper knew how to work a crowd and stayed on after the show to work it some more to cadge enough cash to make up for being booted from the second show.

Next up was Alexander Jackson, a short, horse-hung Latin who Esme introduced simply as "Alexander," saying he had appeared in "Manhattan Latins," a bunch of solo spots featuring kids fresh off the streets, and "Latin Fever," scenes from "Boys Behind the Bars," badly re-edited. Hardly the stuff of porn heaven, prompting me to wisecrack to one of my associates, "Old porn performers never die, they just go dancing." Hapless Alexander knew from nothing about dancing and even less about crowd-working, but it hardly mattered; most in the audience were content just to stare in awe at the almost gross appendage barely concealed by a black fabric G-string.

The only true "star" in the firmament that night turned out to be Cal Thomas of Falcon's "Mission Accomplished." This slim, incredibly hung cutie came on stage in purple, skin-tight sequined leotards and a matching cape, both of which he quickly shed, revealing a black fabric G-string similar to the one Alexander favored, apparently *de rigueur* wear for horse-hung dancers. Periodically through his dance he exposed the full spectacle of his manhood to Esme, who was standing off to the side studying her lines scrawled on a piece of yellow legal paper, and continued the practice as he pranced about in the audience. At show's end, he mounted the tiny platform at the back of the stage and slyly exposed himself completely, which certainly would have got him busted in the backwater, Bible-thumping venue of Tampa. Cal stayed behind to tell Esme about making his first video, Vivid's "Texas Tales," in which he co-starred with Alexander Jackson. "We were all dancing at a club and somebody said we should do a video and so we went out and did it." As such spontaneous things often do, the end product looks it. Noted critic John Rowberry wrote: "Four dull scenes and the slowest circle jerk in recorded history, all set outdoors." As part of the gala birthday celebration, Cal called Alexander back on stage and they proceeded to drive Esme wild before our eyes, the Latin crouched at her crotch and Cal lifting her black lace cover-up then working her into a transvestite tizzy from behind.

Before exiting the stage, Esme promised Vince Cobretti was coming. As the DJ reigned, the owner came by with the kind of look only a disgusted hot-blooded Italian could have, complaining that Vince had indeed arrived, in the promised white stretch limo, but accompanied by five others. The star demanded his guests be admitted compliments of the house. Staring the loss of $17.50 in the face, Al flew into a rage, and rather than see Vince lose his chance to pick up some much-needed cash, the group agreed to pay the cover and were admitted, after which Vince proceeded to the dressing room, which at the Carousel is located across the parking lot, making for messy entrances when it rains.

As Esme came back to the stage, the crew Vince brought with him almost shouted her off the stage with cries of "Vinnie!" But, before long, the jets under the platform on stage were spewing smoke and the DJ had Vince's personal track on the system. At last, to the strains of the James Bond theme done as an overture and then "Goldfinger," the star appeared. With his wild black hair clamped into a pony tail and his cheeks even more sunken than before, he barely resembled the young beauty that adorned the boxcover of "Lust Boys," used on the cover of *A Charmed Life*. But, as soon as his black cloak was tossed aside and he began his patented acrobatic dancing, I saw the splendid, virtually hairless torso I knew so well had not suffered a bit since the last time I ran my hands over every flawless inch of it.

"He still looks good," my friend shouted over the din. I nodded, suddenly to find the star off the stage and gyrating in front of me, his backside wriggling between my legs. But he didn't linger long, slipping from one set of hands to the next and then back on the stage. He lay on his back on the platform and started to slip off the black pants, cueing a great audience participation gimmick, but Vince knows how to seed the crowd and one of his companions rushed to the stage to remove the garment and his boots. Then, clad only in a black, satiny G-string, the star continued his acrobatics and I suddenly found him between my thighs again. I slipped a five-dollar bill in the strap just above his crack and he was off without a word. As he danced about the room collecting his tips, it struck me that, unlike some of the other dancers to work this venue, he seldom made eye contact with anyone. It was as if a zombie was high on coke, spinning like a top through the smoky barroom in search of a reason to put himself through this madness and finding it each time someone shoved a bill next to his sweaty skin. Then, it seemed, it was over, and Alexander was back on stage, his weaponry now ensconced in a green pouch that left nothing to the imagination.

Vince, dressed all in black re-appeared, not to work the crowd but to chat with his companions. "I think," I ventured to one of my associates, "it's time for me to make a graceful exit."

"Aren't you going to talk to him?" he asked incredulously.

I said, "He doesn't have anything to say to me I haven't heard before."

A few minutes later, as I eased my car out of the parking lot, the white stretch limo was pulling up at the front door to ferry Vince and his friends into the night.

All the way home I thought about Vince, about my lips touching his during the ritual of sex as he fucked me until I came. I thought about all the things he said to me over the several years we had been in contact. Vince once told me he was "runnin' low on things to say" to himself. I doubted it. Vince once joked, "As long as I'm here, there'll still be beauty in the world." That I was sure of. He was proud of his beauty, a beauty that time cannot destroy now – it has been preserved on film. We can return to it again and again, savoring it, remembering it. It matters not where Vince is in the world, we have him, at his best, on the VCR whenever we need him. Whenever we want to remember him.

In *A Charmed Life*, I wrote, "Vince is a ghost. Ethereal. A human ectoplasm. He's here, then he's gone. Then you aren't sure he was even here to begin with. You come to realize Vince has had sex with everyone. He has had sex with someone you know or someone who knows someone you know or someone you wish you knew. Vince is famous for sex, he is famous for having sex. In his own world, he is famous. And he has taken advantage of his fame. What you hear about him always centers on the carnal; almost legendary, possibly embellished, certainly superfluous. When you first meet him he seems gentle, respectful, never pushy. Eventually, you realize he is insatiable. He would not mind having sex right now. When he chances upon a pretty woman he says, somewhat shyly, somewhat befuddled, 'Now, I forget your name.' You can imagine him saying, once he has her pussy within reach: 'You're the most beautiful thing I've ever seen.' He's been known to take or make phone calls during sex. His mind swirls with phone numbers, memorized for the ages. To hear him on the phone, his voice a mellifluous purr, instantly conspiratorial, is to hear a master manipulator at work. Vince is as at home in the ear as he is in a mouth, a cunt or in an asshole. He has been inside so many he lost count ages ago.

"'...Yeah, I think I put off posin' or makin' a film just long enough so that I can't put it off any longer. For various reasons. It's like I'm not very fond of schedules. I don't see any point in keepin' to some schedule of life.'

"He grins a reproachful grin. And stares into my eyes. And keeps grinning. He says nothing. It's his canny way of saying he knows. He knows it's time for me again. He knows I want him again. To feel the perfection of his perfect cock between my lips and, perhaps, if I can arouse him enough, between the cheeks of my ass.

"...As he enters me again, stabbing me, I suddenly feel how unfair it is for someone with this much skill to be so stingy with it. So many of the performers give less than their all. If the money is there, Vince comes across. He is an artist at making love and an artist is a man who loves life too intensely, a man who loves life till he hates it and has to strike out to show he knows the tricks. But, in the end, there always will be light.

"'...The kissing is okay," he says, talking about making videos. We've settled back on our respective sides of the bed. I took as much of it as I could. I couldn't cum again but five minutes of having him on top of me was pleasure enough. 'Yeah, I love to kiss. I can handle that, but the sex part, that took some gettin' used to. It was tough. Very tough. They are hard to do, those scenes. There are times I feel a little dirty.

Shit, more than a little dirty. But that wasn't important at all, because that sensation of dirtiness is a moral sensation and morality doesn't go with art.

"Yeah, if you just forget where you really are and look at it as a party.

"Like on the set of 'Lust Boys.' The orgy. God, that was a fuckin' party! Yeah, I liked that one. I didn't have to say a thing!

"In a way, it was more exciting for people when I was unknown. I know I love that feeling when I'm watching a movie and see somebody and, never having seen this face before, I'm not watching a recognizable star, and that's when I can really lose myself in the story. It lives in your mind in such a different way look back at some of that shit now and I say, 'Man, how could I do that?'"

Well, he did do that, and a lot more. I recalled his ad in *The Advocate*: "Vince Cobretti Star of Hard Rock High and Houseboys. This clean-cut 19 year old smooth, Italian, hot top with bronzed body, washboard stomach, can make your fantasy become a reality."

Yes, the fantasy did indeed become a reality, of sorts. Vince is one of those men who looks best without any clothes on. In fact, that's how we got to know him. He is primarily a "boxcover star." By some fluke, the still of him standing in a jockstrap with Marc Radcliffe holding one leg and another blond the other, became the famous box cover pose of "Hard Rock High." And then he was featured as the main illustration for "Houseboys."

Physically, he's no giant. He stands about five-eight and weighs about 134 pounds, with a 28" waist. When pressed, he'll admit, a little self-consciously in a world dominated by huge endowments, that his cock measures about 6 1/2 inches when hard. (A few years ago, Bill Margold, editor of the Hollywood Press for many years and a keen observer of the hardcore industry, gave this advice to would be film studs: "How big does it really have to be? It all depends on your build, whether four inches soft looks big in proportion to the rest of your body. You should be able to at least make a fist around your dick with the head of the dick fully exposed for your dick to look attractive while being blown....It should hit the back of a throat in a deep throat situation. If it can't get past the molars, it's really not big enough.

"The circumference of the dick is not really important as long as the dick has a well- proportioned look."

Therein lies Vince's secret: he may not have a big dick, but it is in perfect proportion to the rest of him. Based on physical description alone, Vince really is nothing special. Each year, thousands of kids get off the bus in L.A. thinking they've found Mecca. They want to become somebody. Most of them would seem to have more to offer than the little Italian from Long Island. But 99 percent of them remain nobody. For one brief moment, the little Italian, christened Vince, has become one of the one percent. Because somebody noticed him, recommended him, passed him on, in the secret world of the sex-obsessed.

"Yeah," Vince says, "I guess why I've been successful is because I like to play a lot of different roles. Like in high school I'd go for the underdog, the person who doesn't expect you to want them. It makes the sex more intense."

I told him once that my dream was to fuck him. I reminded him that he had fingered his slit in "Screen Test Magazine."

"Yeah, well, yah do what the director says to do. I stuck a finger in it. No big deal."

"But it was to me. I'm a guy that would like to stick more than a finger up there!"

"Yeah, maybe some day. I don't know, it really hurts. And with you, shit I know it'd hurt. You got the biggest dick I've ever seen except maybe for Kiko in New York. " (I've left Kiko's name in here because he'd be pleased. In fact, he advertises his size every issue in the *Advocate Classifieds*: 20 y.o. porn star Classic good looks and hung huge. Uncut. 24 hrs. Lve msg. for Kiko. In or Out. (212) XXX-XXXX (18+)"

The last time I talked with him, setting up the aborted meeting in New York, he let me know that he had finally bottomed. Said he, "Yeah, you gotta in this business, you know."

Yes, I knew.

Eearly in 1990, it was with a certain sadness that we saw Vince descend to the hell of Grapik Art's S&M scumbag of tricks, at only $54.95 each, plus $3.00 postage and handling, of course. You could even buy photo sets of the outtakes! This San Francisco direct mail outfit offered two videos starring Vince: "Vince Submits" and 'Tamed." At least they spelled his name right! About "Vince Submits," the copywriter waxed ecstatically: "Vince Cobretti is a street-mart beauty with a strong, muscular body and a classic face. You'll enjoy his submission and training with secure rope bondage, hood, and heavy irons. Easily the hottest slave we've trained yet, this tough lad finds he needs to serve."

And, as our spy in The Big Apple tells us, he's *still* "serving." One tough lad indeed.

THE BEST EROTIC GAY VIDEOS AND SCENES OF THE YEAR

Despite the pleasure they afford, sexual practices tend to be frequently banal, impoverished and doomed to repetition. Therefore, erotic scenes must be shot sparingly, with a good deal of economy. The best directors know this, scouring the carnal operation of its tedium and effort. The best scenes have a preparation, a cruising, an approach, perhaps a little conversation, then the sex. And we do mean *sex*. Two young men do not know each other but they know they are about to become partners in a specific act, or acts, and they are being paid to put on a performance. What ignites the imagination is the passion they put into it even though they are being paid for it. That is what separates the superstars from the wanna-bes and the has-beens, the best videos from the bilge.

And a bigger budget doesn't always make it better. As film critic Bob Satuloff observes, "Maybe I'm unrepresentative of the audience for gay porn but I keep finding that the slicker a video is, the higher the level of production values, the fancier the camera work, the more scoring, the more gleamingly gym-bodied the performers the less I seem to like it, or, to put it more succinctly, the less I'm able to use it. In terms of accessibility, the state of the art stuff I've seen lately puts a thick glass wall between me and what I'm watching."

Perhaps it's passion Bob's missing. When you realize how much of it is programmed, you seek out the exceptions to the rule: The scenes that exude passion, that hold a special charm, a certain magic. From the many scenes that have been shot over the past year, we have picked a few that have practically melted our television sets. These are scenes shot by true artists. We call them artists because it is the artist's gift to see something familiar anew and to make it beautiful, the *creme de la creme* of erotica.

Best Sucking

The finale of Jocks' "Hot Wheels" features one of the most entertaining suck sessions of the year. What makes it so special is that Colby Taylor gets to suck two of the most magnificent performers currently in porn: Falcon's discoveries Jeremy Penn and Eric Hanson. When Jeremy and Eric arrive at Ethan-Michael Ayers's apartment, they find him face-fucking a blindfolded Colby Taylor. They join the action, taking turns letting Taylor suck them. Hanson has a miraculous cock and most of the camera time is spent on this throbbing, perfect member as Hanson teases Taylor with it. Then off comes the blindfold and Taylor is soon on his stomach, taking first Hanson then Penn up his ass. The fucking is not as exciting as the sucking, which continues with Ayers sucking Penn and Taylor sucking Ayers while Hanson fucks, but this one is a keeper.

The other absolute must suck-fest of the year was in George Duroy's "Wide Open," released through Falcon. *In Touch* agreed with us in loving the spirited sucking of Tomas Belko (aka Roman Paulik): "...An amazing performance. In the belly of a riverboat, this cute stud sucks off five guys, one after the other, and then gets plowed up the ass by a hung Alexander Strauss. Bravo Tomas!"

Best Fucking

"I've been noticing lately that different guys have different styles of fucking," Joe McKenna noted in *Inches*. "I suppose I've always known this, but having watched even more porn than usual in recent weeks, I've been aware of just how much men use their cocks as an element of personal style. Some wield their dicks like baseball bats, others like mallets. Still others hold their meat out in front of them like it was, well, a big slab of meat; I think they're my favorites. And the way men clench their asses or suck in their guts, just to show off their stuff to its best advantage. One guy in 'the Anchor Hotel' from Kristen Bjorn goes so far as to undulate his slim, hairless stomach while he thrusts his sausage-like schlong into some other stud's hungry ass. This handsome stud also distinguishes himself by the way he shivers when he comes. His whole body shakes with excitement as his juice shoots up and out, an action the camera records from a beautiful low angle so that his gray juice ends up on the lens."

"Continuing the premise of Catalina's 'Classified Action,' 'Breathless: Classified Action II' is built around connections made through gay personals ads and the j/o fantasies those ads inspire," *The Guide's* Jim D'Entremont says. "All the sex is one-on-one. The first and last encounters both stand out; the first has a definite edge. ...Matt Bradshaw and Drew Andrews are seated on a bed, naked, ravenously kissing as they stroke each other's upthrust cocks. The sexual chemistry between these two is real, intricate, and intense. They seem rapturously turned on by each other's bodies. When Andrews says, as Bradshaw's mouth slides down his shaft, 'I can't believe how good that feels,' you know he means it. When Andrews, a trick from the personals, later makes it clear to Bradshaw that he's only into one-night stands, you can't believe he wouldn't be fiercely eager for more. (You almost certainly will be.) After Andrews obeys the script and leaves, Bradshaw flips through classifieds with headlines like 'Plumber Needs Draining,' and zones out into masturbation reveries.

"...If more of the sex could have reached the erotic pitch of the gorgeous *pas de deux* between Bradshaw and Andrews at the beginning, this could have been a classic."

Andrews had another classic fuck in "A Body to Die For."

"A gay murder mystery porno video? Puhlease!" Sticky Remote in *HX* said about the video which solved "the age-old mystery of how a great set of dicks matched with dirty minds can lead you – the normally rational viewer – to dark and dangerous places your mommy told you to avoid.... Andrews is the oh-so-suave weekend host who turns out to be the hottest top we've seen in a long time. Bravo. ...This group of guys not only has big dicks, and not only gets into sucking and fucking other guys with big dicks, but, surprise, they actually stay hard." The video was highlighted by the "unbelievable pounding of Jeff Dalton by a massive Andrews, whose powerdick rams Dalton 20 feet down a long dining table. See it to believe it!"

In his review of "Portrait of Lust" from All Worlds' new Romance line, Joe Phillips in *The Guide* says, "The scenes and foreplay are romantic, and the sex is highly erotic. The wettest and the wildest point is sincerely delivered by Sam Carson and Eduardo in a shower. Splash! The kissing is tender at first, building to a sloppy tongue bath from the top of their heads to the bottom of their toes and all parts in between. The fuck views are super (it's amazing the cameraman didn't get electrocuted).

"The last scene has Eric York and Ethan Michael Ayers in a tender, yet totally intense, scenario where the canvas is Ethan's ass and the brush strokes are from Eric's paint brush."

In Falcon's "Manhandlers," Jeff Palmer is found "fucking the bejeezus out of Derek Cameron," to quote *Playguy*. "They are so hard, enthusiastic and into each other, that you can't help but get worked up about it." *In Touch's* reviewer: "Mike Branson. His dark hair, rugged good looks and unbelievable body make him the perfect porn star. And then there's his cock. Oh... My...God! It's amazingly big and juicy!

"The runner-up in the cock department is boystud Jeff Palmer. He's got an awesome body and cock, complimented by a pair of alluring and mysterious eyes. And man, is he mean! He shows up in three scenes. First, he teases Mike Branson just enough to make Mike go after his lover, Tony Manchester. Second, he gives in to the seductions of Derek Cameron, but then, if you watched Derek shove an ice cube into his own ass, you'd give in, too. But, Jeff shows us what he's really made of in the last scene, pounding the asses of both Derek Thomas (billed here as Brent Sawyer) and Jordan West, after, of course, grabbing them both by the hair and sadistically pulling their mouths down onto his monstrous prick. Overall, we were extremely impressed with his performance. He got our attention with the way he wields his cock like a weapon: cruelly, but with passion.

"Naturally, we can't leave out Thomas. For the past year he has consistently been one of our favorite bottoms. In 'Manhandlers,' he gives yet another stunning and fully committed performance. With Jordan West as his partner in crime, Thomas manages to take on three very horny men just like a pro.

"This brings us to Falcon's major discovery, Jeremy Penn. Whoa! What a man! He's young and smooth, all-American and totally collegiate. You won't believe your eyes when he first appears in the last five-man fuck scene. From the moment he's first glimpsed, his charming smile and wicked blue eyes capture the audience and never let go. It's evident in this last scene that Jeremy is new to porn, but as he watches Jeff Palmer in action, he catches on quickly and really starts to get into it."

John Erich in *Advocate Men* agreed, in his review of Falcon's "The Player," saying about Palmer that he is "in his element as a top, and uber-bottom Kyle McKenna is a known treasure, though the idea of being plundered in a urinal trough doesn't do much for me."

Palmer can work anybody up, even nominal top man K.C. Hart, who was paired with him in Falcon's "The Player." Hart remembers it: "He's really rough! He fucked me six ways to Sunday!" Hart also was paired with Chad Donovan in "Hot Cops 3" from Centaur. "I don't know why but when they ask me to bottom it's always with these guys with huge, huge dicks! But I got paid, so I guess I can't explain." Hart's own masterful fucking technique has been described by J. Keil in *Mandate* as "fucking like a bunny-rabbit, punching holes left and right with quick little thrusts that set my teeth on edge." Hart says that he has to do that in videos because the sex has to be visually demonstrative, but when he's fucking in real life, he has more energy but he moves more slowly and with greater care. Just so you know.

Best Flip-Flop

One of our favorite things is to find a video wherein we expect to see a notable top do just that and lo and behold, he ends up bottoming! There could be many reasons for this, such as not being able to get wood, but for whatever reason, it's always exciting for us jaded fans. For instance, in his review of "Gold Diggers," Robert Sumners in *Mondo Porno* thought the "stand outs are the fierce Jim Buck (minus his signature Prince Albert), trashy yet tasty Rod Barry and the All-American Sam Dixon. Kevin Gold smolders but is a little pumped up for my taste, and Jay Anthony and Doug Jeffries fare well. Plus relative newcummer Tony Idol is one major hotass. ...The truly jaw-dropping moment was after a major assmunching session, bottom baby Jay Anthony starts fucking regular top Buck! I nearly fainted. Thank goodness for smelling salts."

Rick & Dave at *Frontiers* agreed, but also pointed out the other attraction of flip-flopping, that the stud does, in the end, perform as we expect him to: "Jim begins kissing Jay, roughly at first, Jay goes down on Jim and Jim gives Jay the famous Jim Buck Suck 'N' Rim. Jay does the same for Jim. We are pleasantly surprised to see Jay fucking Jim. Then Jim fucks Jay just like we knew he would. (Remember: Versatility=Love)."

Best Bottoming

In his review of "Beached," from All Worlds, Dana Wells in *The Guide* said, "Homeless cute blonde beach bunny bottom bomps bountifully. Nice outdoor photography full of cute guys. Troy Halston is a standout with that big, big mushroom-headed dip stick. Jake Cannon gives good butt."

Yes, "giving good butt" is an art, and there really are few stand-outs. We tend to immortalize the fuckers not the fuckees because we're so pleased to see the big dick hard and penetrating, for as long as the guy can do it. To see what a difference an aggressive bottom makes, have a look at Drew Kelly in Mustang's "Take Me Home." The sight of Kelly going crazy over Steve Lance's cock, deep throating it, adoring it, nearly making Lance come, is exceeded only by his frenzied fucking of the meat. Seeing those alabaster buttocks slamming back against Lance, taking the cock all the way up, is an incredible turn-on. Kelly, a Derek Powers discovery, made little impression otherwise. As exalted critic Dave Kinnick said, "New York-based Drew gets good gigs based on his boyish looks and his open and willing hole – no one seems to mind that he rarely sprouts wood on-screen for too long." Indeed, the only thing lacking in the sequence in "Take Me Home" is the sight of Kelly coming.

When it comes to bottoming, Chad Knight is, in the words of Kinnick, "a classic," and he hasn't lost his touch. When he's coupled with an outstanding top, the results are truly memorable. The very best example of this can be found at the end of Chip Daniels' "Marine Crucible," with great close-ups of Bo Summers's heroic meat entering Chad's willing hole. Bo stays hard throughout and shows no mercy with his frequent penetrations. Chad, of course, comes after Bo does, completing the sequence. This one's a keeper.

Best Anilingus

In his review of "One Hot Summer" from John Travis's factory, Chris Pomiecko in *The Guide* found "especially appealing" the rimming by Mike Lofton, "a lickable puffy-titted studpuppy who's paired with hairy humpy gardener Logan Reed, in a scene highlighted by some hard-tongued rimming of Lofton's hairy, rosey-sphinctered butthole. Lofton shows up again in the concluding six-man orgy scene, where he's paired with star (and 'Studio 2000 Exclusive') Rick Chase, a dark-haired demi-god. While their action is limited to mutual masturbation, Lofton's guilty hang-dog look and constant looks offscreen (a sure giveaway that the actor's straight), gives this scene a perverse kick. Also noteworthy in this scene are craggy blonds Bobby Golden and Jon Davis with some savage butt-pumping."

In Falcon's "The Player" we have one of the most convincing ass-eating scenes of the year. First, we knew that Sam Dixon thought his bottom Jake Cannon was cute, and he proves it with a spirited sucking of the blond's cock until Jake tells him to "eat my ass." It seems to be music to Sam's ears because he dives right then, then sticks his fingers in, followed by his cock. This is perfect. What we hate more than anything is a bottom boy eating out a top and then having the director cut directly to the top fucking the bottom. You want to say, Wait a second! But not in the case of Sam and Jake.

Matt Bradshaw gets down and dirty with Kyle Hunter and Will Clark in Hot House's "Take One: Guys Like Us." Comments *Torso*: "Fans of rimming will be delighted to see the close-ups of some seriously intense ass-licking, not to mention the butt busting bonanza that ensues."

And, of course, any video is a winner in this category if it has what has now become known as the Famous Jim Buck Suck 'N' Rim (see above).

Best Three-Ways

Jerry Douglas in *Manshots* praised "Dr. Jerkoff & Mr.

Hard's" impressive three-way thus: "...Jim Buck engineers a high-energy threeway with Dax Kelly and Jack Simmons, in which he calls all the shots and proves himself to be quite a pricktease before he gets around to giving head, fucking both of them, and delivering a hailstorm money shot."

"Kristen Bjorn has done it again," Christopher J. Hogan claims in *The Guide*. "This video rules. 'The Anchor Hotel' has the trademark international flair of Bjorn's work. This time, rather than featuring a cast from one country, Bjorn has created an amazing stew of gorgeous men from around the world. Unlike almost all other porn makers, Bjorn has the ability to eroticize all types of men without degrading them. The first scene features Mark Anthony, Pedro Pandilla, and Rafael Perez in one of the best three-ways of recent memory. Not only are these three guys hot beyond belief, they all seem to have unlimited sexual powers."

In "Passage to Berlin" there is a turbulent threeway in which as *Manshots* reported, "C.H. and an older daddy type named Marc take turns reducing a hairy slave, Xerxes, to raw hamburger. Marc, in particular, is an amazing sex engine, clenching his fists and snorting like a stud bull in heat as he explodes into an apocalyptic orgasm. We can't remember having seen a more copious ejaculation."

Best Four (Or More)-Ways

One of the more interesting four-ways of the year can be found in Falcon's "The Freshmen." *In Touch* describes it: "After injuring himself at soccer practice, Tony Idol is taken back to the locker room by hunky coaches Mike Branson and Tom Chase. Now, we don't understand this, but Mike and Tom seem to think that the best cure for an injury is lots of all-male sex. Sure, it sounds strange, but it does seem to work. After thrusting his huge cock down Tony's throat, Mike convinces Chris Berrara to join in on the game. The four of them engage in some sizzling cocksucking, ass rimming and toe sucking. After the four of them cum all over Tom, Tony leaves just as little Jordan Young walks in. Well, the three studs, Tom, Mike and Chris, aren't nearly satisfied yet, and they take the opportunity to get off again in Jordan's pretty little mouth and butt."

And speaking of epics, in his review of Jocks' "Private Parts," Chris Pomiecko says in *The Guide*, "...The concluding five-way is a bonerizing classic. First, beefcakes Doug Jeffries and Vince Skyler work on each other and Nicolas Moore poolside. The are joined by Jeffries' lover (in the movie!), perky bottom Steve Pierce, and they pair off for some intensive rimming. Finally mediterranean dreamboy Dillon Colt joins the action, and the ensuing fuckfest is a real dick-stiffener."

Best Orgasms

To borrow the movie phrase of recent vintage: "Show me the money," "money shot," that is! The point, after all, to all that huffing and puffing in porn is release, and such release, in porn parlance, is "the money shot."

Truly memorable explosions are extremely rare these days, and sometimes the videomakers go to great lengths, as it were, to get even a passable money shot. But occasionally they get lucky and we get something simply unforgettable. For instance, in Centaur Films' "Hot Cops 3," *HX's* reviewer Sticky Remote notes, "Mostly dribbles here, but Steve O'Donnell squirts a prodigious load over K.C. Hart's mouth, face and chest. Dildos are used to pump most of the loads out of these boys, but while the dildos are large, the loads are unimpressive."

In his review of Jocks' "Private Parts," Chris Pomiecko says in *The Guide*, "Special mention must be made for Doug Jeffries' cumshot in scene two. Pulling his substantial pud, Jeffries' loose shaved balls jiggle until he shoots a number of ceiling-splashing loads. Whew! This scene should be nominated for Best Cum Shot of the Year."

In Minotaur's "The Diary," the ever-faithful Brett Winters shoots a wad of ELEVEN spurts all over Aaron Brandt's back.

The money shot is so important it even have its own category at the Gay Video Guide Awards. In 1996, the award went to our absolute favorite everything, Lukas Ridgeston, for his incredible explosion in "Lukas' Story 3." Lukas continued to amaze with several explosions in "Frisky Summer 2." *Manshots* also loved the all-oral scene on the beach where Sebastian Bonnet "treats Lukas to a blowjob of such deliberate force that by the time he reaches his multi-squirt, fountain-like finish, his whole body is trembling with pleasure. Seldom in the history of male erotica have two objects of such pure, unadultered beauty embraced with such simple, yet exquisite perfection."

And then there is the boy known ONLY for his money shot. A boy who could truly make a fortune if he did anything more than just get off: Mike Magik. Mike was so named because of his magical way with his fist, when applied to his own flesh you understand. And he is adorable in "Wacky Wack-Off No. 2." And then there's that porn veteran Brett Winters, who, Robert Sumners said in *Mondo Porno*, "never fails to serve up quite a load."

Of the newer fellas, there is Jim Buck, whose orgasms in "Dr. Jerkoff & Mr. Hard" were praised by Jerry Douglas in *Manshots*: "...He engineers a high-energy threeway with Dax Kelly and Jack Simmons, in which he calls all the shots and proves himself to be quite a pricktease before he gets around to giving head, fucking both of them, and delivering a hailstorm money shot... (In his scene with Matthew Easton) Buck proves that he has learned one can be both gorgeous and giving. And his final money shot, right into the camera, is absolutely atomic!"

J. T. Sloan continued to impress in otherwise undistinguished videos. *Manshots* commented about his turn in "Dino Dreams On," during which he sits on DiMarco's meat and rides: "The only treat here is Sloan's no-handed cum shot, which he delivers while being fucked." The only way to come!

"Cruisin' 3" is "standard stuff" from Falcon, *Manshots* magazine thought, a series of four loops strung loosely together by the ambience of San Francisco and by the mating/dating rituals of the gay men who live there. We liked it because they even go so far as to include the street signs so that, should you go there, you would know where to go. The three-way with Drew Nolan, Dean Spencer, and Mike Nichols produces strong "money shots." Also notable is the finale which features Falcon exclusive Tom Chase (who *Manshots* called "a lean, dark-haired, mega-hung sex machine who reminds one of Lon Flexx and Steve Kennedy"). What makes his scene with Matt Cook is impressive because of Cook's ability to take every inch of Chase's formidable weapon, and Chase's rimming abilities.

When Chase explodes, it's so dazzling that Falcon chooses to rerun it in slow motion."

In their review of "Dirty White Guys," *Manshots* says, "The Fourth of July finale is a sixteen-man, cocksucking daisy chain which is volcanic. The camera slowly moves around the circle allowing us ample views of each cock in each mouth, and it needs to be noted that every one is rockhard. The top shots capturing the entire picture are perfect, as is the cum-athon in which all the players release a storm of spooge. Each and every guy blasts (and we do mean *blasts*) for the crowd. Cum shot fans, take note that we cannot remember when we have seen this much jizz in one scene."

Apparently the success of the Hitchcockian "Flesh and Blood" inspired Studio 2000 to do their own mystery: "A Body to Die For," and it was written with such great camp value that it is unfortunate most of the actors aren't up to that level of acting - shocking," Robert Sumners said in *Mondo Porno*. "Set in a grandiose mansion, lovers Drew Andrews and Gregg Rockwell had planned a 'murder mystery weekend' for their friends only (gosh be darned!) Gregg had to go and get poisoned after the first glass of bubbly. Who is the killer? Who is stealing everyone's stuff? Who's the mysterious guy in the chapel? Who cares as long as there's hot sex! Rick Chase finally bottoms! Sing Hallelujia! But the icing on the cake was that he comes while getting plowed. ...And then there is Rick Price who, after getting nailed by the very well-endowed Mike Nichols (who sports a cute new haircut), shoots several lovely dollops.

"...The movie has such great campy moments including a hysterical hallway scene with doors worthy of a Joe Orton play - it's a shame it tries to take itself so seriously at times. Well, that and the fact that the actors aren't really up to some of the over-the-top dialogue and deliver it like they're trying to do Shakespeare doesn't help either."

Of another video, *In Touch* commented, "With cheap jokes at every turn... for some reason, the lawmen in 'Hung Riders II' never seem to be actually trying to get their man. Instead, they seem to get caught up with sexual diversions at every turn. Imagine that!

"Max Grand and Anthony Mengetti... have a really hot scene in the local jail. Max convinces the hunky deputy to suck his dick in exchange for information about Miss Clitty, and, like the lawmen he is, Anthony completely falls for it. He doesn't seem to mind, however – at least not judging by his cock's impressive eruption." *In Touch* also admired Cody Whiler's orgasm in his fireside fuck with Marc Pierce, while Chris Green strums his guitar, calling it "simply amazing."

In Catalina's "Ranger in the Wild," Eric Stone fucks Tony Cummings. *In Touch* loved the pay-off: "Before stuffing his huge cock into Tony's young ass, Eric fucks the boy with a dildo just to get him good and ready. When the two of them finally blow their loads, we get to see the sticky makings of a budding relationship. The video is greatly enhanced by director Josh Eliot's use of numerous cameras to film the cumshots. Each dramatic explosion of jizz (and there are a lot of them) is filmed from every possible angle and even shown in slowmo. And, some of these orgasms are so big that one really does need to see them over and over again."

In "Heatwave," from Falcon, Steve O'Donnell and Logan Reed are lovers. Joe Phillips in *The Guide* asks, "Donnell wants to fuck Reed - who doesn't? Reed is hesitant to spread his legs. O'Donnell arranges various mini-orgies to try to persuade Reed to put out. Ultimately, however, it's Reed's own fantasy of a mega-orgy that turns the tables. In the end, Reed gets plowed by O'Donnell's sizable endowment just as we knew he would all along. Most of the large cast's members are involved in the dream sequence/swimming pool orgy of the video's penultimate scene. Unlike the dark and serious sex club orgies we see in so many videos these days, this scene is all about playful frolicking. Don't let that fool you, the sex in this orgy is very wild and hot. Hawk McAllister and Adam Wilde are big, fat, messy, pass-around, party bottoms that could hold their own in any dungeon. Just wait until you see what they take up their butts."

Adam Wilde shares his secret: "I can shoot over my head and stuff. It depends on how excited I am. It depends on what you had to drink the day before. If you're dehydrated or if you're not. I can shoot a pretty big load."

Best Orgies

Toby Ross told *Manshots*: "I think when you do an orgy – for me, at least – if you have six people, say – you need two or three that you are personally turned on to, and that's your nucleus. You build everything around them. You cannot do an orgy scene when you're indifferent to the people. I use three cameras. The first two cameras cover the action from different angles, and the third camera is usually just reaction shots."

"Heatwave" boasts "a pool side orgy of fantastical proportions," *In Touch* cheered. "The small conflict that sets up the premise of the video is, in fact, a rather large conflict between Logan Reed and his boyfriend Steve O'Donnell. Logan won't let Steve fuck him, so Logan demonstrates just how good an ass pounding can be. They spy on Tom Chase and Adriano Marquez." *In Touch* says, "The scene is rugged, passionately violent, and even contains some awesome fisting, which Logan watches as he strokes his beautiful cock." Then there is a jacuzzi three-way between Logan, O'Donnell and Derek Cameron. *In Touch* comments, "The two of them go at Derek with pent-up intensity, and Logan gets closer to giving up everything he has to the fiery passion of his lover. Logan's revelations cause his own fantasies to grow, and they soon develop into a nasty nine-man sexfest that takes place both in and out of the water. Logan's dream pushes him over the edge, and Steve finally gets exactly what he was looking for – pounding Logan's hot ass under the burning sun."

Best Rape

"'Balls In Play' is a vaguely disturbing video," Christopher J. Hogan said in *The Guide*, "Perhaps the most upsetting thing about it is that the most disturhing elements are also the hottest. The rather complex plot features an openly gay football player, his homophobic team mate, and lots of rape. Blue Blake is our hero, a tough, queer athlete who stands up for his rights. He's also a top-notch sleuth who solves the mystery of who has been raping and beating hustlers then leaving them for dead in the country. It's his queer-bashing teammate and nemesis, Paul Carrigan. Carrigan sends his thugs, Jack Simmons and Mike

Lamas, to drug Blake. While Blake is semiconscious, they rape him. Blake gets his revenge by arranging a gang rape of Carrigan in the locker room. This time, Nic Collins, Ryan Block, and Jesse Tyler do the honors.

"It's difficult to build a good porn video around all this rape for two reasons. First, the sex we see in the video is clearly not rape. It simply doesn't convey violation or coercion. Second, the film-makers want to have their cake and eat it too which just won't work. You cannot portray rape as evil to advance the plot and try to make it sexy to heat up the sex scenes. For these reasons, both the story and the sex scenes of 'Balls In Play' are mixed successes at best.

"'Balls In Play' is to be commended for two big reasons. It is a veritable ode to sexual versatility. Manly men Blake, Carrigan, and Eric York all top and bottom in the video. Also, this cast has an excellent racial mix. In an industry that continues to shamefully segregate performers, it's great to see someone use such a diverse group of good looking and talented men."

Best Leather

For some years Catalina has been the official videographer of the International Mr. Leather contest, "a yearly event that floods the streets of Chicago with so much cowhide that you'd think the stockyards had exploded," Fred Goss notes in *Advocate Men*. "Besides producing real documentary videos that chronicle the contest itself, Catalina has cagily seen fit to issue three hard-core docudramas set in and around the contest: 'IML Uncut,' 'IML Initiation,' and 'Hell Bent for Leather.'

"Opening with the crowning of Joe Gallagher as International Mr. Leather 1996, 'Hell Bent' goes inside the champ's head as he muses about – what else? – sex. Leather sex, to be precise. After all, Gallagher – the 18th International Mr. Leather in a long line of black-clad, hairy daddies – is to the leather community what the Dalai Lama is to Tibetan Buddhists. Different beings may hold the title in different years, but they are all embodiments of an ideal. With all his IML regalia making him look like King George V – or Czar Nicholas II – with a flattop, Gallagher falls into a reverie after he's been signing autographs, and we're treated to the spectacle of Will

Clark (seriously hot in a buzz cut and, well, leather) going at it with Beau Lyons, 1996's Mr. Boston Leather, who strays from the dress code enough to wear a chrome-plated jockstrap. Perhaps the reason for the metal duds has to do with the fact that Lyons, after getting (and giving) some expert oral service from the ever-accommodating Clark, tosses a big load of Mr. Boston Leather jizz all over his silver codpiece and then licks it up. Hey, no muss, no fuss."

Robert Sumners in *Mondo Porno* comments, "Joe Gallagher, the 1996 International Mr. Leather stars as himself, and he is thrilled to have won the title because it means he has a lot more sex. He watches the pairings of various leather-clad gents in a variety of dark corners, finally joining in the action for the final foursome."

Yes, things do get hot when Gallagher himself finally gets down to business in the finale, when he follows the alluring Steve Rambo behind a curtain and discovers him pigging out with Anthony Gallo and Beau Lyons, that insatiable Mr. Boston. Says Goss, "Sporting a Prince Albert that was a door knocker in a former life, Gallagher manages to keep pace with the two pros and the slightly more experienced Lyons, seeming at ease no matter what raunchy act he's performing (or with whom). Everyone gets fucked by Gallo, and by the looks of it, not a moment too soon. It's great to see real enthusiasm in a sex video, and these four men have that in abundance."

"In 'Leather Obsession, Part 5: Mission Possible,' some sicko is picking up men in leather clubs and killing them in alleys," Christopher J. Hogan says in *The Guide*. "Chase Allen must go undercover to catch the killer. With the help of his intrepid, dreamy lover Will Clark, he does just that. Scooby Snack, anyone?

"The sex scenes are generally very good. Drew Andrews, Max Grand, and Kyle McKenna all give great performances in leather sex club scenes. Ironically, the best scene doesn't involve leather at all: Allen and Clark have really hot sex in and out of vanilla drag. Clark is one of the best bottoms in the business, and Allen is a terrific match for him. Let's face it, they are not hard to look at. They also fuck like it really means something.

"The connection between leather bars and murder is a disquieting one. Of course, part of the allure of leather is 'the danger.' (This vid) tries to walk a fine line between showing homophobia as the cause of the brutal crimes and implying that they are part of the 'leather underground.' Sometimes, the video may cross the line into S/M phobia. Then again, that may all be in the eye of the beholder."

Best Kink

"...Video 10's 'Passage to Berlin,' flawlessly captures the rush of sexual excess to be found in the German capital today," *Manshots* said. "Shot on location in a dance den called The Connection Club, this relentlessly arousing film has been directed by one Jorge Andreas, a name new to us, but whose work in this pulsating production suggests that he may well be the most brilliant director to emerge from the European scene since George Duroy. 'Passage to Berlin' focuses on an enticing blond youth from the moment he enters the cavernous disco and is promptly groped by the doorman. Against a background of vibrating dancers and dizzying lighting effects, he makes his way into the maelstrom and begins his odyssey through the seemingly endless carnival of untrammeled sexuality. The cherubic youth – here using the professional name Michel, although he has worked in BG wrestling tapes under the name Ingo – with his innocent but curious face, boyish body, and thick, man-sized dick seems part Candide, part Alice in Wonderland as he observes, then participates in all manner of sexual variations. And by the time the fast-paced production has run its course, we realize that his evening in this prurient paradise has not been so much an odyssey as it has been his rites of passage."

Best Solos

Anything with Mike Magik (see Best Orgasms, above).

Best Bondage

"Bound and Shaved" from Grapik Art Productions is one of the hottest of this genre. *In Touch* describes the action: "Master Chris McKenzie ties up and dominates beautiful and well-built Jordan Austin. Chris ties Jordan up in various positions using various racks, tables and chairs, all the while stroking Jordan's beautiful plump cock. Eventually, Chris shaves off all of Jordan's armpit and pubic hair, leaving him completely stripped of his masculinity. Once he's been shaved, Chris ties Jordan up in an even more elaborate manner and strokes his cock until he erupts all over himself, after asking for permission first, of course. Chris follows him with a remarkable cumblast that pelts Jordan in the chest.

"The shaving is repeated, but this time it's Jordan's ass that gets cleaned with the razor. Jordan's a real good slave from beginning to end, moaning or crying out whenever his nipples are bitten or whenever the razor touches his skin. After tying him up for total display, Chris strokes Jordan's cock again, bringing him to yet another dramatic climax. Chris then ends the video by taking care of himself once more, spraying all over the boy's stomach and legs. Clearly, Jordan loves every minute of it."

Best Bi-Sex

In "Fly Bi Night," a bisexual romp from All Worlds, The Boy to Watch Out For is, according to Robert Sumners in *Mondo Porno* is Jordan Rivers, "a triple threat with a hot face, a hot body and a hot dick. The words stunning and awesome come to mind whenever he is on screen." Too bad he's straight!

Old reliable Sharon Kane is back in action, this time in a relationship with Jordan where she seems to get as much pleasure from watching people have sex as she does from participating in it herself: "First Sharon gazes on as Jordan bangs Brittany Andrews and later she ogles Troy Halston plowing Sky Thompson all the while diddling with herself. Plus there's a fun threeway with T.J. (a girl), Bo Summers and Shane Thomas. I actually kinda liked the scenes between Sharon and Troy where they were discussing her and Jordan's odd relationship and Troy's fear of eating pussy. And, heaven forgive me, but the best scene was the first between Jordan and Brittany. They are so into it, they look like dogs in heat - moaning and groaning with vigor. When he picks her up and drills her as she's got her legs wrapped around him the hairs on the back of my neck rose to attention. I thought Jordan was going to drown poor Brittany with his spunk. The final scene between Jordan, Troy and Sharon lacked heat but probably because Jordan is a straight boy who felt uncomfortable doing a scene with another guy. Plus why do people hire Sky if he can't get his dick hard? Just wondering."

Biggest Disappointments

Here we waited so long to get our hands on Chi Chi LaRue's "Striptease" and that made our disappointment even more severe. As usual with LaRue's epics, the concept was great. The titling and music are great. Then Jordan Young's "screenplay" kicks in!

The best thing in it isn't even a scene, only a snippet: In one of the continuous short-cuts we see Chad Knight topping a cutie who is kneeling on the bar. Chad is topping as only he can, but we aren't allowed to linger. A stud stands over Chad jacking off and comes, with Chad, meanwhile, giving it his all, which is considerable as his fans know. But how did this start? And, more to the point, why don't we stay on this? No, we are given more of the boring "plot" of two quarreling lovers, and then more cross-cutting to the point of distraction. Even Cole Youngblood's long-awaited, at least by us, plugging of all-time superbottom Knight is spoiled by all this cross-cutting. You can't work up a sweat (or anything else). And of course the mistress Chi Chi LaRue herself has to make an appearance, to announce Chad and Cole. Ugh!

Manshots honcho (and filmmaker himself) Jerry Douglas agreed, and he said the film reminded him of Joe Gage's classic "Closed Set," wherein that legendary director also allowed his camera to wander from one grouping to another as it observed a wide variety of ever-changing sexual configurations. "In an attempt to determine why that film worked (for me) and 'Striptease' did not, I watched them back to back, and came to a number of conclusions.

"The problem with music video editing, when superimposed upon the adult film, is that a single fleeting image, or even a series of them, no matter how electrifying, does not allow the viewer (with Vaseline at the ready and his erection poised for pleasuring) time to savor the image, to share the experience with the performers, or to become aroused. The image is gone before he can connect with it. This is not to say that the MTV experience – as recreated here by editor Tab Lloyd – is not pleasurable, only that it is not titillating. In 'Closed Set,' Gage teases his viewers with fleeting images, but sooner or later, he also allows his camera to pause and luxuriate in the action.

"In 'Striptease,' the camera rarely lands long enough for the viewer to become involved. What a pity that is, for there are many striking images therein: naked models under the spray from working showers on the stage, a dancer squatting on the bar to feed his *hefty* erection to one of the patrons, dancers gyrating like libidinous gymnasts on vertical poles and, finally, the many money shots that appear without warning and all too often remain confusing because we do not know who is delivering them or what prompted them. There are other problems with the film as well. The five-minute-plus title credits sequence, like a trailer for a coming attraction, includes tantalizing shots of the high points of the film, so that by the time it is over, we have seen a truncated version of the entire production. As a result, there are no surprises in the film itself, and very few of these initial images are expanded to provide rewarding payoffs or what has been hinted at initially.

"...Ultimately, 'Striptease' is explicit without being erotic." Yes, this video had everything going for it except a decent director. Think what Jerry Douglas himself ("Flesh and Blood") could have done with it!

"No matter what the title and box cover would have you believe, 'Log Jammer' is not about lumber jacks. Instead, it's about a bunch of fags in some faggotty inn in the woods," *The Guide's* Christopher J. Hogan joked. "The closest these boys have gotten to roughing it is watching 'Wild Kingdom.' All of this would be just fine if there were good sex in the video. Unfortunately, 'Log Jammer' is out of stock in the sexual thrills department too. This is very surprising considering the talent that worked on this video. Any one member of the production team usually guarantees at least a decent video. One would think that will all of them on board we'd have a knockout on our hands. Instead, it feels like the guys at Catalina just went through the motions..."

Best Multi-Racial

"We've all heard that cock size is not important to a good sex life," Jim Boyd said in *Dude*, "but we know better, don't we? An inch or two more (or even three) makes a difference in a star's sexual reputation. And for all the talk about the bottom line in show business, in the bedrooms of the stars, it is measurements of eight to 10 inches and more that really count. For 20 years I have been running the country's most notorious and controversial sex club and dating service, the Hung Jury. In the course of matching thousands of men and women with their ideal Mr. Well Hung, I have met and spoken with scores of men and women in show biz. They all share an aching desire to fuck men with huge cocks who know how to thrust those big, thick inches just right. For them, rulers and tape measures are *de rigueur* equipment."

Boyd says Pamela Anderson Lee is one of many who loves big dicks. He says from the photos taken of her and her hubby, Motley Crue rocker Tommy Lee having sex, Lee clearly measures 10 inches long five-and-a-half inches around. Pamela has had well-publicized flings with other well-hung celebs as actor Scott Baio, David Charvet, Dean Cain, and rocker Bret Michaels from the group Poison. In *Details*, when asked, "Does size count?" Anderson said, "Unfortunately, yes, it does."

For proof that size does count, or at least the perception of size, you need only to go to your corner video emporium. Our local store tells me that their top renters always have color...plenty of color, and we don't mean Technicolor! No, honey, it's the racial thing. We perverts apparently like to fantasize about that which we wouldn't dream of touching in real life. The stereotype of the big black dick, or dark Latino dick, is alive and well across the country, if not the world.

"Legends abound rhapsodizing over the beauty, virility, allure, erotic prowess and overpowering genitalia of the black male," Robert W. Richards said in *HX*. "Yet, incongruously – except for specialty 'chocolate' or 'Bro' videos aimed at a limited audience – this most potent of male sex symbols remains virtually overlooked in gay porn. How often do you see a film in which a Jim Buck or a Logan Reed has an African-American best friend with a name and a home and a life? A character who is woven organically into the storyline and not just used as a big dick in a disposable sequence bearing little or no relation to the rest of the film? To date, almost never."

Yet Jack Simmons has worked to reverse the usual order of onscreen perception for black males. "When I started," Simmons told Richards. "I had very definite ideas about what I wanted from porn, and I've achieved every goal I've set for myself I worked at it; sure, I did the low-end stuff the first few months and it was rough, but I made all the nght contacts while I was doing it. I knew I had a hard road ahead of me because there hadn't been many black models with name value in this business other than Joe Simmons, the man I named myself after. I thought it might be a good thing to create a kind of family thing like the Foxes, the Rocklands, even the Idols. Fifteen years passed between the time Joe started in films and me being hired by Falcon to do 'The Freshmen.' Right from the start I promised myself I wasn't going to be stuck in the 'black only,' 'interracial' or 'specialty' categories. I kept that promise, and I'm proud to say that in most of my movies, I've been the only black man in the movie. When I first started, people said, 'A black guy can't be in a film unless there's a legitimate reason for him to be there.' Although they never said it, I knew they meant like playing the butler or something. I proved them wrong; I can do the same things any other model can do. Maybe people are finally getting over these stereotypes. But would you believe that in some states it's still considered illegal?"

Richards reports that Simmons is one of the busiest men in porn: "He holds down a nine to five job as a receptionist, waits tables by night, sustains his active career as a porn actor, does personal appearances and dancing engagements ('Only down to a jockstrap – if you want to see it, get a video'). Occasionally he'll moonlight as a grip on a movie set. He also directed his first feature, 'Brief Tales.'"

Simmons was part of the ensemble cast that went to Austria for "Tourist Trade" from Titan. In his review, Sticky Remote said that Simmons' big dick "is a real black beauty, and this shows it off. ...We're treated to two full, white, gooey loads of cream that Simmons sprays all over his own torso. Yummmm!" Sticky also enjoyed the "very hot" black-on-white pairing of horse-hung Simmons and eager Austrian bottom Thom Barron.

Seeing an interracial pairing shot so well is a rarity in gay porn and a must-have for all you connoisseurs."

One of the biggest renters of the year was "In the Mix," by Chi Chi LaRue out of All Worlds, which seems to have emerged as Chi Chi's home base of late after long stints producing porn for Catalina and Falcon. Sad to say, it seems as if Chi Chi rolls out a flick every week under all manner of monikers so you just never know if it's going to be worthwhile. "In the Mix" makes up for what it lacks in quality with variety. Indeed, *HX*'s reviewer put it this way: "It represents every color of the rainbow, especially pink. For a LaRue production, 'In the Mix' is a bit unusual… There are no jealous wives, nosy neighbors or adulterous brothers in law. No period costumes or complex plot getting in the way of the fun. There is, however, a lot of steamy sex, including some racy group scenes. Most of the guys are smooth (read: shaved) and muscular… We wouldn't want to be on LaRue's casting couch, but she certainly deserves credit for successfully assembling a crew of color-blind studs, not an easy task in today's homogenized gay porn circles."

Christopher J. Hogan in *The Guide* asked: "What happens when one Latino and three white boys show up at a gay bar that they didn't know was all black? If 'In The Mix' is to be believed, a big orgy ensues. The plot of this video is just that thin, but that's nothing strange for porn. What's more perplexing here is the whole issue of race which this video handles in a curious if not problematic manner. What are we to make of the accidental tourists' initial apprehension at finding themselves surrounded by black men? Does the audience sympathize with them or find them unenlightened? This is all wrapped up with the question of who the audience is for this video. Whose fantasy is it? White men's? Black men's? Who is the object and who the subject?

"Despite all the questions 'In The Mix' raises, it does better than most 'interracial' videos. The sex becomes less about sex between the races and more about sex between men as the video progresses. The roles are somewhat limited. The black men are mostly tops, and the white men bottoms. Still, these roles aren't completely rigid. The major saving grace is that the cast is terrific. They were clearly not chosen simply because of race (or their willingness to have sex with people of other races). Once the premise is out of the way and the orgy is in full swing, the action is hot and well worth watching."

Yes, before LaRue, it was unusual to see such multi-racial carrying on. Generally, if we wanted black, we got all-black. If we wanted Latino, it was all Latino. If all-Latino happens to be your mood, the video 'Learning Latin' (from La Mancha) is a good rent. "Whether we like it or not, this video plays right into the stereotype that men of color have big dicks," says *HX*'s reviewer. "No one minds looking at a big dick, but it's kind of sad that audiences would expect it just because the models are Latino. In any case, Kiko, the movie's star attraction, is hung like a fire hose, and he just loves lying back and having his throbbing meat sucked and fucked. Raymond, Kiko's partner in the opening scene, actually manages to shove all of Kiko's ten inches up his butt. It hurts just watching these antics! After that, it's pretty easy to lose track of who's who. All the guys are running around either naked or showing off their Tommy Hilfiger underwear. (Good taste, this crew.) The dialogue is terrible, of course, but no worse than you would find in any other porn flick. In fact, it's pretty realistic. These guys are tough and butch, and they look great while getting it on."

The focus of "White Nuts and Black Bolts" from All Worlds is, as its title implies, the screwing of white ass by black cock. Derek Thomas and his white lover are fighting and when a black construction crew arrives at their house, we expect things to heat up. *Manshots* said, "The fourth scene is, of course, the one for which the viewer has been waiting. The immovable object (Thomas's well-plowed asshole) meets the irresistible force (Bam's huge cock). Certainly this is the most exciting scene in the video; even so, it is marred by predictability, mediocre videography, and less than memorable grunts and moans. When Thomas's lover unexpectedly comes upon the two men right after they have shot their loads, he throws a queenly fit, firing Bam on the spot and giving Thomas his walking papers. Although Bam's character is straight and has a wife, he invites Thomas to sleep on their couch until he can find a new home." What bothered us more than anything about this scene (and Bam's other scene earlier) is that the mega-endowed black just couldn't seem to get too excited and had to hold his cock throughout.

You expect a lot from a major studio such as Catalina, but when it comes to black videos, even they can't get it together. Consider "Black in the Saddle," in which all kinds of technical gimmicks "do nothing to elevate the sexual heat or the production values above the bargain basement level," claimed *Manshots*. "Technically, the tape has dull videography, desperate editing, and virtually no evidence of direction. Furthermore, the all-oral action reduces the sexual heat. Someday, perhaps, some company will produce an all-black tape that offers first-rate action and first-rate support to the actors. Until that time, viewers are stuck with bottom-of-the-line exploitation videos that ultimately serve no purpose at all."

But things are looking up. Ixor Kleb in *The Guide* found "Black Secret" from All Worlds rather clever in conception and execution: "The secret of 'Black Secret' is at once the identity of a mysterious stud with a 13-inch dick at the local bath house as well as the way to win the heart of this horse-hung mystery man. T-Spoon, the hero of the story, is smitten with him searching the baths only to have his dream lover cum and go before they can exchange words.

"(The video) maintains a sense of place at the baths. T-Spoon and Kevin Kemp are sucking and fucking when joined by 13-inch Bam. T-Spoon takes Bam's dick in his mouth and up his ass and just after Bam shoots his load, he mysteriously disappears. T-Spoon is consoled the next day by his roommate and also tells his story to friend Shean Black who is too busy sucking off Bobby Blake to give much sympathy. T-Spoon's roommate discusses the mystery man with Panama who gets horny, stroking his own huge cock. Gene Lamar handles Panama's ample dick in a well-filmed outdoor scene. The climax of the film comes as Spoon encounters the mystery man in his own home with Richard Reyes who valiantly takes the 13 inches in his mouth and ass. The all black stars are well built and amazingly well-hung."

Upon seeing this video, an *Inches* reader in Manhattan wrote, "Wow, loved the black studs Bobby Blake and those other 'Black Secret' studs like Kevin Kemp. I have seen Bobby Blake's videos around in the video store. They have a lot of gay videos at the store I know and I rented one about the guy from Belgium who gets gangbanged by a bunch of black studs. They teach him what a punk like him is for: To take big black

American dick. I would have loved to watch them make that video. It was good for a lot of cums. I still jerk off just thinking about it."

In his review of "Huge Black Delicious" from All Worlds, Robert Sumners in *Mondo Porno* says, "The video is basically an interview with Bobby Blake who talks about his numerous sexual exploits as a cocky, hot top boy in the industry. The highlight is when he tells the interviewer about seeing Flex Gamble outside his window and inviting him up to his photo studio and getting him to bottom - Flex's first time! - on the stairs."

Another encouraging entry was "Black and Blue." Although modest in production values and plot, Michael Lynch in *Manshots* thought it was one of the best interracial gay videos in recent memory: The story is simple: two white men (Chad Connors and Blue Blake) discuss the attraction of black men and exchange stories about their own experiences or observations.

"Blake begins with the tale of his encounter with a black cop (Gene Lamar) in an alleyway behind the bar at which he has been drinking. When Lamar threatens to arrest him for public drunkenness, Blake offers mouth and ass to change his mind. As usual, Lamar is a fine actor as well as first-rate top.

"Connors counters with the tale of his encounter with a black student (T-Spoon) in his drama class. Amid the props of the drama club, the two young men exchange blowjobs, and then Connors tops him, first with a dildo, then with his cock. Unfortunately, the dildo footage is more exciting than the cock footage.

"Blake then shares a fantasy he had while in the U.S. Marine Corps: three black dicks appear through glory holes, and Blake services each in turn. Then the three men (Paul Hansen, T-Spoon, and Duke Johnson) appear in the flesh as Blake jacks himself off and shoots.

"Connors' second story concerns an interracial couple (Paul Hansen and Georgio Falconi) who live across the courtyard: he has watched them make love. After an exchange of blowjobs, Hansen tops Falconi with his usual enthusiasm, and both men come.

"For the final scene, the story-telling ends. Delivery man Ryan Block arrives at the door, and a spirited three-way ensues. After a variety of pairings for oral sex, Block and Connors take turns fucking Blake, and soon all three shoot copious loads. After Block leaves, Blake spells out the thematic, message for Connors: 'The truth about race is that it makes no difference.' In the highly segregated world of gay video, this message needs to be repeated until it is heard clearly by every major producer and director.

"'Black and Blue' certainly has its heart on the right side, and the sexual action is solid. Block is equally proficient as actor and director. As for Gene Lamar, his talent as an actor and his sexual charisma suggest that he should be a major star. He certainly steals the show, hands down.

"Connors and Blake are special cases. Both men have their followings, but neither has what is naively known in the video industry as 'universal appeal.' Blake depends on the sheer energy of his performances for his effect – either you like him a lot, or you find him over the top. And Connors is so pretty that his lackluster performances are easy to forgive – if his brand of prettiness pushes your buttons."

The sequel to French porn *auteur* Jean Daniel Cadinot's "Service Actif" provides additional insights into "life on a military compound in Cadinot Neverland," Jim D'Entremont said in *The Guide*. "Here, where *tout le monde* is irrepressibly horny, there's no need to ask who's queer, and to tell would be a redundancy. The daily routine consists of sex followed by exercise followed by more sex followed by more exercise followed by still more sex. These guys' dicks, at least, strive mightily to be all that they can be.

"Sex happens in the stockade, the infirmary, offices, the base kitchen, and a supply room. It happens in ones, twos, threes, and fours. Aside from the standard oral, anal, and manual activities – all performed with panache – we're offered bootlicking, occasional rough stuff, and rape fantasies. Opening, middle, and closing sequences that would have appealed to Jean Genet involve prisoners in the camp lockup. Probably the best sexual production number features Jerome Terrade, Florent Carpentier, Serge Charnay, and Salvator Merida, on KP duty, devising new uses for certain root vegetables and inventing a brand-new recipe for soup. There are also two good passages that document the treatment of Patrick Rameau's turned ankle, which keeps requiring the removal of his pants.

"The absence of subtitles may bother American viewers too impatient to avail themselves of direct-method lessons in such useful phrases as *'Donnes ton cul!'* and *'Suces-moi!'* The absence of condoms in this 1990 film will bother some viewers even more. Many will find the presence of an American Confederate flag on the set less than amusing, especially in a sequence where a black recruit (Jocelyn Cheroux) is coerced into servicing nasty white corporal Elyes Ardini. Others may welcome the general lack of political correctness. Much of the sex is wonderfully directed, acted, and shot. This is not Jean Daniel Cadinot at his nearly peerless best, but second-tier Cadinot surpasses the work of most American porn directors."

*The year's VERY BIG sensation: BAM,
courtesy Titan Media. (It's hard to keep it in his underpants.)*

THE PICTURES OF THE YEAR

In these annual reviews we have always found the finest, sexiest photos of gorgeous guys in advertising, especially those ads run in magazines directed to gays. Ads for jeans and underwear continue to fascinate. In fact, it seems every designer is trying to top the other with the sexiest guys around.

"For those with a vested interest in such things, pop cultures greatest contribution to the late 20th century surely has to be ads for men's designer underwear," David Colman said in *OUT*. "For while it has been argued that almost everything, from glossy decor layouts to haute women's fashion spreads, is basically pornography only the men's designer underwear ad has taken the pains to translate the actual visual vocabulary of porn into retail sales stardom.

"The phenomenon started rather innocently in the early 1980s with Jim Palmer shucking his baseball uniform for a pair of Jockey bikini briefs. Calvin Klein followed suit with pole vaulter Tom Hintnaus sporting clingy white briefs and a steady stream of similarly anonymous bronzed beauts. For years no one challenged Klein, but after Marky Mark's multi-media assault, underwear was suddenly everything. Gianni Versace came out with Latin lotharios and clean-cut boys wearing his Greek-key patterned waistbands; 2(x)ist arrived not only with torrid hunks but with claims that its brand was more gay positive. Even preppy old Abercrombie & Fitch hiked up its skirts for a football locker-room scenario right out of a Kristen Bjorn video.

"Not to be outdone, Calvin Klein countered with Wayne Maser's photographs of Antonio Sabato Jr. In frank mimicry of the models of Bruce of Los Angeles – whose 1960s bodybuilder magazine *The Male Figure* was a standard-bearer for safe, jockey-short skin rags – Sabato is posed as if fresh from the Hollywood bus station. With a lecherous smile-for-the-camera amateur look and retro Superman-style underwear, the photos manage in their sophistication to be less wholesome than the porn they imitate – a plus or a minus, as you like it."

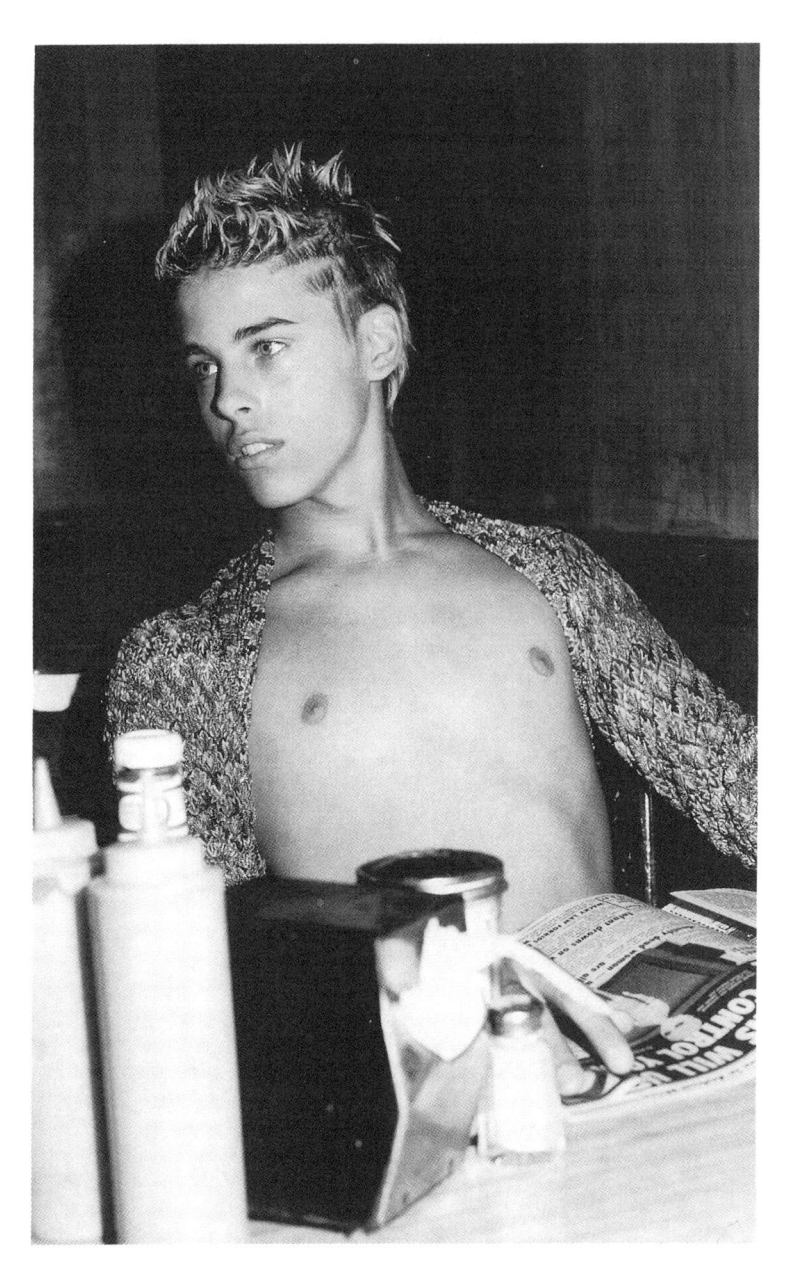

Before we get to the undies, this cutie caught our eye in a fashion layout in *Detour* magazine by Ben Watts

Zane model Craig Anthony, photographed by Kenneth Rothman in shorts by Todd Oldham, dazzled.

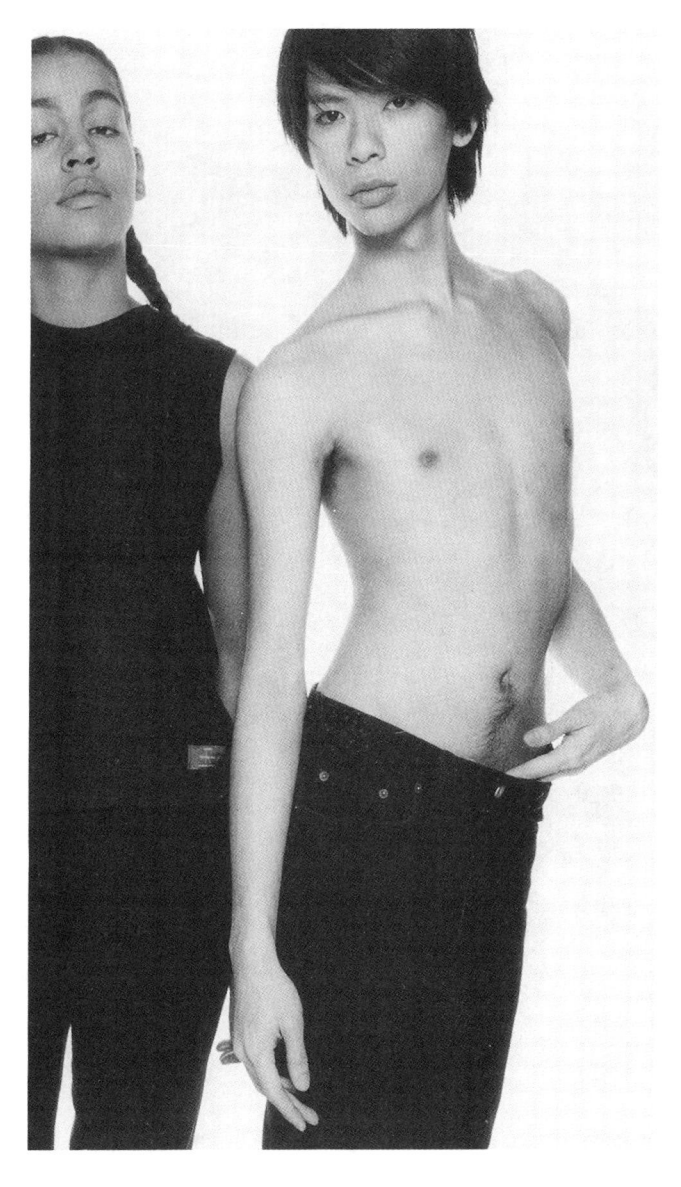

Calvin Klein has no racial barriers for CK One

Brendan Sexton III, of the movie "Hurricane," directed by Morgan J. Freeman, modelling a Calvin Klein turtleneck, photographed by Bettina Rheims.

Model Drake from Tyler Models posed for DKNY, photographed by David Hawe in *Icon* magazine

And now, the best of the best, in Helmut Lang underwear, photographed by Lee Strickland

Nature Boy
917-858-9886

Ivy League college boy.
Attractive. I'm looking for a
sugar daddy.

In Rate: 250

Out Rate: 250

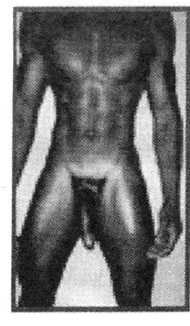

Chase
917-768-9547

Tough but friendly! 5' 11", 170 lbs.
Model who has 10" by 6" around. If you
don't want dissappointments, lies, or
games then I am the one. What you see is
what you get, so relax and enjoy. Disease
free, Discreet and safe. 24 hours. 7 Days.

In Rate: 200

Out Rate: 200

Peddling flesh on the Web,
as reported by the Village Voice

THE LAST WORD:
IN THE AGE OF CYERBSEX

"Ken Augustan doesn't really look like a hustler, at least not any more so than the average sexed-up clubgoer at Jackie 60, the Tuesday-night party at Mother in the meatpacking district," comments Tom Dolby in *The Village Voice*. "Blond, 23, and cute in a college-boy sort of way, Augustan is one of the escorts on www.rentboy.com, the Web site celebrating its launch at the club with go-go boys and notables like the Misstress Formika.

"Rentboy is the first Web site in New York established exclusively to advertise male hustlers. While there are a few other New York-area sites, such as MasterVu and Hardbodies, that combine listings for 'escorts' with those for phone-sex services and exotic dancers, Rentboy is the first to be so bold in its intent. And multi-hustler sites launched in other cities bear euphemistic names like 'Dreamboys' and 'PeopleMale.'"

"This is an entirely unique service in the community for escorts, models, and bodyworkers (massage specialists not necessarily licensed as masseurs)," promotions director Tom Weise, an actor-dancer, says initially, though later he becomes more honest about the site. "These days, we're able to handle things like this without hiding them," he says. He is, after all, wearing a name tag that says "Cyber-pimp." Weise and his partner, computer consultant Jeffrey Davids, are offering hustlers the first three months of ads for free; all future revenue will be generated from ad sales.

"Legally," Colby notes, "advertising on the site should be protected under the First Amendment in the same way as ads in the back of the *Voice* or *HX* and *Next*, two gay-bar publications. The site's promotional packet notes, however, that ads may not refer to illegal activities such as drugs or – surprise – prostitution. Ads also may not mention prices for specific services, though they do list ballpark numbers for 'in' or 'out' appointments. Rentboy's ads are often more visually explicit than print publications permit (about 60 percent of the ads on Rentboy contain full nudity), and are also less expensive, at $50 a month. The site has received nearly 35,000 hits so far, and it's still under construction. Weise and Davids are committed to promoting safer sex. Weise says the site will contain links to information about creative ways for rentboys to have safer sex.

"Absent from the site is any indication that what it's promoting is probably technically illegal."

"This is not something that's a big concern for us," Weise says. "It's not like we're the first people to put rentboys in ads."

"This *laissez-faire* approach to hustling seems a sign of the times," Dolby says, "as well as what seems to be decreased enforcement of prostitution laws. The Internet has already proved indispensable to the s/m community and it appears likely that it will do the same for the culture of hustlers and johns."

To say nothing of pedophiles, who will have to get a bit smarter if they want to stay out of jail. For instance, last October a Myrtle Beach, Florida man sent a bulletin to "all parents" using America Online, a computer messaging service. In the message, the man solicited parents for sexual liaisons with their children. Hard to believe offers such as that are zooming around the Internet and showing up on peoples' computer screens virtually every minute of every day, but they are, according to Dan Curry, who works in the Crimes Against Children Unit of the Manatee County, Florida, Sheriff's Office. And, as the cost of computer equipment decreases while access to worldwide computer systems increases, law-enforcement officials say sending and receiving child pornography through cyberspace soon will be silently spreading out of control. "This is not a trend," said Ruben Rodriguez, supervisor of the child exploitation unit at the National Center for Missing and Exploited Children in Washington. "It's something that's here to stay."

According to Center statistics, 44 million people use the Internet every day and there are currently 150,000 pornographic images of children circulating in cyberspace, Rodriguez said. In addition, as technology advances and perpetrators find more ways of hiding their tracks – with encryption and password protected software – finding the bad guys gets tougher, Rodriguez said.

Doug Rehman is a special agent with the Florida Department of Law Enforcement and the president of the Florida Association of Computer Crime Investigators. He says most pedophiles suppress their desires, but put a computer in a pedophile's lap, and he is more likely to carry out his urges, Rehman said. "They get online, and they see all the inter-generational sex rooms, and they go into chat rooms with other pedophiles who have had sex with minors," he said. "And they start to feel it's not that wrong . . . that society is the bad guy." They use the same psychology when trying to court youngsters online. They know children, especially teen boys, are confused about their sexuality and want to talk to someone about it. Pedophiles will enter search words to locate young people online, especially boys from single-parent homes and with expressed interests in gay or alternate lifestyles, Curry said. Once they have gained the child's trust, they will start sending them pornographic pictures, mainly pictures exploiting children. This helps convince the child that it is normal for kids and adults to have sex, Rehman said. And, the pursuit continues from there, with planned meetings for sex. "Pedophiles are like the used car salesman of the Internet," he said. "They can convince someone who is not sure about their sexuality that they are gay or bisexual." "Innocent Images" is the name of the FBI's international child porn eradication effort, which has gotten national attention.

At the National Center in Washington, Rodriguez is putting together a database of the law-enforcement agencies with computer-trained detectives, so local, state and federal officials can work together. The problem is that there are very few law-enforcement agencies with the money or the staffing to train their staffs on computer crimes, especially when they have so many other crimes to investigate. But Rehman warns: "Law enforcement in general is going to have to pay a lot more attention to computer crimes to keep up with tomorrow's criminal."

TRIBUTE

"With astonishment, I suddenly found myself on the roster of familiar faces Diana wanted to meet. There she was, right in front of me, and I instantly realized that no kind of film, whether still or moving, had done her justice. She wasn't just beautiful. She was like the sun coming up: coming up giggling. She was giggling as if she had just remembered something funny."
– British TV's Clive James,
upon meeting Princess Diana for the first time.

Princess Diana (shown above with a patient in 1991) "took on AIDS because she saw this group of people for whom nothing was being done," according to a friend.
(Photo by Hans Deryk, AP.)

ACKNOWLEDGEMENTS AND SOURCES

The editor thanks the many video companies and other sources featured for their participation in providing most of the illustrations in this volume. Also, we acknowledge the other photographers featured, as noted.

For more information:

Bel Ami (films of George Duroy), 484-B Washington St #342, Monterey CA 93940.

Leisure Time Entertainment; call 1-800-874-8960.

Falcon Studios, which can be contacted at 1-800-227-3717; catalogue is $15, refundable with purchase.

Catalina Video, providing a catalogue for $15: 1-800-708-9200.

All Worlds Video, which also offers a catalogue: 1-800-537-8024.

Studio 2000, which has a catalogue service for one year at $10 by calling 1-800-435-2445.

Vivid Video, which offers a free catalogue: 1-800-822-8339.

Rogofsky: Rare issues of celebrity nude magazines are available. Box 107-CS, Glen Oaks NY 11004. Catalogue is $3.

Mike Esser's Pride Videos are available from STARbooks Press. Write for complete list and other free information about imported, soft-core video releases.

Other cover photography for STARbooks Press' releases occasionally provided through the courtesy of the celebrated English photographer David Butt. Mr. Butt's photographs may be purchased through Suntown, Post Office Box 151, Danbury, Oxfordshire, OX16 8GN, United Kingdom. Ask for a full catalogue.

THE SUPERSTAR INDEX

Allen, Chad............236-238
Andrews, Drew...........312, 362, 470, 478, 482
Ashfield, David...........426-432, 434

Bam......................490, 495
Banderas, Antonio.........21, 171-176
Beckford, Tyson.......278-280
Bell, Joshua............259-262
Bergin, Michael.......270-271
Bjorn, Kristen.........469, 475
Blake, Blue......312, 364, 480
Block, Ryan............287-492
Bootlickers.....................247
Bowie, David..........255-258
Bradshaw, Matt...........340-347, 365, 390, 470
Brandon, Kyle...............384
Branson, Mike................475
Brewer Twins............275-277
Brock, Daryl....................311
Buck, Jim.................308, 391-397, 477
Burns, Chris.......423, 425-426
Burroughs, William......10-12

Cain, Dean.........113-116, 161
Cameron, Derek.............310, 361, 471, 480
Cannon, Jake.................337, 398-401, 473, 474
Caulfield, Maxwell..........195
Chandler, Rex.................199
Charvet, David..........231-235
Chase, Tom..............445-447

Cobretti, Vince..........458-467
Colbert, Gino.........286-7, 301
Connors, Chad.........282, 312, 337, 448-449, 451, 492
Crisp, Quentin.................12
Cruise, Tom......67, 70, 73-77
Cummings, Tony............355, 377, 479

Davis, Brad...............163-167
DiCaprio, Leonardo............9, 157, 177-179
Dior, Karen (Rick Van)..15-16
Dixon, Sam...............337, 368, 400, 472
Donovan, Chad........350, 376
Duchovny, David......219-220

Everett, Rupert.............45-53

Fine, Richie...............451-453
Ford, Leo..................437-444
Fox, Ty...............286, 289-294
Fraser, Brendan.........118-122

Gallagher, Joe............481-482
Gallo, Anthony...............311
Ginsberg, Allen............10-12
Grand, Max...................311, 312, 450, 478, 482
Grant, Cary............22-24, 30

Haas, Lukas.................58-62
Halston, Troy...........282, 400
Hanson.....................263-266
Hanson, Johnny...........214-215, 218

Hart, K. C....349-357, 472, 476
Hart, Adam..............305-308

Jackson, Michael......130-135
Jordan, Jeremy...........63-66

Katt, Tom.....................284-285, 368, 397, 450
King, Jon..........420-421, 433
Knight, Chad...........281-282, 370-380, 473, 485
Kramer, Kevin............200, 202-205, 374, 512

Lamas, Mike.............282-283
Law, Jude....................38-44
Leto, Jared...................94-98
Lopez, Mario............168-170
Louganis, Greg..........168-170

Magik, Mike.............477, 483
Markham, Sonny.......213-214, 365
McAllistar, Hawk...........201, 205-206, 479
McGregor, Ewan.......185-189
McKenna, Kyle........343, 482
Michael, George.........20, 244
Murphy, Eddie.............14-17

O'Donnell, Steve............368, 385, 479, 480
O'Hara, Scott............404-422

Palmer, Jeff...............361, 471
Pansy Division....247, 249-251
Paulik, Johan................1, 309, 313, 314-324
Penn, Jeremy...................471
Pet Shop Boys............252-254
Pitt, Brad...............70, 90-93
Prince, Pagan............454-457

Reed, Logan.......359-369, 480
Reeves, Steve......103, 105-110
Reeves, Marcello.......330-336
Reeves, Keanu...66, 70, 78-85
Renfro, Brad............153-156
Rex, Simon....................223
Ridgeston, Lukas...........312, 314-324, 476
Rockland Brothers.....300-304
Rossi, Marco...................451
Ruiz, Mike....................33-36
Ryker, Ken.....................301

Sabato Jr, Antonio....70, 86-89
Sawa, Devon.............150-153
Schaech, Johnathan.....99-102
Serbo, Kevin.............111-113
Shaw, Aiden.............325-329
Simmons, Jack 477, 488-489
Stanton, Derrick........424-425
Stefano, Kurt...................311
Stevens, Marc...........435-436
Stevens, Todd...........339-341
Stryker, Jeff...............294-299
Summers, Bo.....367, 371, 473

Thomas, J. Taylor.......143-149
Thomas, Derek..........293-294, 358, 360-369, 471, 490

Ulrich, Skeet...........190-192
Wahlberg, Mark...68, 123-129
Ward, Tony.................54-57
Wayne, Anthony.....272-274
William, Prince.......136-142
Winters, Brett..287, 366, 399
Wyle, Noah............224-230

Young, Kurt............342,348-357, 385
Youngblood, Cole.........341-342, 370-380, 485

THIS IS AS GOOD AS IT GETS...INDULGE!

beautiful boys

An Extravagant Collection of Erotica
Plus A Scandalous Porn Star Expose

Now available at bookstores or by mail: BEAUTIFUL BOYS, John Patrick's enormously entertaining look at boys who are really much more than just a pretty face. This unusual collection of hot erotic tales includes two big bonus books: "The Blessing," a sizzling novella by Leo Cardini, and another of John Patrick's revealing looks at the lives of porn stars, this one featuring the incredible bottom boy Kevin Kramer. This huge book is $14.95, plus $2.75 post from STARbooks Press, P.O. Box 2737-B, Sarasota FL 34230-2737 USA. *Or at your bookseller now.*

About the Editor

The editor with his favorite boy-toy Kevin Kramer

John Patrick is a prolific, prize-winning author of fiction and non-fiction. One of his short stories, "The Well," was honored by PEN American Center as one of the best of 1987. His novels and anthologies, as well as his non-fiction works, including *Legends* and *The Best of the Superstars* series, continue to gain him new fans every day. One of his stories appears in the Badboy collection *Southern Comfort* and another is included in *The Mammoth Collection of Gay Short Stories*.

A divorced father of two, the author is a longtime member of the American Booksellers Association, the Florida Publishers' Association, American Civil Liberties Union, and the Adult Video Association. He resides in Florida.